D0067970

Santa Fe, Taos
& Albuquerque

Kim Grant

Taos Pueblo (p156)
Tour the ancient adobe city built at the foot of a deeply spiritual mountain

Canyon Road (p70)
Stroll amidst more fine art in Santa Fe than the wealthiest museums can afford

San Francisco de Asis Church (p141)
Scan the silhouette that launched scores of photography careers

Museum Hill (p67)
Visit the four fine museums, just a quick ride from Santa Fe's plaza

Abiquiú (p122)
Drink in the undulating landscape that inspired Georgia O'Keeffe and visit Ghost Ranch

Chimayó (p126)
Make your own pilgrimage to the sacred santuario and enjoy lunch at the Rancho de Chimayó

Indian Pueblo Cultural Center (p177)
Learn about Pueblo Indian culture before visiting individual pueblos near Albuquerque

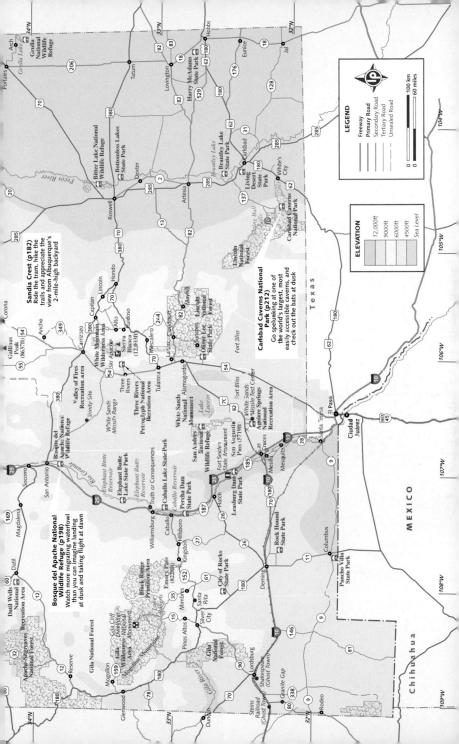

Sandia Crest (p182)
Ride the tram, hike the trails and appreciate the view from Albuquerque's 2-mile-high backyard

Carlsbad Caverns National Park (p212)
Go spelunking at one of the world's largest, most easily accessible caverns, and check out the bats at dusk

Bosque del Apache National Wildlife Refuge (p198)
Watch more migrating waterfowl than you can imagine landing at dusk and taking flight at dawn

LEGEND

	Freeway
	Primary Road
	Secondary Road
	Tertiary Road
	Unsealed Road

0   100 km
0   60 miles

ELEVATION

12,000ft
9000ft
6000ft
4500ft
Sea Level

Destination Santa Fe, Taos & Albuquerque

San Francisco has its Golden Gate Bridge and New York has its Statue of Liberty, but New Mexico has its fair share of iconic imagery, too – earthen adobe buildings, kiva fireplaces, yellow aspens, green chile, blue turquoise and red *ristras*.

Sit atop a mesa in O'Keeffe country or climb into cliff dwellings; admire lowriders or watch fiestas in ancient plazas. Hike to your soul's content in the autumn; ski a world-renowned mountain in the winter; soak your cares away in the spring(s); take it easy in the summer. Let the love affair begin. It may have already washed over you like a flash flood.

Enliven your senses listening to coyotes and the Santa Fe Opera; watching pastel sunsets and ever-changing art exhibits; tasting raw piñon and homemade *biscochito*; smelling dirt during a summer monsoon and roasting chile during an autumnal harvest; feeling *farolitos* warm a night sky and feeling smooth-as-silk pueblo pots.

From the coziness of your rented hacienda, watch lightning storms and thunder clouds. Sip a margarita at sunset surrounded by the brightest profusion of flowers you've ever seen. Ponder centuries of Native history and tradition at Taos Pueblo. Float your cares away on a hot-air balloon in Albuquerque or leave them in the dust, driving the back roads.

Oh yeah, and along the way you'll learn a thing or two about a millennia of Native American culture, centuries of Spanish influence and decades of Anglo incursions. New Age spirituality and Old World religion will reveal themselves, too.

Go ahead and sign that old-fashioned picture postcard from the edge of nowhere: 'Wish you were here.'

OPPOSITE: JOHN HAY   RICHARD CUMMINS

Santa Fe

Local produce fills the Santa Fe Farmers Market (p101) with vibrant colors

At Christmas Eve, Canyon Rd (p92) is softly lit with twinkling *farolitos*

JOHN HAY

RALPH LEE HOPKINS

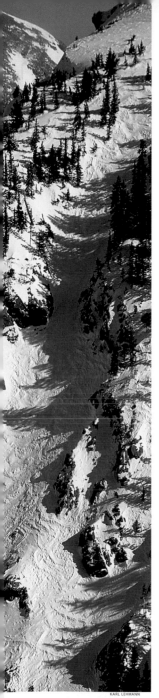

KARL LEHMANN

Taos Ski Valley (p158) is
spectacular all year round

Taos

JOHN NEUBAUER

The adobe San Francisco de Asis Church (p141) is an artistic
study of the interplay between shadow and light

Albuquerque

Central Ave is one of the most buzzing sections of Route 66 (p178)

Albuquerque is famous for its public art (p179); this 'Fruits of Expression' mural is downtown

Contents

Regional Map Contents

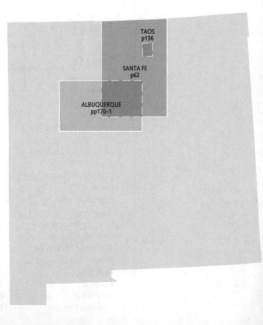

The Author

KIM GRANT

There's no denying the region's magnetism for Kim Grant – after 20 years in Boston she moved to Albuquerque in late 2005. Although she'd been making quarterly pilgrimages since the early 1990s, by mid-2003 the frequency had tripled. And the writing was on the wall (er… the canyon.) Kim is happiest in three places: cruising on wide open roads, scrambling along mountain trails and relaxing at sunset with a margarita. All three conditions are easily met living in the foothills of the Sandias. New Mexico is a natural fit. Alongside her partner, she cultivates a xeriscape garden, bikes the Tramway before the sun bursts over the Sandias and provides refuge for mourning doves and quail.

My Santa Fe, Taos & Albuquerque

As a new resident of (but longtime visitor to) Albuquerque, it's been a joy to more deeply discover all the reasons I was drawn to this region in the first place. Since I live at the base of the Sandias, I can hike in Elena Gallegos (p178) year-round. After the *New York Times* features it prominently, visitors spend thousands of dollars to visit Santa Fe during the holidays, but I can drive an hour to walk Canyon Rd at Christmas time (p92). I can people-watch over margaritas for as long as I want at the Adobe Bar (p153).

In the autumn, nothing beats cruising the Chama River Valley (p214), when aspens turn yellow and cottonwoods rustle. In the spring, nothing compares to hundreds of thousands of migrating waterfowl landing and taking off at Bosque del Apache National Wildlife Refuge (p198). No matter the season, I'm always up for camping at White Sands National Monument (p207), with a warm piñon fire and a frosty Roswell Alien Amber Ale.

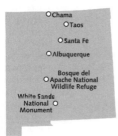

Getting Started

Ninety-nine percent of visitors to New Mexico begin their journey by flying into the Albuquerque Sunport, and 98% of those head straight for Santa Fe. Try instead to relax into the slower pace of New Mexico by staying the first night in Albuquerque. Let your body begin acclimating to the high altitude, let your eyes begin adjusting to the bright desert light and let your stomach become acquainted with the ubiquitous green chili.

Decide how much time you'd like to spend getting off the beaten path – there are plenty of ways to do it. Although this book covers all the high points of New Mexico's corners, most visitors confine their explorations to the Santa Fe–Taos–Albuquerque corridor. Try branching out.

Remember, though, that distances can be lengthy in this part of the world, so plan accordingly. Driving time between Albuquerque and Carlsbad is six hours, but then again, the Enchanted Circle is only an hour from Taos. Welcome to the Land of Extremes – er, the Land of Enchantment.

If you're used to following a strict itinerary, keep in mind that here, more than many places, plans tend to go absurdly awry. To quote former New Mexico governor Lew Wallace, 'All calculations based on our experiences elsewhere fail in New Mexico.' If you're visiting for a specific event, particularly during the jam-packed late-summer months of Santa Fe's Indian Market and opera season, planning ahead is crucial – reserve your rental car and hotel room as far in advance as possible.

But if you're simply exploring, reserve a rental car in advance, and perhaps just reserve a hotel room for the first couple of nights. Create a loose itinerary of preferences, but don't be determined to stick to it. Temptations arise, mañana time happens and some New Mexican you meet will probably point you toward an experience that will change your life. Use us as a guide, but don't be shy about doing it yourself.

WHEN TO GO

Northern New Mexico is a year-round destination, with four distinct seasons and 300 days of sunshine annually. Spring is unpredictable, and visitors from March to early June should bring both winter coats and shorts to wear while meandering among lilacs and blooming fruit trees.

DON'T LEAVE HOME WITHOUT...

- Comfortable footwear for hiking in remote areas and walking along Canyon Rd
- Strong sunscreen, high-quality sunglasses and a wide-brimmed hat
- One spiffy outfit for a big splurge at dinnertime
- Your favorite CDs for long drives
- A bathing suit (for hot springs)
- Binoculars for bird-watching
- A copy of your passport, driver's license and 800 numbers for your credit cards
- Packing your Swiss army knife and traditional film in your checked luggage (not carry-on)
- Room in your carry-on to bring home Native American pottery and jewelry
- A high-quality water bottle

Summer is a great time to spend in Santa Fe galleries, at the opera, in the cool Sangre de Cristos and at Indian Market. Summer is also a great time to frolic in the mountains and rivers of Taos, where temperatures are easily 20 degrees lower than in Albuquerque. The desert heat will slow you down in many towns, but give in and bask, the way locals do. And you can often count on cooling afternoon storms that arrive in the July and August 'monsoon season' to make things more pleasant in the early evening.

In the cooler fall, aspens shimmer yellow across mountainsides above Santa Fe, Taos and Albuquerque; the scent of roasting green chiles wafts across towns everywhere; and hot-air balloons crowd the skies above Albuquerque during the October fiesta.

From late November through March, it's ski season. Early December and mid-January are the lulls, with good deals on lift tickets. But Christmas holidays are a peak period, when room rates skyrocket and rental cars are difficult to find.

See Climate Charts (p229) for more information.

Spring brings a profusion of desert wildflowers; legions of purple, pink and white trees blossom unabashedly. Sure, everyone knows about flocking to Washington, DC during cherry blossom season, but locals stay home in New Mexico to witness the state bursting wide open.

All said, there's no bad time to visit. The sun will always be shining, no matter when you cruise through.

COSTS & MONEY

Unless you plan to stick to the cities and have some extra time on your hands to navigate public transportation systems, travel by car is de rigueur – it's the most convenient, and often the only, way to get around. Greyhound is affordable, but the private shuttles and tours you'll need in order to get off the beaten path cost money and time.

Off-season rental rates run as low as $150 a week for economy cars, $200 or more during peak season, plus $12 to $25 a day for insurance. Four-wheel-drive vehicles can be as high as $90 a day; keep in mind that only two roads mentioned in this book – to abandoned gold mines – require them.

You can camp for free on Bureau of Land Management (BLM) land, pay $6 to $15 for developed wilderness sites, or $20 to $30 at full-service campgrounds with convenient in-town locations. Youth hostels charge $15 to $20 for a dorm bed, and sleazier motels (not really available in Santa Fe or Taos) can be yours for $40 a double.

Motels charging $75 for a double tend to be well kept, if basic. Hotels close to the plazas start at around $100 and go way, way up, while B&B prices start at $100 or so for small rooms serving continental breakfasts and $150 to $225 for the real, antique-packed deal. A luxury suite – and Santa Fe has some truly fine accommodations – usually runs $350 to $450, though you can certainly spend more.

Good Southwestern fast food (healthy if you're careful) can be as cheap as $4 to $8 for a substantial meal. Full-service restaurants will still fill you up for $12 or less, while fine cuisine will start at $25 per main (not including wine).

TRAVEL LITERATURE

A little background reading can go a long way toward enriching and deepening your experience of a place.

Travelers' Tales American Southwest, edited by Sean and James O'Reilly, is a collection of regional essays, which will infuse your impending adventure with rich detail.

TOP TENS

Top Ten Festivals & Events

New Mexico doesn't settle for the average celebration. This is a creative culture – three of them, actually – and there's always something spectacular happening. For more listings, check the Santa Fe, Taos and Albuquerque chapters, as well as sections on smaller towns and pueblos.

- Taos Spring Arts Festival (p146), April, Taos
- Gathering of Nations Powwow (p180), April, Albuquerque
- San Felipe Feast Day and Green Corn Dances (p193), May, San Felipe Pueblo
- Solar Music Festival (p147), June, Taos
- UFO Encounter (p211), July, Roswell

- Spanish Market (p91), July, Santa Fe
- Indian Market (p91), August, Santa Fe
- Santa Fe Fiestas (p91), September, Santa Fe
- International Balloon Fiesta (p194), October, Albuquerque
- Canyon Road Walk (p91), December, Santa Fe

Top Ten Spots to Transcend

Whether you're a dedicated spiritual seeker or just casually interested in keeping your karma clean, there are plenty of places for miracles and meditation in this state.

- El Santuario de Chimayó (p127), Chimayó
- Ghost Ranch (p125), Abiquiú
- Zozobra (p90), Santa Fe
- Shrine of the Stone Lions (p133), Bandelier
- Sandia Tram (p177), Albuquerque
- Loretto Chapel (p82), Santa Fe

- Pecos Benedictine Monastery (p224), Pecos National Historical Park
- T'ai Chi Chih Center (p183), Albuquerque
- Earthships (p142), Taos
- Vietnam Veterans Memorial (p167), Eagle Nest

Top Ten Places to get in the water

The desert is beautiful (and dry and hot). Into every life, though, a little water must fall. When you need a soak, paddle, swim, foot dipping or dive, you have options. Don't discount the value of seeing and hearing water in the desert, either.

- Ojo Caliente Hot Springs Resort (p124), Ojo Caliente
- Eagle Nest Lake (p166), Eagle Nest
- Genoveva Chavez Community Center (p86), Santa Fe
- Cochiti Lake (p193), Pueblo de Cochiti
- Jemez Springs Bath House (p192), Jemez Springs

- Sierra Grande Lodge & Spa (p200), Truth or Consequences
- Elephant Butte Reservoir (p199), Elephant Butte, Truth or Consequences
- Gila Hot Springs Vacation Center (p203), Gila National Forest
- Blue Hole (p225), Santa Rosa
- Lake Nambé (p118), Nambé Pueblo

Pueblos of the Rio Grande is Daniel Gibson's indispensable guide for anyone interested in Native New Mexico. Others offering insight into Pueblo culture include *Almanac of the Dead* by Leslie Marmon Silko, who grew up on Laguna Pueblo near Albuquerque, and Kiowa Indian N Scott Momaday's Pulitzer Prize–winning *House Made of Dawn.*

Martin & Meditations on the South Valley, by gifted local Jimmy Santiago Baca, gives voice to Chicanos struggling here in one of the poorest states in the nation.

If you've already discounted pleas to conserve water as mere handwringing by Lonely Planet lefties, read *Cadillac Desert: The American West and Its Disappearing Water,* by Marc Reisner, a thorough and entertaining account of this land's dripping-to-dry history. *Touring New Mexico Hot Springs,* by Matt Bischoff, with maps and reviews of the state's finest soaks, will cheer you up afterward.

New Mexico's Sanctuaries, Retreats and Sacred Places, by Christina Nealson, is a predictably New Agey but fabulous rundown of spiritual spots, with maps and lore galore.

The laugh-out-loud *Turn Left at the Sleeping Dog: Scripting the Santa Fe Legend 1920–1955,* by John Pen La Farge, is oral history at its finest, with interviews with local characters who discuss Dennis Chávez, Georgia O'Keeffe and the whole 'Old Santa Fe Trail' thing with absolutely no respect for the tourist bureau's rosy tricultural rap.

INTERNET RESOURCES

Lonely Planet (www.lonelyplanet.com) An online guide with up-to-date visa regulations, events that could affect your visit and the Thorn Tree forum, where you can ask other travelers what they think.

New Mexico CultureNet (www.nmcn.org) Articles about the artists, writers and history of New Mexico, with events listings of the most enriching sort.

New Mexico Department of Tourism (www.newmexico.org) Information and links to accommodations, attractions and other useful sites.

Santa Fe New Mexican (www.santafenewmexican.com) Online visitor information and top local stories from Santa Fe's newspaper.

State of New Mexico (www.newmexico.gov) Facts, stats and state government sites, plus links to public transportation, USGS (US Geological Survey) and street maps, and other official business.

Itineraries
CLASSIC ROUTES

ALBUQUERQUE–SANTA FE–TAOS LOOP
One Week

Hit the ground running by heading over to Albuquerque's **Indian Pueblo Cultural Center** (p177) for an immersion course in Puebloan culture. Take the **tram** (p182) just before dusk to Sandia Peak and have dinner at **Sadie's** (p186). Take an early morning walk along the **Rio Grande** (p176) before hightailing it up to Santa Fe via **Madrid** (p194) and the **Turquoise Trail** (p194).

Stretch your legs around the plaza, map out a plan of attack for restaurants and galleries and eventually watch the sun set from **La Fonda** (p94). Spend **three days and nights** (p61) exploring Santa Fe. Then jump on the **High Road** (p125), poking around **Truchas** (p127) and **Las Trampas** (p127), before beginning a **two-day and -night tour** (p135) of Taos.

Wake up early and head down the I-25 to **Kasha-Katuwe Tent Rocks** (p193) for a hike. Then go upscale in Albuquerque for dinner at **Artichoke Café** (p184) or savor your last green chile at the **Frontier** (p184).

This round trip will put about 325 miles on your car and is book-ended by overnights in Albuquerque. The three-day tour of Santa Fe includes one full day of exploration; take more time in town if you can afford it.

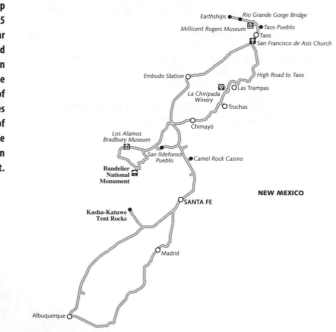

NORTHERN NEW MEXICO: THE GRAND TOUR   Two Weeks

Don't leave Albuquerque so quickly; depending on when your flight arrives, stay two or three nights. Ride the **tram** (p182), visit the **Indian Pueblo Cultural Center** (p177), decipher carvings at **Petroglyph National Monument** (p177) and hike the foothills at **Elena Gallegos** (p178). Then, without hesitation, head out to **Acoma Pueblo** (p214). Feeling adventurous? Take the bumpy road to **Chaco Cultural National Historical Park** (p220) and camp overnight. (The park is best explored early or late in the day.)

Take a late-morning soak at **Jemez Springs** (p192) and an afternoon walk at **Kasha-Katuwe Tent Rocks** (p193) before pulling into **Santa Fe** (p60) for a **four-day tour** (p61).

When it's time to get out of Dodge, hit the **High Road** (p125) to Taos, and take our **five-day tour** (p135) of Taos. With a couple of nights to spare, it's time to take a whirlwind cruise of a quarter of the state. For the biggest bang, head southeast.

Soak in hot springs in **Truth or Consequences** (p199), watch a dusky sky merge with the horizon at **White Sands National Monument** (p207), catch a performance in **Ruidoso** (p208), hike in **Cloudcroft** (p207), communicate with aliens in **Roswell** (p211) and go underground at **Carlsbad** (p213).

A circle tour of southeastern New Mexico will add 800 miles onto your trip. If you're not up to it, spend another day in Santa Fe and another on the 84-mile Enchanted Circle tour, part of the five-day Taos tour.

TAILORED TRIPS

NATIVE AMERICAN

The Rio Grande Valley is one of very few places where Native Americans have continuously held their ancestral lands. In Albuquerque start at the **Indian Pueblo Cultural Center** (p177) for Pueblo Art and History 101, then hike around **Petroglyph National Monument** (p177) or **Coronado State Monument** (p192) to experience both up close.

End the day at **Prairie Star Restaurant** (p192) in Santa Ana Pueblo or with a show at Sandia Pueblo's casino before exploring the many pueblos, book-

ended by dramatic **Acoma Pueblo** (p214) and stunning **Taos Pueblo** (p156). Six Tewa-speaking pueblos are clustered around **Española** (p120), making it the perfect base for exploration.

Detour to **Bandelier National Monument** (p133), or continue into the volcanic wilderness to **Jemez State Monument** (p192), once home to the Jemez Pueblo, and the **Museum of Pueblo Culture** (p192), both near **Jemez Springs** (p192).

On the High Road, don't skip **Picuris Pueblo** (p128), which gets remarkably few tourists, and explore the many fine Native art galleries in **Taos** (p134). End by checking out **Santa Fe** (p60), which has the **Museum of Indian Arts & Culture** (p69) and **Institute of American Indian Arts Museum** (p72).

ARTFUL PURSUITS

Art oozes from every pore of New Mexico's soul. Start in Santa Fe, with **Museum Hill** (p67), which boasts four museums bursting with fine arts, Indian arts and folk art. Other worthy contenders include the **Georgia O'Keeffe Museum** (p69). (Serious fans head out to O'Keeffe country in **Abiquiú**; p122.) **Canyon Rd** (p70) offers more galleries than you could shake a stick at, while the **Santa Fe Opera** (p107) and **Maria Benitez Teatro Flamenco** (p107) have few peers. Visitors come from thousands of miles away to attend **Indian Market** (p91).

Heading north, you can sample the weaving on the **High Road to Taos** (p125) before plunging into art big-time in Taos itself. And make sure

you don't miss the **Millicent Rogers Museum** (p139), **Harwood Foundation Museum** (p139), **Taos Art Museum & Fechin House** (p140) and **Blumenschein Home & Museum** (p140). Literature buffs make pilgrimages to the **DH Lawrence Ranch & Memorial** (p161).

Located in Albuquerque, the **Indian Pueblo Cultural Center** (p177) offers a great introduction to Pueblo arts, while the **National Hispanic Cultural Center** (p177) does the same for its people.

A multitude of art courses are offered in **Santa Fe** (p88) and **Taos** (p146). Architecture fans will make the effort to reach **Spencer Theater** (p210) in Ruidoso.

SPIRITUAL PILGRIMAGES

Taos Pueblo (p156), set at the base of a deeply mystical mountain, is an ancient place full of spirit. Ride a steed from the **Taos Indian Horse Ranch** (p157) on sacred lands. Questions posed at **Chaco Culture National Historical Park** (p220) will bury themselves deep within your core.

Traditionalists pop their souls into Taos' **San Francisco de Asis Church** (p141) – before taking requisite exterior photos. In Santa Fe, old missions and small chapels give way to **St Francis Cathedral** (p82), an enduring symbol downtown. Many visitors continue on to the **Cross of the Martyrs** (p83). Real seekers give it up at **Santuario de Chimayó** (p127), where miracles can happen. New Agers won't overlook the **Absolute Nirvana Spa & Tea Room** (p98), but all should seek refuge in adobe churches on the **High Road to Taos** (p125).

Non-Christian pilgrims have a place here, too, at the **Lama Foundation** (p161) near Taos, and in Abiquiú at **Ghost Ranch** (p125), **Christ in the Desert Monastery** (p125) and **Dar al Islam Mosque & Madressa** (p124).

Less traditional pilgrimages take many forms. Foodies flock to Mark Miller's **Coyote Café** (p100) in Santa Fe and prideful GLBT tribe members time a visit with Albuquerque's **Pride Parade** (p180). Not to sound blasphemous, but the quest for the ultimate margarita is something of a spiritual pursuit for many; if that describes you, look no further than **Adobe Bar** (p153). Moving meditators visit the **T'ai Chi Chih Center** (p183) in Albuquerque, environmentalists pay homage at Taos' **Earthships** (p142), while spacey visitors tune into aliens at **Roswell** (p211). Spirit takes many forms in New Mexico.

NATIONAL PARKS & MONUMENTS

Connect the dots on these winners and you'll have a handy and handsome excuse to explore three corners of the state. Start at **Petroglyph National Monument** (p177), just 10 easy miles from Albuquerque's Sunport. Then visit the well-worn walls of the **Kasha-Katuwe Tent Rocks** (p193), which offer ready-made travelogue highlights. **Bandelier National Monument** (p133), in the heart of an old volcano, is threaded with ancient trails.

Head southwest to clamber around the desolate **Gila Cliff Dwellings** (p202) and then head due east to **White Sands National Monument** (p207), where expansive gypsum dunes resemble something out of the bleached sub-Sahara. Forge on to explore deep beneath the earth's surface at **Carlsbad Caverns** (p213), an immense caving network.

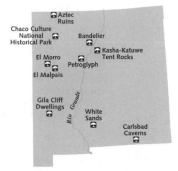

Then it's up to northwestern New Mexico to wander lava fields at **El Malpais National Monument** (p214) and marvel at the sandstone **El Morro National Monument** (p216). Even more remote, **Chaco Culture National Historical Park** (p220) barely gives up her secrets to quiet visitors. **Aztec Ruins** (p220), a mini Chaco, has the largest reconstructed kiva in the country. Don't forget to sprinkle in a few national wildlife refuges and state parks along the way; there are plenty.

Snapshot

Put your ear to the ground in New Mexico and what are you likely to hear? The scuttlebutt depends on where you do the asking: Santa Fe, Taos, Albuquerque or the hinterlands (er…the four, far reaches of the state).

Amble into a bar (except it's not a bar, it's a free-trade coffee-café) in Taos and you'll likely hear a vigorous conversation about the subtle nuances of passive solar energy and the US addiction to oil. Except the far-left-of-center off-the-grid types here are actually doing something about it, rather than Mr Bush and the neo-cons just talking sound bites.

Saunter into a divey bar (except it's more like a hundred-year-old gathering place) miles from nowhere and you'll find generations of Hispanic friends and family strengthening ties and bonding in ways that middle-class Anglos generally do not.

March into a rez or casino bar and you'll come face-to-face with the impact of gaming on Indian lands, newfound wealth and alcoholism.

Head into a scenester bar (one that doubles as a hip bistro) in Santa Fe and you'll hear liberals talking about locally grown organic veggies and the price of real estate. Have a micro beer at an in-the-know dive and eavesdrop on activist politicians actually doing something about raising minimum wages in Santa Fe (to $10.50 an hour in 2008). The majority of voters in Albuquerque (in October 2005) thought workers could get by on $5.15 an hour.

Stroll into a suburban-style bar in Rio Rancho and someone will bend your ear about the need for commercial and residential development, dwindling water resources be damned. Rio Rancho is one of the fastest-growing small cities in the country (and the fastest in New Mexico).

And although it's hardly an issue reserved for border communities, walk into any small town way south of Albuquerque and immigration issues (border patrols and illegal aliens) loom large as they come under the scrutiny of a national microscope. Illegals were the 2006 electoral cycle's gays – the litmus test for the strength of a politician's conservative conviction.

Water, of course, inspires the steadiest stream of commentary. It's most certainly not everywhere, and if you want a drop to drink at any restaurant, you'll have to ask for it – by law. What really gets folks in a lather is that Las Campañas, where President George W Bush golfs when he's in town, has been awarded water rights more suitable for Seattle while the rest of the capital suffers Stage III Water Restrictions, which forbid planting new grass or watering existing (brown) yards more than twice a week.

Above all, remember that this is no ordinary place. In the *Albuquerque Journal*'s 'Albu-Quirky' section you'll find stories about the right to dance naked in one's own house and about a Catholic diocese holding a novena to pray for rain. Open the *Santa Fean* and you'll read about a judge who forced drunk drivers to wear pink hats in public as a form of punishment. On any given day, whether you keep the shutter open for 1/60 of a second or for a long timed exposure, a snapshot of New Mexico is highly unpredictable. Bring a big memory chip to capture all of its nuances.

History

About the same time that the Brits were building Stonehenge and Indians (in India) were beginning to weave cotton, New Mexicans were learning to farm and organizing into permanent settlements. By the time Charlemagne was crowned emperor in Europe and Nara was named the first capital of Japan, Chaco Canyon, Bandelier and other major regional cities were thriving metropolises regularly trading with Central America and the US Midwest. Heck, the first cities in Mesopotamia may not be much older than some of the irrigation ditches around here.

And as the Pilgrims settled down to that first Thanksgiving, bustling Santa Fe was celebrating its second decade as the Spanish capital of New Mexico, complete with political tensions involving the surrounding, and far older, cities. The USA may be a young country in some respects, but New Mexico is ancient and enamored of its rich cultural inheritance, which is so well preserved in the dry desert air.

The New Mexico Office of the State Historian (www .newmexicohistory .org) is an elegant site that offers an online searchable database of historical documents.

HUNTER-GATHERER PERIOD

Though you may know that humans first came to the Americas atop a land bridge formed along Alaska's Aleutian chain during the last ice age, consider the potential for a grain of truth in the Native American version: that people around here originally emerged from the Sipapú, a cavern somewhere in the mountains of Northern New Mexico.

Because, oddly enough, the oldest evidence of human habitation on the continent wasn't discovered in Alaska. Spearheads, dating back at least 12,000 years, found near Clovis, New Mexico, are widely accepted as the oldest human remains on the continent.

Here's the official version: nomadic Paleo-Indians first settled Northern New Mexico in about 10,000 BC (a suspiciously round number that experts from various fields argue over constantly). About 2000 years later, the ancestors of the linguistically distinct Zuñi tribe came from the Midwest to join them.

The shift from hunter-gatherer existence to a more settled agricultural economy took place between 6000 and 3000 BC, when techniques and crops introduced from Mexico became widespread. By this time, trade routes with civilizations in Central America, California and the Midwest were well established. One of the first cultivated crops was tobacco, and by 1500 BC thriving farms along the Rio Grande were producing corn, beans and squash – a reliable diet diversified with hunting and gathering.

RISE OF THE CITY-STATES

The growing agricultural economy gave people more time to pursue arts and sciences, including manufacturing goods for trade. One of the most valuable items available in Northern New Mexico was turquoise, taken from surface deposits that were eventually depleted.

In about AD 100, engineers dug North America's first mine, near Cerrillos; you can see stone taken from these mines at the Cerrillos

TIMELINE	12,000 BC	AD 850
	Hunters near Clovis leave behind a few broken spearheads	Chaco Canyon founded; would later become the most important city-state in Northern New Mexico

Turquoise Mining Museum & Petting Zoo, which also has tools that were used there. Jewelry made with Cerrillos turquoise has been unearthed all over North America.

Basketry, ceramics and other arts also improved rapidly during this period, and by AD 600 locally produced redware pottery was being traded as far as California and Mexico.

Cities were springing up throughout the region, as advances in materials and design allowed complexes to reach five stories tall. Chaco Canyon – founded in the late 800s east of modern-day Cuba – was the capital of a city-state, immediately housing some 1200 people, while the surrounding communities may have had a population of 5000 more.

By AD 1000 Chaco was the region's most important financial and administrative center, facilitating communications and trade via some 400 miles of roads that connected it with other cities throughout the region, including Puyé and Bandelier. In turn, these cities probably acted as local centers of government for surrounding communities.

Religious iconography of the period bears a strong resemblance to that of the Aztec empire. This empire was built in the 1200s by people who called their ancestral home, which is usually traced to this region, Aztlán (Nahuatl for 'Land of the Blue Herons'), indicating a much moister environment.

Like all empires, Chaco fell. Modern research suggests that long-term warming trends and increasingly depleted resources, including lumber and fertile soil, may have led to a period of civil unrest. The abandonment of Chaco and other major cities between 1150 and 1270 remains somewhat mysterious, however.

Many of the 19 modern pueblos were founded in the wake of this exodus, including Ohkay Owingeh (formerly San Juan Pueblo). There, a central government for a loose confederation of regional city-states was established as early as the 1200s. It is still the seat of both the Eight Northern Indian Pueblos Council and Bureau of Indian Affairs Northern Pueblo Agency.

The Jicarilla Apache Indians, whose reservation is in north-central New Mexico, first migrated into the state's northeast plains between AD 1300 and 1500.

THE SPANISH INCURSION

In about 1400, groups of Diné (Navajo) and Apache emigrated from Colorado to the region. Though many of these nomadic peoples pursued a peaceful and profitable relationship with the Pueblo Indians, this was, overall, a violent period. Skirmishes inspired advances in defensive architecture that would prove useful when the next new neighbors moved in.

The Spanish government sent two preliminary teams into the area, one in 1536 and another in 1539, when missionary Fray Marcos de Niza erected a cross at Zuñi Pueblo and claimed the territory for Spain. It was the 1540 expedition led by Francisco Vasquez de Coronado, however, that fundamentally transformed the region.

Coronado was searching for the Seven Cities of Gold but found only heavily fortified cities of gold-toned adobe. He stopped first at Acoma Pueblo's mesa-top fortress, calling it among the strongest cities he'd ever seen. He then moved on to easier pickings, wintering at less-fortified Kuau'a, on which the present-day Coronado State Monument is built.

Coronado and his men began appropriating food and clothing from area residents. Though most grudgingly acceded, one group, probably from Sandia Pueblo, drove off several of their horses. Enraged, Coronado ordered an attack on the pueblo, burning it to the ground.

Several other explorers followed, and in 1598 Don Juan de Oñate set out to colonize the region. When his contingent of some 400 priests and soldiers wintered near Acoma Pueblo, several men attempted to scale the fortress's cliffs and raid its winter stores; 13 were killed, including Oñate's nephew.

According to Acoma historians, retribution was severe: Oñate chopped one foot off every man over 25. Others call this exaggeration, as Oñate needed slave labor, and this would have cost him manpower. Whatever the truth, when a statue in Oñate's honor was erected in Española in 1998, clever vandals made off with one of its feet.

It was close to modern-day Española that Oñate founded the first permanent Spanish settlement of San Gabriel, declaring it the capital of the Kingdom of New Mexico, with himself as governor. About 800 Spaniards and lots of Mexican Indian laborers were joined by 18 Franciscan friars, who got to work converting the locals by any means necessary.

These friars had been born into and trained during the most brutal wave of the Spanish Inquisition. After successfully driving the Moors from Spain, an entrenched theocracy continued to torture and kill accused heretics in the name of God. This was something these men had lived their entire lives considering normal. Oñate likely encouraged them to do their worst. Beautiful missions were built using forced labor, children were sold as slaves in Mexico, and that was not the worst of it.

Eventually Oñate was removed from office, both for his failure to find gold and for his mistreatment of the locals. His replacement, Don Pedro de Peralta, chose to move the capital entirely, founding La Villa de Santa Fe (City of Holy Faith) in 1609. There he and those first families built La Fonda; the Casas Reales (Royal Houses), today called the Palace of the Governors; and eventually a thriving agricultural sector, built around present-day Canyon Rd and Barrio de Analco.

In the pueblos, however, echoes of the Inquisition only intensified.

PUEBLO REVOLT OF 1680

According to Native traditions, the only place a pan-Pueblo war could be declared was San Juan Pueblo, and only by one who lived there. In the 1670s, friars punished, publicly and horribly, perhaps 50 Native religious leaders who continued practicing the old religion, including a San Juan priest named Popé. Popé organized a meeting of pueblo representatives and told them they could beat the Spanish. They agreed to try.

San Juan was too close to Santa Fe, so Popé moved his base of operations to Taos Pueblo. He worked closely with other military leaders throughout the state, most notably Domingo Naranjo from Santa Clara and Catiti from Santo Domingo, who marshaled the Keres-speaking tribes.

They used the tools of the conquistadors against them: the Spanish language facilitated communication between the linguistically different tribes, and runners distributed yucca cords with knots untied each morning in a universal countdown.

The Spanish suspected subterfuge, and shortly before the uprising was due to begin two Tesuque messengers were intercepted. When Fray Juan

The Genealogical Society of Hispanic America (www.gsha.net) provides access to historical records, maps, family histories and books with New Mexico as a major focus.

1680	1693
The Pueblo Indians organize a successful revolt, driving the Spanish settlers back to El Paso for 12 years	Don Diego DeVargas, after talking things over with the locals, returns with more Spanish settlers to Santa Fe

---

THE USA'S OLDEST CAPITAL CITY – BUT HOW OLD?

You'd think that a city so storied (and so proud of it) would have its own history down pat. But any firm account of Santa Fe's foundation has remained elusive, thanks to the Pueblo Revolt of 1680, which destroyed all documentation of the city's inauguration.

Regardless, as late as the 1880s, Santa Fe's ever-diligent tourism professionals were touting that Francisco Vasquez de Coronado himself had left a handful of settlers/soldiers at an Indian pueblo right here in 1540 or so. There was just one problem – there was absolutely no proof of any area pueblos, much less that Coronado had left any of his gold-seeking companions here.

But Santa Fe's promoters and publicists were nothing if not resilient, and quickly pinned the city's nativity on explorer Antonio de Espejo, who rode through New Mexico in 1883. Once again, however, not one record reflected that Espejo had even come close to town.

Regardless, the tourists had a lovely time at the various anniversary parties, and thus, the city stuck to its story for several decades. Then evidence uncovered in Spain during the 1920s fixed the long-contested date at 1608, when the Crown had ordered Don Pedro de Peralta to found the villa (or town) of Santa Fe in that lush little valley. Finally, beleaguered city historians could relax.

Or could they? In the 1940s documentation turned up that one Don Juan Martinez de Montoya, appointed interim governor after Oñate was recalled to Mexico City, founded the plaza (or village) of Santa Fe in 1607. Peralta had only upgraded the already existing site. At long last, the mystery was solved.

Not so fast: recent excavations at the Palace of the Governors seem to confirm rumors that have been going around for half a millennium. Yes, it seems that there really was once a pueblo right beneath where the plaza now stands. And one can't help but wonder whether a few of Coronado's bedraggled troops weren't enchanted enough to stay behind.

Pío arrived at Tesuque the next morning to give Mass, he was assassinated. It was too soon, and too late. Runners fanned out across the state.

The following day, Indians began laying siege to Santa Fe. San Miguel Mission was the first to fall. Santa Feans barricaded themselves inside the Palace of the Governors as Indians torched homes and businesses.

Though the better-armed Spanish killed scores of Indian troops, reinforcements from the surrounding pueblos poured into the capital. For nine days the battle raged, until Indians diverted the palace's water supply.

Thirsty and exhausted, the Spanish surrendered. Pueblo leadership defined the terms of the truce: immediate removal of the Spanish from tribal lands. A rag-tag column of refugees made their way south to El Paso, more than 300 backbreaking miles.

The Indians occupied Santa Fe for 12 years, though old political rivalries quickly resurfaced, weakening the tenuous system of alliances formed during the occupation. Many returned to their homes.

The Spanish settlers were plotting their own return, and with the arrival of Don Diego DeVargas, a seasoned soldier and negotiator, set their plans into motion. DeVargas visited all the pueblos with a heavily armed contingent, basically aiming cannons at the city walls while asking for peace.

Popular history calls the Reconquista 'almost bloodless,' yet many tribes abandoned their pueblos entirely for several years, retreating to

1821	1826
Mexico's (and New Mexico's) independence from Spain finally allows the opening of the Santa Fe Trail for business	A young Kit Carson joins a wagon train to Santa Fe; he would settle in Taos in 1843

live with Apache and Plains Indian allies rather than face retribution. At least 80 people died resisting DeVargas, and that's according to historical accounts written by the Spanish.

But pueblos were negotiating from a difficult position, and since the revolt, the Indians have worshipped however they chose without interference (well, not as much). Many chose Catholicism or some combination of Christian and Native belief systems.

In October 1693, 70 families, 100 soldiers and 18 friars returned to Santa Fe.

EUROPEAN EXPANSION

After securing Santa Fe, Spanish settlers began populating the Rio Grande Valley in earnest. By the 1700s Spanish control of the continent was being threatened by growing British and French colonies to the east, and the government encouraged settlers with land grants. Truchas, Taos, Albuquerque and many other cities were incorporated.

The region remained isolated from Spain, and agricultural communities were basically self-sufficient, developing distinctive crafts, in particular the colorful reredos and retablos – sacred art – which were markedly different from the European traditions.

Though the pueblos had been largely subdued, retribution for the Pueblo Revolt was exacted in the form of high taxes and annexed land, and the Comanche, Apache and Navajo tribes began increasingly coordinated attacks on these homesteads. Plazas and large haciendas, such as Chimayó's original plaza and La Hacienda de los Martinez in Taos, were designed to protect entire communities from these raids.

New Mexicans were becoming increasingly independent from Spain, and despite laws against trade with the newly independent United States of America, illegal trade along the Santa Fe Trail became more common. When peace treaties were signed with the Comanche in 1804, only one barrier remained to free trade.

MEXICAN INDEPENDENCE

Though most New Mexicans were comfortable with – or, at least, could ignore – Spanish rule, revolution had been fomenting in central Mexico for decades. In September 1821 Mexican separatists declared victory. Santa Fe celebrated, and the end of the Santa Fe Trail became a popular spot for traders led by William Becknell, who brought in wares like nails, metal tools and new technologies that the isolated region had long done without.

Businesspeople like Doña Tules began building a formidable economy, opening saloons and gambling halls where these traders could come and lose their profits. By the 1840s Rio Grande weavers were exporting some 21,000 pieces annually; trade increased twentyfold in every sector.

Even as cultural and economic ties with the Americans strengthened, the local population was growing disenchanted with Mexican rule. Governor Manuel Armijo attached increasingly higher taxes on every transaction, and his corruption and cruelty won him few friends. When the US declared war on Mexico in 1846, ostensibly because of skirmishes on the Texas border (but in reality because of a strategy to extend US control

The 12 essays in Marc Simmons's *Spanish Pathways: Readings In the History of Hispanic New Mexico* use original scholarship to tell of real people's lives during colonial times.

1846	1847
Mexican-American War arrives with General Stephen W Kearny, to little resistance from locals disenchanted with Mexican rule	Governor Charles Bent killed; some 150 Pueblo Indians are killed and 400 captured in retribution

to Pacific ports), General Stephen Kearny was able to take Santa Fe and all of New Mexico with relative ease.

US RULE

Pockets of resistance remained after the state was annexed as a US territory. The first US governor, Charles Bent, was attacked and scalped at his home in Taos by a contingent of Spanish and Indians loyal to Armijo.

The event touched off a bloody reprisal on Taos Pueblo, where 150 women, children and elders were burned alive as they huddled inside the pueblo's mission. Today only the bell tower remains.

Scour the exhaustive history bibliography and obtain access to photo archives at www.cabq .gov/museum/history.

Relations between the US government and Native peoples continued to deteriorate, and in 1851 Governor James C Calhoun issued a proclamation authorizing volunteer forces to kill any Native American who looked threatening. The Diné and Apache 'Long Walk,' in which 10,000 POWs and civilian detainees were marched by Kit Carson, starving, for 400 miles to a concentration camp near Fort Sumner, was probably the worst episode.

Most of the state thrived under US rule, however, despite tensions between the largely Spanish-speaking population and their new government. A new wave of settlers began pouring in: young Jewish men, escaping persecution in Central Europe, set up shop here. Solomon Jacob Spiegelberg arrived with Union forces in 1846 and operated a mercantile in Santa Fe until the 1870s. Solomon Bibo, who arrived in the region in the 1870s, married a Laguna Pueblo woman and was later elected governor of the tribe.

You can still have drinks in the home of prominent Santa Fean Abraham Staab, who helped finance Archbishop Jean-Baptiste Lamy in the construction of St Francis Cathedral. According to legend, Staab forgave the massive debts its construction incurred, inspiring the addition of the tetragrammaton (JHVH) above the entrance.

Lamy, a newly arrived French archbishop less than enchanted by the territory's independent Catholic leadership, suspended Albuquerque Padre José Manuel Gallegos, who went on to represent New Mexico in the US Congress. Lamy later excommunicated the beloved Padre Antonio José Martinez of Taos, who ignored him and continued to preach.

The archbishop also ordered many of the traditional retablos and reredos removed from New Mexico churches; they were squirreled away in private homes and returned to their altars after his death in 1888.

By this time, the railroad linked Santa Fe and Albuquerque to the rest of the country; it was only a matter of time before the territory gained full statehood.

STATEHOOD

After New Mexico finally achieved statehood in 1912, writers and artists began coming to the arid state to recuperate from tuberculosis and ended up falling in love with the place, then inviting their friends out to visit. Folks like Mabel Dodge Luhan, the Taos Society of Artists and Los Cincos Pintores in Santa Fe began adding their own surreal twists to local culture.

1853	1879
The Gadsden Purchase adds another sliver of (train-friendly) land to New Mexico's southern border	The Santa Fe Railroad is established but (a boon to trivia fans everywhere) bypassed Santa Fe for Lamy

The growing Anglo community made several popular contributions to the increasingly pluralistic society, including Zozobra at the annual Santa Fe Fiestas. Though some saw this as the erosion of New Mexico's essentially Hispanic character by its latest nation, in 1936 the state returned the favor, sending the USA's first Hispanic senator, Dennis Chávez, to Washington.

New Mexico was a primarily agricultural economy, so most folks didn't feel much of a pinch during the Great Depression. But when the Works Progress Administration (WPA) began, New Mexicans began getting training and opportunities they'd never had before, new roads and buildings were built, and most people did better than ever – and changed their votes. Prior to 1936 New Mexico was a Republican state; ever since, it's voted Democrat in two out of three elections.

WWII transformed the state even more fundamentally. In 1943 the federal government took over an isolated mesa east of Santa Fe and built a secret city to construct a nuclear device, code-named the Manhattan Project. In 1945 Los Alamos unleashed its secret on Hiroshima and then Nagasaki, bringing WWII to an end. The blasts killed 120,000 people immediately, and perhaps three times as many in the years that followed.

Santa Fe and Taos, in the meantime, were experiencing a cultural bloom. Since the 1920s Taos patron Mabel Dodge Luhan and Santa Fe's Alice Corbin had been bringing writers and artists to the state. In the 1960s they were joined by a new breed of counterculture archetype: the hippie. New Buffalo Commune, made famous in the movie *Easy Rider*, was but one groovy Taos outpost where folks farmed naked, drove rattling VW buses around and in general irritated the traditionally conservative Catholic residents.

There were incidents of violence and vandalism in Taos throughout the late 1960s and early 1970s as the two very different groups learned to get along. Things eventually settled down, particularly after the newcomers began donning clothing. The precedent was set, and both Santa Fe and Taos were firmly entrenched on the hippie trail.

But it wasn't just the hippies. New Mexico, like the rest of the Southwest, was experiencing a huge general population boom, coinciding with the widespread availability of swamp coolers and air-conditioning. The state's population has tripled since 1950.

In the 1980s New Agers, convinced that Santa Fe was at the crossroads of invisible lines of power, brought holistic healing, organic grocers and feng shui to the state capital. Microchip manufacturer Intel, convinced that Albuquerque's underground aquifer would never be depleted, built the world's largest chip manufacturing plant in the suburb of Rio Rancho in the 1980s.

CURRENT ISSUES

The jury's still out on the New Agers, but Intel was wrong, and Albuquerque's primary source of water is being rapidly depleted. Water remains the state's single most important issue, and as this book went to press the state had entered its sixth year of drought. There are several stop-gap measures in place, such as restrictions on watering lawns and laws requiring restaurants to supply patrons water only on request,

The Man Who Killed the Deer, first published in 1942 when author Frank Waters lived in Taos, is a transcendent story of Pueblo Indian culture that raises moral questions about the conflicts between Indian and white laws.

In *Off the Map*, directed by Campbell Scott in 2003, an entrancing storyline and stunning panoramic cinematography help tell the tale of an idealistic 1970s family dropping out in Taos.

1912	1945
New Mexico becomes the 47th state in the USA after years of debate about slavery, Spanish speakers and other issues	The world's first nuclear bomb, built in Los Alamos, is successfully detonated near White Sands National Monument

but the main problems – population growth and increased reliance on often water-dependent industries – are all but impossible to regulate effectively.

Luckily, there are plenty of other issues keeping New Mexicans thinking – or not. Former Republican governor Gary Johnson made national headlines in the late 1990s after saying on national TV that, 'I don't think you should go to jail for smoking marijuana,' and calling the War on Drugs 'a miserable failure.' The former owner of Big J Construction became a regular on the talk-show circuit and introduced eight legalization bills to the state legislature, from medical marijuana to full decriminalization of all drugs. Not one of them passed.

Johnson's successor, popular Democratic governor Bill Richardson, has decided to take the state's reputation even higher. In December 2005 he signed a contract with Virgin Galactic to build the world's first private spaceport near White Sands National Monument. As of 2009, for the first time in history, you'll be able to take your high-altitude New Mexico vacation out past the stratosphere.

In 2005 the Navajo Nation signed a tribal law banning uranium mining on their land, part of which is in New Mexico.

1981	2005
Intel Corporation opens the world's largest chip manufacturing plant in Rio Rancho, Albuquerque	Deal for the construction of the first purpose-built commercial spaceport struck between Virgin Galactic and New Mexico state

The Culture

New Mexico pitches itself as proudly tricultural, a place where Native Americans, Hispanics, Anglos and everyone else gets along, if not in perfect harmony, then at least better than most places. In general this is true, with a few simmering caveats. But most folks make a genuine effort to understand and respect one another, something that extends to growing populations of African-Americans, Asians and other groups drawn to the region.

Most people who have been here a while think of themselves as New Mexicans, often distinct from Americans, and in a different category altogether from the rest of the Southwest, which tends to be more conservative politically and socially. It's a consciously open-minded place, where a variety of traditional cultures are preserved in an atmosphere of mutual respect and where creative careers, fostered from an early age in the public schools, are encouraged and venerated. The result is a region of unusual diversity and impressive eclecticism.

Population centers are still distributed along major rivers and waterways, as water remains the limiting factor to all New Mexican development, as it has been for centuries. Rural communities of a few thousand people or less tend to be more traditional (read: unpaved roads and real, often ancient adobes), and in the northern part of the state Spanish remains spoken as often as English, though this is evidently diluting with each successive generation.

Major cities are more mainstream (and Albuquerque almost cosmopolitan), with most population centers boasting modern downtowns, Vietnamese restaurants, Starbucks galore and English spoken in almost every business. But look hard enough and you'll still find old Spanish plazas lost among the strip malls and skyscrapers.

Santa Fe, dating back to at least 1607, is the oldest US capital. Since heritage preservation can be a challenge in such an old state, check out www.nmheritage.org.

REGIONAL IDENTITY

Though describing the three major New Mexican cultures is a good introduction to the state, keep in mind that many people hail from more than one of them, and most of the rest feel little need to judge their neighbors by the color of their skin.

With so many characters around, that's the barometer folks have been relying on for centuries.

Native Americans

There are about 150,000 Native Americans officially enrolled in tribes in New Mexico, making up around 10% of the population. Most are Diné/Navajo, with around 40,000 Pueblo Indians and 6000 Jicarilla and Mescalero Apaches. Indians account for only about 1% of the US population, thus New Mexico has become something of a stronghold, politically and economically, of Native pride and power.

The approximately 800-year-old San Juan Pueblo changed its name in 2005 back to Ohkay Owingeh, as it was known before Spanish possession in 1598.

Area Indian tribes are only now coming into their own economically. Until gaming became widespread in the early 1990s, the vast majority of Native New Mexicans lived beneath the poverty level, many subsisting on bare-bones federal stipends that were, as one person put it, 'the government's way of proving that socialism doesn't work.' Though some criticize casino culture as destroying the traditional Native way of life, the trade-off is obvious when watching luxurious homes rise from where doublewide trailers once parked.

All pueblos and reservations are diversifying their economies, adding everything from business parks to resorts and golf courses, and gaming profits have also been efficiently invested in schools, roads, clinics and other long-needed infrastructure. Many tribes have undertaken buffalo reintroduction programs, while others are working for environmental protection and cleanup. Their effect on the state and nation has been profound, and continues to grow.

Hispanics

About 43.3% of New Mexico's population is Hispanic, the highest proportion of any state in the USA (about 15% Hispanic overall). New Mexico's Hispanics also command more wealth, own more businesses and are better represented in politics than anyplace else in the country. In the northern half of the state, most come from Spanish-speaking families who have been here since well before statehood; in the south, a recent influx of Latin American immigrants – legal and illegal – form a distinct Spanish-speaking population.

New Mexico is the only officially bilingual state, though some historians have recently argued that this provision, outlined in the 1912 Constitution, was meant to be temporary. Nevertheless, about 30% of New Mexicans speak Spanish at home, all government publications are bilingual, and there are three state songs, in Spanish, English and Spanglish. New Mexico's Hispanics exert their political and economic influence not only in New Mexico but also throughout the country.

The country's first Hispanic senator, Dennis Chávez, was a fierce proponent of civil rights, while Dolores Huerta, cofounder of the United Farm Workers, negotiated the first contract for immigrant farm workers. Today, the country's only Hispanic governor, Democrat Bill Richardson, looks ready to make a run for the presidency.

WHAT'S IN A NAME?

Though the stereotypes that too often accompany racial labels are largely ignored in New Mexico, it's still a challenge for publishers to figure out the most accurate (and politically correct) term for various ethnic groups. Listed here is the rundown on our terminology for New Mexico's big three:

- Native American – after introducing themselves to one very confused Christopher Columbus, the original Americans were labeled 'Indians.' The name stuck, and 500 years later folks from Mumbai are still trying to explain that, no, they don't speak a word of Tewa. 'Native American' is recommended by every major news organization, but in New Mexico most tribal members remain comfortable with the term 'Indian.' Both terms are used in this book.

- Anglo – though 'Caucasian' is the preferred moniker (even if their ancestors hailed from nowhere near the Caucuses) and 'White' is the broadest and most useful word for European-Americans, in New Mexico the label for non-Iberian Europeans is 'Anglo' ('of England'). Even English speakers of Norwegian-Polish ancestry are Anglo around here, so get used to it.

- Hispanic – this is the one that has editors pulling their hair out. Associated Press prefers hyphens: 'Mexican-American,' 'Venezuelan-American' – and are Spanish-speaking US citizens more properly 'American-Americans'? Obviously, it's easier, if less precise, to use 'Latino' to describe people hailing from the Spanish-speaking Americas. Then add to that list 'Chicano,' 'Raza' and 'Hispano,' a de-anglicized term currently gaining popularity, and everyone's confused. But, because New Mexico was part of Spain for 225 years and Mexico only 25, and many folks can trace an unbroken ancestry back to Spain, 'Hispanic' ('of Spain') is the term used throughout this state and book, sprinkled with 'Spanish' and all the rest.

Anglos

Anglos (more properly, non-Hispanic Whites) make up 43.5% of the state's population, a number that has grown disproportionately over the past 50 years. Most live in Southern New Mexico and in major population centers throughout the rest of the state, and recent waves of arrivals include wealthy retirees, scientists, defense workers and, most famously, the artists, hippies and spiritual types who feel drawn here.

Racial roles are in some ways reversed in New Mexico compared to the rest of the United States: many Anglos feel that they are the outsiders, working to fit into a still largely Hispanic culture. But Anglo contributions to the arts, sciences and progressive politics of Northern New Mexico are seen as cultural markers that few would want to erase.

LIFESTYLE

The lifestyle in Northern New Mexico can best be described as laid-back. Although many folks have a taste for the finer things – the number of excellent gourmet restaurants is your first clue – you can wear jeans absolutely anywhere. Locals are casual and community-oriented, people know their neighbors and you'll get smiles anywhere you go.

Rural communities tend to be artsy and insular, while cities like Santa Fe and Albuquerque offer all sorts of activities that tend toward the creative and outdoorsy. While the person scraping off the 'too-hot' chile you just sent back may mutter about 'tourons,' New Mexico has a tourist economy, which means that your dollars create much-needed jobs.

And, like many tourist economies, the region has a drug problem, exacerbated by proximity to the rather porous border with Mexico. The attendant crime is relative high, and New Mexico ranks near the top in violent crimes, burglary and aggravated assault, not to mention car accidents, drunk driving and other scary social indicators.

It's still the Wild West, but bravado here comes fabulously accessorized. Individuality (even eccentricity) is highly regarded, and 'keeping up with the Joneses' often translates into having the neighborhood's best yard art, welded or raku-fired by hand in the studio out back. There's a sense of freedom beneath the enormous sky, and a big part of the unspoken social contract is to live and let live.

POPULATION

Like most Southwestern states, New Mexico has a relatively young population, with the median age of 34 somewhat skewed by the number of retirees who choose to live here. Because water availability is a constant concern, most people are concentrated in urban areas such as Santa Fe (pop 65,100), Taos (4700) and Albuquerque (712,700); almost half the state population lives in Albuquerque and the endless suburbs of tract housing that surround it.

New Mexico is one of the most culturally, racially and religiously diverse regions in the USA, with higher percentages of Hispanics, Native Americans and Catholics than other states.

No race or religion claims an absolute majority in New Mexico, and neither does a major political party. About 30% of New Mexicans speak Spanish at home, almost 9% speak an indigenous language fluently, and recent immigrants speak all sorts of languages. While in some spots all this diversity might lead to some sort of social Balkanization, in New Mexico it's become a point of pride that so many peoples have decided just to get along.

Bookmobiles bring NM State Library materials to readers in 134 rural counties, serving almost 25,000 readers annually. Find free internet through www.publiclibraries.com/newmexico.

Acoma Pueblo's new 40,000-sq-ft Sky City Cultural Center and Haak'u Museum (www.skycity.com) showcases vibrant tribal culture, ongoing since the 12th century.

RELIGION

Perhaps because of its enforced isolation and (since 1680, anyway) tradition of tolerance, Northern New Mexico is considered a spiritual center to a variety of faiths, which exist here in unusual harmony, particularly considering how things are elsewhere in the world. The cultural geography that this has engendered is inspiring.

Native American Religions

The specifics of Pueblo Indian religious practices are not generally revealed to outsiders, and each tribe has its own traditions. But spiritual life centers on the kiva, a circular sacred space buried partially underground as a reminder of humanity's essential connection to the earth. All Native practices are characterized by a respect for nature that is often de-emphasized in modern interpretations of Western religions.

In *Fire in the Mind*, George Johnson asks if fact and belief, magic and science differ? This gifted writer juxtaposes groundbreaking scientific theories with Tewa Indian beliefs in northern New Mexico. Prepare to be dazzled.

Dances held on saints' feast days nominally praise each mission's Catholic patron, but also honor more ancient deities; other dances don't bother with the saint. Visitors are welcome to observe some dances as long as proper respect is maintained.

Festivities center on the plaza, where long lines of dancers move to drums and chanting provided primarily by men. The dancers are sometimes painted in earth and wearing pine boughs, fur pelts and fetching dresses – the costuming is different for each tribe and celebration. The gatherings are prayers, but are also festive, so expect food stands and plenty of roaming about after the prayer is complete.

Catholicism

The dominant religion in New Mexico is Roman Catholicism, and about 41% of the population is baptized Catholic, making this the most Catholic of all western states. Traditions remain stronger here than most places in the USA.

In the Holy Week leading up to Easter, some 75,000 pilgrims from as far away as Albuquerque make the pilgrimage to the Santuario de Chimayó. Christmas traditions, called Las Posadas, go way beyond Santa Claus: *farolitos* and luminarias line streets and cemeteries, and many families celebrate not on December 25 (though most businesses are closed that day) but on King's Day, January 6, as in Spain. Some businesses, particularly in rural areas, are closed during the weeks between.

In *Jemez Spring*, Rudolfo Anaya, the heralded Chicano novelist and UNM professor emeritus, combines poetic descriptions of New Mexico with politics, religion and culture as seen through the eyes of a wise, spiritual private detective investigating the governor's death.

Judaism

Many original Spanish settlers were probably Crypto-Jews, who converted to Catholicism to avoid persecution under the Inquisition. In the 1850s, a wave of openly Jewish young men, fleeing persecution in Central Europe, established businesses and homes here, particularly in Santa Fe. According to legend, the tetragrammaton (JHVH) above the entrance of St Francis Cathedral was to give thanks for the Staab family's financial contribution to its construction, but it may also honor those for whom Catholicism and Judaism have been intertwined for 400 years.

Other Religions

In the 1970s and 1980s, Santa Fe in particular became a mecca for New Age types. This migration has led to a proliferation of pagan and other traditions: 'What's your sign?' isn't just a pickup line around here; be prepared to know your ascendant and moon signs as well.

Large communities of Muslims, Sikhs, Quakers and most other major Protestant sects have been joined by the recent diaspora from Tibet, refugees who note the prophesy of Padmasambhava, founder of Tibetan Buddhism: 'When the iron bird flies and horses run on wheels…the Dharma will come to the land of the Red Man.'

And when a contingent of maroon-clad monks approached area tribes to tell their strange tale, they learned of a parallel Hopi prophesy: A 'tribe of red hat and red cloaked people' would arrive from the east 'by air.' Both, unfortunately, are evidently precursors to the cleansing of the Earth by fire; see the Los Alamos section for more about that.

ECONOMY

With little arable land, water that's been stringently regulated since at least 2000 BC, not to mention a merciless desert separating the region from trading partners, New Mexico has always been poor. Until the 1930s, the New Mexican economy was primarily subsistence farming; hence, the Great Depression had little effect on the population (it's hard to get fired from the family farm). President Roosevelt's 'New Deal,' however, finally provided high-paying jobs, building much needed infrastructure – highways, bridges, schools – and implemented WPA programs that launched artists, including Maria Martinez and Peter Hurd.

New Mexico reached a new level of sophistication (read: consumerism) in 2006 when Pottery Barn and the Sharper Image opened their first NM stores in Albuquerque.

WWII set off the state's biggest economic boom, and today the defense industry has two national labs, three air-force bases and White Sands Missile Range, all economic pillars. More than 25% of New Mexicans work for the government, with other top employers including Immigration Services, the Navajo nation, gas companies and public schools. New Mexico is the USA's largest per capita recipient of public funds.

SOUTHWEST REGIONAL SPACEPORT: THE ULTIMATE SIDE TRIP

White Sands earned its nickname 'Birthplace of the Race to Space' In 1947, when humanity, courtesy of NASA's Werner von Braun, successfully hurled its first missile out past the stratosphere from among those rolling, pure white dunes. Today, thanks to Virgin Galactic CEO Sir Richard Branson, Governor Bill Richardson and lots of other pie-in-the-sky visionaries (not to mention state taxpayers who'll foot most of the projected $225 million bill), the world's first private spaceport has opened right next door.

Space tourism, till now restricted to adventurers willing to shell out US$2 million a pop aboard Russia's Soyuz, may well involve a simple 62-mile (straight up) add-on to your New Mexico vacation package. For just $200,000, you can book your flight on the VSS Enterprise online, for a 90-minute ride in a plush cruiser with reclining seats, big windows and a pressurized cabin so you won't need space suits. The vessel is currently being built by legendary aerospace engineer Bob Rutan, whose SpaceShipOne was the first privately funded (by Microsoft cofounder Paul Allen) manned vehicle to reach outer space twice in a row, winning him the $10 million 2004 Ansari X-Prize.

It's not all about tourism, however. The Southwest Regional Spaceport (SRS), which is set to be renamed Spaceport America, has been used by UP Aerospace to launch cheap cargo carriers into low Earth orbit since 2006. The SRS is also the new home of the X-Prize competition, as well as other aerospace-themed expositions to be held throughout the year. But it's Virgin Galactic's maiden voyage, projected for early 2009, that promises to bring in the real press.

The New Mexico Office for Space Commercialization, founded by forward thinkers in 1994, estimates that the SRS will pump US$500 million into the state economy annually, primarily in the neighboring towns of Upham, Alamagordo and Truth or Consequences. Officials also hope to raise international awareness of New Mexico as a serious high-tech center: 'The planet will be watching as we reach for the stars,' noted New Mexico Tourism Secretary Michael Cerletti.

'We might even be able to allow those aliens who landed at Roswell 50 years ago in a UFO a chance to go home,' adds Richard Branson.

Important private industries include Intel, cattle ranching, farming (hay, pecans, chile, sorghum and piñon nuts), mining (turquoise, uranium, copper and beryllium) and pine wood. The art industry is important throughout Northern New Mexico, as is tourism. Regardless, the state ranks 48th in the USA for per capita income, with more than a quarter of children under 18 living in poverty. Employment opportunities are so scarce that the state forecasts a growth rate of only 12% between now and 2030.

GOVERNMENT

Though not everyone realizes it, New Mexico is part of the USA. The state maintains close ties with old Mexico, as well as strong cultural ties with the rest of Latin America and Spain, facilitated by the fact that many in state government speak Spanish with some degree of fluency.

About 300 Native American tribes in the USA are technically recognized as sovereign nations, but in reality are subject to most US laws and lots of red tape spewed forth with every attempt at economic development. Tribal members are also full US citizens and hold several important offices in US and New Mexico government. Internal Native governments vary from tribe to tribe, but are usually led by a governor, normally appointed by a council of elders rather than voted into office.

GOVERNOR BILL RICHARDSON

Right Wing News recently rated New Mexico Governor Bill Richardson number two on their 'Top Ten Most Dangerous Democrats' list, as America heads toward the 2008 presidential elections. His easy-going charisma and solid record as an antiwar, progay, negotiations-loving liberal, they noted, came nicely paired with the conservative CATO Institute ranking him the most fiscally responsible Democratic governor.

Richardson is perhaps best known as a seasoned diplomat with a 'knack for finding a warm spot in even the surliest of despots,' according to *Time* magazine. Richardson has gone to the mat with some of the USA's most dedicated antagonists, including Cuba, North Korea, Bangladesh and Sudan, famously convincing Iraqi President Saddam Hussein to release two American engineers who had wandered in from Kuwait.

As a border governor, Richardson has also been heavily involved with the immigration debate, and was the first to ask President Bush for federal resources to aid enforcement. But that tough stance is belied by the belief in 'an earned legalization program that has benchmarks of law-abidingness, that has benchmarks of working hard.' This merit-based citizenship could be 'a clear path toward some kind of legal status.'

His insights come via life experience quite different from most US officials. Born in Pasadena, California, to a Mexican national and an Anglo US citizen, he was raised between Mexico City and Boston. After earning his masters degree in Law and Diplomacy from Tufts University, Richardson worked for the US State Department and Senate Foreign Relations Committee. In 1978, he moved to Santa Fe (where he had never lived before) and promptly lost his first run for public office. Four years later, however, Richardson won the newly formed third district easily. He spent the next 14 years in congress before being appointed UN Ambassador and later Secretary of Energy under President Bill Clinton.

Like his good friend Clinton, Richardson has a reputation as a man of appetites: in 2005 he somehow managed to convince the legislature to purchase 'the state' a $5.5 million private jet – with leather seats and a wet bar. More recently, after getting yet another speeding ticket, he deadpanned, 'I am the first to admit that I try to cram as much business as possible into each and every day.' Democratic brass worry that what plays as fun-loving in New Mexico may read as irresponsible on the national stage. Regardless, Richardson's noted diplomatic skills, experience in energy legislation and familiarity with Latin America – of which the rest of the USA is only now realizing it is an integral part – may make him just the guy for the presidency in 2008.

The New Mexico state legislature (www.legis.state.nm.us) goes into session the third Tuesday of January and lasts two months during odd years, one during even years, at the Roundhouse. You're welcome to watch as any citizen is allowed to talk for as long as they want about anything, then ask audience members what they think. The possibilities, clearly, are endless.

Though registered Democrats make up the majority of New Mexican voters, voters have elected a 50-50 split of Democratic and Republican politicians. In any event, the politics of personality remain more important than party affiliations: many folks tick off six-term Republican US Senator Pete Dominici right along with Democrats Senator Jeff Bingaman and Representative Tom Udall. New Mexico was the only state to support Al Gore in the 2000 elections and go on to support George Bush in 2004. (Gore won by a margin of 366 votes after a tense Florida-esque recount that didn't really matter, since New Mexico has only five electoral college votes; four years later Bush won by 5000 votes.) Three minority parties – the Green, Constitution and Libertarian Parties – have also mustered the required 5% of the vote in recent elections in order to qualify for federal funding.

Cruise over to the annual Route 66 Preservation Foundation's Car Show and Neon Cruise (www .oldrt66.com).

Thanks in part to the Green Party's record turnout, maverick Republican Gary 'Big J' Johnson became governor in 1994, slashing budgets, freezing pay raises and becoming a Republican Party darling – until his maverick crusade to legalize marijuana during his second term.

Johnson's successor, popular Democratic Governor Bill Richardson, has played it a bit more conservatively (for New Mexico), merely speaking out on the once-popular Iraq War and signing legislation like the nation's most comprehensive civil rights law protecting gays, lesbians and transsexuals. The international power player was up for re-election as this book went to press, with no signs Richardson would lose the Roundhouse.

Arts

New Mexico's arts history is legendary and today's contemporary artists expand and explode that legacy. Native American writers, Chicano poets, Anglo architects, legions of painters and photographers, writers of every genre, and globally known classical and popular musicians make this sparsely populated state a major spot on the world's culture maps.

Santa Fe is no ordinary art colony: it's the third-largest art market in the US, after New York City and Los Angeles. The town's 250 galleries and other arts-related businesses support one in six people living there, and it boasts the highest number of arts businesses per capita in the country.

While most Americans consider the pursuit of art an interesting hobby, at best, in New Mexico it's a respected vocation. Art is heavily promoted in both public and private schools, and kids are encouraged to develop their skills through a variety of programs and special events.

The region's museums and galleries are a feast for the eyes, but the number of options can be overwhelming. So set priorities. Grab at least one of the elegant but free publications available everywhere: the **Collector's Guide** (www.collectorsguide.com) has gallery, accommodations and events listings for Taos, Santa Fe and Albuquerque; the **Essential Guide** (www.essentialguide.com) covers galleries and restaurants in Taos and Santa Fe; and the **Magazine** (www.themagazineonline.com) has more of the same for Santa Fe.

Arts aficionados can log onto www.santafearts andculture.org to browse gallery shows, view individual artists' work, read recent articles and use the interactive cultural-sites map.

VISUAL ARTS

You can spend days wandering the many galleries and museums and still not see everything, so if you're here to look at specific types of art, do some advance homework. If you're here to buy, do even more research to be sure the investments you make are worthwhile.

Native American Arts

From painting and sculpture to pottery, weaving and basketry, each New Mexico tribe has a specialty, though artisans at each pueblo pursue different – sometimes radically so – directions. The Indian Pueblo Cultural Center (p177) located in Albuquerque is a fantastic introduction

---

TURQUOISE – OR NOT?

Though New Mexico is famed for its high-quality Native American jewelry, those 'authentic' Zuñi and Navajo pieces aren't always what they seem. Several Southeast Asian countries have created quite a cottage industry imitating the fine work. Manufacturers use synthetic turquoise in pieces that appear almost identical to originals. Though required by law to display an import sticker, many unscrupulous dealers continue to market the jewelry as genuine.

Even if the piece is made in New Mexico by Native artisans, you still might not be getting the turquoise you think you are. There are five 'grades' of turquoise: expensive natural turquoise, which is quite difficult to simply cut and set; stabilized turquoise, softer stone treated with an epoxy resin, which makes up the bulk of fine jewelry; treated turquoise, which has been dyed; reconstituted turquoise, ground stone that has been colored and formed into cakes; and imitation turquoise, an entirely different stone, usually howlite, dyed to look like the real thing.

How do you tell the difference? Educate yourself at Albuquerque's Turquoise Museum (p174) before spending any serious money, and buy from either reputable shops or direct from the artisan. Genuine pieces are generally stamped and signed (though counterfeiters are clued into this as well), and tend to cost a bundle. If a deal seems too good to be true, it probably is.

ALLAN HOUSER: AN AMERICAN TREASURE

Chiricahua Apache artist Allan Houser's final work of art is the moving, 10-foot-tall bronze sculpture, *Unconquered*, standing at the entrance to the Oklahoma History Center. The pair of Apache warriors personify the Apache Nation's – and all tribes' – enduring history, pride and survival despite the Spanish and American world's betrayals.

Born in 1914 in Oklahoma to parents who had been held as prisoners of war by the US government, Houser brought his strong sense of cultural heritage to his work, which was selected for exhibition at the New York World's Fair in 1936. Major art-world recognition followed.

The prolific Houser completed some 450 bronze statues and 500 more in metal, wood and stone, as well as numerous paintings and drawings during his lifetime. Honored with the National Medal for the Arts in 1992 and showcased at the opening of the Smithsonian's National Museum of the American Indian in September 1994, Houser was, indeed, widely regarded as a national treasure.

For over 50 years his paintings, drawings and sculptures toured the US, Europe and Asia, putting Native American images and sensibilities before audiences worldwide. He also was devoted to cultivating other Native artists (during the 13 years he taught at the Institute of American Indian Arts Museum, p72, in Santa Fe), often remembering his own beginnings as a student in 1934 at what then was called the Painting School of the Santa Fe Indian School. In 1993, a year before his death, a permanent sculpture garden (p72) dedicated to his work opened at the Institute.

to the finest art of each tribe, broken down pueblo by pueblo, while the Institute of American Indian Arts Museum (p72) in Santa Fe shows the community's cutting-edge pieces. Indian Market (p91), Santa Fe's annual juried show, attracts the very best Native artists from across the continent.

Several other museums feature great Native work, but galleries are better endowed: Santa Fe's Canyon Rd (p70) has more of Maria Martinez's black-on-black pottery than the museum dedicated to her work at San Ildefonso Pueblo (p119).

The best places for shopping are the pueblos and reservations, where beautiful pottery and other work often are sold from artists' homes. Fine jewelry is sold outside the Palace of the Governors (p68) in Santa Fe, but Albuquerque shops carry pawn at good prices. If you just want to look, the Millicent Rogers Museum (p139) collection in Taos is outstanding.

New Mexico Masters

Between roughly 1910 and 1940, Northern New Mexico attracted and inspired some of the finest painters in the world. Georgia O'Keeffe (p125) is probably the most famous, and the largest collection of her work anywhere is on display at her namesake museum (p69) in Santa Fe.

Santa Fe's first serious Anglo collective, Los Cincos Pintores (Freemont Ellis, Willard Nash, Jozef Bakos, Walter Mruk and Will Shuster) and members of the Taos Society of Artists (p141) also command large followings – and high prices. Several museums have excellent collections of their paintings, particularly the Blumenschein (p140) and Harwood (p139) in Taos and the Museum of Fine Arts (p68) in Santa Fe. The Gerald Peters Gallery (p109) and Nedra Matteucci Galleries (p110) in Santa Fe also display their work.

Western realists, including cowboy sculptor Frederic Remington and landscape artists Maynard Dixon and Charlie Russell, are also best found on Canyon Rd; try the Altermann Galleries (p70). The work of Native American sculptor and painter Allen Houser is displayed at the sculpture gardens and gallery of the same name (p72) in Santa Fe.

Even cars are folk art here – a local entomologist covered hers in hundreds of plastic, metal and ceramic bees and another creative type plastered his VW with colorful gravel. Check out cool NM cars at www .artcaragency.com.

PATROCIÑO BARELA: MASTER WOOD CARVER

Patrociño Barela, *Time* magazine's 1936 'discovery of the year,' was lauded worldwide as a genius and master after his rounded and emotional pieces took center stage at a WPA show at New York City's Museum of Modern Art. His fluid forms, carved from a single piece of wood, are clearly anchored in the *santero* tradition, but markedly different: this is what art historians now call Barela style.

Probably born in 1900 (he wasn't sure), Barela worked at steel mills and picked vegetables until moving to Taos in 1930. There, an elderly neighbor asked Barela to repair her San Antonio. He did it with a pocketknife, then carved his own Santa Rita.

Area churches, taken by his heartfelt interpretations of saints and martyrs, began asking him to fill their own altars with his creations. His work caught the attention of New Deal representatives, who trained him for one week – perhaps his only formal education – and began collecting his art for government shows.

Barela never attended those openings in Washington, DC, New York City or Paris; he seemed unconcerned with his following among critics and collectors. Instead, he worked in his Taos studio, often donating prized pieces to churches and sanctuaries.

Both the Harwood Foundation Museum (p139) and Millicent Rogers Museum (p139) in Taos have excellent collections of his work.

Spanish Arts

Many of New Mexico's traditional Spanish arts focus on sacred art. Painted altar pieces, called *retablos* and *reredos*, and carved saints (*santos*) are well worth seeing, particularly those by artists selected by the Works Progress Administration (WPA) during the 1930s, including Santiago Matta, José Dolores López and most famously Patrociño Barela (above).

You'll find collections of their work at the Harwood Foundation Museum (p139) and Millicent Rogers Museum (p139) in Taos and at the Museum of Spanish Colonial Art (p72) in Santa Fe.

Córdova (p126) is renowned for its distinct woodcarvings, while Chimayó (p126) has been producing some of the world's finest wool weavings for 400 years.

Contemporary Art

Photography, painting, sculpture, ceramics, performance art and mixed media – just try to avoid them: in every hotel, coffee shop, bar and restaurant, fine art by local artisans is on display and often on sale. Collectors make Santa Fe a regular destination, and many internationally known artists, both local and otherwise, show in galleries in Santa Fe, specifically close to the plaza or Canyon Rd, and downtown Taos.

The railyard area on S Guadalupe St and Baca St in Santa Fe, less touristy spots in both the capital and Taos, and small galleries in Albuquerque are great places to find cutting-edge artists. Several small communities in the region have almost become art colonies: Truchas (p127), Dixon (p131), Abiquiú (p122), Madrid (p194) and Arroyo Seco (p157).

ARCHITECTURE

Adobe houses anchor the world's image of New Mexico architecture and to a great extent that's correct, though modernist influences are making headway in places other than Santa Fe. Albuquerque-based Antoine Predock won the illustrious American Institute of Architects' Gold Medal in 2006 – see why at the Spencer Theater for the Performing Arts (p210) in Ruidoso. 'I don't think of New Mexico as a region,' he says. 'I think of it as a force that has entered my system.'

The conservatory at the Rio Grande Botanic Gardens (p176) in Albuquerque showcases another modernist trend – cutting energy consumption and carbon dioxide emissions by selective use of materials and methods, including passive solar, all of which are mainstays of Edward Mazria of Santa Fe, who designed the building.

New Mexicans have been working closely with the environment as a matter of survival since Nomadic Paleo-Indians first wandered here, and have been building with adobe for 6000 years or more. Well-preserved examples at Chaco Culture National Historical Park (p220) and Bandelier (p133) date back to about AD 800; the loveliest and best-preserved example is Taos Pueblo (p156), built around 1100.

The Spanish introduced improvements to adobe building, mixing mud with straw to form more easily transportable brick rather than just cutting it from riverbanks. Spanish colonial architecture was simple: usually single-story homes with dirt floors and walls plastered with a mixture of oxblood and clay or *tierra blanca*, wheat paste mixed with white micaceous clay, to keep dust under control.

After US annexation in 1846, the less curvaceous Territorial style was introduced. Also adobe, this featured wooden porches and columns, including Santa Fe's famed Palace of the Governors (p68) portico and framework.

In 1912 Santa Fe enacted its famous adobe-only law, requiring new buildings to return to that pristine pueblo look. The Museum of Fine Arts was one of the first, inspiring architect John Gaw Meem (p68) to create what's now known as Pueblo Revival, or Santa Fe style.

That style today is combined with alternative technologies and modern materials and sometimes abandoned altogether for strong lines, refined geometry and bright colors. Trendy residential lofts springing up in downtown Albuquerque are just one example of things to come.

LITERATURE

Strong, passionate, modern voices from New Mexico include Santa Fe–born Jimmy Santiago Baca, who first learned to read and write in prison and then used those tools to take the literary world by storm. 'I don't know if I would have lived had I not found poetry,' he says. He has written books and poems, such as *The Importance of a Piece of Paper* and *A Place to Stand*, that are rooted in his Spanish and Apache ancestry, and has won the Pushcart Prize, American Book Award and National Poetry Award.

New Mexico–born Laguna Sioux and Lebanese poet and novelist Paula Gunn Allen's work, including *Spider Women's Granddaughters: Traditional Tales and Contemporary Writing by Native American Women* and other works, brought tribal women's voices to the world's attention.

Best-selling Anglo author and New Mexico resident Tony Hillerman expresses a deep appreciation for Native American culture, especially Hopi and Diné/Navajo, in his detective novels set in the Southwest, including *The Shape Shifter*.

The precedents for these and many other unique works are many. Immediately after the US annexed New Mexico in 1853, the state began to attract an unusual assortment of literati. During his term as governor, Lew Wallace wrote part of his popular passion play *Ben Hur: A Tale of Christ*, published in 1880. His wife, Susan Wallace, recorded her own impressions of the territory, collected as *The Land of the Pueblos*.

It was Alice Corbin, however, who established what's now termed 'The Writer's Era' in Northern New Mexico. Like many artists, she came

New Mexico architect Antoine Predock (www.predock.com) received the American Institute of Architects' illustrious Gold Medal in 2005 for his visionary international work, joining the ranks of Santiago Calatrava and IM Pei.

The Small Adobe House, by Agnesa Reeve and Robert Heck, documents endless design possibilities for floors, ceilings, doors, windows, walls and fireplaces and gives advice to those who'd like to build their own.

to convalesce from tuberculosis in 1916, bringing her husband, William Penhallow Henderson, illustrator of *Brothers of Light: The Penitentes of the Southwest.*

Corbin's 1928 anthology of poetry, *The Turquoise Trail,* included pieces by many of the writers she hosted in the city: Carl Sandburg, Ezra Pound, Paul Horgan and Witter Bynner, the poet who would go on to found his own collective of kooky characters. Together Corbin and Henderson founded Santa Fe's first publisher, Rydal Press, in 1932. The growing literary culture racked up some unusual accomplishments: in addition to Willa Cather's *Death Comes for the Archbishop,* one of Lynn Riggs' plays was adapted into the musical *Oklahoma!,* and Boy Scout cofounder Ernest Thomas Seton's short stories became the basis of the Disney classic *Bambi.*

Mabel Dodge Luhan (p150) was something like a rival to Corbin. Indeed, the heiress was known for her bitter insults to the Santa Fe crowd. Her own collective included such notables such as DH Lawrence, Robinson Jeffers and Jean Toomer.

Focus on writers lessened during WWII but gradually increased again in the late 20th century, and today New Mexico writers are again at center stage.

A world of small presses awaits at www.santafe.net/books_and_publishers/index.htm, including Azro, producers of charmingly illustrated children's books with Southwest themes.

FILM

Ever since Tom Mix arrived in 1915 to commit cowboy mythology to the silver screen, New Mexico has had its endless vistas and picturesque ghost towns captured on camera.

Politicos are sweetening the deal these days – anyone filming here gets a 25% rebate from the state for all direct production costs incurred on New Mexico soil. Support for burgeoning filmmakers also is strong: Governor Bill Richardson awarded $500,000 in 2006 to a new program for Hispanic and Native American filmmakers.

The movie-making industry has transformed New Mexico in many ways. *Easy Rider,* which popularized the hip 1960s scene in Taos, inspired a youthful immigration that painted the town tie-dye. *The Milagro Beanfield War,* the excellent adaptation of John Nichols' book, forced star and director Robert Redford to build an authentic-looking plaza in Truchas, after the town of Chimayó declined to allow movie crews to overrun their own. Even the road to Acoma Pueblo, previously accessible only via a steep footpath, was built for a John Wayne flick.

More than 300 major films – including *21 Grams* with Sean Penn in 2003 – and countless smaller ones have been made in New Mexico, and many of them are screened at film festivals throughout the year. The Santa Fe Film Festival (p91) runs each December and the Center for Contemporary Art hosts the Native Cinema Showcase (p91) in August, coinciding with Indian Market (p91).

Grace your coffee table with Phillip Huscher's *The Santa Fe Opera – An American Pioneer,* a sumptuously photographed, impression-filled book about one of the world's most unique opera houses.

PERFORMING ARTS

All New Mexico is a stage: from the elaborate ceremonial dances of the Pueblo Indians and pageantry of the Santa Fe Fiestas (p91), ritual as performance art has long been an integral part of life.

Traditional urban culture came to Albuquerque with the Civic Symphony debut in 1932 when community musicians were also students, homemakers and business people. Today the all-professional New Mexico Symphony Orchestra (p187), led by noted conductor Guillermo Figueroa, plays to 130,000 fans a year.

The Santa Fe Opera (p107), established in 1957, is world-famous for its glorious open-air stage in a spectacular setting. The Santa Fe Chamber

Music Festival (p107) began in 1972, with performances by top musicians and composers that roughly coincide with the opera's late-summer season. Together they attract hundreds of thousands of culture mavens annually.

The best dance outside the pueblos in New Mexico is Spanish. One of Santa Fe's most renowned dance troupes is Maria Benitez Teatro Flamenco (p107), while the National Institute of Flamenco in Albuquerque hosts the spectacular annual Festival Flamenco Internacional (p180), drawing the world's premier performers in dance, guitar, percussion and *cante*.

Some of the best locally produced popular music is Spanish, too. Al Hurricane, for example, known for his rockin' guitar, released his first album in 1967 and is still going strong. Having played guitar for Fats Domino and Marvin Gaye, he mostly toured the world with his own band and is still a favorite at Albuquerque's Summerfest. Ramón Bermudez Jr calls his unique sound 'flamenco fusion' – check out his award-winning *Fuego en Alma*. Also give a listen to Wayne Wesley Johnson, who specializes in 'jazzmenco,' and the Nuevo Latino band Manzanares, one of the best in the country. Try to catch a performance while you're here.

Albuquerque resident Otono Silva makes beautiful didgeridoos from agaves, yuccas and other New Mexico plants and sells them in music stores under the label Rhythm Tree.

Environment

Folks from less arid climes often think the term 'desert' refers to vast wastelands, uninspiring tracts of hot sand where the occasional cactus provides the only shade. If all you do is cross the state on I-40, that, indeed, is what you'll think you're seeing.

The Nature Conservancy protects more than 1.3 million acres in New Mexico.

But set foot in a desert for any length of time and you'll find that it is richly varied. And in New Mexico, deserts can even rise to scenic heights, arrayed with flora and fauna adapted to the extreme variations in aridity and temperature brought on by the region's climatic mood swings.

But that's not all that's moving and shaking in New Mexico. This is where the tectonic plates that make up North America meet, on either shore of the Rio Grande, and their interaction has inspired geological wonders – from the stunning volcanic features of the Jemez Mountains, to the highlands of the Enchanted Circle, alive with creatures that would feel more at home in the Alps than anything portrayed in those Roadrunner cartoons.

If you have environmental misconceptions, leave them behind as you make your way toward the 'deserts' of Northern New Mexico, where ski slopes, streams and shady trails invite you to redefine what that word actually means.

THE LAND

The barren geographic non sequitur of White Sands National Monument and the cactus-studded landscape of tumbleweed, jackalopes and stunted buttes often spring to mind when thinking of New Mexico. That topography indeed holds sway in the southern reaches of the state. But in

---

RESPONSIBLE TRAVEL

All the usual rules of responsible travel apply in New Mexico: don't litter, tip well, respect the locals and appreciate and enjoy the land. Indian pueblos in particular ask for more sensitivity from visitors.

Common sense also applies when camping and hiking. The desert may seem tough, but is extremely sensitive to overuse. Simple acts of carelessness can require many years of delicate reclamation; stay on trails and practice low-impact camping. Take special care with campfires (and cigarettes), as droughts have turned the region into a tinderbox.

Recreational opportunities abound, so why not choose from among those that wreak the least environmental havoc? Use of all terrain vehicles (ATVs) in the national forests is causing serious damage, and 'varmint hunts,' which target coyotes, bobcats and other inedible animals, remove necessary predators from the ecosystem.

The most important contributions you can make revolve around New Mexico's most precious resource: water. Keep conservation in mind at all times: this is not the place to indulge in long showers, let the faucet run while you brush your teeth, or ask hotel staff to wash towels used only once.

Consider carefully before patronizing golf courses: sure, many are on Native American land, use gray water systems and so on, but there are probably better uses for all that water. Golf courses belong in Scotland, where it rains.

Northern New Mexico has been experiencing a renaissance (of sorts) in sustainable agriculture based on small farms often growing heirloom and other rare crops. These are available at roadside stands and **farmers markets** (☎ 505-983-4010, 888-983-4400; www.farmersmarketsnm.org). A dollar spent there is a vote for New Mexico's future.

the north, where the Rocky Mountains are just thinking about handing the horizon over to the lowlands, there are forests of ponderosa pine and aspen spilling down the flanks of 12,000ft peaks. The high-desert plateau from which these mountains rise loses elevation as the state slants to the south; Albuquerque, at more than 5000ft, is only slightly lower than Denver, Colorado.

To Albuquerque's east are the rose-tinted granite cliffs of Sandia Crest, rising another mile from the Earth's crust like a trap door, opening at the crumpled-granite hinge of Cedar Crest.

The uplift that began about 10 million years ago continues to grow another couple of centimeters each year. At the top, hardened, layered limestone formed by the ocean that covered the region during the Paleozoic Era (544 million to 245 million years ago) is studded with the fossils of sea creatures.

The uplift and granite are volcanic in origin, and the region is defined by tectonic activity along the Rio Grande Rift, marked by the great river coursing through the gorge, most dramatically displayed on the Low Road to Taos. This is where tectonic plates floating atop a sea of magma chafe against one another, pulling apart to create the Rio Grande Valley and sometimes inspiring enormous, violent eruptions.

The Jemez Mountains (where volcanoes began rising 13 million years ago) are one of the largest volcanic fields in the world, forming the pyroclastic tuffs of Bandelier National Monument and the unusual formations of Kasha-Katuwe Tent Rocks. Valles Caldera is at the heart of a huge volcano that once reached perhaps 30,000ft. Much as the ancient spirit of this area may seem vanquished to outsiders, these volcanoes are dormant but far from dead.

East of the Continental Divide are the high plains of the Llano Estacado, which are watered by the Pecos River. The river pours down from the Sangre de Cristo Mountains, one of the world's longest chains, which rose from the Earth about 27 million years ago, forming 13,101ft Truchas and 12,280ft Baldy Peaks.

The granddaddy of New Mexico mountains is 13,161ft Wheeler Peak, surrounded by alpine plains populated with wildlife suited to Canada.

WILDLIFE

Northern New Mexico's flora and fauna are fascinating but difficult to observe. Adapted to the aridity and extremes in temperature, many creatures are nocturnal and quite timid.

Plant life is not limited to cacti, which actually are rather rare in the northern highlands. But all plants here must be able to survive for quite some time without water, a trait in particular demand in light of the extended drought that seems here to stay. Plants and animals in these parts rely on a fascinating armory of wily and weird tricks to thrive no matter what nature throws their way.

Animals

The New Mexico state bird, the roadrunner, bears little resemblance to its cartoon mascot. For one, *Geococcyx californianus* isn't purple; the 2ft-long critters are dusty brown and cruise low to the ground. While fairly common, you're likely to miss the well-camouflaged birds as they race around looking for tasty lizards.

The mountains are home to black bears that seem more familiar with garbage pickup schedules than their human counterparts. Bobcats are more elusive.

Check out 1500 New Mexico rock specimens at www.nmfossils.org, part of the NM Museum of Natural History and Science.

The NM Environment Department's Pollution Prevention Program (www.nmenv.state .nm.us/green_zia_web site/index.html) uses the eco guidelines to assist pueblo and tribal communities.

Stan Tekiela's *Birds of New Mexico Field Guide* will get you up to speed on spirited roadrunners and quail, then refine your abilities to distinguish between red-breasted and pygmy nuthatches.

Those exploring north of Santa Fe and Taos may see squirrels, turkeys, quails, elks, mule deers, javelinas (small boars) and, if you're lucky, those adorable, fat little marmots of the Enchanted Circle.

Big-horned sheep became extinct in New Mexico in the early 1900s, the victims of overhunting and diseases introduced by domesticated sheep. They were reintroduced into the Pecos Wilderness and Wheeler Peak region in the 1990s and are now thriving to the point where some of the herd is being used to help restore populations in other western states.

The Southwest Research & Information Center (www.sric.org) works with Navajo communities affected by uranium mining.

Trout still ply the waters in abundance, as New Mexico stocks rivers and lakes, although they are falling victim in increasing numbers to a handful of debilitating diseases. Wetlands have several unusual birds, but it's the rare rosy finch, which winters in the Sandias, that brings in the birders.

Insect and reptile lovers have a ball in the lower elevation deserts surrounding Albuquerque, where creepy crawlies like tarantulas, scorpions, rattlesnakes and lizards make their home. Perhaps the most reviled insect at present is the piñon bark beetle, which is killing off great swaths of evergreens.

Plants

Vegetation of the high desert must survive serious extremes in temperature and a lack of water. Though cacti are less common in the region north of Albuquerque, most plants have similar survival strategies: they collect sunlight during the day and process it at night, when evaporation is less of an issue. On the whole, they sport smaller leaves with less surface area to reduce the amount of hard-won water exhaled back into the arid atmosphere. Other plants, like the omnipresent sage bushes, have volatile oils that protect their stores of water from marauding deer, who don't like the taste.

At higher elevations, large stands of ponderosas encompass Santa Fe and Taos.

A Climate Change Advisory Group established by Governor Bill Richardson is developing recommendations on ways to reduce greenhouse emissions in the state 75% by 2050.

From about 8000ft to 9500ft white fir, juniper, Douglas firs and aspens, which turn a dramatic gold in the fall, grow thickly, shading out competitors.

From 9500ft to 11,500ft conifers predominate, including Engelmann spruce and subalpine fir. Bristlecone pine put in a rare appearance in the steppes of the Enchanted Circle. Above tree line (11,500ft) is the alpine zone, characterized by small tundra-like plants.

The state tree is the piñon. Long the dominant feature of the high deserts between the moister regions of Northern New Mexico, these trees are the most visible victims of the ongoing drought and piñon bark beetle onslaught.

NATIONAL, STATE & REGIONAL PARKS

The best place to start your exploration of New Mexico's wilderness is the **Public Lands Information Center** (Map p62; ☎ 505-438-7542, 877-276-9404; www.public lands.org; 1474 Rodeo Rd, Santa Fe; ☺ 8am-5pm Mon-Fri Nov-Mar, Mon-Sat Apr-Oct), which has information about all public lands.

There are nearly nine-million acres of state lands in New Mexico, which encompasses 32 state parks and five historic monuments. Of that, only about 1.6 million acres are protected as wilderness. Indian lands are protected, but in general, access is either highly restricted, available only through a guided tour or administrated in conjunction with the Bureau of Land Management.

PIÑON BARK BEETLES

Squat, green piñon trees silhouetted against a turquoise sky – this is the enduring image of New Mexico captured by O'Keeffe and others, forever etched in the memory of visitors. The scent of burning piñon wood, the rich flavor of its nut – this tree, the state tree, is deeply rooted in the heart of New Mexico.

Its nemesis, the tiny *Ips pini*, is no larger than a grain of rice. Together with its cousins in the *Ips* and *Dendrodoctonus* genii, this bug has become a scourge. The piñon bark beetle, as it's known in New Mexico, burrows under the bark of the tree, laying eggs that will hatch into larva, devour the tender wood (leaving it a tinder-dry husk of deadwood) and take to the air to start the cycle once again.

Long a part of every healthy pine ecosystem, the beetles have always targeted trees weakened by age and drought and no longer able to cast the larva out in a flood of pitch. But in the 1980s, the beetles began reproducing more rapidly, as evergreens wilted in the globally increasing heat. Los Alamos, the Enchanted Circle and other regions are hard hit. More menacingly, the beetle has jumped species in the Jemez, now attacking the Ponderosa pine.

The economic impact, from shrinking piñon nut crops and growing wildfire risk, is as yet incalculable. The Forest Service philosophically opines that this is just part of a natural cycle. Years of fire suppression have led to more piñon than this region was ever supposed to cradle, they say, and this plague, though hard to watch, will restore an ancient balance. Besides, only plentiful rain or a hard winter could possibly reverse it, and Mother Nature has not been forthcoming.

Due to severe drought conditions, restrictions on fires, smoking, campsite location and use of cookstoves vary daily. Some areas have been closed entirely. Call about restrictions and closures before you head for the hills.

State Parks

The New Mexico State Parks office (p67) in Santa Fe has information on the state's 32 state parks, most of which offer camping that can be reserved by phone or online. Campgrounds are usually open May through September. Not all have running water, but all have access to water that can be treated. Some are restricting activities to day use only due to fire danger posed by the drought. Call ahead to make sure.

Hyde Memorial (p84), close to Santa Fe, is New Mexico's highest state park (9400ft), with aspen forests perfect for hiking, mountain biking, Nordic skiing and llama trekking. Cimarron Canyon (p166) features gold mines, the Cimarron Palisades and developed campsites. Fish, hike or rock climb here from May to November.

National Forests

National forests are multiuse areas, which include logging, ATV and snowmobile trails, hunting and private ski areas. Developed campsites are administrated independently; you can pick up a backcountry pass and camp for free, usually within 30ft of an established trail. Many national forests include wilderness areas, which are off-limits to most development. Off-highway vehicle use is under scrutiny in national forests, so call ahead to make sure your loud machine of choice will still be welcome.

Santa Fe (p89) spans 1.6-million acres and boasts hot springs, ancient ruins, Rio Chama, Truchas and Baldy Peaks, plus 28 campgrounds and about 1000 miles of trails. After you hike, ski, scale a few rocks or ride the rapids, you can soak away your aches year-round.

Carson (p168) offers some 1.5-million acres of opportunities all throughout the year: ski, boat, hike, snowmobile, go horseback riding or

200,000 acres in southern Dona Ana County are temporarily protected as federal wilderness study areas, but the NM Wilderness Alliance (www.donaanawild.org) wants it permanently protected.

wildlife-watching (look for elk, deer, marmots and big-horned sheep). Near Wheeler Peak and the Red River, the forest includes four ski areas and campgrounds.

Cibola, close to Albuquerque, grants access to Sandia Crest, Sandia Ski Park and Sandia Man Cave. It offers hiking, skiing, wildlife-watching and even fine dining year-round within its 1.9-million-acre reach. At press time, portions of Cibola were closed due to the drought; check at the **Cibola National Forest Mount Taylor Ranger Station** (☎ 505-287-8833; 1800 Lobo Canyon Rd; ☽ 8am-noon & 1-5pm Mon-Fri).

Wilderness Areas

Generally, wilderness areas are those portions of a national forest set aside to remain pristine. Some commercial activity, including grazing animals and approved mining, is allowed, but ATVs, hunting, ski areas and logging are banned. Campsites don't often have running water or campfire grills, and usually their costs range from free to around $10.

Wheeler Peak, just north of Taos, offers hiking, rock climbing, fishing in alpine lakes and wildlife-watching on 19,661 acres; watch out for marmots, elk and big-horned sheep. Wheeler is at its best from June to September. Cross-country ski trails open up a whole new world in winter. Inquire at the **Public Lands Information Center** (Map p62; ☎ 505-438-7542, 877-276-9404; www.publiclands.org; 1474 Rodeo Rd, Santa Fe; ☽ 8am-5pm Mon-Fri Nov-Mar, 8am-5pm Mon-Sat Apr-Oct) about avalanche danger.

Sandia Mountain (p182) has pine-forest trails with eagles, bears and archaeological sites. You can backcountry camp, mountain bike and lose the Albuquerque crowds on 117 miles of trails.

Chama Valley features incredible desert scenery, with access to Pedernal, El Vado Lake, Rio Chama and Abiquiú. Go for great camping, white-water rafting and fishing May to September.

Gila (p202) offers cliff dwellings, out-of-the-way hiking and ghost towns.

ENVIRONMENTAL ISSUES

With an annual average precipitation of a mere 13in per year, New Mexico is the third most arid state in the union. At the same time, this fragile region has also become the 11th fastest-growing state. In combination with an epic drought and federal policies at odds with sound land use, New Mexico is positioning itself to play the big loser in 'Revenge of the Ecosystem' in the coming decades.

Water is, of course, the hot-button issue. Massive aquifers – porous sediment that accumulates at the foothills of large granite peaks like the Sandias – are New Mexico's primary water source. Politicians, who compared Albuquerque's aquifer to the Great Lakes in an effort to lure businesses to the area, have long been cheerfully overestimating reserves. Water tables throughout the region are dropping, and there is no effective policy to deal with it. However, that hasn't stopped developers from building more golf courses.

The drought, combined with a long-standing policy of fire suppression that has allowed more vegetation to accumulate than is theoretically natural, has led to outbreaks of massive forest fires. New federal forest-thinning policies that could have had a positive impact if applied judiciously are little more than thinly veiled gimmies for politically connected extractive industries.

Rangers and wildlife experts explain that fires are normal and healthy, and a program of controlled burns has been implemented – with some

Vandana Shiva's *Water Wars: Privatization, Pollution & Profit* makes for great desert reading. Increasing droughts, desertification, damming and mining may well lead to international water wars yet this century, according to this political activist and physicist.

New Mexico still boasts more lawns and golf courses than it should, but there's an alternative. Learn about water-wise cactuses and grasses in Gayle Weinstein's *Xeriscape Handbook*.

WATER: NEW MEXICO'S MOST VALUABLE RESOURCE *Annette Rodriguez*

Northern New Mexico's varied topography and abundance of plant and wildlife make it easy to forget that this is a desert. And like other Southwestern states, this region has experienced enormous metropolitan growth that pits a diminishing water supply against inexorable population expansion. Ground water is the state's principal source for agricultural, industrial and public water. About 90% of the population relies on this source, and it has been extracted far more quickly than nature has been able to replenish it.

The average annual precipitation ranges between 7in in the high desert of the northwest to about 20in in the central mountain region. During recent years of extended drought, many parts of the state have received less than half of that meager allotment. Most falls during what New Mexicans call the 'monsoon season,' characterized by afternoon thunderstorms in July and August. While the dry climate makes for vast blue skies and a horizon line that seems just feet off the ground, extended periods of little rainfall or snowmelt have resulted in states of emergency throughout New Mexico – conditions expected to persist.

Widespread wildfires, state park closings and water-use restrictions in both urban and rural areas are now part of daily life. Skirmishes regarding water use include bitter interstate water rights disputes and political finger-pointing.

What does this mean for you? Municipalities have their ways of letting you know when water restrictions are in force, usually with friendly signs, full-page ads and banners hanging in hotels that announce how often they'll be able to legally wash your linens (during a Stage III alert, that's every four days).

Many communities have begun replacing lush, grassy lawns with xeriscaping, a specialty that promotes the use of native or desert-adapted plants.

There are public xeriscape demonstration gardens throughout the state, the largest of which is at El Rancho de las Golondrinas (p81). Don't expect acres of cacti, but a peek at these xerophytes is worthwhile; their diversity and beauty are quite remarkable.

setbacks. The Cerro Grande fire of 2000 resulted from a controlled burn near Los Alamos and raged through 43,000 acres that surrounded Los Alamos National Laboratory (LANL). The federal government refused to tell residents what is – or was – stored out there, but folks familiar with nuclear weapons have made educated guesses. Plutonium and uranium, both incredibly toxic, as well as radioactive isotopes of beryllium and cesium, were dumped in the area throughout the Cold War, and there is neither accountability nor information from any quarter. What was in that smoke, and what continues to flow down the mountain to Española, Santa Fe and the surrounding pueblos following heavy rains, is the subject of much uninformed debate. It can't be good.

New Mexico Outdoors

New Mexico has an irresistible outdoor mojo dimmed only slightly by the ongoing drought. The state ranks 45th in population density, which means that there are plenty of unspoiled natural places, no matter the climate. Some parcels have been closed because of drought and fire danger, and some rivers and ski areas might be running a little thin. So it's wise to hitch a ride on the information highway of choice before setting out.

The **Public Lands Information Center** (Map p62; ☎ 505-438-7542; www.publiclands .org; Santa Fe Map p62; 1474 Rodeo Rd, Santa Fe; Albuquerque ☎ 505-345-9498, 877-851-8946; 6501 4th St NW, Albuquerque) and **Carson National Forest Supervisor's Office** (Map p136; ☎ 505-758-6200; www.fs.fed.us/r3/carson; 208 Cruz Alta Rd, Taos) are the best places to start. But ranger stations and visitors centers always have information on the finest regional trails and outfitters.

Download free maps from the **National Forest Service** (☎ 505-842-3292; http://sar.lanl.gov/maps_by_name.html).

In Taos, the gateway to the wild northeast, **Taos Outdoor Recreation** (www .taosoutdoorrecreation.com) provides a comprehensive online rundown of all your options, and **Native Sons Adventures** (Map p138; ☎ 505-758-9342, 800-753-7559; www.nativesonsadventures.com; 1033-A Paseo del Pueblo Sur) offers advice and guided tours of every stripe.

Faust Transportation (☎ 505-758-3410, 888-830-3410; www.newmexiconet.com/trans /faust/faust.html) gets you to trailheads for less than most outfitters.

HIKING

You can choose a lovely stroll or a butt-kicking trek when you ride your shank's mare deep into the heart of the New Mexico wilderness. Sturdy shoes make rough walking less of an ankle-twisting proposition, and by now you don't need to be reminded about bringing a gallon of water per day per person, a hat and lots of sunscreen (do you?). With a little more preparation, you could stay out for several sunsets.

Day Hikes

Every visitor center and ranger station, not to mention gear shop and bookstore, has maps and advice for the asking.

The Atalaya Trail (p85) is perfect at sunset. This 7-mile loop connected to the Dale Ball Trails (not far from downtown Santa Fe) tops the 9121ft Atalaya Mountain.

A quarter of New Mexico is forested, including the 3.3-million-acre Gila National Forest (www .fs.fed.US/r3/gila), the sixth largest national forest in the US.

For super up-to-date hiking info, click on www.sandiahiking.com, written by local enthusiast and Mt Kilimanjaro veteran Mike Coltrin.

A WORD OF CAUTION

There are reasons why this beautiful land hasn't sprouted the usual varicose veins of interstates and tract housing: altitude, aridity and extremes in temperature.

Don't underestimate the importance of altitude acclimation before any serious activity, and of carrying (and drinking!) at least a gallon of water per person, per day. Try not to rely on 'reliable' water sources, particularly in summer and while the drought persists; they have a dangerous tendency to dry up right when you need them.

Temperatures can vary up to 50°F (28°C) between day and night, and hikers have been known to get hypothermia on top of their sunburns. At these altitudes there's a lot less atmosphere to protect you from the sun – wear a hat, sunscreen and shades at all times. For more information, see the Health chapter.

Perhaps the prettiest day hike on the Enchanted Circle, Clear Creek Canyon Trail (p166) is a golden tunnel of aspen in fall.

Magnificent Kasha-Katuwe Tent Rocks National Monument (p193) offers two short (under 2 miles) and incredible day hikes with bizarre rock formations and a narrow canyon.

An 8-mile hike from the desert to the woods, La Luz Trail (p182) includes a 3800ft altitude gain. Bonus: you can take the tram back down.

Hikes with Kids

These hikes are easy enough for even small children. But remember that tears flow more easily at high altitudes, and always pack sunscreen, shades and plenty of liquids.

Randall Davey Audubon Center (p84), just 3 miles north of the plaza, is a 135-acre preserve offering two trails, one descending Santa Fe Canyon.

Two great 20-minute hikes end up at lovely Nambé Falls (Nambé Pueblo; p118). The high trail beckons photographers with views, and the easier low trail follows a river and petroglyphs.

Follow the Rio Grande through a cottonwood forest on short nature trails and cruise the wetlands for migratory birds at Rio Grande Nature Center (Albuquerque; p176).

In *Best Hikes with Children in New Mexico,* father and veteran outdoorsman Bob Julyan outlines 60 hikes rated by difficulty and kid-friendly features. He even suggests turning-back points when junior hikers begin protesting.

Hikes Through History

New Mexico is an open book of time, and each trail peruses a fascinating new chapter.

Bandelier National Monument (p133) boasts 70 miles of trails, and you can climb a ladder to Ceremonial Cave or follow footsteps worn into the mesa bedrock.

Three-mile Pioneer Canyon Trail and 8-mile Placer Creek Trail (p165) pass dozens of dilapidated gold mines with rusting equipment, old machinery and abandoned shafts.

Petroglyph National Monument (p177) holds intriguing hikes wending by volcanic cones and thousands of ancient petroglyphs.

Perfect for all ages, Sandia Man Cave (Albuquerque; p182) is where Boy Scouts discovered the oldest human encampment in North America.

Hiking around old volcanoes? Find out which ones might erupt again at the NM Bureau of Geology and Mineral Resources (www.geoinfo .nmt.edu/faq/volcanoes /home.html).

Serious Hikes

You'll need all the equipment – sturdy boots, water-filtration systems, permits, USGS maps and more information than this book provides – for these stunning hikes.

The sacred, 28-mile, three-day **Stone Lion Shrine** (☎ 505-672-3861; www .nps.gov/band; Los Alamos; car $10 for 7 days; ⏱ 7am-7:30pm) walkabout through the Jemez Mountains takes you by ladder and canyon to two ancient and sacred stone carvings.

The most scenic route to the top of 13,101ft **Truchas Peak** (☎ 505-757-6121; NM 63; ⏱ 8am-4:30pm Mon-Fri, & Sat in summer) is via Trailriders Wall trail, which courses through flowery alpine meadows with stunning views to forever.

Start at first light for the prettiest trail to the highest point in New Mexico – 13,161ft Wheeler Peak. It also happens to be relatively easy (although long), running through Bull-of-the-Woods pasture.

Hiking, skiing, fishing, dog sledding? Peruse www.newmexico.org/go /loc/outdoors for locations and seasons for every intrepid (or not) sport.

BIKING

After you acclimate to the altitude for a few days, exchange four wheels for two on back roads and scenic byways.

You can rent bikes in Santa Fe, Taos and Albuquerque; rates drop for longer rentals. Santa Fe rates are about double those elsewhere.

Road Biking

While interstates are off-limits to cyclists, the scenic byways are all yours. Top tours include the Enchanted Circle (with 84 miles of alpine intensity) near Taos and the Turquoise Trail near Albuquerque. Park next to the Harleys in Madrid (on the Turquoise Trail) and show 'em how far an alternative form of internal combustion can take you.

Albuquerque has an elaborate system of bike trails throughout the city, many of which are isolated from automobiles. The Santa Fe Rail Trail (p85) offers a fun 18-mile trail, almost entirely paved, that follows the rail line to Lamy.

SKI (AND MORE) IN NEW MEXICO

Time to stop equating aridity with desiccation; in fact, aridity brings that fluffy powder that draws schushers from around the world to these mountains. As long as the drought persists there'll be a drop in flake footage, but we're talking maybe 15 feet of coverage instead of the usual 20.

North-central New Mexico, almost entirely enfolded in the Rocky Mountains, boasts all sorts of opportunities for frolicking. Take snowmobile tours to abandoned mining towns from Red River; ice skate on lakes near Questa; or finally learn funky telemark turns at a ski resort.

Ski season generally runs from November through March, depending on altitude and weather, and resort schools will show you the slopes if you need lessons. There are a dozen or so free ski guides (available at visitors centers). **Ski New Mexico** (www.skinewmexico.com) provides ski reports, links to resorts and discount cards.

Enchanted Forest (p164) is the most beloved Nordic ski area, with some 25 miles of groomed trails lit up with luminarias at Christmas. Less-developed options include ski-in yurts at the Southwest Nordic Center (p165) and dozens of trails in the Carson National Forest.

The main attraction, however, is the cool collection of ski resorts scattered across New Mexico's sunny peaks. Here's a rundown of the basics:

- Ski Santa Fe (p85) Just 16 miles from the capital, lifts take you to the top of the highest skiable slope in the state – 12,053ft. The views of the Sangre de Cristos are legendary. The 1600ft vertical drop is blanketed with 225in of powder, and 67 trails are rated for every level; new lifts help alleviate the crowds.

- Sipapú Ski & Summer Resort (p128) Family-owned and out of the way, this small resort in Peñasco with a 1055ft vertical drop and 37 trails smothered in 170in of snow (a decent showing) has lots of little-used acreage and some of the least expensive rates in the state.

- Pajarito Mountain Ski Area (p132) Short lines, long lifts, all-natural snow, beautiful bumps, glades galore and a 10,440ft peak elevation make this a hidden gem.

- Taos Ski Valley (p158) Among the nation's top ski areas, with 305in of natural snow, 110 trails, 12 lifts, a 2612ft vertical drop (or 3274ft, if you're willing to hike 662ft to the 12,481ft peak), instructors and all the amenities. You can snowshoe, inner-tube, grab some air in the terrain park, and even snowmobile in various outreaches here – but, dude, leave the board behind.

- Angel Fire Resort (p167) With 210in of snowfall (pretty darn good for a drought) enhanced with many machines, this sprawling, all-inclusive resort boasts a 2077ft vertical drop, two terrain parks (including a 400ft half-pipe), 9 acres of glade skiing, 22km of Nordic trails, and special areas and amenities for kids and families.

- Red River Ski Area (p164) Though it doesn't have the most challenging slopes, this adorable resort community gets a head start on Mother Nature with snowmaking machines to cover its easy-to-tackle runs. Family packages and activities are ideal for kids – plus, it's close to Enchanted Forest and opportunities for snowmobiling.

- Sandia Peak Ski Park (www.sandiapeak.com; p182) Close proximity to downtown Albuquerque and the world's longest tram to get you there make this a sweet treat with nice, long runs. But recent mild winters have left it a bit barren.

Native Sons (p142) has several guided tours that take you two-wheeling all over the state.

Mountain Biking

Many mountain-biking trails, including Santa Fe's Dale Ball Trails (p84) and Atalaya Trail (p85), are open to a variety of uses. Forest roads are maintained with mountain bikers in mind and tend to be rated beginner or moderate – except after it rains, when they can quickly become intermediate or holy-moley.

Other options run the gamut of abilities, from easy to most challenging, and represent only a taste of what's out there.

All downhill ski areas offer up their trails to summertime mountain bikers, providing a lung-busting challenge going up (or an exquisite chairlift ride) before a bone-rattling descent.

Windsor Trail (p85) is a 10-mile intermediate trail through the aspens and views of Santa Fe Ski Area; the path forms the spine of several other trails, and some folks say they're best when snow is on the ground; we say find yourself there in foliage season.

The moderate 9-mile West Rim Trail (p129) offers stunning views of the Rio Grande Gorge.

In Carson National Forest (p168) the USFS maintains a huge system of mountain-bike and multiuse trails between Taos, Angel Fire and Picuris Peak.

South Boundary Trail (Taos; p144) is a must, as it's hallowed among the trail-riding tribe. The 28-mile adventure is only for experienced bikers with maps, survival and repair gear, and up-to-date trail information.

Angel Fire Resort (p168) has a wild assortment of terrain, including forests, meadows and lava fields, with jumps and easy cruising trails; Pajarito Mountain Ski Area (p132) offers guided rides and clinics; and Sandia Peak Ski Park's (p182) 30 miles of trails offer every level of adventure.

You'll need more skills than you have now to survive for three days if you get stranded in the middle of nowhere in NM. Download Jack Purcell's *Desert Emergency Survival Basics*, a 31-page e-book, and take it seriously.

WHITE-WATER RAFTING

Desert dwellers make the best river rats; they'll lead you to some rip-snortin' rapids. The screamer is the Class IV Taos Box ($109), for rafters 12 years and older, while the Class III Racecourse ($48) and even mellower Class III Lower Gorge ($50) are suitable for anyone over the age of six.

These last two trips put in at Pilar (p129), but a variety of outfitters in Santa Fe and Taos take busloads of wide-eyed neophytes and seasoned rodeo paddlers there daily from April through October. May and June, when all that snowmelt really gets things rolling, are tops. You will get wet. You will scream yourself hoarse.

More relaxed options include a leisurely float to Embudo Station (p129) and an all-ages trip offered by Los Rios River Runners (p143).

The Class III Rio Chama ($360 to $750), near Abiquiú, is usually run as a three-day all-inclusive excursion, with meals and tents included. Far Flung Adventures (Pilar; p129) offers custom trips that could also include horseback riding.

New Mexico boasts the lowest water-to-land ratio in the US, with just 0.002% of the state's surface area covered by lakes and rivers.

FISHING

If you plan to spend much time outdoors, bring your fishing pole. Many lakes and streams are stocked with rainbow, German brown and cutthroat trout (the state fish!), and some lakes even have salmon. There are fishing holes with full wheelchair access, and others you'll hike all day to find. You'll need a license on all but the two free-fishing days: the first Saturday in June and the last Saturday in September.

New Mexico Game & Fish (☎ in Santa Fe 505-476-8000, in Albuquerque 222-4700; www
.wildlife.state.nm.us) issues several licenses for nonresidents: one year (adult/
child $56/28), five days ($24) and one day ($12), including the $5 WHI
(Wildlife Habitat Improvement) stamp that's required to fish on USFS
and BLM lands. They'll also give you the lowdown on the latest diseases
to watch out for, such as the rampant whirling disease. Find out where
stocked fish lurk by calling ☎ 800-ASK-FISH.

Craig Martin's *Fly Fishing in New Mexico* tells where to find bountiful waters and what to do with it when you get there.

Your bag limit is five fish for trout and salmon, with a maximum of
two cutthroat trout per day. Sporting-goods stores, tackle shops and RV
parks (and some gas stations near popular fishing areas) sell licenses, and
you can often rent a rod and tackle for about $25.

The Enchanted Circle (p160) has the best access and is lined with
campsites known for fishing. Red River (p163) and the Rio Grande are
tops September through April, while Cimarron Canyon State Park (p166)
has area lakes that are best fished between May and September. **Ed Adams**
(www.edadamsflyfishing.com; Questa), **High Desert Angler** (www.highdesertangler.com; Santa
Fe), and **Taos High Mountain Angler** (www.highmountainangler.com) lead guided fly-
fishing trips and are great sources of fishing information.

Closer to Santa Fe, Abiquiú, Nambé Lakes and Rio Chama can also
hook you up with dinner. Jemez Springs, the Las Vegas Gallinas Canyon
Complex and Pecos Wilderness are great places to reel one in, and many
pueblos maintain stocked fishing ponds where you can catch a fish or
five for $7 to $10 a day.

If you're looking to learn the fine art of fly-fishing, or just want access to less-crowded private lands, several outfitters lead the way. Prices,
which are just a bit higher for an extra person, vary widely ($175 to $250),
so shop around. Independent guides are generally much less expensive
and they generally leave flyers at ranger stations and visitors centers.
When considering hiring any outfitter, ask around for recommendations
to make sure you actually get the experience you're expecting.

In Santa Fe look into **High Desert Angler** (Map pp64-5; ☎ 505-988-7688, 888-988-
7688; www.highdesertangler.com; 451 Cerrillos Rd); Taos sports **Los Rios Anglers** (Map p138;
☎ 505-758-2798, 800-748-1707; www.losrios.com; 126 W Plaza Dr).

Food & Drink

Food in New Mexico is a lively mix of the ancient, the historic and the now. Dishes here trace the state's history back thousands of years to a time when Native Americans raised corn, squash, chiles and beans along the Rio Grande and crossed the Sangre de Cristo Mountains to hunt bison grazing on the Eastern Plains. Mix in hundreds of years of Spanish and more recent Anglo influences and you have one unique cuisine.

The unofficial state question, 'Red or green?,' is your first clue to culinary priorities. More than balloon fiestas, Pueblo Revival architecture or even art galleries, chile is the modern-day pride of New Mexico. Not Mexican – and most definitely not Texan – these fiery flavors have won adherents the world over.

On any given night, your heavenly meal won't arrive at the table as a distinct main with a couple of neatly arranged side dishes. It'll all be piled together – richly seasoned rice or potatoes, beans, the pride of any serious cook, and something like a chile-and-cheese-covered burrito bursting with gooey goodness. You are expected to mix all this together and enjoy it as a symphony rather than a series of solos.

The exception to this rule is contemporary, upscale New Mexican cuisine that takes the same ingredients but parcels them out quite differently – say, in a rabbit tart at world-famous Geronimo (p100) in Santa Fe or a rack of local lamb at Artichoke Café (p184) in Albuquerque.

Originally sold to help low-income New Mexicans pay their utility bills, the collection of old-time, authentic recipes (found on www.vivanewmexico.com/food.recipes.cocinas.html) is timeless, although the cookbook is no longer available.

STAPLES & SPECIALTIES

Most dishes here go back to basics. Corn is ground and patted into tortillas or made into *masa*, which is elaborately folded into cornhusks with some sweet or savory filling to create tamales, steamed to perfection. Sometimes corn is soaked in lime or lye water until tender and used in a rich stew called posole. Kernels also are roasted to create dried chicos, used in soups and stews.

Beans have long been the staple protein of New Mexicans from every culture, and come in many colors, shapes and preparations. Often stewed with onions, chiles and spices (many say the micaceous pottery of the pueblo tribes is the best vessel for such preparations), they're served somewhat intact or refried to a creamy consistency, for scooping with corn chips.

Squash is no longer a real staple, as imported produce from more accommodating climes has largely replaced this desert standard, but if you

FRITOS PIE

Not everyone can whip up an edible green chili stew, but even die-hard bachelorettes should be able to re-create this classic Santa Fe treat.
Ingredients:

- 1 single-serving-sized bag of Fritos corn chips
- 1 can chili con carne (substitute vegetarian chili, if desired)
- Grated cheddar cheese and/or diced onion (optional)

Heat chili on a stove or space heater. Open Frito bag. Pour warm chili into the bag as desired, taking care not to smother the chips entirely. Garnish with cheese and onion. Grab a fork and enjoy!

see *calabasas* on the menu, give it a try. The popular dish *calabacitas*, a combination of squash, corn and green chile, is ancient.

The Spanish brought with them a whole new world of ingredients, hauling across the sands the first grapevines, ostensibly for sacramental wine; sheep, pigs and cattle; fruit trees; grains like rye and wheat; spices introduced by the Moors from North Africa, including the omnipresent cumin; and most importantly, chile.

New Mexico has more than 17,500 farms, whose specialty crops include piñon nuts, chile peppers – red and green – and pinto beans.

Chile

From the sweet red bell pepper to brutish jalapeño, smoky chipotle to potent serrano, chiles are carefully cultivated across the globe. Hardy sources of vitamin C, flourishing where lesser plants fail, they are revered as much for their health benefits as their bite.

None can match the Hatch green chile, New Mexicans will tell you, but though the Chimayó red chile is perhaps not as revered, discriminating critics often prefer its more elegant flavor. Both are from the same plant but are harvested at different times. While the Chimayó is a close cousin to the mild Anaheim chile, the fruit's flavor is as much a reflection of environment and technique as mere genealogy.

Chiles are picked green in September and October, an event that fills every town in the state with the scent of the roast, done outdoors in special barrel-shaped contraptions designed for the task. Forty-pound burlap bags are hoisted onto the shoulders of slavering locals, who roast them at home. After the roasted peppers have cooled just enough to handle, friends and families spend a long evening carefully removing the outer skins and inner seeds, leaving just the soft, slightly cooked meat of the chile to be used in cooking all year long. It's a definite autumnal ritual.

New Mexico grows more chiles than any other state, and Hatch – the 'green chile capital of the world' – hosts the Chile Festival each Labor Day weekend.

Chiles left on the plant are allowed to mature to a deep ruby red, then strung on ristras to dry – making outdoor ornaments gracing many New Mexico homes until used as spice – and then they're laboriously ground into a paste that becomes the basis of rich red sauces, or a piquant spice for sprinkling atop almost anything.

When taking your order, waitstaff straightaway offer the most important choice: 'Red or green?' If you don't yet have a favorite, simply say 'Christmas' and you'll get it half-and-half, a bit of both.

As a side note, chili is a word that refers not to New Mexico's most important harvest, but to a bean-and-meat stew classified as Texan around here.

Breakfast

The hearty breakfasts here are capital-M Meals, probably because this is a culture only recently divorced – well, amicably separated, anyway – from a subsistence farming economy. Even omelets and other egg breakfasts usually come with beans and some kind of potatoes on the side, plus a couple of flour tortillas and, of course, chile. Breakfast meats include all the usual suspects, plus chorizo, a soft and spicy sausage often scrambled right into the eggs.

Huevos rancheros are the quintessential New Mexican breakfast: eggs prepared to order are served on top of two fried corn tortillas, loaded with beans and potatoes, sprinkled with cheese, and served swimming in chile. Slightly less massive are breakfast burritos – a flour tortilla filled with eggs, bacon or chorizo, cheese, chile and sometimes beans, and usually served à la carte. Somewhere in between are *migas,* prepared by stirring crunchy tortilla chips, lots of cheese and spices into scrambled eggs, served everywhere from local diners to the finest B&Bs.

A TASTE OF NEW MEXICO *Beth Penland*

Already hungry, but your flight doesn't leave for five more months? Begin preparing your taste buds today for the flavors of Santa Fe with this recipe.

Green Chile Stew

½lb ground beef, pork or turkey
½lb boneless sirloin, cubed
1 medium onion, chopped
1 clove garlic, minced
½ cup fresh cilantro, chopped
4 cups chicken broth
½ cup beer
2lb fresh green chiles, roasted, peeled and chopped
1 tomato, chopped
1½ tsp oregano
2½ tsp cumin
1/8 cup parsley, chopped
1 tsp salt
1 tsp pepper

In a large pot, sauté ground meat and sirloin until done. Remove from pot. Add onions, garlic and cilantro to pot and cook for three to five minutes or until onions are softened. Add chicken broth, beer, green chiles and tomato. Bring to a boil and reduce to a simmer. Add meat, oregano, cumin, parsley, salt and pepper. Simmer for two hours, stirring occasionally.

Main Dishes

You'll start just about every meal with a big bowl of corn chips and salsa. Almost everything comes with beans, rice and your choice of warm flour or corn tortillas, topped with chile, cheese and sometimes sour cream. Blue corn tortillas are one colorful New Mexican contribution to the art of cooking – they're just like regular tortillas but – drum roll please – they're made with blue corn.

Enchiladas are made with your choice of blue or regular corn tortillas (blue usually costs a bit extra) and they are served either rolled Mexican style around the filling (usually cheese or chicken) or flat, which is a New Mexican preference, layered like a lasagna with the filling and then baked.

Burritos are the staple: flour tortillas rolled around just about everything – beans, lamb, chicken, vegetables, cheese, whatever. Try the *carne adovada*: tender, slow-cooked pork baked in savory red chile. A *chimichanga* is a deep-fried burrito, just in case you're trying to gain weight for your next movie role. Stuffed *sopapillas* are similar to burritos, but all that good stuff comes inside a *sopapilla* (deep-fried bread), which makes them that much better.

Chile rellenos really are the food of the gods. Usually green or serrano chiles are stuffed with cheese and sometimes other ingredients, thickly breaded and fried, then topped with more chile. Northern New Mexico's version is more delicate and eggy, while Albuquerque and points south tend to use a thicker, firmer cornmeal breading.

Green chile stew is, perhaps, the ultimate expression of chile cuisine, and most certainly the pride of every New Mexican cook. Chiles are joined by potatoes, corn and other vegetables, and usually ground beef, though recipes vary.

Local cooks at the Whole Enchilada Festival (www .twefie.com) in Las Cruces build the world's largest enchilada in October.

Sopapillas & Desserts

A culinary culture boasting some form of chile in almost every dish would not last very long without the hot and delicate *sopapilla*, a deep-fried bread. These fragrant pillows of dough serve two primary purposes: first, as an alternative to tortillas for scooping up dinner; and second, as a receptacle for honey, available at every table in handy squeezable plastic bottles. Together with the honey, *sopapillas* cool off your palate after a fiery meal.

Other than *sopapillas*, dessert is something of a side note in New Mexican cooking, probably because meals are so huge. *Biscochitos* – the New Mexico state cookie – are simple sugar cookies with anise flavoring. You'll also find traditional Spanish flan, rich custard with a caramelized sugar topping, on many menus. Empanadas, pastries folded around fruit, spices and other fillings (sometimes savory), are almost a meal in themselves and *natillas*, soft custard topped with cinnamon-dusted meringue, make a great finish to any meal.

<aside>
Cookbook writers extraordinaire, Cheryl and Bill Jamison reveal the secrets behind fusing Native American, Spanish and Western foods in *The Border Cookbook: Authentic Home Cooking of the American Southwest and Northern Mexico.*
</aside>

Native Cuisine

Modern Indian cuisine bears little resemblance to food eaten prior to the Spanish conquest, but it is distinctive from New Mexican cuisine nonetheless. Navajo and Indian tacos – fry bread usually topped with beans, meat, tomatoes, chile and lettuce – are the most readily available. Chewy *horno* bread is baked in beehive-shaped outdoor adobe ovens (*hornos*) using remnant heat from a fire built inside, then cleared out before cooking.

Most other Native cooking is game-based and usually involves fry bread, beans, squash and locally harvested ingredients like berries and piñon nuts. Overall it's difficult to find; your best bets are stands at festivals and markets, casino restaurants or people's pueblo homes, where meals might include Picuris Pueblo's grass-fed bison, sometimes also available at the Santa Fe Farmers Market (p101).

The Tewa Kitchen (p157), at Taos Pueblo, and Pueblo Harvest Café (p185), at the Indian Pueblo Cultural Center in Albuquerque, are authentic exceptions. You could also attend a pueblo feast day, where you might be lucky enough to be invited to someone's table for serious home cooking or (more likely) can grab good grub at a stand set up prior to every dance.

<aside>
In *Cooking with Café Pasqual's,* Katharine Kagel ('The Luddite Chef') shares her passion for experimentation as well as fresh and fabulous contemporary recipes from the café.
</aside>

DRINKS

In case you hadn't noticed, New Mexico's in the middle of a drought. You can help save the state's golf courses, however, by drinking more fine New Mexican wine, a margarita or one of the excellent beers made right here.

Microbreweries for your sampling pleasure include the state's first, Embudo Station (p129), and Eske's (p154) in Taos. Both make great green chile beers. Or try Kelly's Brewery (p187) in Albuquerque. Santa Fe's Blue Corn Café (p105) and Second Street Brewery (p105) make up for their ambiance with a fine selection of quality brews. At the grocery store, pick up a six-pack of Roswell Alien Amber Ale, with perhaps the best label ever printed.

CELEBRATIONS

Visions of sugarplums don't dance in the heads of New Mexican kids at Christmas. Instead, families get together for big tamale-making parties, where *biscochitos* are baked by the hundreds. Specially spiced hot chocolate is served all around town, and many restaurants feature Christmas specials – usually the cook's family recipes – on the menu.

But it's the pueblos that really know how to throw a ceremony. Feast days, replete with dances, pole climbs, races and whatnot, are topped off with lots of great food. The biggest events are noted throughout the book,

---

ON THE VINE

Award-wining vineyards in New Mexico grow at some of the highest altitudes in the country, ensuring night-time temperatures that cool the grapes after a long day in the hot desert sun, slowing maturation of the coveted grapes in this state's short growing season. Sandy, loamy soil adds its blessings and the extremely dry air inhibits the scourge of grape rot that threatens in more humid climes.

According to the **New Mexico Wine Growers Association** (☎ 866-494-6366; www.nmwine.com), the state's 29 wineries produce some 350,000 gallons of various vintages annually – and a lot of it, according to both *Wine Spectator* and local wine connoisseurs, is top-notch. That's not surprising when you learn that the first grapevines were planted here in 1629 south of Socorro by a Franciscan friar and a Capuchin monk, some 150 years before Californians began to grow grapes in the 1770s.

The star of the show is Gruet (p177), in Albuquerque, with outstanding Blanc de Noirs sparkling wine and several award-winning whites, though it's the rosé pinot noir that vintner Laurent Gruet calls 'the juice of love.' La Chiripada (p131), in Dixon, is well known for its riesling and cabernet sauvignon, while Casa Rondeña (p177), another Albuquerque entry, boasts a cabernet franc that's earned plenty of kudos.

But that's just the beginning. Stop at any fine winery and taste for yourself. Better yet, build your vacation around one of these festivals:

Albuquerque Wine Festival (Balloon Fiesta Park) Tickets $15. This festival is held in late May, with arts, crafts and gourmet grub.

Santa Fe Wine Festival (Rancho de los Golondrinas) Tickets $12. This wine festival is held early July, with jazz, blues, mariachis and art.

New Mexico Wine Festival (Loretto Park, Bernalillo) Tickets $10. Still the biggest and best, this festival is held in early September.

---

but refer to the website of the **Indian Pueblo Cultural Center** (www.indianpueblo .org) for more complete listings. Be sure to familiarize yourself with the etiquette and have fun.

On Saturday evenings all summer, Albuquerque throws a party called Summerfest (p181), with food and entertainment. Santa Fe offers upscale food-related events, including late-February's Artfeast Edible Art Tour (p91), with art, jazz, wine and gourmet cuisine. The Santa Fe Wine & Chile Fiesta (p91) features wine tastings and dinner events in late September.

WHERE TO EAT & DRINK

As in cities and villages the world around, you can't always tell the quality of a restaurant's food just by looking at the establishment's exterior. Towns in New Mexico enjoy a wealth of strip malls and faux adobe concrete buildings side-by-side-by-side, so except in central Santa Fe, you won't find glitz and glam or elegant entrances, but you will find more great food than you can sample in one vacation if you follow a few simple rules.

First and foremost – and this is less true in Santa Fe than elsewhere, but generally still applies – get the heck away from the plaza. The food won't be bad, but you'll often pay extra for something less than spectacular.

Phenomenal four-star cuisine is available everywhere, although you'll pay through the nose for it. But if you're looking for quality New Mexican grub, ask the locals where they're having lunch. Places that gussy themselves up – this is not done for locals – are unlikely to be your best bets for authentic cuisine. Look for simple places with chipped Formica tables, Naugahyde booths and lines out the door. The Frontier (p184) in Albuquerque is a great place to start – and end. (They'll even pack frozen chile to take on the plane ride home.)

Fabiola Cabeza De Baca Gilbert, who was born in New Mexico in 1895 and wrote *Good Life: New Mexico Traditions and Food*, was recognized among Hispanic and pueblo villages as a food expert.

AT THE GROCERY STORE

You can't import New Mexico's sunshine, vistas or laid-back attitude, but luckily you can import the food.

Bueno (☎ 800-952-4453; www.buenofoods.com) This Albuquerque company ships frozen green chile with red and green salsas anywhere you have an address.

505 Southwestern (☎ 888-505-2445; www.505chile.com) Based in Las Cruces, these folks will ship fajita marinade, salsas and green chiles. They'll also 'send a friend a free chile' – no kidding.

Santa Fe Chile Company (☎ 505-995-9667; www.chileco.com) This outfit spreads the gospel of chipotle garlic salsa worldwide, fresh from Santa Fe's only salsa factory.

Tamale Molly (☎ 877-509-1800; www.tamalemolly.com) Proceeds from this Santa Fe enterprise go to feed the homeless. All the while, you're fed all-veggie, all-natural, hand-tied tamales, made with everything from goat cheese with mint to honey pecan.

Tamaya Blue (☎ 888-867-5198; www.cookingpost.com) Chefs from the Bernalillo-based Santa Ana Pueblo ship their own blue corn muffin mix, deer jerky and other Native treats to your door. Online recipes show you how to cook them.

VEGETARIANS & VEGANS

This edition of *Lonely Planet Santa Fe, Taos & Albuquerque* makes hunting and gathering easy for vegetarians with the Ⓥ icon in the Eating sections. It indicates which restaurants serve vegetarian mains. Thanks to the prevalence of rice and delicious beans, as well as the area's long-standing appeal to hippie-types, vegetarians and vegans will have no problem finding something delicious on most menus, even at fast-food drive-throughs and tiny dives. There is a potential pitfall though: traditional New Mexican cuisine uses lard in beans, tamales, *sopapillas* and flour (but not corn) tortillas, among other things, so be sure to ask.

Almost every large town has a natural foods grocer, and Happy Cow's Vegetarian Guide (www.happycow.net) will help you locate them and veggie-friendly restaurants as well. You'll eat better here than almost anywhere in the Southwest, so go nuts (as in piñon).

EATING WITH KIDS

Put the hot desert sun to work by cooking solar. Buy a box cooker from AAA Solar in Albuquerque (www.aaasolar.com) and get started (www.solarcooking.org) frying those eggs on the sidewalk.

Families are an important part of New Mexico culture, so all but the most upscale restaurants are kid-friendly and generally have children's menus (indicated by a 🄵 icon), high chairs, large booths for big families and often crayons or other toys to amuse the tots. Most folks will know to automatically omit the chile for younger kids; tweens and teens should specifically ask for it on the side, if necessary.

If the kids are feeling rambunctious, it's easiest to avoid the crowds by eating between 2pm and 5pm, just to give yourself a little more room. Remember, though, that not all restaurants are open straight through lunch and dinner.

COOKING COURSES

Taking home new recipes and special techniques not only makes your New Mexico vacation memories last, it keeps them as fresh as a newly minted mango and habanero chile salsa.

Santa Fe School of Cooking (Map pp64-5; ☎ 505-983-4511, 800-982-4688; www.santafeschoolofcooking.com; 116 W San Francisco St, Santa Fe; $35-95), the capital's most acclaimed cooking school, offers classes on New Mexican favorites and Native American cuisine. Feeling lazy? Try the afternoon tapas demonstration, where experts cook and you eat.

Area chefs at **Las Cosas Kitchen Shoppe & Cooking School** (Map pp64-5; ☎ 505-988-3394, 877-229-7184; www.lascosascooking.com; 181 Paseo de Peralta, DeVargas Center, Santa Fe; $55-70) teach you to cook at high altitudes, master New Mexico faves, grill meat-lovers' specialties or whip up vegetarian or Thai masterpieces. There's also a four-day kid's camp ($275). It's never too early to teach them to do more than wash the dishes!

Weekend cooking courses are held at **Jane Butel's Cooking School** (Map pp170-1; ☎ 505-243-2622, 800-473-8226; www.janebutel.com; 2655 Pan American Fwy NE, Albuquerque; $900-1650) in Butel's Albuquerque-area home, while week-long courses take place in Santa Fe and come packaged with hotel stays. Jane will teach you to prepare basics like guacamole, blue cornbread and salsas before moving onto more ultimate New Mexico dishes like enchiladas, tamales and posole.

Santa Fe

Your first glimpse of Santa Fe may feel like seeing the Golden Gate Bridge or Grand Canyon for the first time. It's so familiar that you swear you've been there, done that.

It's all here: abstract adobe architecture, carved wooden doorways, wizened Native American faces selling turquoise jewelry, well-to-do Anglo women wearing concha belts, ristras hanging from vigas. There are authentic celebrations here for art, heart, belly and soul; there are trails into mountains held sacred for millennia.

On the surface, Santa Fe is a laid-back place. Beneath the surface there is age-old tension between newcomers and old timers, between those who can afford and those who cannot. There is a convergence of Native American, Hispanic and Anglo culture; the heroic triad is writ large here. At the same time, this high-desert enclave, her growth long limited by a lack of precious water, remains a beacon of progressive thought and creative culture.

In Santa Fe, start with margaritas. Like pilgrims tasting pie in Key West, sip a salty rimmed glass in Santa Fe until you can sip no more.

HIGHLIGHTS

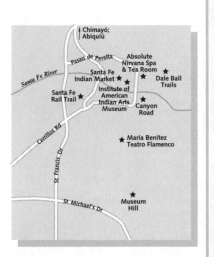

- Sample the twin delights of art and history on **Museum Hill** (p67)
- Immerse yourself in modern art and ancient Native wonders along **Canyon Rd** (p70)
- Send temperatures soaring at **Maria Benitez Teatro Flamenco** (p107)
- Spoil yourself at **Absolute Nirvana Spa & Tea Room** (p98)
- Savor the art of Georgia O'Keeffe at **Abiquiú** (p122)
- Witness the multiplicity of Native American art at the **Institute of American Indian Arts Museum** (p72)
- Turn your home into a museum after shopping at **Santa Fe Indian Market** (p91)
- Pay your respects at the Santuario in **Chimayó** (p126)
- Follow the **Dale Ball Trails** (p84) through the high desert
- Mountain bike along railroad tracks on the **Santa Fe Rail Trail** (p85)

| ■ TELEPHONE CODE: 505 | ■ POPULATION: 65,100 | ■ ELEVATION: 7200FT |

SANTA FE IN...

Two Days

After breakfast at **Cafe Pasqual's** (p99), take in the plaza – particularly the excellent offerings of the **Museum of Fine Arts** (p68), the **Palace of the Governors** (p68) and the **Native American jewelry** out front. All your official tourist duties are over, and it's not even noon.

Take the **Santa Fe walking tour** (p87) – the route is a suggestion, not an itinerary. Pick up a *Reporter* to see what's up. If nothing strikes your fancy, head to the **La Fonda Belltower Bar** (p105) and watch the sun set.

The next morning, it's up and at 'em at **Tia Sophia's** (p98). Make reservations at **10,000 Waves** (p97), then catch the M-line to **Museum Hill** (p67), where you can't skip the **Museum of International Folk Art** (p69). Hungry for more art? Then it's **Canyon Rd** (p70), with a pick-me-up at the **Teahouse** (p98). Reached art saturation? Then it's the **Dale Ball Trails** (p84). Now you deserve to relax in a hillside hot tub at **10,000 Waves** and watch the moon rise over Santa Fe.

Three Days

After two days of wandering Santa Fe, it's time to get out of town. Hop onto US 285/84 north and NM 502 toward Los Alamos, stopping at **San Ildefonso Pueblo** (p118) for the **Maria Poveka Martinez Museum** (p118).

Cruise through **Los Alamos** (p129), pausing at the **Bradbury Science Museum** (p131) to learn all about WMDs – it's a blast. Then it's onto **Bandelier National Monument** (p133) for a hike into history and a climb to **Ceremonial Cave** (p133). Wind your way back to **Chimayó** (p126) and dine at **Rancho de Chimayó** (p126).

Are you so enchanted that you want to move here? You'll need money: stop at **Camel Rock Casino** (p117) and take your best shot. Then it's back to Santa Fe for a brew at the **Cowgirl Hall of Fame** (p102).

Four Days

Follow the two-day schedule. Wake up, grab coffee and magazines at **Downtown Subscription** (p98) and hit the road. First, brunch at **Angelina's** (p122) in Española. Mmm...chile. Grab some local produce from a roadside stand and head to **Ojo Caliente Mineral Springs** (p124).

Get a massage, then head past El Rito, on the back road to **Abiquiú** (p122). Drop your stuff at the **Abiquiú Inn** (p125) and head to **Ghost Ranch** (p125). The museums are fine, but you must hike **Chimney Rock** (p124), playing 'Name That O'Keeffe Painting' as you drink in the views. The winner gets dinner at the inn.

The next morning, detour to **San Ildefonso**, the **Bradbury Museum** in Los Alamos and **Bandelier**. And then it's back to Santa Fe, perhaps for one last sunset from the **Belltower Bar**.

ORIENTATION

Built long before cars were an issue, downtown Santa Fe, bounded by St Francis Dr to the west and horseshoe-shaped Paseo de Peralta on all other sides, seems to the recent arrival like a warren of narrow, confusing streets, which become narrower and more confusing the closer you get to the plaza. The plaza is most easily accessible via the well-signed turnoff from St Francis Dr.

If you get lost driving in this area, your best bet is to find Paseo de Peralta, which will return you to car-friendly St Francis Dr no matter which way you turn. Then follow the signs for another try.

Both Cerrillos (pronounced ser-ree-yos) Rd and St Francis Dr intersect I-25 at the southern end of downtown, forming a triangle. Cerrillos Rd is a 7-mile, neon-lit strip of motels and businesses, while St Francis Dr takes you more directly to the plaza. Connecting these two main drags are Rodeo Rd, heading west to the airport; St Michael's Dr, with challenging on-ramps; and Cordova Rd, which is very close to downtown.

St Francis Dr becomes US 84/285 north of Santa Fe, connecting the city to Española and points north. Cerrillos Rd is the northernmost stretch of NM 14, also called the Turquoise Trail; you can continue south

SANTA FE

SANTA FE

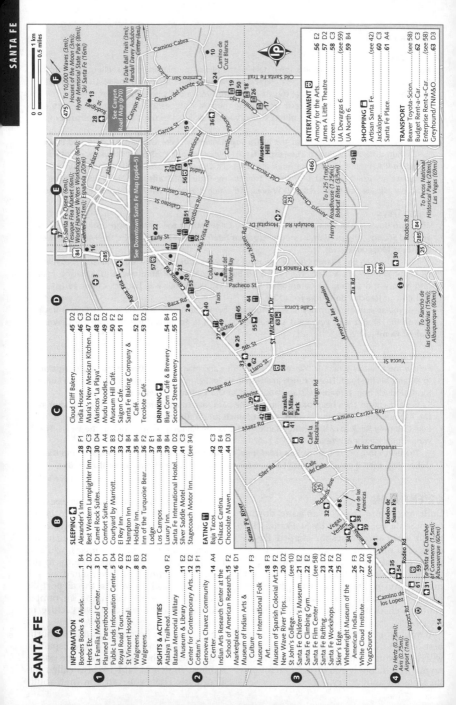

INFORMATION
Borders Books & Music....................1	B4
Herbs Etc.....................................2	D2
La Familia Medical Center................3	D1
Planned Parenthood.......................4	D1
Public Lands Information Center.........5	D4
Royal Road Tours...........................6	D2
St Vincent Hospital.........................7	E3
Walgreens....................................8	B3
Walgreens....................................9	D2

SIGHTS & ACTIVITIES
Atalaya Trailhead.........................10	F2
Bataan Memorial Military	
Museum & Library......................11	E2
Center for Contemporary Arts.......12	E2
Cottam's....................................13	F1
Genoveva Chavez Community	
Center...................................14	A4
Indian Arts Research Center at the	
School of American Research....15	F2
Marketplace...............................16	D1
Museum of Indian Arts &	
Culture..................................17	F3
Museum of International Folk	
Art...18	F3
Museum of Spanish Colonial Art...19	F2
New Wave River Trips...................20	D2
St John's College..............................(see 10)
Santa Fe Children's Museum.........21	E2
Santa Fe Climbing Gym................22	E2
Santa Fe Film Center.........................(see 58)
Santa Fe Rafting.........................23	D2
Santa Fe Workshops....................24	F2
Skier's Edge...............................25	D2
Wheelwright Museum of the	
American Indian.....................26	F3
White Cloud Institute..................27	D2
YogaSource.....................................(see 44)

SLEEPING
Alexander's Inn...........................28	F1
Best Western Lamplighter Inn.......29	C3
Camel Rock Suites.......................30	D4
Comfort Suites............................31	A4
Courtyard by Marriott..................32	B3
El Rey Inn...................................33	C2
Hampton Inn..............................34	B4
Holiday Inn................................35	B4
Inn of the Turquoise Bear	
Lodge....................................36	F2
Los Campos................................37	E1
Luxury Inn.................................38	B4
Santa Fe International Hostel.........39	B4
Silver Saddle Motel......................40	D2
Stagecoach Motor Inn..................41	C3

EATING
Baja Tacos................................42	C3
Chilacas Cantina........................43	E4
Chocolate Maven.......................44	D3
Cloud Cliff Bakery......................45	D2
India House................................46	F1
Maria's New Mexican Kitchen......47	D2
Mariscos 'La Playa'.....................48	E2
Mudu Noodles...........................49	D2
Museum Hill Café.......................50	F2
Saigon Cafe...............................51	E2
Santa Fe Baking Company &	
Café..52	E2
Tecolote Café............................53	D2

DRINKING
Blue Corn Café & Brewery............54	B4
Second Street Brewery.................55	D3

ENTERTAINMENT
Armory for the Arts.....................56	E2
James A Little Theatre...................57	D2
Screen......................................58	C3
UA Devargas 6...............................(see 59)
UA North 6................................59	B4

SHOPPING
Artisan Santa Fe..............................(see 42)
Jackalope..................................60	C3
Santa Fe Place...........................61	A4

TRANSPORT
Beaver Toyota–Scion.......................(see 58)
Budget Rent-a-Car......................62	C3
Enterprise Rent-a-Car.....................(see 58)
Greyhound/TNM&O.....................63	D3

on Cerrillos Rd past I-25 for the scenic back road to Albuquerque. I-25 South is the fastest route to Albuquerque, while I-25 North actually takes you southeast to Las Vegas, New Mexico.

Paseo de Peralta is the hub for other major roads. Old Santa Fe Trail (which becomes Old Pecos Trail) heads south to I-25 and the old road to Las Vegas. Bishops Lodge Rd (also called Washington Ave; just look for the pink Scottish Rite Temple) runs north to Tesuque, eventually joining US 84/285, or you can make an almost immediate right from Bishops Lodge Rd onto Hyde Park Rd (NM 475, also called Artist Rd) for well-signed access to Hyde Park and Ski Santa Fe.

The train station on Guadalupe St is easily accessible from the plaza on foot but handles primarily tourist excursions. The main train station is 18 miles east in Lamy and is served by a shuttle from Santa Fe. The bus station is centrally located but miles from the plaza on St Michael's Dr, while the airport is closer to the Cerrillos Rd exit off I-25 than downtown. Both are served by Santa Fe Trails buses.

Maps

The visitors centers stock several free maps, most of them cutesy and advertising-based. If you plan to explore, invest in Rand McNally's *Santa Fe/Taos Local Street Detail* folding map (it's the green one) with insets covering Española, Las Vegas and Los Alamos. There are several others, available at any gas station, which are almost as good.

Rand McNally also publishes the exhaustive atlas *Albuquerque, Santa Fe & Taos: Street Guide*, but go for the locally produced version by Horton Family Maps, a slightly thinner black-and-white book of street maps covering the area.

If you plan to get out into the wilderness, the *Benchmark New Mexico Road & Recreation Atlas* is indispensable; if you're only going to dip your toes into the great outdoors, the excellent *Highroads of North Central New Mexico Map* is a great folding map covering northern New Mexico.

Travel Bug (right) has every map you want or need, including USGS and custom hiking maps, aerial photography and lots of travel guides.

INFORMATION
Bookstores

Ark Bookstore (Map pp64-5; ☎ 988-3709; www.ark books.com; 133 Romero St) This place is out to enlighten, covering all your spiritual needs from chakra to chakra.

Borders Books & Music (Montezuma Ave Map pp64-5; ☎ 954-4707; 500 Montezuma Ave; Zafarano Dr Map p62; ☎ 474-9450; 3513 Zafarano Dr) This big-chain entry features an expansive selection of Southwestern reading. The larger branch on Zafarano Dr is off Cerrillos Rd.

Collected Works Book Store (Map pp64-5; ☎ 988-4226; www.collectedworksbookstore.com; 208B W San Francisco St) Walls lined with literature, New Mexicana and lots of maps make this a fine place to pick up a quality vacation read.

Downtown Subscription (Map pp64-5) Next door to Garcia Street Books, this has the best newsstand in town.

Garcia Street Books (Map p70; ☎ 986-0151; www .garciastreetbooks.com; 376 Garcia St) Shelves packed with heavily illustrated art and architecture books could have you perusing for hours.

Leo's Art Books (Map pp64-5; ☎ 989-7554; 225 Montezuma Ave) Leo has an enormous selection of new and used art books, from verbose histories to sumptuous coffee-table tomes.

Photo-Eye Books & Prints (Map pp64-5; ☎ 988-5152; www.photoeye.com; 370/376 Garcia St) Photo-Eye claims (and it's probably true) to stock more photography books than anyplace else in the USA. It also has a great adjacent gallery!

Travel Bug (Map pp64-5; ☎ 992-0418; www.maps ofnewmexico.com; 839 Paseo de Peralta) With guidebooks to most of the planet and maps covering every inch of New Mexico, this place rules. Also espresso, pastries, wireless internet access, USGS topographical maps, GPS units and mapping software.

Emergency

Fire & Ambulance Dispatch (☎ 955-5144)
Fire, Police, Ambulance Immediate Dispatch (☎ 911)
NM Poison Control Center (☎ 800-432-6866)
Police – nonemergency (☎ 955-5080)
Santa Fe Rape Crisis Center (☎ 986-9111)
St Vincent Hospital Emergency Room (Map p62; ☎ 983-3361; 455 St Michael's Dr)

Internet Access

CD Café (Map pp64-5; ☎ 986-0735; 301 N Guadalupe St) Bring your laptop for free wireless internet while you have lunch, or pay $10 to use a café computer. Bonus: sample CDs for sale at listening stations.

Santa Fe Public Library (Map pp64-5; ☎ 955-6780; 145 Washington Ave) Make reservations for a free half hour of internet access.

DOWNTOWN SANTA FE

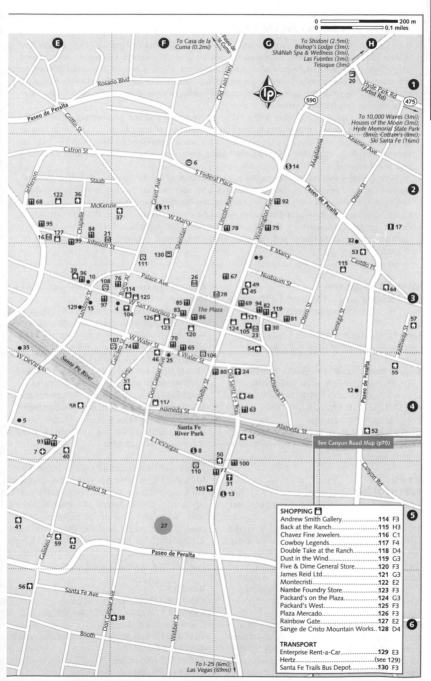

0   200 m
0   0.1 miles

To Casa de la
Cuma (0.2mi)

Paseo de la Cuma

To Shidoni (2.5mi);
Bishop's Lodge (3mi);
ShaNah Spa & Wellness (3mi);
Las Fuentes (3mi);
Tesuque (3mi)

Hyde Park Rd
(Artist Rd)

To 10,000 Waves (3mi);
Houses of the Moon (3mi);
Hyde Memorial State Park
(8mi); Cottam's (8mi);
Ski Santa Fe (16mi)

Rosario Blvd

Paseo de Peralta

Griffin St

Catron St

Jefferson

Staab

McKenzie

Chapelle

Johnson St

Sandoval St

Galisteo St

Ortiz

Don Gaspar Ave

Shelby St

Old Santa Fe Trail

Cathedral Pl

Canyon Rd

Paseo de Peralta

S Federal Place

Grant Ave

W Marcy

Lincoln Ave

Washington Ave

Sheridan

Palace Ave

W San Francisco St

The Plaza

W Water St

E Water St

Alameda St

Santa Fe River Park

E DeVargas

W DeVargas

Santa Fe River

S Capitol St

Galisteo St

Paseo de Peralta

Santa Fe Ave

Don Gaspar Ave

Webber St

Booth

To I-25 (6mi);
Las Vegas (69mi)

See Canyon Road Map (p70)

E Marcy

Nusbaum St

Castillo Pl

Oteto St

Magdalena

Kearney Ave

Paseo de Peralta

Cerrillos St

Faithway St

Staab

SHOPPING		
Andrew Smith Gallery	114	F3
Back at the Ranch	115	H3
Chavez Fine Jewelers	116	C1
Cowboy Legends	117	F4
Double Take at the Ranch	118	D4
Dust in the Wind	119	G3
Five & Dime General Store	120	F3
James Reid Ltd	121	G3
Montecristi	122	E2
Nambe Foundry Store	123	F3
Packard's on the Plaza	124	G3
Packard's West	125	F3
Plaza Mercado	126	F3
Rainbow Gate	127	E2
Sange de Cristo Mountain Works	128	D4

TRANSPORT		
Enterprise Rent-a-Car	129	E3
Hertz	(see 129)	
Santa Fe Trails Bus Depot	130	F3

IT'S OFFICIAL – SANTA FE IS CREATIVE

It was an honor, but really no surprise, when the UN named Santa Fe America's first Creative City in July 2005. The designation, bestowed by Unesco, the UN Education, Scientific and Cultural Organization, made Santa Fe part of a growing network of cities around the world offering to link artists from developing countries and emerging markets with patrons in well-established art markets. The network also promotes information- and expertise-sharing among member cities to grow their arts-related economies.

As the third-largest art market in the US (only New York and Los Angeles sell more art annually), and the highest rate of arts businesses per resident of any city in the US, Santa Fe also caught the attention of Unesco's Creative Cities Network, established in 2004, with the popular International Folk Art Market (p91), an ideal place for artists from around the world to display and sell their work.

'With a history that traces back to the pueblo cultures of the Rio Grande, abundant spirituality and beautiful landscapes, Santa Fe inspires and nurtures creative talent in a multicultural setting that cultivates a unique and organic cultural sensibility and industry,' says Milagros del Corral, Unesco's deputy assistant director general for culture. Other cities in the network include Aswan, Egypt; Berlin, Germany; Bologna, Italy; Buenos Aires, Argentina; Seville, Spain; Montreal, Canada; Edinburgh, Scotland; and Popayan, Colombia. Several countries, too, have applied for the status.

Internet Resources

City of Santa Fe (www.santafenm.gov) The city's official website has information on public transportation and more.

Santa Fe (www.santafe.org) This site is designed for event planners and business travelers as well as vacationers.

Santa Fe Always Online (www.sfaol.com) You'll find links to everything Santa Fe, as well as Southwest tales under 'Articles and Stories' to entertain adults and kids alike.

Visit Santa Fe (www.visitsantafe.com) This site has easy-to-navigate links and reviews.

What's Happening in Santa Fe (www.santafeartsand culture.org) Check out the calendar and buy tickets online for events you just can't miss.

Media
PUBLICATIONS

The City Different is also the City Literate, hence the many glossy, often upscale art and photography gallery guides, magazines, alternative weekly newspapers and conventional daily newspapers – some of them free.

New Mexico Kids! (www.newmexico-kids.com) Face it – traveling with kids is different; consult the calendar of events in this free bimonthly newspaper to keep them happy.

Santa Fe New Mexican (www.santafenewmexican .com) Santa Fe's daily record has water stats, tourist information, fishing reports and a Saturday 'Spiritual Community Directory' with rundowns on everything from Catholic masses to Sufi Circles of Prayer. On Friday, it publishes

Pasatiempo, a pullout arts and entertainment insert with comprehensive events listings.

Santa Fe Reporter (www.sfreporter.com) This spirited free weekly comes out on Wednesday, and has all the events listings, reviews, clever columns and spicy articles you need.

Santa Fe Trend (www.santafetrend.com; $6) This elegant bi-annual magazine explores 'where art and design meet' and aims for an even more exclusive audience.

Santa Fean (www.santafean.com; $5) Glossy and beautifully illustrated, this monthly magazine has outstanding writing that focuses on the posh side of Santa Fe, including art, history, dining and shopping – plus exhaustive listings of events and gallery openings.

Other free monthlies available around town include *The* magazine, with arts coverage such as reviews of galleries, artists and openings; the **El Dorado Sun** (www.eldoradosun .com), with lefty and green news; *Broad Issues,* published by and for the Warehouse 21 crowd (p106); and *Sun Monthly,* a New Age publication focusing on progressive politics and holistic health.

RADIO
KABQ 104.1 FM Contemporary Hispanic.
KANW 89.1 FM National Public Radio (NPR) plus jazz, New Mexican and Mexican music.
KBAC 98.1 FM Radio Free Santa Fe: great alternative music.
KBQI 107.9 FM Country.
KDRF 103.3 FM Hard rock.
KFLQ 91.5 FM Christian.

KNML 610 AM Sports.

KSFQ 101.1 FM Classic rock.

KSFR 90.7 FM Santa Fe Public Radio: wacky music, lots of jazz, classical and lefty talk radio.

KSWV 810 AM Mexican and Tex-Mex.

KUNM 89.9 FM NPR, Native American programming, fine arts and student DJs spinning wild and free.

KYBR 950 AM Mariachi, norteño and Tex-Mex.

KZNM 106.7 FM Spanish-language with great area musicians.

TELEVISION

KAOT 7 ABC.

KASA 2 Fox.

KASY 50 UPN.

KCHF 11 Christian.

KLUZ 41 Univision.

KNME 5 PBS.

KOB 4 NBC.

KRQE 13 CBS.

KTEL 53 Telemundo.

KWBQ 19 WB.

Santa Fe Community Television 8 The local community access station is worth watching for its performance art, spiritual talk shows and Los Alamos National Laboratory lectures.

Medical Services

Herbs etc (Map p62; ☎ 888-694-3727; 1345 Cerrillos Rd) Natural medications are available here in both packaged formulas and bulk.

La Familia Medical Center (Map p62; ☎ 989-5934, emergency 982-4425; 1035 Alto St) You'll wait in line for quality care, paid up-front on a sliding scale, if you don't have insurance.

New Mexico Alternative Health Center (Map pp64-5; ☎ 983-3003; 436 Cerrillos Rd) Chinese medicine, acupuncture homeopathy, midwifery and more are available.

Planned Parenthood (Map p62; ☎ 982-3684; 514 Oñate Pl) Make an appointment for women's reproductive health services.

St Vincent's Hospital (Map p62; ☎ 983-3361; www .stvin.org; 455 St Michael's Dr) This is the major full-service hospital for northern New Mexico.

Walgreens (Cerrillos Rd Map p62; ☎ 474-3507; 3298 Cerrillos Rd; S St Francis Dr Map p62; ☎ 982-4643; 1096 S St Francis Dr) The Cerillos Rd branch of this all-night pharmacy is convenient to the budget-hotel strip.

Money

It's a tourist town, and all-too-convenient ATMs are everywhere. **Wells Fargo** (Map pp64-5; ☎ 984-0424; 241 Washington Ave), like most area banks, changes foreign currency.

Post

Main post office (Map pp64-5; ☎ 988-2239; 120 S Federal Place) Convenient to the plaza.

Tourist Information

New Mexico State Parks (Map pp64-5; ☎ 827-1470; www.nmparks.com; 141 E DeVargas St; ☼ 8am-5pm Mon-Fri) This office has information on all state parks and recreation areas. Reserve campsites through www.new mexico.reserveworld.com.

Public Lands Information Center (Map p62; ☎ 438-7542, 877-276-9404; www.publiclands.org; 1474 Rodeo Rd; ☼ 8am-5pm Mon-Fri Nov-Mar, 8am-5pm Mon-Sat Apr-Oct) Come here first for comprehensive information about all state and national parks, national monuments and BLM lands; hunting, fishing and backcountry camping permits; up-to-date information on trails, roads and closures (a list is posted on the door); and a wide selection of books and maps.

Santa Fe Chamber of Commerce (Map p116; ☎ 988-3279; www.santafechamber.com; 8380 Cerrillos Rd; ☼ 8am-5pm) Inconveniently located at the Cerrillos exit from I-25, in the Santa Fe Outlets Mall, this office has information geared toward residents and visitors.

Visitors Center (Lamy Bldg Map pp64-5; ☎ 827-7336; Lamy Bldg, 491 Old Santa Fe Trail; ☼ 8am-5pm; W Marcy St Map pp64-5; ☎ 955-6200, 800-777-2489; 201 W Marcy St; ☼ 8am-5pm Mon-Fri) In the historic 1878 Lamy Building (site of the state's first private college), the main center has flyers, information, a hotel reservation line, free coffee and free internet access. The W Marcy St branch in the Sweeney Convention Center is smaller, but more convenient.

SIGHTS

While you're here in one of the top-rated arts towns in the United States, plan to spend time in some of the city's museums. Choices range from confrontational, political, Native American art to eye-popping modern art to Spanish and international folk art. In 2005, the UN officially designated Santa Fe one of the world's premiere Creative Cities, the first US city to be so recognized.

Most museums are clustered in two primary locations – around the downtown plaza and on **Museum Hill**, where four excellent museums, a research library and a recommended café all are linked by a sculpture-lined trail. Since it's almost 3 miles southwest of the plaza, unless you're really up for the walk, take the M Line – a Santa Fe Trails bus geared toward visitors – that winds through historic neighborhoods.

Many museums and other attractions offer discounts to senior citizens and free

SANTA FE

JOHN GAW MEEM *Bridgette Wagner*

The father of Pueblo Revival style, architect John Gaw Meem was instrumental in building Santa Fe. Meem came, like so many others, to convalesce from tuberculosis, then fell in love with 'those graceful little mud houses everybody lives in.' After his recovery he left to study architecture, returning two years later to open up shop.

Only a few years had elapsed since the city had passed the controversial 1912 adobe-only building laws. Meem took the side of the preservationists and developed architectural designs and methods based on pueblo architecture. He got a few jobs designing homes, including that of writer Mary Austin, but it was the 1928 commission for Maria Vilura Conkey that ignited his career. By combining the vigas, beams and rounded corners of the Spanish Pueblo Revival with the brick cornices, white painted windows and tall posts of the Territorial Revival, Meem inspired a renaissance in Southwestern architecture.

Meem was contracted to design the Laboratory of Anthropology, refurbish La Fonda Hotel and build the Museum of Spanish Colonial Art in Santa Fe, Fuller Lodge in Los Alamos, and more than 35 buildings at UNM's Albuquerque campus. His projects also included restoring the missions at Laguna and Santa Ana Pueblos. Meem's architectural elements have since become popular throughout the Southwest, but remain quintessentially Santa Fe style.

---

admission or discounts to New Mexico residents, at least on certain days of the week. Also, log onto www.museumhill.org for special events calendars and links to all four Museum Hill institutions.

Museum of New Mexico

A collection of four very different **museums** (☎ 827-6463; www.museumofnewmexico.org; per museum $8, 4-day pass to all 4 $18, 1-day pass to 2 $12, under 16 free; ☻ 10am-5pm Tue-Sun, 10am-5pm Mon in summer), two of them on Museum Hill, also offer seminars, musical events and a variety of guided tours with historic or artistic focuses, many designed for children. Both the Palace of the Governors and Museum of Fine Arts, the two located on the plaza, are free on Friday from 5pm to 8pm. Some are open on Mondays during the summer and all have fabulous on-site gift shops and online shopping at www.shopmuseum .com.

PALACE OF THE GOVERNORS

Begin your voyage into Santa Fe's rich past right here at the **Palace of the Governors** (Map pp64-5; ☎ 476-5100; www.palaceofthegovernors.org; 105 W Palace Ave), built in 1610 as the Casas Reales (Royal Houses) and home to more than 100 governors – 60 of them Spanish – before becoming a museum in 1909.

This is where Spanish colonists waited out the Pueblo Revolt of 1680, and where Governor Lew Wallace wrote part of *Ben Hur*. This is also where the first museum

director, Jesse L Nusbaum, displayed the first public collection of Native artifacts west of the Mississippi, an exhibit that's been re-installed alongside many other treasures: a state seal made entirely of recycled hardware and cutlery, religious items brought by early Jewish settlers, 400-year-old Spanish armor and the impressive Segesser Hide Paintings, which portray a bitter 1720s battle between Spanish and French-Indian coalition forces.

Volunteers lead free, highly recommended **palace tours** in the mornings, April through October; call ahead for exact times. Volunteers also lead downtown walking tours (p90).

The **Portal Program** (www.newmexicoindianart .org) allows artisans with tribal enrollment to sell jewelry and art in front of the palace. It's a tradition that began in the 1880s, when Tesuque artisans began meeting the train with all manner of wares; today more than 1000 members representing almost every New Mexico tribe exhibit here at various times, alternating schedules to fill nearly 80 spaces beneath the vigas each morning.

MUSEUM OF FINE ARTS

Brush up on your knowledge of New Mexico's manifold artists and art movements at the country's oldest contemporary arts museum, the **Museum of Fine Arts** (Map pp64-5; ☎ 476-5072; mfasantafe.org; 107 W Palace Ave). The 1917 building is itself among the finest examples of Pueblo Revival architecture anywhere and served as a starting point from which architects like John Gaw Meem (opposite) would go on to transform the city in 'Santa Fe style.'

With more than 20,000 pieces – including collections of the Taos Society of Artists (p141), Santa Fe Society of Artists, Los Cincos Pintores and other legendary collectives – it's a veritable who's who of the geniuses who put this dusty town on a par with Paris and New York. Docents, who give **tours** (🕑 1:30pm), are far less likely to roll their eyes than gallery owners while you're learning to appreciate the state's finest offerings from the likes of Georgia O'Keeffe, Elias Rivera and Ansel Adams.

The museum also hosts free concerts by the **Santa Fe Community Orchestra** (☎ 466-2516; www.sfco.org) and others from July through August in **St Francis Auditorium** (Map pp64–5), an elegant venue designed to look like the interior of a Spanish mission, where you can enjoy classical music and new works by New Mexico composers.

MUSEUM OF INDIAN ARTS & CULTURE

Impressive displays, almost installation-art pieces, were designed by Diné (Navajo), Hopi, Apache and Pueblo tribal members for the **Museum of Indian Arts & Culture** (Map p62; ☎ 476-1250; www.miaclab.org; 710 Camino Lejo). Exhibits draw you through 10,000 years of Indian history, from efficient hide tents perfect for the nomadic lifestyle and adobe apartment complexes that grew along with regional agriculture to modern, HUD-approved hogans with prefab kitchens stocking Navajo tacos and government-issued 'Wheat Square Cereal.' The juxtaposition of centuries is a bit jarring.

Your introduction to Native America comprises incredible art, from the ancient and antique to 1960s psychedelic, including musical instruments, jewelry, weavings, pottery and more. Catch traveling exhibits like the nine outdoor sculptures by famed Chiricahua Apache artist Allan Houser, patriarch of Native Modernism, who was honored with a retrospective at the Smithsonian when the National Museum of the American Indian opened in Washington, DC in 2004.

Many exhibits are accompanied by informative and sometimes sobering testimonials from the elders who have lived through so many changes. It's a must. There are also guided **tours** (🕑 10:15am, 1:30pm & 3pm).

MUSEUM OF INTERNATIONAL FOLK ART

Prepare to have your mind jarred out of submission: no craft is too colorful, no medium too wacky, no object too insane to join this wonderful collection at the **Museum of International Folk Art** (Map p62; ☎ 476-1200; www.moifa.org; Camino Lejo), begun by Florence Dibell Bartlett in 1953.

More than 135,000 objects now pack the place, arranged without regard for time or place but rather by the spirit of the piece. It's all quite refreshing. The beadwork of Victorian England is alongside that of West Africa; castles of Mexican tin preside over townships of Chinese ceramic; rooms and rooms of outrageous crafts and toys in the Girard Wing hail from more than 100 countries. Kids go crazy (or catatonic) at the sight.

Excellent traveling exhibitions are shown in galleries adjacent to those celebrating Native American and Hispanic crafts, and don't miss Lloyd's Treasure Chest, downstairs, a behind-the-scenes look at out-of-rotation pieces in storage. There are also guided **tours** (🕑 10:15am & 2pm Tue-Wed, 10:15am, 1pm & 3pm Thu-Sun).

Other Museums
GEORGIA O'KEEFFE MUSEUM

Possessing the largest collection of the master painter's work in the world, this **museum** (Map pp64–5; ☎ 946-1000; www.okeeffemuseum.org; 217 Johnson St, admission $8, free for students & 5-8pm Fri; 🕑 10am-5pm Mon-Tue, Thu, Sat & Sun, 10am-8pm Fri) is the most visited art attraction in Santa Fe. Seeing these paintings in person will move even the most casual O'Keeffe fans. Her thick brushwork and luminous colors don't always come through on the peeling posters you've kept since college; relish them here firsthand.

You'll recognize some of the canvases straightaway: *Abstraction White* (1927) and *Jimson Weed* (1932) are practically cultural icons. And if you've already visited Abiquiú (p125), O'Keeffe's home and studio for half a century, you'll marvel at how her artistic vision was able to render the area's ghostly intangibles, woven into landscapes and bones.

Docents lead free **tours** (10:30am), and for $5 you can rent an audio guide. During 2007, declared the Year of Georgia O'Keeffe by the Santa Fe City Council, the museum will sponsor several special events throughout the city.

EXPLORING CANYON ROAD

Once a footpath used by Pueblo Indians, then the main street through a Spanish farming community, Canyon Rd began its current incarnation – as art-gallery central – in the 1920s: artists led by Los Cincos Pintores moved in to take advantage of the cheap rent.

Believe it or not, this opulent stretch of painstakingly remodeled adobes was, until rather recently, the 'hood. Kids of struggling single moms dislocated 20 years ago still can't go into excellent **Nüart Gallery** (☎ 988-3888; www.nuartgallery.com; 670 Canyon Rd), now specializing in magical realism, without telling tales of Gormley Market, where they used to buy 10¢ candy.

Today Canyon Rd is a can't-miss attraction: 90+ galleries at the epicenter of the nation's healthiest art scene display rare Indian antiquities, Santa Fe School masterpieces and wild contemporary work. It's a little overwhelming, but sooth your battered brain with the requisite wine and cheese on Friday, at 5pm or so, when glittering art openings clog the narrow street with elegant art collectors (and those cheese-filching starving artists).

Here are some strip favorites; check Shopping (p109) for more. A handful of upscale restaurants and a couple of cool coffee shops will sustain you on this most inspiring of hikes, but don't expect to find parking. Bring your walking shoes (and credit cards), and get ready to be impressed.

Adobe Gallery (☎ 955-0550; www.adobegallery.com; 221 Canyon Rd) includes pieces by the 'Five Matriarchs' of the pueblo pottery renaissance: Maria Martinez, Margaret Tofoya, Maria Nampeyo, Lucy Lewis and Helen Cordero, among many other famed Indian artisans.

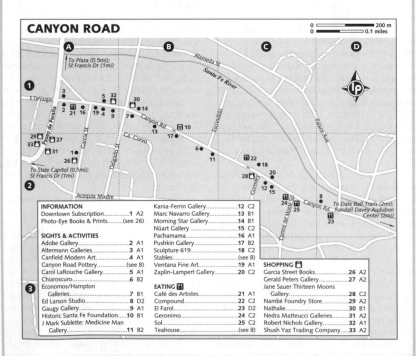

CANYON ROAD

INFORMATION		
Downtown Subscription	1	A2
Photo-Eye Books & Prints	(see 26)	

SIGHTS & ACTIVITIES		
Adobe Gallery	2	A1
Altermann Galleries	3	A1
Canfield Modern Art	4	A1
Canyon Road Pottery	(see 8)	
Carol LaRouche Gallery	5	A1
Chiaroscuro	6	B2
Economos/Hampton Galleries	7	B1
Ed Larson Studio	8	D2
Gaugy Gallery	9	A1
Historic Santa Fe Foundation	10	B1
J Mark Sublette: Medicine Man Gallery	11	B2

Kania-Ferrin Gallery	12	C2
Marc Navarro Gallery	13	B1
Morning Star Gallery	14	B1
Nüart Gallery	15	C2
Pachamama	16	A1
Pushkin Gallery	17	B2
Sculpture 619	18	C2
Stables	(see 8)	
Ventana Fine Art	19	A1
Zaplin-Lampert Gallery	20	C2

EATING		
Café des Artistes	21	A1
Compound	22	C2
El Farol	23	D2
Geronimo	24	C2
Sol	25	C2
Teahouse	(see 8)	

SHOPPING		
Garcia Street Books	26	A2
Gerald Peters Gallery	27	A2
Jane Sauer Thirteen Moons Gallery	28	C2
Nambé Foundry Store	29	A2
Nathalie	30	B1
Nedra Matteucci Galleries	31	A2
Robert Nichols Gallery	32	A1
Shush Yaz Trading Company	33	A2

Whether you have $5 milagrosas or $50,000 santos and retablos to spend, there's something for everyone in the vibrant collection of Latin American folk art at **Pachamama** (☎ 983-4020; 223 Canyon Rd).

Altermann Galleries (☎ 820-1644; www.altermanngalleries.com; 225 Canyon Rd) is the absolute classic venue to find legendary Southwestern fine art – cowboys, Indians and landscapes from (art) household names such as Fredric Remington, Kim Wiggins and Charlie Russell.

Stroll the sculpture garden at **Ventana Fine Art** (☎ 983-8815; www.ventanafineart.com; 400 Canyon Rd) and then step inside for contemporary American painting, including the color-saturated work of Native American artist John Nieto, available in poster form as well.

Canfield Modern Art (☎ 988-4199; www.canfieldgallery.com; 414 Canyon Rd) has modern art – the challenging kind, which can be a little unnerving – from top Taos and Santa Fe artists of the post-WWII era.

Children are entranced by wolves, tigers and other engaging animals ready to stare you down at **Carol LaRouche Gallery** (☎ 982-1186; www.laroche-gallery.com; 415 Canyon Rd).

Economos/Hampton Galleries (☎ 982-6347; 500 Canyon Rd) is where all of the museums actually come to purchase fantastic examples of retablos, ancient Native American art, pre-Columbian Mexican pieces and much, much more, all crammed onto two huge floors aswirl with history.

Collectors come to **Marc Navarro Gallery** (☎ 986-8191; 520 Canyon Rd) to find antique Spanish and Mexican silver pieces, including jewelry studded with onyx and amethyst.

Owned by the family of poet Alexander Pushkin, **Pushkin Gallery** (☎ 982-1990; www.pushkingallery.com; 550 Canyon Rd) shows Russian masters including Nikolai Timkov and Vasily Golubev, who are outshined by newcomer Alexy Smirnov Vokressensky; museum-quality Orthodox icons and lacquer boxes are also on display.

Chiaroscuro Gallery (☎ 992-1100; www.chiaroscurosantafe.com; 558 Canyon Rd) has a sophisticated and often abstract collection moved recently into this glorious large space, all the better to showcase extravagant yet minimalist modernism like the work of Udo Noger.

J Mark Sublette: Medicine Man Gallery (☎ 820-7451; www.medicinemangallery.com; 602-A Canyon Rd) shows quality antique retablos, Navajo blankets, $5000 kachinas and more Maria Martinez (p119) pottery than her San Ildefonso museum. You'll also find artwork by seminal Western landscape artist Maynard Dixon.

When you tire of abstraction and minimalism, wander through the bronzes in the sculpture garden and gallery of **Sculpture 619** (☎ 983-8600; www.sculpture619.com; 619 Canyon Rd) , where Geno Miles worships the human figure.

The renowned collection of Santa Fe and Taos School masters at **Zaplin-Lampert Gallery** (☎ 982-6100; www.zaplinlampert.com; 651 Canyon Rd) is nothing short of phenomenal – check out the Gene Kloss artwork downstairs.

Kania-Ferrin Gallery (☎ 982-8767; www.collectorsguide.com/kaniaferrin; 662 Canyon Rd) has antique Native American basketry from the 1800s through the 1940s elevate the everyday to art.

You can still see artists at work at the cool collection of studios/galleries at **Stables** (821 Canyon Rd). Standouts include **Canyon Rd Pottery** (☎ 983-9426), with excellent and affordable hand-thrown work, and the amazing **Ed Larson Studio** (☎ 983-7269) with illustrated political poetry and the biggest, bestest fish around, all right under the sign reading 'Jesus said buy folk art.'

SANTA FE

INSTITUTE OF AMERICAN INDIAN ARTS MUSEUM

Primarily showing work by students and faculty of the esteemed four-year Institute of American Indian Arts, this revealing **museum** (Map pp64-5; ☎ 983-8900; www.iaiancad .org; 108 Cathedral Pl; adult/student $4/2, under 16 free; ☯ 10am-5pm Mon-Sat, noon-5pm Sun) also features the finest offerings of Native artists from tribes across the US. It's eclectic: traditional weavings, basketry and jewelry are juxtaposed with more modern statements.

The work can be uneven – this is a student gallery, after all – but much of it is spectacular, and all offer insight into the evolution and integration of classical techniques and symbolism into a contemporary culture, consciously developing on its own terms.

Outdoor **Allan Houser Art Park** (☎ 471-1528) features massive sculptures by this patriarch of Native American contemporary art (p37), and the five-star gift shop features work by alumni, plus plenty of Native kitsch.

WHEELWRIGHT MUSEUM OF THE AMERICAN INDIAN

Another Museum Hill entry, the **Wheelwright Museum of the American Indian** (Map p62; ☎ 982-4636, 800-607-4636; www.wheelwright.org; 704 Camino Lejo; admission by donation; ☯ 10am-5pm Mon-Sat, 1-5pm Sun) is an eight-sided hogan-style structure that houses three galleries packed with rotating exhibitions of Native American art, both historic and modern.

Many events are geared toward kids, including free storytelling by area elders and the annual All Children's Powwow, held in October, designed to introduce kids to Native culture. Docent-led free **tours** (2pm Mon-Fri, 1pm Sat) will send you away much wiser.

MUSEUM OF SPANISH COLONIAL ART

Ranging from the Middle Ages to today, and set in one of John Gaw Meem's (p68) finest buildings, the **Museum of Spanish Colonial Art** (Map p62; ☎ 982-2226; www.spanishcolonial.org; 750 Camino Lejo; admission $6, under 16 free; ☯ 10am-5pm Tue-Sun) traces the history of Spanish New Mexico. Straw appliqué, popular among gold-poor settlers who wanted their religious objects to gleam, joins jewelry and other treasures that made the three-year trip from Spain, as well as contemporary crafts like *ramilletes* (colorful paper garlands) by local artist Estrellita Carillo-Garcia.

The surreal collection of *santos* (religious figures) in the form of retablos (paintings on wood) and bultos (small sculptures) includes not only New Mexican examples, but also pieces from Spain, Brazil, Mexico and many other countries. There are guided **tours** (☯ 10:30am & 2:30pm).

BATAAN MEMORIAL MILITARY MUSEUM & LIBRARY

A labor of both love and war, the **Bataan Memorial Military Museum & Library** (Map p62; ☎ 474-1670; 1050 Old Pecos Trail; donation; ☯ 9am-4pm Tue-Wed & Fri, 9am-1pm Sat) exhibits an unusual collection of military mementoes. It began in 1947 as a display in the state capitol honoring the 'Battling Bastards of Bataan.'

The museum occupies the former home base of the NM 200th Coast Artillery, captured when the Japanese invaded the Philippines in 1942, and the very last unit to surrender. Some 70,000 POWs, most Filipino, were forced to walk the 75-mile Bataan Death March. Of 1800 mostly Hispanic New Mexicans stationed in Bataan, 900 returned.

In addition to exhibits that tell their story, interesting examples of psychological-warfare leaflets from WWII to the first Gulf War plaster the walls, along with an amazing collection of military patches. Uniforms, weaponry and other gear date as far back as the Spanish conquest. It's the old photos and letters, however, that really hammer the point home and tug at your heart.

AWAKENING MUSEUM

The **Awakening Museum** (Map pp64-5; ☎ 954-4025; www.theawakeningmuseum.com; 125 N Guadalupe St; adult/child $3/free; ☯ 10am-4:30pm) boasts some 8000 sq ft of mahogany panels, which originally covered the interior of a West Virginia gymnasium. They are emblazoned with artist Jean-Claude Gaugy's roughly hewn, gem-toned figures. Thirteen years of his life were poured into this chronicle of the Passion of Christ, the State of Grace and the Book of Revelations, all of them exploding around you. There is no crucifixion here, only resurrection. And you can touch it.

A recommended audio tour explains the imagery in detail, while **Gaugy Gallery** (Map p70; ☎ 984-2800; www.gaugy.com; 418 Canyon Rd; ☯ 10am-5pm) has more of the artist's work.

(Continued on page 81)

WITOLD SKRYPCZAK

Sandia Peak Tramway (p177), Sandia Crest, Albuquerque

White Sands National Monument (p207), southeastern New Mexico

CAROL POLICH

Acoma Pueblo (p214), northwestern New Mexico

ANN CECIL

Rio Grande Gorge Bridge (p141) viewed from West Rim Trail, Taos

KARL LEHMANN

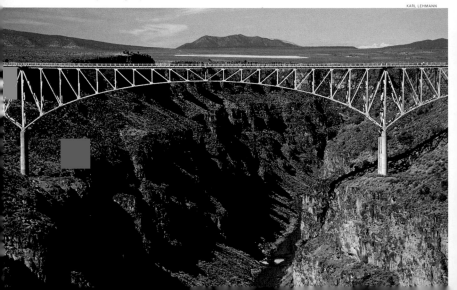

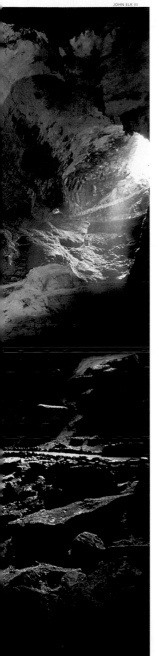

Carlsbad Caverns National Park
(p212), southeastern New Mexico
JOHN ELK III

RICHARD CUMMINS

Gila Cliff Dwellings (p202), Gila National Forest,
southwestern New Mexico

Mabel Dodge Luhan House (p149), Taos

Native American turquoise (p36) jewelry pieces

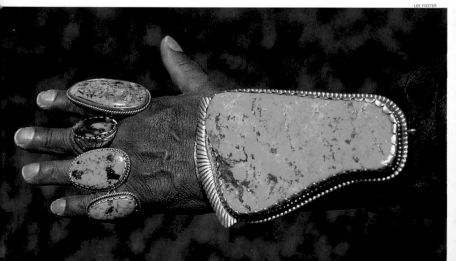

Interior of a hat shop, downtown Albuquerque

Woven Native American handicrafts (p111), Santa Fe

Taos Pueblo (p156), near Taos

Corn Dance performers, Ohkay Owingeh (p119), near Santa Fe

Local outside his shack, in laid-back New Mexico style (p31)

OLIVER STREWE

Classical Gas Museum (p129), Embudo

KARL LEHMANN

Extraterrestrial souvenirs, Roswell (p211)

KARL LEHMANN

Next page:
San Miguel Mission (p82), Santa Fe
RICHARD CUMMINS

(Continued from page 72)

SANTA FE CHILDREN'S MUSEUM

Reward younger kids by bringing them to this **museum** (Map p62; ☎ 989-8359; www.santa fechildrensmuseum.org; 1050 Old Pecos Trail; admission $4; ☺ 10am-5pm Wed-Sat, noon-5pm Sun) to hang out with things and people they can relate to. Giant bubble makers, pint-sized looms and climbing structures are great for working off all that excess energy, and even more opportunities for play exist outside.

The museum runs daily two-hour programs (call ahead for times) led by local scientists, artists and teachers, who take on subjects like solar energy or offer dance and art workshops.

EL MUSEO CULTURAL DE SANTA FE

In a huge warehouse at the developing Santa Fe Railyard site, the kid-friendly **El Museo Cultural de Santa Fe** (Map pp64-5; ☎ 992-0591; www .elmuseocultural.org; 1615 Paseo de Peralta; admission free; ☺ 1-5pm Tue-Fri, 10am 5pm Sat) is an all-in-one museum, gallery, performance space and community arts center designed for local Hispanic youth.

With exhibits by internationally known artists and others still in grade school, plus all manner of displays geared toward home schooled kids, this is a great place to introduce your own children to *la cultura* Nuevomexicana.

The huge warehouse space hosts art openings, live music and theater. The Santa Fe Farmers Market (p101) is also ensconced here in the winter.

HISTORIC SANTA FE FOUNDATION

On the site of El Zagúan, an expansive Territorial-style mansion purchased in 1849 by Anglo entrepreneur James Johnson, the unassuming little **Historic Santa Fe Foundation** (Map p70; ☎ 983-2567; www.historicsantafe.com; 545 Canyon Rd; admission by donation; ☺ 10am-4pm Tue-Sun), on Canyon Rd, has a few interesting exhibits – old photos, potsherds and whatnot. The lovely gardens outside are also worth a look.

Create your own walking or driving tour of Santa Fe's historic best by consulting the foundation's registry (available on-site and on the website) of more than 70 Santa Fe buildings considered worthy of historical preservation. Each is marked by a bronze plaque.

RANCHO DE LAS GOLONDRINAS

About 15 miles south of downtown Santa Fe, in the town of La Cienega, **Rancho de las Golondrinas** (Ranch of the Swallows; ☎ 471-2261; www.golondrinas.org; 334 Los Pinos Rd, La Cienega; adult/child $5/2; ☺ 10am-4pm Wed-Sun Jun-Sep) is a grassy oasis that has been a popular overnight stop for weary travelers for at least 10,000 years, and many of the historic structures housing this living-history museum were built by Spanish explorers who fortified the area in 1625.

The 200-acre preserve has rescued dozens more original Spanish buildings from the bulldozers of progress and brought them from all over the Southwest for respectful renovation. Volunteers use centuries-old equipment to re-create colonial life, and blacksmiths, weavers and lots of cuddly livestock – including rare Churro sheep sheared annually at the Spring Festival, in early June – keep the kids entertained.

Special events include Civil War reenactments in May, a popular Wine Festival in July and a Harvest Festival in October with dancing, grape crushing, an arts market and more. Kids aged seven to 12 and accompanying adults can go on private group excursions with **Josefina's guided tours** (☎ 473-4169; adult/child $10/7; ☺ 10:30am Wed-Sun, scheduled in advance), which include snacks and craft making. Take I-25 south from Santa Fe to exit 276, making a hard right at NM 599.

HISTORIC LINE CAMP GALLERY & HUICHOL INDIAN MUSEUM

About 15 miles north of Santa Fe, the one-of-a-kind **Historic Line Camp Gallery & Huichol Indian Museum** (Map p116; ☎ 455-3600; www .tribesgallery.com; US 84/285; admission $1; ☺ 10:30am-6pm Tue-Sun) is a gift shop and museum that claims the largest collection of Huichol Indian art in North America. *Nearika*, unbroken strands of colorful yarn coiled into tales of life and death, and *chaquira*, sculptures of animals covered in tiny, obsessively patterned beads, are said to depict the understandably wild dreams of the 'People of Peyote.' Westerners didn't encounter the tribe, which lives in a remote region of the Sierra Madre, until the 1930s.

The small museum has a video as well as artifacts, including clothing, musical instruments, old photos and art, but the most impressive pieces are on sale in the gallery.

Churches

The original Spanish settlers drawn to the Royal City of Holy Faith were a devout bunch, and Santa Fe boasts many of the nation's oldest and finest Catholic churches, many with miracles adorning their rich histories.

ST FRANCIS CATHEDRAL

Archbishop Jean-Baptiste Lamy had a dream to build a French Romanesque cathedral worthy of any archdiocese back in Europe, right here in Santa Fe. From 1869 to 1886, imported artists and architects (Lamy wasn't too fond of local retablo-style decor) erected one of the city's most enduring symbols, **St Francis Cathedral** (Map pp64-5; ☎ 982-5619; 213 Cathedral Pl; admission free; ⏰ 6:30am-6pm, English mass 7am & 5pm Mon-Sat, Spanish mass 8am, 10am, noon & 5:15pm Sun).

The archbishop, buried beneath the altar, didn't survive to see its completion; indeed, original plans called for spires that have yet to be added. Massive bronze doors chronicle the centuries (and martyrs) of New Mexican Catholicism, and above them, the tetragrammaton, reading 'JHVH,' honors the area's Jewish community.

The cathedral was built on the site of the small adobe **Our Lady of the Rosary Chapel**, extant on the northeast side of the cathedral, honoring the USA's oldest statuette of the Madonna, 'La Conquistadora,' declared New Mexico's Patron Saint in 1770. Originally brought from Mexico in 1625, the statue was rescued shortly before the Pueblo Revolt of 1680 by Josefina Lopez, who abandoned her own possessions and carried the effigy all the way to El Paso.

After negotiations with Pueblo leadership were resolved in 1692, DeVargas led some 70 families on the arduous trek back home. Upon hitting La Bajada, the steep escarpment that still overheats cars on I-25, the caravan got stuck. Hopeless and cold, DeVargas made a vow: if the Virgin would just get his oxen moving, he'd build her a chapel in Santa Fe. Almost immediately, his charges were released from the mud.

During Fiestas (Zozobra; p90), La Conquistadora is still carried in procession around the old city. The rest of the year she resides, surrounded by fine retablos, inside the cathedral. The small **Archdiocese of Santa Fe Museum** (Map pp64-5; ☎ 983-3811; 223 Cathedral Pl; admission by donation; ⏰ 9am-noon, 1-4pm Mon-Fri) has more information, and also has pleasant gardens out back.

LORETTO CHAPEL

The small Gothic **Loretto Chapel** (Map pp64-5; ☎ 982-0092; www.lorettochapel.com; 207 Old Santa Fe Trail; admission $2; ⏰ 9am-6pm Mon-Sat, 10:30am-5pm Sun summer, 9am-5pm Mon-Sat, 10:30am-5pm Sun winter), modeled after Sainte Chapelle in Paris, was also commissioned by Archbishop Lamy. But when architect Projectus Mouly (hired after his father, the original architect, went blind) began 'courting' the archbishop's niece-in-law, well, the chapel was left without an architect. And a staircase. And so the Sisters of Loretto prayed to St Joseph, patron of carpenters, for divine intercession, or at least something to replace the darned ladder.

Sure enough, a mysterious man with a burro, T-square and hammer appeared, asking for two tubs of water and perfect solitude. The sisters complied, and using neither nails nor any obvious support structure, the white-haired stranger completed the famously graceful spiral staircase. Then he disappeared. Of course.

Today **St Joseph's Miraculous Staircase** is popular among tourists and wedding photographers, but regular services are no longer held here. The adjacent gift shop is packed with Catholic kitsch.

SAN MIGUEL MISSION

Enter through the gift shop to experience what's probably *not* quite the oldest church in the USA, as the folks down in Acoma (p214) will explain. Still, the adobe walls of **San Miguel Mission** (Map pp64-5; ☎ 983-3974; 401 Old Santa Fe Trail; admission $1; ⏰ 9am-5pm Mon-Sat, 10am-4pm Sun, mass 5pm Sun) have watched Santa Fe grow since 1610.

Tlaxcalan Indian servants brought here by Fray Alonso de Benavidez constructed the church atop even older Native structures; this is also where, according to legend, the 1680 Pueblo Revolt began with the burning of the mission's original patron saint, San Miguel.

Artistic treasures abound, including the 17th-century statue of St Michael, but the most famous artifact is the almost 800-pound **San Jose Bell**, cast in the 14th century in Andalusia, Spain.

SANTA FE

SANTUARIO DE GUADALUPE

The chapel of **Santuario de Guadalupe** (Map pp64-5; ☎ 988-2027; 100 Guadalupe St; admission free; ☒ 9am-noon & 1-4pm Mon-Sat; English mass 10am Mon-Sat, Spanish mass 4pm & 6pm Mon-Sat, 8am Sun) looks much as it did when it was built between 1776 and 1796 but has actually gone through several transformations. You can see photos of its previous and very different facades, as well as what remains of the original, 200-year-old adobe walls, in the tiny **museum**. The oldest shrine to the Virgin of Guadalupe in the USA, it's sometimes closed for weddings and funerals.

The star attraction is the amazing **altar piece**, brought here from Mexico City by José de Alzíbar in 1783.

CROSS OF THE MARTYRS

More a quick climb than a religious shrine, the **Cross of the Martyrs** (Map pp64-5; Paseo de Peralta btwn Marcy & Otero Sts) was erected to commemorate the 21 Franciscan friars who lost their lives in the Pueblo Revolt of 1680. Historic plaques explain 400 years of Santa Fe history, and the view from the top really makes you appreciate those adobe only laws.

Other Attractions

INDIAN ARTS RESEARCH CENTER AT THE SCHOOL OF AMERICAN RESEARCH

Make reservations to tour the vaulted collection at the **Indian Arts Research Center** (Map p62; ☎ 954-7205; www.sarweb.org/iarc/iarc.htm; 660 Garcia St; $15 tour; ☒ 2pm Fri). The collection consists of more than 11,000 Native American artifacts, much of it precolonial, including textiles, baskets, jewelry and lots of pottery. It's not really displayed for public consumption, which makes the tour through the climate-controlled collection that much more interesting; you'll be surrounded by shelves packed with remnants of a time long past. The **gift shop** (☒ 8am-noon & 1-5pm) has an outstanding selection of collection-related books by associates, faculty members and others.

SITE SANTA FE

Enormous whitewashed spaces of **Site Santa Fe** (Map pp64-5; ☎ 989-1199; www.sitesantafe.org; 1606 Paseo de Peralta; adult/student $8/4, free Fri; ☒ 10am-5pm Wed-Thu & Sat, 10am-7pm Fri, noon-5pm Sun) are perfect for radical installation pieces, painters and photographers who love a large scale. The hybrid museum-gallery space offers **guided tours** (☒ 6pm Fri, 2pm Sat & Sun) and hosts wine-splashed openings, artist talks, film screenings and performances of all kinds. It's the ultimate cure for Canyon Rd overkill.

NEW MEXICO STATE CAPITOL

Inside the Zia Indian–inspired **Roundhouse** (Map pp64-5; ☎ 986-4589; cnr Paseo de Peralta & Old Santa Fe Trail; admission free; ☒ 8am-5pm Mon-Fri) is one of the best art collections in New Mexico –

ZIA SUNSET?

It's on the flag. It's on the license plate. Heck, it's the 'o' on the sign at that sleazy motel where you'll never stay again. It's the ubiquitous Zia sun symbol, sacred to Keresen-speaking Zia Pueblo, where the pot emblazoned with the emblem was first found.

New Mexico adopted the Zia as its state symbol in 1925, inspired by its four-fold meaning: the four directions, the four seasons, the four times of day and the four ages of man – well, according to the pamphlet describing the Zia-shaped state capitol, anyway. Zia Pueblo elders have no comment.

They have, however, made one thing very clear: 'The people of Zia were never compensated or consulted about the use of the Zia sun symbol,' Zia Governor Amado Shije told the state legislature in 1999, adding that the sign had been 'diminished by its casual use.' The tribe then requested $74 million in compensation, $1 million for every year the Zia had been in official use.

The battle raged quietly for three years, reaching a temporary stalemate in 2001, when legislators formed a committee to discuss the issue further. In the meantime, you can still pick up key chains, shot glasses and other Zia-covered kitsch anywhere, or even fly here in a Zia-clad plane.

Southwest Airlines actually approached Zia Pueblo in 2000 with a request to use the sacred symbol. And, after making a hefty donation to the pueblo's college fund, the company was granted not only permission, but also a prayer by Zia elders when the plane was commissioned. It's just amazing what respect for culture – and copyrights – will get you.

and it's free! There are **guided tours** in the summer (schedule varies) and you can always grab a flyer with a bare-bones self-guided tour at the visitors desk, then peruse hundreds of sculptures, paintings and photos by the state's best- (and least-) known artists.

SANTA FE COMMUNITY COLLEGE PLANETARIUM

The stars shine brightly in Santa Fe, thanks to the high altitude and arid climate, so take advantage at the **Santa Fe Community College Planetarium** (Map p116; ☎ 428-1677; Richards Dr; adult/child $5/3), which offers indoor programs and outdoor tours of the skies outside after dark. Programs and times vary, so call ahead. Between June and November, reservations are required for various 8pm presentations, many linking ancient Native American cultures with modern astronomy.

ACTIVITIES

Santa Fe's urban attractions – museums, churches, galleries, restaurants and shops – are first rate, but don't forget to play outdoors. The fifth largest US state at nearly 122,000 sq miles, New Mexico enjoys one of the lowest population densities – an average of 15 people per square mile, compared with, say, New York state's average of 402 people per square mile. That means a lot more room on the hiking and biking trails.

Hiking

The Public Lands Information Center (p67) has maps and information on area hikes. Also check out *Day Hikes in the Santa Fe Area,* published by the Sierra Club, available in local bookstores like Travel Bug (p63).

Check the site of the **Sierra Club** (www.riogrande .sierraclub.org/santafe/outings.asp) for weekly guided hikes and leaders' contact phone numbers. Several multiuse trails are also listed under Mountain Biking (opposite). During especially dry seasons, some parks are closed and campfire building is severely restricted, so check locally before heading out.

RANDALL DAVEY AUDUBON CENTER

Protecting 135 acres along the acequias of Santa Fe Canyon, just 3 miles north of the plaza, this preserve's **visitors center** (☎ 983-4609; 1800 Upper Canyon Rd; trail-use donation $2; ☼ 8am-5pm) has information on the juniper and piñon

forest's coyotes, bobcats and other wildlife. It's close to the trailhead for the half-mile interpretive **El Temporal Trail** and the 3-mile round-trip **Bear Canyon Trail**, which leads into the steep-sided canyon itself.

Guided tours are also available at the 1847 **Randall Davey Home** (admission $5; ☼ 2pm Mon), which has a small but excellent collection of Spanish art and antiques. Plus, there are free guided bird walks and nature walks some Saturday mornings; call in advance.

DALE BALL TRAILS

A great opportunity for day hikers and intermediate mountain bikers (the switchbacks can be challenging, particularly the South Trails), the **North** and **South Dale Ball Trails** run more than 20 miles and circumnavigate some of Santa Fe's most exclusive neighborhoods, eventually winding past the 'no trespassing' signs to views of unspoiled mountains and deserts. Trails range from several 3-mile loops to a 1500ft climb to Picasho Peak. Eventually the trail hooks into **Atalaya Trail** (opposite) and the **Windsor Trail** (opposite), creating an unparalleled opportunity for urban adventure, just a 10-minute bike ride from the plaza.

To get here, follow Upper Canyon Rd north to the well-signed parking lot at Cerro Gordo Rd, or follow Hyde Park Rd and make a left on Sierra del Norte, then park on your right.

HYDE MEMORIAL STATE PARK

Located eight miles north of Santa Fe, nestled in the Sangre de Cristo Mountains at 8500ft, Hyde (Map p116) offers several hikes through 350 acres of aspen and pine. The **visitors center** (☎ 983-7175; 740 Hyde Park Rd; day use $5) has information and is close to the trailhead for 3-mile **Hyde Park Circle Trail**, with a 1000ft elevation gain to outstanding views. With 125in of annual snowfall, this often is also a good place for snowshoeing and cross-country skiing.

Chamiza Trail Loops begin about 1 mile southwest of the visitors center, following a picturesque canyon to join up with the Windsor Trail after 3 miles; you can hike 5 miles to Big Tesuque campground (p96) for a 1400ft elevation gain and more aspen views.

Bear Wallow Trail begins just north of the visitors center, at the parking lot on the northern edge of the park, and is the first leg of the Triangle Trails, joining Windsor and Borrego Trails for what could be a 4-mile loop or a serious 8-mile hike into the wilderness.

BISHOP'S LODGE RESORT & SPA
This luxury resort (Map p116) sits astride 450 acres of classic high desert piñon forest, with spectacular views from the 7700ft crest, and graciously allows free public access to scenic trails, many of which are tame enough for smaller kids. The staff do ask that you check in at the lodge (hey, there's a shooting range out there), where they'll give you maps and trail information.

Skiing
Sure, Taos Ski Valley gets all the glory, but **Ski Santa Fe** (Map p116; ☎ 982-4429, snow report 983-9155; www.skisantafe.com; lift tickets adult/child $47/34; ☺ 9am-4pm late Nov–mid-Apr) delivers you to the highest skiable peak in the state – 12,053ft. The setting atop the Sangre de Cristos is breathtaking, the runs are challenging and, best of all, it's only 16 miles from downtown Santa Fe.

With 67 runs on 660 acres, a 1703ft vertical drop and about 225in of snow per year, this is serious skiing – and unlike in Taos, snowboarders are welcome. Ski Santa Fe has restaurants, equipment rentals, and lessons for all ages and abilities, plus package deals that include accommodation in Santa Fe, lessons and/or equipment. **Chipmunk Corner** (☎ 988-9636), near the lifts, offers daycare for kids from three months to four years old, but make reservations in advance.

Alpine Sports (Map pp64-5; ☎ 983-5155; www.alpinesports-santafe.org; 127 Sandoval St; ☺ 7:30am-6pm winter, 9:30am-6pm Mon-Sat other seasons), one of the USA's top ski shops, rents ski packages (regular/high performance $12/39) as well as snowboards ($30); **Skier's Edge** (Map p62; ☎ 983-1025; 1836 Cerrillos Rd) also rents packages for skiers ($20), snowboarders ($30) and kids ($15). **Cottam's** (Map p62; ☎ 982-0495; www.cottamsskishops.com; 740 Hyde Park Rd; ☺ 7am-6pm), on the way to the slopes, has packages (adult/child $25/15), and also rents snowboard packages ($28), snowblades ($25) and snowshoes ($10). It is recommened that you make reservations for equipment rental everywhere.

If you prefer cross-country skiing, **Norski Trail**, about a mile past the Aspen Vista

Picnic Ground in Hyde State Park, has almost 3 miles of free, volunteer-maintained trails with the same great views.

Roadrunner Shuttle (☎ 424-3367; one way/round trip $15/20; ☺ 8am & 11:30am) runs buses from the plaza and some larger hotels to the ski area twice daily in winter.

Mountain Biking
Melo Velo Bicycles (Map pp64-5; ☎ 982-8986; www.sunmountainbikeco.com; 102 E Water St, El Centro Gallery; rental per hr/day $9/45; ☺ 9:30am-5pm Mon-Sat, 10am-4pm Sun) is a great outfit, which has information about trails throughout the region, rents bikes and offers half-day to 10-day tours. *Santa Fe Area Mountain Bike Trails*, by Craig Martin, is another good source of trail info. Here are a few, though, to get you started:

Atalaya Trail (Map p116) This popular trail leaves from the first St John's College parking lot for a 7-mile loop that will have you gasping – if not from the climb to the top of 9121ft Atalaya Mountain, then from the views. Note that the trail gets packed with hikers, dog walkers and stoned liberal arts students as sunset approaches.

Windsor Trail (Map p116) This 10-mile trail for intermediate bikers is one of the most renowned treks in the state; though hard-core folks may find it overrated, the scenery – particularly in the fall and winter – is outstanding. The route begins at Little Tesuque In Hyde Park and climbs steadily upward to serve as the spine of several other multiuse trails, including the bike-friendly Chamiza Loops.

Tesuque Peak Rd (Aspen Vista Trail; Map p116) Beginning at Aspen Vista Picnic ground in Hyde Park, this 6-mile abandoned dirt logging road makes for a nontechnical but steep (2200ft) ride to eagle-eye views of the Sangre de Cristos and Santa Fe. It's also open to hikers, horses and llamas.

Santa Fe Rail Trail Beginning at the Santa Fe Southern Railway Depot, this 18-mile trail follows the rail line clear to Lamy. The trail is unpaved until you hit Agua Fria St, then paved the rest of the way, though mountain bikers can take a dirt turnoff at the intersection with US 285 to avoid following CR 33 into Lamy.

Rafting
Santa Fe's white-water rafting outfits head to Pilar (p129) for the renowned Class IV **Taos Box**, an adventure for folks 12 and up; and the Class III **Racecourse**, which is fine for active kids over six. The Class III **Rio Chama** is often rafted as a multiday trip with camping supplies and food included. The day trips, through dramatic Rio Grande Gorge,

are great excursions and are easily arranged from May through October.

New Wave River Trips (Map p62; ☎ 984-1444, 800-984-1444; www.newwaverafting.com; 1101 Cerrillos Rd; 🕑 9am-5pm) Stay cool on day trips through the Rio Grande Gorge (adult/child $96/77 full day) or Taos Box ($115), a half-day trip down the Racecourse (adult/child $48/40), or go for a three-day Rio Chama float ($357). Bonus: you can take on the white-water in a 'funyak,' an inflatable kayak that leaves the driving up to you.

Santa Fe Rafting (Map p62; ☎ 988-4914, 800-467-7238; www.santaferafting.com; 1000 Cerrillos Rd) Adjacent to New Wave and offering similar trips for similar prices, it's been keeping the competition going for more than 15 years.

Rock Climbing

Santa Fe Climbing Gym (Map p62; ☎ 986-8944; 825 Early St; adult/child $12/8; 🕑 5-10pm Mon-Fri, 1-8pm Sat, 1-6pm Sun) has two floors of indoor climbing, rents and sells gear and guidebooks, and can offer personal tips about nearby outdoor climbing opportunities ($90 to $450) if you're ready to hit the rocks.

Top outdoor sites close to Santa Fe include the **Overlook**, in White Rock's Overlook Park, with more than 30 routes scaling the basalt cliffs; **Las Conchas** and **Cochiti Mesa Crags**, administrated by the Jemez Ranger Station; and plenty of places throughout the **Sandia Mountains** (p182). For information on more opportunities for adventure, pick up a copy of *Rock Climbing New Mexico* by Dennis Jackson.

If you don't feel comfortable climbing on your own, Arroyo Seco's **Mountain Skills Rock Climbing Adventures** (☎ 776-2222; www.climbingschoolusa.com) offers instruction and guided climbs about a 1½-hour drive outside Santa Fe. Call a few weeks in advance to schedule.

Wings West Birding Tours (☎ 800-583-6928) offers half-day ($95 for one to two people, $15 for each additional person) and full-day tours ($175 one to two people, $25 for each additional person), including binoculars and field guides, to the Santa Fe Ski Basin from May to July, and to other locations at other times. The Randall Davey Audubon Center (p84) offers programs and self-guided tours.

On your own, head to **Hyde Memorial State Park** (p84) and walk the trails while looking up. You're likely to see Western Tanagers, various Nuthatches, Clark's Nutcrackers, and more – especially in the 12,600ft Santa Fe Baldy forests.

Fishing

New Mexico's truly outstanding fishing holes are better accessed from Taos (p143) and the Enchanted Circle, but there are plenty of opportunities around Santa Fe, including Abiquiú, Nambé Lakes and Rio Chama. You'll need a license (p51).

In addition to a wide selection of gear, the **High Desert Angler** (Map pp64-5; ☎ 988-7688, 888-988-7688; www.highdesertangler.com; 451 Cerrillos Rd; 🕑 8am-6pm Mon-Sat, 11am-4pm Sun summer, 10am-6pm Mon-Sat other seasons) offers guided excursions to private streams (one person/two $275/350) and a variety of multiday trips. A one-day, state-required license is $22. **Reel Life** (Map pp64-5; ☎ 995-8114, 877-733-5543; www.reellifesantafe.com; 500 Montezuma Ave; 🕑 10am-6pm Mon-Sat, noon-5pm Sun) offers similar excursions as well as a private, daylong introduction to fly-fishing course (one person/two $275/300) and a 1½-hour private fly-casting class ($40).

Golfing

With 300 days of sunshine, even some Green Party voters can't always resist a round of golf in this thirsty state, particularly considering those fine greens, generally available from 7am until dusk daily.

Marty Sanchez Links (Map p116; ☎ 955-4400; 205 Caja del Rio Rd; fees $27-51) Just 20 minutes from Santa Fe, these nine- and 18-hole courses have great views, graywater systems and some of the best golfing in New Mexico.

Pueblo de Cochiti Golf Course (☎ 465-2239; 5200 Cochiti Hwy; fees $15-40) Cochiti Pueblo's offering, about 40 minutes from Santa Fe, may be the most challenging course in the state.

Other Activities

Genoveva Chavez Community Center (Map p62; ☎ 955-4001; www.gccommunitycenter.com; 3221 Rodeo Rd; adult/child $5/2; 🕑 6am-10pm Mon-Fri, 8am-10pm Sat, 10am-6pm Sun) is a real bargain. This state-of-the-art facility includes a large heated indoor pool with lots of swim lanes (and the largest kids' area this side of Orlando), a hot tub, sauna, weight room, indoor jogging track, basketball courts, year-round ice-skating and a wide variety of yoga and fitness classes. Where can you beat that?

Water is entirely essential to our psyches in the desert. If you're longing to see shimmering water, there are four other **public pools** (☎ 955-2511; adult/child $2/1) in town, including an indoor one at **Fort Marcy** (☎ 955-4998; 490

DO-IT-YOURSELF

It's all the rage these days – Do It Yourself (DIY) home remodeling, DIY home brewing, DIY robot building, DIY computer hacking. So come on – it's time for DIY itinerary planning in Santa Fe. Eager *Lonely Planet* writers have mapped every possible step for you and suggested ways to fill every waking minute. Now put the book down, and escape the lovely confines of Paseo de Peralta for some truly purposeless wandering.

Need some help getting started? If you're in a car, head straight up Washington Ave, which becomes Bishop's Lodge Rd. Fantasize about which estate you'll buy after winning the lottery (you'll have to decide based on creative Southwestern-style entry gates because most haciendas are perched at the end of secluded private drives) as you continue into the leafy, horsy village of Tesuque. Lunch at the upscale, down-home Tesuque Village Market (p104) and then venture down any (public) dirt road. Local finds range from small, solar-topped condo complexes with pools to sprawling ranches boasting 300-year-old adobe haciendas worth millions of dollars, to small cabins snapped up years ago by folks staffing visionary, local nonprofit organizations.

On foot? Walk to Canyon Rd (p70) and then take any right-hand turn onto any side street and you'll intersect with the elegant and curvaceous 250-year-old road, Acequia Madre (Spanish for 'mother ditch'). Amble along this graceful, shady street, home to Santa Fe's first irrigation ditch, which today still transports water and creates a lovely burbling sound to counteract the dryness. To pass the time, count Sotheby Realty signs; count the countless shades of turquoise used to paint front doors; count the number of small guest casitas you glimpse behind large adobe homes.

Take any right-hand turn off Acequia Madre (if you're heading east) and walk along the dusty roads. There's a saying in Santa Fe: you can tell an outsider by how shiny their shoes are – even most pricey houses require a short walk across a dusty, unpaved drive. Go ahead: let your shoes get dusty.

When you start fantasizing about building your own hand-crafted adobe home (see, it's that DIY thing again), head back to the plaza for a margarita. Those you can mix on your own!

Washington Ave; adult/child $2/1; 6am-8:30pm Mon-Fri, 8am-6:30pm Sat, noon-5:30pm Sun).

YogaSource (Map p62; 982-0990; www.yogasource-santafe.com; 901 W San Mateo Rd; 1/5 classes $15/65) can stretch your horizons with five different styles of yoga, chanting sessions and classes for every level.

Broken Saddle Riding Company (424-7774; www.brokensaddle.com; 26 Vicksville Rd; 1/3hr $50/90; 8am-sunset) offers day-trip horseback rides at Bishop's Lodge (p85) and in Cerrillos as well as sunset ($75) and moonlight ($90) options. Also check out **Galarosa Stables** (Map p116; 466-4654; www.galarosastables.com; NM 41 S; 2hr $70).

Skater dudes and dudettes can check out the ramps during daylight hours at the **Skateboard Park** (Map pp64-5; 955-2100; 302 W DeVargas St) and **Franklin E Miles Park** (1027 Camino Carlos Rey).

SANTA FE WALKING TOUR

Begin at the **Palace of the Governors** (1; p68) for a crash course in Santa Fe history – you'll appreciate the city even more. Peruse the Native American jewelry out front, then do the obligatory circuit around the plaza, taking careful note of the difference between Santa Fe–style fashions displayed in the windows and what actual Santa Feans, playing Hacky Sack outside, are wearing.

Head west on Palace Ave to the **Museum of Fine Arts** (2; p68) – ah, Pueblo Revival architecture! Step into the museum for artistic inspiration, then continue east, with a quick detour down Burro Alley to the **French Pastry Shop** (3) for a quick pick-me-up.

Return to and cross Palace Ave to Grant St, making a left onto Johnson St, continuing past the **O'Keeffe Museum** (4; p69). More art, perhaps? The **Awakening Museum** (5; p72), a block further west, is a much shorter (and cheaper) commitment and has comfy seats for relaxing while you take in a single, phenomenal masterpiece.

Make a left onto Guadalupe St, noting the occasional brick building (this area predates the adobe-only laws), and cross the Santa Fe River. The **Santuario de Guadalupe** (6; p83) is on your right, the **Cowgirl Hall of Fame** (7; p102) is on your left – which feminist

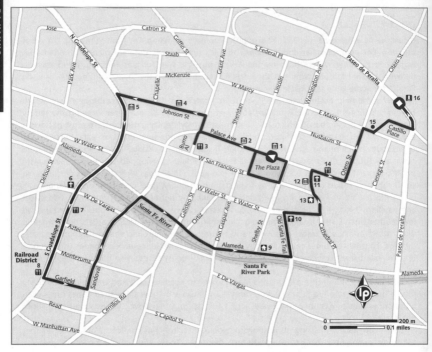

WALK FACTS

Distance 2.5 miles
Duration Two to four hours

icon would you prefer to explore? Continue to Garfield St, noting the old Railroad District and **Tomasita's** (**8**; p102), both historic and delicious.

Hang a left on Garfield St, another left on Sandoval and a right on Alameda. If you can't make it to Taos, snap a picture of the **Inn at Loretto** (**9**; p94); the folks back home won't know the difference.

Keep following the river east until you reach the Old Santa Fe Trail, then make a left. In the mood for a miracle? Try your luck at the **Loretto Chapel** (**10**; p82). Make a right onto Water St, then a left onto Cathedral Place. Then visit **St Francis Cathedral** (**11**; p82) to see La Conquistadora, or the **Institute of American Indian Arts Museum** (**12**; p72) for more cutting-edge contemporary work.

Tired again? This is an excellent place to end the tour, backtracking to **La Fonda** (**13**; p94), where you can relax atop the city at the Belltower Bar (p105), with the second-best view in town.

Hardier souls can make a right onto Palace Ave, popping in to take a look at Sena Plaza and perhaps make reservations at **La Cantina at La Casa Sena** (**14**; p99), then make a left on Otero St for **Back at the Ranch** (**15**; p110), where you can buy fabulous boots (or explore any number of several upscale shops).

Take a shortcut across the empty lot out back to Castillo Place, then make a left on Paseo de Peralta, crossing the road to the **Cross of the Martyrs** (**16**; p83). Climb the steep hill, reading the plaques for more history, and enjoy the best view in town from the top.

COURSES

One of the best excuses to spend time in Santa Fe – and away from the plaza – is by enrolling in a course. Check out several culinary courses (p58) offering classes, or attend one of these:

Art Adventures in the Southwest (☎ 986-1108; www.skyfields.net; various outdoor locations) Jane Schoenfeld conducts a six-day pastel and mixed-media landscapes class at Ghost Ranch in Abiquiú ($595). Join small groups to sketch around Santa Fe ($125), or call to arrange private one-on-one intensives.

St John's College – Summer Classics (Map p62; ☎ 984-6117; www.sjca.edu; 1160 Camino Cruz Blanca) Join 15 other intellectually inclined adults in one of three weeklong seminars ($1100 plus lodging) to study some of Western civilization's greats – Aristotle, Milton, Mozart, Shakespeare, and more. Faculty are some of the best in the nation and extracurricular events include nights at the Santa Fe Opera.

Santa Fe Workshops (Map p62; ☎ 983-1400; www .santafeworkshops.com; 50 Mt Carmel Rd) Get in touch with your inner Ansel Adams at these highly regarded week-long photography and digital-imagery workshops (classes $800 to $1700). Meals and lodging are available for an extra fee.

Santa Fe School of Weaving (Map pp64-5; ☎ 982-6312; www.sfschoolofweaving.com; 614 Paseo de Peralta) Danish-born and Israeli-trained weaver Miriam Leith-Espensen teaches small classes – usually in four half-day sessions ($350 plus materials).

White Cloud Institute (Map p62; ☎ 471-9330; www .whitecloudinstitute.com; 1221 Luisa St) If your aura needs adjusting, try an evening group spiritual healing class ($15), a weeklong Qigong seminar ($450) or a yearlong Taoist studies program.

Word Harvest Writers Workshops (☎ 471-1565; sfworkshops.com; 304 Calle Oso) Learn the ancient art of ekphrastic poetry from master Arthur Sze, named Santa Fe's first poet laureate in 2006; polish your fiction-writing skills with National Book Award nominee Lynn Stegner; or sharpen your command of written dialogue with *New York Times* best-selling author Margaret Cole ($130 per class). Word Harvest also sponsors a mystery writers' conference ($400) with acclaimed author Tony Hillerman in Albuquerque each November.

SANTA FE FOR CHILDREN

Check *Pasatiempo*, the Friday arts and entertainment section of the *Santa Fe New Mexican*, for its 'Bring the Kids' column, which has a rundown on area events for children. Also get a copy of the free local newspaper *New Mexico Kids*, published six times a year, for great day-by-day event calendars.

The **Santa Fe Children's Museum** (p81) is wonderful, with interactive and educational activities for kids up to 10 or so. Kids of all ages shouldn't miss the amazing **Museum of International Folk Art** (p69); for more color, including some you can take home, a shopping trip to **Jackalope** (p111) is most definitely in order.

Expose your children to the diversity of cultures Santa Fe is so proud of: **Rancho de las Golondrinas** (p81) is Spanish colonial history made real, while **El Museo Cultural de Santa Fe** (p81) has artwork and other exhibits by kids and for kids.

The **Santa Fe Opera** (p107) does backstage tours during opera season, free for folks under 17, and a visit to the **Wheelwright Museum of the American Indian** (p72) will introduce them early to Native culture, with events and even an annual powwow designed for children.

Older kids in touch with their inner nerd will enjoy the **Santa Fe Community College Planetarium** (p84), while eye-rolling teens itching for their first tattoo may prefer all-ages **Warehouse 21** (p106), though you probably won't be invited.

Several hiking trails, particularly those at **Randall Davey Audubon Center** (p84), are perfect for active children; just be sure to coat them with sunscreen and make sure they don't get dehydrated. The **Genoveva Chavez Community Center** (p86) has a heated indoor pool and an ice-skating rink if the weather's not cooperating.

Most restaurants, except those that are seriously upscale, are happy to host your kids, and most have special menus – but only the **Cowgirl Hall of Fame** (p102) has a playground *and* a full bar.

If you want to get out on your own, **Magical Happenings Babysitting** (☎ 982-9327) can have sitters stay with your kids in your hotel room; it's $16 an hour for one child, $18 an hour for two, with a four-hour minimum, and reservations should be made in advance, particularly during the high season.

TOURS
Ecotours

Learn why the Andean people of South America have revered gentle, wooly llamas for thousands of years. Just go ahead, let one of the nimble creatures at **Wild Earth Llama Adventures** (☎ 800-758-5262; www.llamaadventures.com) nibble your ear and carry your pack through peaceful remote areas of the Santa Fe National Forest and you'll be a goner. Learn about local ecology, natural history and wilderness skills on a daylong trek ($89), an overnight pack trip ($299) or a five-day wilderness expedition ($749). Call in advance to request a child-friendly or family-focused tour.

Walking Tours

Knowledgeable Museum of New Mexico docents lead 1¾-hour tours of the **Palace of the Governors** (Map pp64-5; 105 W Palace Ave; tours $10; ☺ 10:15am Mon-Sat Apr-Oct). The tours can be somewhat customized, depending on the group, around downtown Santa Fe. Meet at the Blue Gate on Lincoln Ave at 10am.

Aboot About Historic Walks (☎ 988-2774; www.abootabout.com; adult/under 12 $10/free; ☺ 9:30am & 1:30pm) tours begin at Hotel St Francis and El Dorado, covering the plaza, St Francis Cathedral, Loretto Chapel and more. The same company runs **Aspook About Walks** (tour $10; ☺ 5:30pm Mon, Tue, Fri & Sat), which includes ghost stories.

Loretto Line (☎ 983-3701; adult/child $14/7; ☺ 10am, noon & 2pm May-Oct) operates an open-air bus tour of the downtown area and historic neighborhoods. They depart from the Loretto Chapel area; you can't miss 'em.

Stephanie Beninato Southwest Tours (☎ 988-8022; www.swguides.com; tours $18) Make reservations for in-depth custom tours of Santa Fe's Jewish historical sites, haunted places, hidden gardens and even former brothels.

Vehicle Tours

Though the **Santa Fe Southern Railway** (Map pp64-5; ☎ 989-8600, 888-989-8600; www.sfsr.com; 410 S Guadalupe St) doesn't run through town, several scenic train rides use the 120-year-old spur line to take you 18 miles, past the Galisteo Basin to the fairly ghostly town of Lamy. The four-hour trip (adult $28 to $50, child $14 to $35) is the most popular run, but there are also several themed trips like the Barbecue Train (adult $58 to $80, child $38 to $65), with live music and a campfire.

In addition to the standard 1½-hour tours of Santa Fe sites, including stops at several art galleries, **Custom Tours by Clarice** (☎ 438-7116; www.santafecustomtours.com; ☺ 9am, 11am, 1pm, 3pm & 5pm) arranges group tours of art studios ($10), Bandelier ($65) and Taos Pueblo ($95).

If you are having a really great time with your vacation mate, **Fairytale Weddings** (☎ 438-7116; www.santafewedding.com) can arrange your entire wedding at an area chapel ($1085 for the ceremony and up to $20,000 for a reception).

ZOZOBRA

Have you had a lousy year? Dry your eyes and put on your party clothes, for it is to bid such sorrows farewell that the Santa Fe Fiestas' monumental centerpiece will be sacrificed in fireworks and flames.

Fiestas started out as a solemn affair, begun in 1712 to commemorate the city's 1692 resettlement after the Pueblo Revolt. Fast forward to the 1920s: Santa Fe is home to not only a rollicking Spanish scene and traditional Native quarter, but also a recent influx of some conspicuously eccentric Anglo artists.

Artist Will Shuster and fellow members of Los Cincos Pintores decided in 1926 that something was needed to bring all these celebrants together. Taking a cue from the Yaqui Indians of Mexico, who stuff an effigy of Judas with fireworks to dispel their woes, they built a 6ft-tall puppet in a field where the library now stands.

Poet Witter Bynner led a mob of fiesta-goers to the park and began the chant as dark-robed Kiwanis set torches at its base. When that first Zozobra – loosely translated from Spanish as 'the gloomy one' – went up in shocking green flames, the crowd went crazy. It was a hit.

Today the scene is set at Fort Marcy Park, where some 30,000 people gather each year beneath 50ft-tall Old Man Gloom's accusing glare. As dusk becomes pitch black, the crowd begins to chant: 'Burn him! Burn him!' The hillsides, packed with people who refused to pay the entry fee, echo the cries with gusto. Ghosts – the year's sorrows – mill about at Zozobra's feet. Then the fire dancer prances in, his wand ablaze, teasing and taunting, tempting all hell to break loose. Finally, *finally,* an eruption consumes the massive creature, all Santa Fe lending voice to the roar.

And that, folks, is what you call catharsis.

All bitterness is burned away by the inferno, fueled by police reports, divorce papers and paid-off mortgages. The four days of Fiestas have officially begun.

And once Fiestas are over, it's the first day of the rest of your life. All those dramas and traumas? Forgotten. Your sins? Forgiven. The eternal soap opera of life will continue unabated, but this dawn, your soul is fresh.

Need a good rest after your Canyon Rd gallery hike? Try an informative 1¼-hour tour ($10) or a three-hour tour ($30) by bus with **Santa Fe Detours** (☎ 983-6565, 800-338-6877; www.sfdetours.com). Need to get out of town? Tired of planning everything yourself? The company will also arrange ski trips, opera nights and more.

Outback Tours (☎ 820-9375, 888-772-3274; www.outbacktours.com) will help you climb to the 9000ft Jemez volcano looking for elk, deer and bear ($65), explore Georgia O'Keeffe's red-rock country near Abiquiú ($85) or travel off-road to 10,000ft in the Sangre de Cristo Mountains ($55) in 4WD SUVs.

FESTIVALS & EVENTS

Santa Fe often serves up more cultural events in a day than many towns do in a year. Here's a sampling of major happenings, but check the *Santa Fe Reporter*, the various freebies and the *Pasatiempo* insert in the Friday *New Mexican* for up-to-the-minute info on area happenings, including the locations of the swanky but friendly Friday-night art openings, usually held between 5pm and 7pm.

February
Artfeast Edible Art Tour (☎ 982-1648, www.artfeast .com; tour $25) Savoring gourmet food, sampling fine wines and touring world-class art galleries serves an even greater purpose than indulging pure personal pleasure – benefiting arts programs in Santa Fe schools. Held in late February.

April
Chimayó Pilgrimage On Easter week join – or pay respects to – the tens of thousands of pilgrims, mostly Native American and Hispanic, who trek anywhere from a few to a few hundred miles on a journey of personal penance, prayer and hope to the tiny Santuario de Chimayó (p127), 40 miles north of Santa Fe.

June
Gay/Lesbian/Bisexual/Transgender Pride on the Plaza (www.santafehra.org) Join pilgrims of another sort for an entirely different procession – the gay, lesbian, bisexual, transgender parade during mid-June. Look for a whole host of special music, comedy and other events; area bars and restaurants throw special bashes for a full week when everyone flies the rainbow flag.
Rodeo de Santa Fe (☎ 471-4300; www.rodeodesanta fe.org; adult $10-20, child $5) This is the real deal, you visitin' city slickers! In late June, join wranglers, ranchers, cowpokes and plenty of rhinestone cowpersons to see

what cowboys and girls really mean when they say they wrestle steer, ride bulls and race barrels.

July
International Folk Art Market (☎ 476-1166; www .folkartmarket.org) If your travel budget doesn't include a trip to Japan, India, China, Laos, Mexico, Zimbabwe, Tibet, Uzbekistan or Zimbabwe this year, this wildly popular market with more than 100 artists from around the globe will fit your passport perfectly. Held in early July.
Eight Northern Indian Pueblos Arts & Crafts Show Excellent outdoor art show, going strong since 1972 at Ohkay Owingeh (formerly San Juan Pueblo). Come for the traditional dances, music and food, too.
Spanish Market (☎ 982-2226; www.spanishmarket .org) Handcrafted furniture, tin, precious metal and bone-work are offered alongside traditional retablos and bultos at this juried extravaganza of traditional Spanish colonial arts in late July. Another Spanish Market is held in early December at the Sweeney Convention Center.

August
Santa Fe Indian Market (☎ 983-5220; www.swaia .org) Only the best get approved to show their work at this world-famous juried show (held the weekend after the third Thursday in August), where more than 1000 artists from 100 tribes and pueblos exhibit. As if that's not enough, a hundred thousand visitors converge on the plaza, at open studios and gallery shows. Get there Friday or Saturday to see pieces competing for the prestigious top prizes (they get snapped up by collectors). But wait until Sunday if you want to try bargaining.
Native Cinema Showcase (www.ccasantafe.org) Part of the Santa Fe Indian Market.

September
Santa Fe Fiestas (☎ 988-7575; www.santafefiesta.org) In the first week in September, a full eight days of events celebrate the September 4, 1692, resettlement of Santa Fe. Don't miss Zozobra (opposite), but also look for Don Diego DeVargas, the Procession of La Conquistadora, a mass at St Francis Cathedral, concerts and a pet parade.
Santa Fe Wine & Chile Fiesta (☎ 483-8060; www .santafewineandchile.org) It's a gourmet's fantasy fiesta, with wine tastings and fine cuisine; dinner events ($50 to $150) sell out early. Held in late September.

December
Canyon Road Walk (p92) Join thousands of quiet revelers on December 24 in one of the loveliest holiday celebrations anywhere on earth.
Santa Fe Film Festival This five-day, mid-month extravaganza presents world cinema in a noncommercial context and premiers New Mexican, new American and foreign films.

CHRISTMAS EVE ON CANYON ROAD

Whatever the airfare costs, being in Santa Fe at Christmastime is worth it – just to experience the overwhelming grace and elegance of the Canyon Rd Walk on December 24. Come for frosty air, miles of glowing pathways of tiny candles and comradely quiet. Come to see a night sky meeting gallery windows filled with fine art. This other world is, simply, Santa Fe at its best.

Partly it's the intoxicating sights and scents of small piñon and cedar wood bonfires that line the road, offering guiding light and memories that meld into your bone marrow. Partly it's a few equestrians prancing on horseback, jingle bells jingling, clackity-clacking along the narrow street, evoking memories of early Santa Feans who led their burros up the 'Road of the Canyon' to gather firewood in mountain forests. Partly it's the silhouettes of 250-year-old adobes softly lit by rows of twinkling *farolitos*, small candles anchored in sand inside brown paper bags.

Dress warmly and beat the crowds by arriving early, say by 6pm. Park in one of the public lots near the Capitol (p83), and walk over to warm yourself by early bonfires. You'll still be able to walk the road without mobs at this point. As night falls, the streets fill, in a nice way, with happy and friendly revelers. Small groups of carolers sing remarkably in tune; gracious locals offer spiced cider, hot chocolate and cookies from small tables set out along the way.

Just when you think your senses are delicately sated, at around 8pm 'flying *farolitos*,' beloved gifts born of a local science teacher, begin ascending into the velvet sky, one-by-one. You'll know he's started when you hear folks pointing and whispering, 'Hey, there's one.' Then you too will start scanning the stars above the tree line. Pay attention, because each *farolito* has a short life span, trailing embers falling earthward.

Meander through the welcoming, adobe-lined streets along Acequia Madre St, just off Canyon Rd, to trace these floating candles to their source. See how they're made – it's astonishingly simple – and how they manage to gain such altitude.

Most likely your evening will trail off like a bright *farolito*, and with a heartfelt promise to begin a tradition of Christmas Eve in Santa Fe. And if you're lucky, you will.

SLEEPING

Standards are high in Santa Fe, but prices don't have to be if you're willing to sleep in basic accommodations. On the other hand, world-class luxury can also be yours, so just decide your priorities and choose accordingly. Most of the low-budget and national chain options line Cerrillos Rd between I-25 and downtown; luxury options live closer to the Plaza or on the outskirts of town in glorious settings; midrange options are sprinkled around town.

Options vary widely in the midrange price category – from motels to inns that resemble hotels to B&Bs with four or five rooms. Most offer complimentary breakfasts ranging from packaged Danish at motel chains to gourmet green chile omelets at more charming B&Bs. Some hotels and motels offer free shuttles to the plaza or are well situated near the Santa Fe Trails bus line. Most B&Bs offer off-street parking so you can leave your car and walk to the center of the action – a good choice during high season because Santa Fe is small and finding parking near the plaza can be frustrating.

In December and during the summer (particularly during Indian Market in August and on Opera nights), expect to pay premium prices. Make reservations well in advance. Remember: prices do not include taxes and other add-ons of 11% to 15%.

The neighborhoods described are subjective: Plaza & Canyon Rd is the downtown area bounded by the Santa Fe River, Guadalupe St and Paseo de Peralta; Guadalupe St Area runs from Guadalupe St to the Capitol, including parts of Cerrillos Rd; Cerrillos Rd covers the strip south of Guadalupe St plus side streets; Metropolitan Santa Fe covers everything else.

RESERVATION SERVICES

All Santa Fe Reservations (☎ 877-737-7366; www .all-santafe.com) Personal assistance by phone and internet; helps you choose among 100 hotels, motels and B&Bs. Arrange car rentals, airport shuttles, ski packages and more.
New Mexico Lodging Association (www.nmlodging .org) Search by city or region, cost and amenities.
New Mexico Bed & Breakfast Association (☎ 800-661-6649; www.nmbba.org) More than a dozen Santa Fe B&Bs, plus others all over the state.

Kokopelli Property Management (☎ 988-7244, 888-988-7244; www.kokoproperty.com) A wide variety of vacation casitas, condos and homes in the city and country.

Santa Fe Detours – Emergency Lodging Assistance (☎ 986-0038) Call this number after 4pm daily to get help finding last-minute lodging in any price category, though the more you can pay, the more plentiful your options.

Plaza & Canyon Road
MIDRANGE
Garrett's Desert Inn (Map pp64-5; ☎ 982-1851, 800-888-2145; www.garrettsdesertinn.com; 311 Old Santa Fe Trail; r low $79-109, high $99-139, ste low $99-124, high $129-139; P ⊠ ⊛) Though this inn's heyday passed in the 1960s, the price for a basic room next to the plaza makes it a deal, and there's wireless internet in the on-site restaurant (open 7am to 2pm Sunday and Wednesday to Saturday, 5pm to midnight Monday and Thusday to Saturday).

Madeleine (Map pp64-5; ☎ 986-1431, 888-877-7622; www.madeleineinn.com; 106 Faithway St; r shared bath $90-105, private bath $120-200; P ⊠ ⊛) The fabulously indulgent Absolute Nirvana Spa & Tea Room (p98) puts this B&B over the top, along with lovely Victorian architecture, Queen Anne antiques, decadent homemade snacks, lush gardens and private cottages. Wireless internet runs throughout.

Hotel St Francis (Map pp64-5; ☎ 983-5700, 800-529-5700; www.hotelstfrancis.com; 210 Don Gaspar Ave; r low $90-219, high $125-300; P ⊛ ⊡) Rates are pretty good for being plaza-side, but this hotel's glory days were the 1930s and '40s. Guest rooms still whisper elegance in a decadently aging way and the trademark afternoon tea continues in the lobby.

Casa de la Cuma (☎ 216-7516, 877-741-7928; www.casacuma.com; 105 Paseo de la Cuma; r low $95-135, high $125-170; P ⊠ ⊛) The friendly hosts here have built a reputation for warmth and great homemade granola and baked goods. Guests return year after year to these four rooms, one with a kitchenette, two with wood-burning fireplaces, all with wireless internet.

Inn of the Governors (Map pp64-5; ☎ 982-4333, 800-234-4534; www.innofthegovernors.com; 101 W Alameda; r low/high $129/189; P ⊠ ⊛ ⊡ ⊛) Ambitious decorating in elegant rooms, suites with fireplaces, wireless internet and the popular Del Churro Saloon (snacks $5 to $11; open 11:30am to midnight, bar until 2am) conspire to make this a perfect location.

Water Street Inn (Map pp64-5; ☎ 984-1193, 800-646-6752; www.waterstreetinn.com; 427 W Water St; r low $100-190, high $135-205; P ⊠ ⊛ ⊡) Step off bustling Water St to enter this cheery world where relaxing beneath an umbrella-shaded sundeck is an art form. Historic brick floors are a nice counterpoint to the flat-screen TVs with DVD players in rooms accented with Spanish, Native American and Anglo art. Wireless internet in guest rooms keeps you connected.

Hacienda Nicholas (Map pp64-5; ☎ 888-284-3170; www.haciendanicholas.com; 320 E Marcy St; r $110-220; P ⊠ ⊛) Sumptuous beds await within this quiet, authentic adobe hacienda B&B where the focus is on organic and vegetarian food and a hypo-allergenic and 'green' environment.

Adobe Star Inn (Map pp64-5; ☎ 988-3024, 800-647-0530; www.adobestarinn.com; 222 McKenzie St; r $149, ste $165-195; P ⊠ ⊛) Under same ownership as Adobe Abode, these bright, basic rooms and casitas (small houses) offer lodging at affordable prices in a convenient location within walking distance of the plaza. The Hacienda Grande room has a large wood-burning fireplace and full kitchen; all guest rooms have wireless internet.

Adobe Abode (Map pp64-5; ☎ 983-3133; www.adobeabode.com; 202 Chapelle St; r $149-189; P ⊠ ⊛) Color is the watchword here, where Southwest kitsch rules in rooms recently upgraded in response to guests' feedback. They're nothing fancy, but wireless internet and a good night's sleep can be yours just a block from the Georgia O'Keeffe Museum.

TOP END
Inn on the Alameda (Map pp64-5; ☎ 984-2121, 888-984-2121; www.innonthealameda.com; 303 E Alameda St; r low $120-135, high $205-220, ste $255-375; P ⊛ ⊡ ⊛) Hand-made furniture, luxe linens, elegant breakfasts and afternoon wine-and-cheese receptions bring B&B-style elegance to a pleasantly efficient hotel. The staff can also arrange cooking classes, fly-fishing, outdoor adventures and more, all with local experts.

Hotel Plaza Real (Map pp64-5; ☎ 988-4900, 877-901-7666; www.buynewmexico.com; 125 Washington Ave; r low/high $137/199, ste low $157-179, high $227-249; P ⊠ ⊛ ⊛) This former Radisson still feels like a chain but offers nice Territorial architectural style, some wood-burning fireplaces and several 2nd-floor suites with small outdoor balconies boasting mountain views. A lively bar downstairs and wireless internet in guest rooms complete the package.

Inn at Loretto (Map pp64-5; ☎ 988-5531, 800-727-5531; www.hotelloretto.com; 211 Old Santa Fe Trail; r low/high $160/360; P ⊠ 🖳 🅡) Everyone feels creative in this gorgeous hotel that resembles Taos Pueblo and is filled with stunningly luxurious rooms and suites, all with wireless internet. So why not make the most of it by attending the hotel's exclusive tours, hands-on classes and lectures with local artists? On-site Baleen Restaurant (dishes $8 to $42; open 7am to 2:30pm and 5:30pm to 10pm) is celebrated for its seafood and discerning wine list, while the pampering at SpaTerre (p97) is world renowned.

La Posada de Santa Fe (Map pp64-5; ☎ 986-0000, 866-331-7625; www.laposada.rockresorts.com; 330 E Palace Ave; r low $169-259, high $239-339; P ⊠ 🖳 🅡) World-class service puts this hotel in a league of its own. Your every need is catered to on this beautiful, shady, 6-acre property a few blocks from the plaza. Elegantly furnished adobe casitas are outfitted with gas fireplaces. More historic (and smaller) rooms, some with views, are located in the Staab House and all have wireless internet. Onsite Avanyu Spa (p97) and the heralded restaurant Fuego are both deservedly fabulous, while the cigar-friendly Staab House Lounge (open 11:30am to 11pm) is a local favorite for its leather-chaired ambiance and single-malt scotch.

El Dorado Hotel (Map pp64-5; ☎ 988-4455, 800-955-4455; www.eldoradohotel.com; 309 W San Francisco St; r $175-300; P ⊠ 🖳 ♿ 🅡) Popular for meetings as well as weddings, this somewhat conventional hotel's rooftop pool and luxury spa add elegance – as do the exclusive packages. For $600, you can secure two nights' lodging and tickets to the Santa Fe Opera for two, along with dinner at the mah-vellous Old House Restaurant (p103).

Inn of the Anasazi (Map pp64-5; ☎ 988-3030, 800-688-8100; www.innoftheanasazi.com; 113 Washington Ave; r low $200-469, high $325-525; P ⊠ 🖳) Ancient blends seamlessly with ultramodern in this elegant, Navajo-themed property. For a deal as well as a boost, try the 'Better Business Package' ($200) – a night's lodging, a power breakfast, laundering and an optional session with a Native American mystic.

La Fonda (Map pp64-5; ☎ 982-5511, 800-523-5002; www.lafondasantafe.com; 100 E San Francisco St; r low/high $219/319; P ⊠ 🖳 🅡) Staff artist Ernest Martinez has been painting thousands of windows and other fixtures since 1954,

giving La Fonda its unique folk-art character. Claiming to be the original 'Inn at the end of the Santa Fe Trail,' here since 1610, the hotel also features Southwest murals and paintings commissioned in the 1920s and '30s. Rooms are sometimes odd but all have wireless internet. The top-floor luxury suites in La Terraza are lovely, and sunset views from the Belltower Bar (p105) are the best in town.

Guadalupe St Area

BUDGET

Santa Fe Motel & Inn (Map pp64-5; ☎ 982-1039, 800-930-5002; www.santafemotel.com; 510 Cerrillos Rd; r $79-119; P ⊠ 🖳) Colors and tiles in these simple yet stylish rooms are not for the faint of heart. Kitchenettes and casitas are available, also in assertive hues, with delightful accents and wireless internet beaming throughout.

MIDRANGE

El Paradero (Map pp64-5; ☎ 988-1177; www.elparadero.com; 220 W Manhattan Ave; r low $80-150, high $95-160; P ⊠ 🖳) When you're ready for a break from the ubiquitous shades of earthen brown, this historic building's brick facade is a relief – it predates the city's adobe-only laws. This very traditional B&B has small but airy rooms, suites with kitchenettes, a lovely courtyard and wireless internet in the common areas.

Old Santa Fe Inn (Map pp64-5; ☎ 995-0400, 800-745-9910; www.oldsantafeinn.com; 320 Galisteo St; r low $89-179, high $164-254; P ⊠ 🖳) Good-looking though smallish rooms, wireless internet and a great breakfast burrito bar prepare you well for a day of sightseeing. And the plaza is just blocks away.

Pueblo Bonito Inn (Map pp64-5; ☎ 984-8001, 800-461-4599; www.pueblobonitoinn.com; 138 W Manhattan Ave; r $90-135, ste $120-165; P ⊠ 🖳) Surrounding a small estate built in the 1930s, complete with horse stalls and barn, the inn's 18in-thick adobe walls lend authenticity and a certain quietude to these simple, beautiful, white-walled rooms and casitas. Wood-burning kiva fireplaces in the bedrooms and living rooms amp up the charm factor and make this a preferred place to stay in winter as well as the milder seasons.

Don Gaspar Inn (Map pp64-5; ☎ 986-8664, 888-986-8664; www.dongaspar.com; 621 Don Gaspar Ave; r low $105-145, high $125-195, ste $175-355; P ⊠ 🖳)

In this quiet residential neighborhood just choose a room, a suite or even an entire home from among three elegant houses – Arts and Crafts bungalow, Pueblo Revival and Territorial styles. Save plenty of time to lounge in front of the large fireplace in cooler months or follow the (red) brick road through lush gardens in warmer times. You'll have to leave the grounds to remember you're in a desert state.

Hotel Santa Fe (Map pp64–5; ☎ 800-825-9876; www.hotelsantafe.com; 1501 Paseo de Peralta; r low/high $110/159, ste low/high $175/235; P ⌘ ⌨ ♨) There are no hotels at Picuris Pueblo so your best chance to experience Pikuri hospitality is in this pretty adobe, several blocks from the plaza. It's one of the best deals for resort-style accommodations downtown. Decorated with Native American art, the hotel is home to a small spa and Amaya restaurant (p103). Rooms are basic, sure, but that keeps ski packages and suites with fireplaces well priced.

Four Kachinas Inn (Map pp64–5; ☎ 982-2550, 800-397-2564; www.fourkachinas.com; 512 Weber St; r low $110-175, high $170-215; P ⌘ ⌨) Individual entrances to each of these bright, basic rooms create a nice feeling of privacy, and it's just a short walk from Canyon Rd. Individual decorating – like wrought-iron beds in the Old Mexico room – and wireless internet are nice touches. Small private gardens and a sunny courtyard provide focal points for relaxation and optional socializing.

El Farolito (Map pp64–5; ☎ 988-1631, 888-634-8782; www.farolito.com; 514 Galisteo St; casita $150-180; P ⌘ ⌨) Relax in your own private, elegant casita (some with patios), and enjoy all the amenities you expect from a fine B&B, including a well-stocked fridge and a TV/DVD player.

TOP END

Las Brisas (Map pp64–5; ☎ 982-5795, 800-449-6231; www.lasbrisasdesantafe.com; 624 Galisteo St; ste low $155-255, high $230-330; P ⌘) Find just about every home comfort in these one-, two- and three-bedroom condos with fully equipped kitchens. They're individually owned and are decorated accordingly, and they're popular with the opera crowd.

our pick Inn of the Five Graces (Map pp64–5; ☎ 992-0957; www.fivegraces.com; 150 E DeVargas St; ste $295-750; P ⌘ ⌨) Much more than an ordinary luxury getaway, this exquisite, exclusive gem offers an upscale gypsy-style escape. Sumptuous suites are decorated in a lavish Persian/Indian/Asian–fusion theme, complete with fireplaces, beautifully tiled kitchenettes and a courtyard behind river-rock walls. Say Scheherazade sent you.

Cerrillos Rd
BUDGET

Santa Fe International Hostel (Map p62; ☎ 988-1153; 1415 Cerrillos Rd; dm $15, s/d with shared bath $25/35, s/d with private bath $33/43; P ⌘ ⌨ ⌨) A cherry tree shades the patio and grill outside this mural-covered building. In exchange for very inexpensive simple quarters (private rooms and sex-separated dorms), free continental breakfast, an open kitchen, linens and no lockout, there are mandatory morning chores. Reservations are accepted only by mail.

Los Campos (Map p62; ☎ 473-1949, 800-852-8160; 3574 Cerrillos Rd; RV $25-35; P ⌨ ♨) This in-town place has full RV hookups, wireless internet and a pool, but no tents are allowed.

Silver Saddle Motel (Map p62; ☎ 471-7663; 2810 Cerrillos Rd; r low/high $45/65; P ⌘) This rustic subject of the 1988 documentary film *Motel* has Southwestern comfy-rustic decor, with attractively tiled kitchenettes, a good location (for Cerrillos Rd) and lots of kitschy appeal.

Luxury Inn (Map p62; ☎ 473-0567; 3752 Cerrillos Rd; r $50-199; P ⌘ ♨) All rooms at this fine, independently operated inn have free wireless internet. And some of the huge suites have kitchenettes.

Santa Fe Sage Inn (Map pp64–5; ☎ 982-5952, 866-433-0335; www.santafesageinn.com; 725 Cerrillos Rd; r low $55-80, high $95-125; P ⌘ ⌨ ♨) This newly refurbished (bargain) gem has great curb appeal, a stylish, cheerful interior and wireless internet, all within walking distance of the plaza.

Holiday Inn (Map p62; ☎ 473-4646; www.holidayinn.com; 4048 Cerrillos Rd; r low $73-82, high $98-107; P ⌘ ⌨ ♨) This perfectly adequate chain hotel features a fabulous indoor/outdoor pool and wireless internet.

Best Western Lamplighter Inn (Map p62; ☎ 471-8000, 800-767-5267; www.bwlamplighter.com; 2405 Cerrillos Rd; r $89-109; P ⌘ ⌨ ♨) Guest rooms in this aging but very well maintained hotel include refrigerators and coffeemakers; wireless internet is available in the larger rooms with kitchenette. The pool is open year-round, while a recreation room offers table tennis.

MIDRANGE

Comfort Suites (Map p62; ☎ 473-9004; www.choice hotels.com; 3348 Cerrillos Rd; r low/high $53/80, ste low/high $80/171; P 🅿️ 🖥️ 🛗) This three-story, good-quality chain hotel offers great rates, reliable service, wireless internet and the choice of a kitchenette.

Hampton Inn (Map p62; ☎ 474-3900, 800-426-7866; www.hamptoninn.com; 3625 Cerrillos Rd; r low/high $69/$129; P 🅿️ 🖥️ 🛗) Security-minded guests will appreciate that room access is through the lobby only; everyone with an enabled laptop appreciates the wireless internet.

Stagecoach Motor Inn (Map p62; ☎ 471-0707; 3360 Cerrillos Rd; r $78-150; P 🅇 🅿️) Looking for character among the chain hotels on Cerrillos Rd? This nice spot has Santa Fe–style rooms, complete with vigas and saltillo tiles, a colorful garden, a shady courtyard and a good breakfast.

El Rey Inn (Map p62; ☎ 982-1931, 800-521-1349; www.elreyinnsantafe.com; 1862 Cerrillos Rd; r $95-150; P 🅇 🅿️ 🖥️ 🛗) An eye-catching white-washed compound, this 70-year-old classic has large rooms (try the updated deluxe versions), a great pool and a kids' playground on 5 acres of greenery. It's highly recommended.

Courtyard by Marriott (Map p62; ☎ 473-2800, 800-777-3347; www.marriott.com; 3347 Cerrillos Rd; r low $89-109, high $109-189; P 🅿️ 🖥️ 🛗) Very professional, businesslike and attractive, this amenity-laden hotel has an on-site bar and restaurant, wireless internet and free shuttles to downtown.

Metropolitan Santa Fe

BUDGET

Along Hyde Park Rd (NM 475) to Ski Santa Fe, the National Forest Service operates both **Black Canyon** (Map p116; ☎ 438-7840, 877-444-6777; www.reserveusa.com; sites $10; P), 8 miles from town with fir trees and a pretty stream, and nearby **Big Tesuque Campground** (Map p116; ☎ 438-7840, 877-444-6777; www.reserveusa.com; sites free; P), sitting pretty at 9700ft with great views of the aspens but no drinking water, so bring your own. Both are open April to November; reservations are recommended in summer.

Rancheros de Santa Fe Campground (Map p116; ☎ 466-3482, 800-426-9259; 736 Old Las Vegas Hwy; tent/RV $20/32; 🕙 Mar-Oct; P 🛗) Seven miles southeast of town, off exit 290 from I-25 North, Rancheros has nice views, a convenience store and wireless internet. Oh yeah, its sites are wooded and open.

MIDRANGE

Camel Rock Suites (Map p62; ☎ 989-3600, 877-989-3600; www.camelrocksuites.com; 3007 S St Francis Dr; ste low/high $89/119; P 🅇 🖥️) The Tesuque Pueblo Indians own this collection of large apartment-like suites just off I-25. They come with full kitchens, fold-out sofas, a free shuttle downtown and free day passes to the outstanding nearby Genoveva Chavez Community Center (p86). All combined, it's a fantastic deal.

Alexander's Inn (Map p62; ☎ 986-1431, 888-321-5123; www.alexanders-inn.com; 529 E Palace Ave; r $90-210, casita $165-220; P 🅇 🅇) In a historic neighborhood five blocks from the plaza, Alexander's is a beautiful 1903 Arts and Crafts home. Most rooms are decorated for a frilly romantic escape, while casitas (some of which are located several blocks away) boast fireplaces and full kitchens.

Sunrise Springs (Map p116; ☎ 471-3600, 800-955-0028; www.sunrisesprings.com; 242 Los Pinos Rd; r low $90-145, high $125-175; P 🅇 🅇 🛗) Secluded in the high desert just 15 minutes from downtown, this mix of basic retreat-center rooms and casitas provide access to 69 lush acres of spring-fed ponds, fountains and resident wildlife. With yoga, tai chi and ceramics classes, an on-site spa, and the Blue Heron Restaurant (p104) whipping up phenomenal meals, you might never want to leave the grounds.

Houses of the Moon (☎ 982-9304; www.ten thousandwaves.com; 3451 Hyde Park Rd; r $99-279; P 🅇 🅇) You can make your own resort vacation simply by staying in these beautiful, Zen-inspired, freestanding accommodations. How? They're within walking distance of the mountainside hot tubs and massage cabins at adjacent 10,000 Waves (opposite). Lodging choices range from a tiny Airstream trailer named Silver Moon to a 1100-sq-ft Tsuki suite with a full kitchen. The latter is a contender for nicest room in Santa Fe, though you'll swear you're in Japan. Make reservations two months in advance.

RELAX INTO MAÑANA TIME

Many Santa Fe spas offer spectacular natural settings and mountain views; all offer world-class pampering.

Absolute Nirvana Spa & Tea Room (Map pp64-5; ☎ 983-7942, 888-877-7622; www.absolutenirvana .com; 106 Faithway St; ☯ 10am-6pm Sun-Thu, 10am-8pm Fri & Sat) Rose-petal baths and sumptuous Indonesian- and Thai-style massage ($145 to $220) await you inside the Madeleine (p93).

Avanyu Spa (Map pp64-5; ☎ 986-0000, 866-331-7625; www.laposada.rockresorts.com; 330 E Palace Ave; ☯ 7am-8pm) Choose from sophisticated massage techniques, including craniosacral therapy, polarity, Reiki and shiatsu ($115 to $180) at this swanky spot within La Posada de Santa Fe (p94).

Ojo Caliente (p124) An hour north of Santa Fe, this is Mother Nature's original New Mexico spa, where stressed-out Comanche and Pueblo Indians have been soaking for millennia.

Santa Fe Massage (☎ 995-5105; www.santafemassage.com; ☯ 9am-9pm) These folks come to your hotel room, massage table in hand ($100).

SháNah Spa & Wellness (☎ 983-6377, 800-974-2624; www.bishopslodge.com; 1297 Bishops Lodge Rd; ☯ 8am-8pm) This Bishop's Lodge (p85) spa has a watsu pool for floating shiatsu ($105), two outdoor massage gardens and indoor services too. General services cost $105 to $125.

SpaTerre (Map pp64-5; ☎ 988-5531; www.innatloretto.com; 211 Old Santa Fe Trail; ☯ 9am-9pm) Melt your cares away at this Inn at Loretto (p94) spa with Native American–themed decor and absolutely delectable massages with herbs and aromatherapy ($110 to $225).

Samadhi Spa (☎ 471-3600, 800-955-0028; 242 Los Pinos Rd; ☯ 9am-7pm Wed-Sun, 9am-2pm Mon-Tue) This Sunrise Springs (opposite) spa sits among trees and spring-fed ponds on 65 lush acres.

10,000 Waves (☎ 992-5025; www.tenthousandwaves.com; 3451 Hyde Park Rd; communal tubs $15, private tubs $20-27 per person, premium private tub $59; ☯ 9:15am-9:30pm daily except 4-9:30pm Tue Jul-Oct, 10:15am-8:30pm Mon & Wed-Thu, 4-8:30pm Tue, 9:15am-9:30pm Fri-Sun Nov-Jun) Even if you can't keep the hours straight, you'll probably end up at these tubs done in a smooth Zen style with cold plunges, saunas and two swimsuit-optional tubs, one reserved for women (open noon to 8pm daily except 4:15pm to closing on Tuesday). Massages ($92 to $139) are also available throughout the day.

TOP END

Inn of the Turquoise Bear (Map p62; ☎ 983-0798, 800-396-4104; www.turquoisebear.com; 342 E Buena Vista St; r $100-230, ste $160-335; ☷ ☒ ☷) Visitors enjoy the quiet now, but this expansive adobe party palace built by local legend Witter Bynner and domestic partner Robert Hunt was once home to legendary parties hosting Thornton Wilder, Robert Oppenheimer, Edna St Vincent Millay, Robert Frost and many, many others. It's now a B&B surrounded by an acre of sculpted gardens, combining authentic ambiance and modern amenities. It is, as always, straight-friendly but remains a cozy place for gays and lesbians to relax into historic Santa Fe. The inn can arrange commitment ceremonies and weddings in the gardens.

Bishop's Lodge Resort & Spa (☎ 983-6377, 800-7419-0492; www.bishopslodge.com; 1297 Bishops Lodge Rd; r low $149-279, high $299-429; ☷ ☷ ☷ ☷) Come play (upscale) cowboy/cowgirl on 450 acres of almost untouched piñon wilderness just 3 miles from the plaza. This family-friendly spot boasts huge, luxurious rooms and casitas, many with patios, kitchenettes, fireplaces and more. From yoga and pilates classes at SháNah Spa & Wellness (above) to a skeet and trap range to a magnificent outdoor pool overlooking the mountains, there truly is something for everyone. When you add miles of trails, free shuttles downtown and the excellent on-site restaurant, Las Fuentes (breakfast and lunch $8 to $7, dinner $24 to $34; open 7am to 2pm and 6pm to 9:30pm), it adds up to one excellent vacation.

EATING

Food is another art form in Santa Fe, just as world-class as the galleries. From spicy, traditional Southwest favorites to cutting-edge cuisine, it's all here. Reservations are always recommended for the more expensive venues, especially during summer and ski season. All Santa Fe restaurants and bars are nonsmoking.

Check for au courant reviews in the *Santa Fe Reporter*, which often has coupons for area eateries, or the free monthly *Local Flavor*, with reviews and news about area restaurants. The **Santa Fe Restaurant Association** (www.santaferestaurants.net) publishes a free booklet with sparkling reviews of their members and has a searchable online index. And www.999dine.com offers substantial discount coupons for even the top spots.

Plaza & Canyon Road

BUDGET

Downtown Subscription (Map p70; ☎ 983-3085; 376 Garcia St; snacks $3-8; ☻ 7am-6pm; P ✕ & V ♿) Excellent coffee, scores of teas, pastries and a few savory offerings are complimented by a truly spectacular newsstand and flagstone patio, just a few blocks off Canyon Rd.

Plaza-side vendors (Map pp64-5; dishes $3-9; ☻ 11am-7pm in summer; & V ♿) Tacos, burritos and fajitas are specialties at these city-licensed stalls where you can dispense with table manners entirely.

Teahouse (Map p70; ☎ 992-0972; 821 Canyon Rd; dishes $3-9; ☻ 8:30am-7pm; ✕ & V ♿) Enjoy more than 100 varieties of tea and creative coffee drinks alongside pastries, soups and salads in the cozy, relaxed interior or the outdoor rock garden. Fortify yourself for a long gallery stroll with smoky Lapsang souchong tea or coffee spiced with red chili and chocolate. Whew.

Tia Sophia's (Map pp64-5; ☎ 983-9880; 210 W San Francisco St; dishes $3-9; ☻ 7am-2pm Mon-Sat; ✕ V ♿) Locals outnumber tourists at this top spot. They've come to savor New Mexican *chile rellenos* and hearty and flavorful lunch specials. The shelf of kids' books helps little ones pass the time.

Burrito Company (Map pp64-5; ☎ 982-4453; 111 Washington Ave; dishes $3-9; ☻ 7am-5pm; ✕ & V ♿) Because of its prices, this pleasant, plaza-side favorite will allow you to spend more money on art. Enjoy budget blue corn enchiladas and chorizo burritos that compete with the best of 'em.

Café des Artistes (Map p70; ☎ 820-2535; 223B Canyon Rd; dishes $4-8; ☻ 10am-5pm; ✕ V ♿) Tour world-class art galleries on Canyon Rd, splurge on original art, then eat on an art-student's budget. These folks serve up delicious sandwiches ($6) and French-inspired dishes like a Brie-and-berry salad ($6) served in a cheerful café or on the sunny patio.

Absolute Nirvana Spa & Tea Room (Map pp64-5; ☎ 983-7942; 106 E Faithway St; tea & snacks $5-10; ☻ 10am-5:30pm; ✕ V) Find absolute tranquility at this elegant tea spot offering teacakes, scones and organic lunches. Choose from 50 varieties of tea to help you peacefully unwind overlooking a lush garden. It borders a B&B and a world-class spa (p97).

Upper Crust Pizza (Map pp64-5; ☎ 982-0000; 329 Old Santa Fe Trail; dishes $7-8, pizza $10-24; ☻ 11am-11pm; P ✕ & V ♿) Relax on a nice outdoor patio or in a cozy interior over pizza piled with green chile, piñon or traditional favorites like pesto and pepperoni. This is considered by many (including us) to be Santa Fe's best.

Atomic Grill (Map pp64-5; ☎ 820-2866; 103 E Water St; dishes $7-10; ☻ 11am-3am Mon-Fri, 9am-3am Sat, 9am-midnight Sun; ✕ & V ♿) Pull a plastic chair up to a Formica-top table on the shaded patio, order a sandwich and a local ale, and watch the world walk by at one of Santa Fe's only late-night venues.

MIDRANGE

Sol (Map p70; ☎ 989-1949; 802 Canyon Rd; lunch $6-11, dinner $13-18; ☻ 11:30am-8pm Wed-Thu, 11:30am-9pm Fri & Sat, 9am-3pm Sun; P ✕ & V ♿) Burgers are the raison d'être here, yet vegetarians aren't slighted. The Sol Burger ($9) is massive, the crab-cake sandwich and smoked-salmon burger solid ($10). Mac with five cheeses, nachos and salads also make great choices as you survey galleries and passersby from the patio.

Plaza Café (Map pp64-5; ☎ 982-1664; 54 Lincoln Ave; dishes $7-38; ☻ 7am-9pm; ✕ V ♿) Serving hearty meals since before the roads were paved, this Formica-furnished 1918 establishment still makes one of the best breakfasts around and offers great New Mexican food. (The café's 'not responsible for chile that is too hot.') It prides itself on a varied menu, welcomes kids and offers an unusual perk – a list of New Mexico politicians' phone numbers. Give someone a ring and let them know what you think.

La Cantina at Coyote Café (Map pp64-5; ☎ 983-1615; 132 Water St; dishes $7-18; ☻ 11:30am-9pm Apr-Oct; ✕ V) This lively rooftop cantina atop famed sister restaurant Coyote Café (p100) welcomes budget gourmets to sample chef Mark Miller's cut-rate creations. Try the Oaxacan chicken mole ($11), spit-roasted pork tacos with pineapple ($13) and the signature mango margarita ($8).

India Palace (Map pp64-5; ☎ 986-5859; 227 Don Gaspar Ave; dishes $8-13; ☻ 11:30am-2:30pm & 5-10pm; ✕ & V ♿) Cloth napkins and stemware add ambiance, but it's the recommended lamb *sagwala*, *baingan bartha* (tandoori eggplant) and buffet lunch ($9) that pack these pretty tables with locals and tourists who long for a change from burritos and tacos.

Jinja (Map pp64-5; ☎ 982-4321; 510 N Guadalupe St; lunch $8-11, dinner $8-18; ⏰ 11am-10pm; P ⊠ ⟨ V ⟨) The Asian-fusion cuisine and tropical cocktails here make this bright spot a place to linger. Choose from among Thai, Vietnamese, Japanese, Chinese and Malaysian-style mains, but whatever else you do, don't miss the wasabi mashed potatoes. The kids' menu keeps young ones happy and the drinks menu inspires adults to be bold – try a Polynesian 'party bowl' with four straws ($29) or a Thai martini ($9) with lime vodka and house-made lemongrass syrup.

Il Piatto Cucina Italiana (Map pp64-5; ☎ 984-1091; 95 W Marcy St; lunch $8-10, dinner $9-18; ⏰ 11:30am-2pm Mon-Fri, 5:30-10pm daily; ⊠ ⟨ V ⟨) This crowded, spirited establishment serves up creative Italian fare. When you want a night off from red and green chile sauces, a pasta dish with sun-dried tomatoes may be just the thing.

Shed (Map pp64-5; ☎ 982-9030; 113½ E Palace Ave; lunch $8-10, dinner $9-19; ⏰ 11am-2:30pm & 5:30-9pm Mon-Sat; ⊠ ⟨ V ⟨) This family-run, James Beard Award–winning restaurant has been serving New Mexican fare in a 1692 adobe since 1953. Order anything – it's all fantastic – but get it red. Spicy posole soup comes with many of the mains, and trust us, the rich chocolate mocha cake ($4) provides an outstanding end to any meal.

Cafe Pasqual's (Map pp64-5; ☎ 983-9340; 121 Don Gaspar Ave; breakfast & lunch $8-15, dinner $19-37; ⏰ 7am-3pm & 5:30-9pm; ⊠ V ⟨) Make reservations for dinner if you'd like, but definitely wait in line to enjoy the famous breakfasts. We highly recommend *huevos motuleños* ($12), made with eggs and black beans, sautéed bananas, feta cheese and more; *tamal dulce* ($12), a sweet corn tamale with fruit, beans and Mexican chocolate; or the enormous Durango ham-and-cheese omelet ($13). They're all served up in a festive, if crowded, interior. Jump ahead in line by sitting at the community table, where tourists and locals mix it up daily.

La Plazuela (Map pp64-5; ☎ 982-5511, 800-523-5002; 100 E San Francisco St; lunch $10-16, dinner $15-26; P ⊠ ⟨ V ⟨) Make reservations to dine on pork medallions in prickly pear Tecate barbecue sauce ($26), chipotle-glazed filet mignon ($36) and other gourmet goodies at this lovely spot in the painted-glass heart of La Fonda hotel, where local artist Ernest Martinez has graced more than 400 windows with his paintings over the last 50 years.

La Cantina at La Casa Sena (Map pp64-5; ☎ 988-9232; 125 E Palace; dishes $13-28; ⏰ seatings 5:30pm & 8pm May-Oct, 6:30pm Sun-Thu, 5:30pm & 8pm Fri & Sat Nov-Apr; P ⊠ ⟨ V) Expect an abbreviated menu of La Casa Sena's finest. Make reservations for this serious visitor magnet, which offers one huge bonus: the waitstaff get dressed up and sing show tunes and jazz!

TOP END

Fuego (Map pp64-5; ☎ 986-0000; www.laposada.rockresorts.com; 330 E Palace Ave; breakfast $10-22, lunch $15-28, 4-course tasting dinners $85, bistro dishes $12-24; ⏰ 7-11am, 11:30am-2:30pm & 6-9pm; P ⊠ ⟨ V) Remember the old adage 'location, location, location?' Here it's all about service, service, service. Special events are exclusive – scotch and cigar tastings ($85 per person) anyone? – but the classy Sunday brunches ($45) also pamper palates with Dungeoness crab strudel and asparagus lobster omelets. Lighter dishes like bouillabaisse ($24) and ginger soup ($12) are offered at the bar (aka the Staab House). Prepare to be spoiled – in a good way.

Julians (Map pp64-5; ☎ 988-2355; www.juliansofsantafe.com; 221 Shelby St; dishes $16-36; ⏰ 5:30-9:30pm, P ⊠ ⟨ V) Bring a date to one of Santa Fe's most romantic dining rooms and together enjoy authentic Italian creations and a fine wine list in a soft, jazzy atmosphere. You can't get a more delicious seafood stew outside of Italy than the *caciucco alla* Livornese, a mix of shrimp, lobster, clams, mussels, halibut and squid cooked to perfection in a distinctive tomato sauce ($36). Veal aficionados can order the tender, rich osso buco *alla* Milanese ($28).

El Mesón (Map pp64-5; ☎ 983-6756; www.elmeson-santafe.com; 213 Washington Ave; tapas $3-12, mains $18-26; ⏰ 5-10pm Tue-Sat; P ⊠ ⟨ V ⟨) Chef/owner David Huertas brings the flavors of his native Spain to the table with famous paella and fine Spanish wines. Solo travelers can find conversation at the communal table. Within El Mesón, ¡Chispas! is known for excellent tapas, live music Wednesday evening and flamenco (cover $8) at 8pm on the first Saturday of the month.

O'Keeffe Café (Map pp64-5; ☎ 946-1065; www .okeeffecafe.com; 217 Johnson St; lunch $10-17, dinner $18-30; ☺ 11am-10pm; ☒ �& ⓥ) An elegant eatery with shaded patio dining, this fine café boasts an exceptional wine list and exquisite, mostly organic mains like the Colorado lamb chops with a red chile honey glaze ($29). And it's all right next to the O'Keeffe Museum (p69). The café also offers wine tastings and 'Emerging Oenophile' classes.

Ore House (Map pp64-5; ☎ 983-8687; www.ore houseontheplaza.com; 50 Lincoln Ave; lunch $7-11, dinner $18-32; ☺ 11:30am-2:30pm Mon-Fri, noon-2:30pm Sun, 5:30-10pm daily; ☒ �& ⓥ) Folks willing to indulge their inner tourist should stop here for its 40 different margaritas and balcony tables overlooking the plaza. Oh yeah, and good, hearty food – but that's almost beside the point.

SantaCafé (Map pp64-5; ☎ 984-1788; www .santacafé.com; 231 Washington Ave; lunch $10-14, dinner $18-38; ☺ 11:30am-2pm Mon-Sat, 5:30-9pm daily; ☒ �& ⓥ) Chef David Sellars is practically an international celebrity because of dishes like roasted poblano *chile rellenos* with three mushroom quinoa and chipotle cream ($19), served in an 1850s adobe built by the infamous Padre Gallegos. Lunch is a deal, the wine list flawless and the dining room historic. In short, it's perfect.

Bull Ring (Map pp64-5; ☎ 983-3328; 150 Washington Ave; lunch $9-18, dinner $21-38; ☺ 11:30am-9:30pm Mon-Fri, 5-9:30pm Sat & Sun; ☒ ☒ �& ⓥ ☹) This is the seat of state government, and lobbyists lather up their prey over thick steaks and single-malt scotches at places like the Bull Ring, where fast and friendly staff serve aged Angus in either the Naugahyde dining room or rustic saloon (open until 11pm).

Compound (Map p70; ☎ 982-4353; www.compound restaurant.com; 635 Canyon Rd; lunch $12-20, dinner $24-31; ☺ noon-2pm Mon-Fri, 6-9pm daily; ☒ ☒ �& ⓥ) Chef/owner Mark Kiffin, the James Beard Foundation's Best Chef of the Southwest in 2005, emphasizes elegant flavors, fresh ingredients and exquisite presentations at dinner. The first-course offerings include a rich buttery scallop and morel mushroom stew ($18) and a perfect tuna tartare with caviar ($16). Come when there's reason to celebrate – the wine list includes several top-notch champagnes.

315 Restaurant & Wine Bar (Map pp64-5; ☎ 986-9190; www.315santafe.com; 315 Old Santa Fe Trail; dinner $20-28; ☺ 5:30-9pm; ☒ �& ⓥ) Chef/owner

Louis Moskow creates Provencal-inspired sensations like braised veal with truffle jus ($20) and duck breast with fried cherries ($24). The prix fixe menu ($27) served Sunday through Thursday (5:30pm to 7pm) is a great deal. And while the excellent wine list alone is adequate reason to visit the wine bar, call ahead about special food and wine events.

Coyote Cafe (Map pp64-5; ☎ 983-1615; www.coyote cafe.com; 132 Water St; dishes $23-45; ☺ 5:30-9pm; ☒ ☒ ⓥ) Superstar chef Mark Miller keeps serious foodies returning year after year for stellar interpretations of New Mexico cuisine. Try the garden sampler ($22) or rabbit tart ($20) for appetizers; mains change every couple of weeks but might include a tenderloin of pork with apple and red chile chutney. For dessert, the chocolate mousse ($8) is always deliciously over the top.

Trattoria Nostrani (Map pp64-5; ☎ 983-3800; www.trattorianostrani.com; 304 Johnson Ave; dinner $26-40; ☺ 5:30-9:30pm Mon-Sat; ☒ ☒ ☒ ☒ ⓥ) Dinner at this trattoria is like a trip to Italy, complete with fresh pastas made by hand daily. The menu changes often, so return trips are a delight. Choose a theme to guide you through artful food – for a seaside vacation, start with the seared rare scallop salad ($14), followed by the talierini with clams ($20) or the sautéed shrimp with toasted orzo ($26).

Geronimo (Map p70; ☎ 982-1500; www.geronimo restaurant.com; 724 Canyon Rd; lunch $13-24, dinner $26-43; ☺ 11:30am-2pm & 6-9:30pm Tue-Sun; ☒ ☒ ⓥ) Chef Eric DiStefana presents Santa Fe's most exclusive dining experience in a 1756 adobe on Canyon Rd. In warm weather months the front porch is a great place for lunch while gallery hopping. (It's also a very good 'bargain.') Sample the elk tenderloin ($22) and delightful lobster salad ($17).

ourpick La Casa Sena (Map pp64-5; ☎ 988-9232; www.lacasasena.com; 125 E Palace; lunch $12-20, dinner $24-53; ☺ 11:30am-3pm & 5:30-10pm; ☒ ☒ ⓥ) Housed in an 1880s-era adobe fronted by arguably the most idyllic restaurant patio in Santa Fe, this restaurant serves gourmet cuisine with Southwestern flair, like the Jackelope mixed grill of mesquite-grilled antelope loin, smoked rabbit sausage and sun-dried cherry coulis ($38). Next door, the newly expanded, award-winning wine shop (☎ 982-2121; open from 11am to 6pm) offers more than 1000 international wines.

SANTA FE

El Farol (Map p70; ☎ 983-9912; www.elfarolsf.com; 808 Canyon Rd; lunch $8-18, dinner $25-50; ⊙ 11:30am-late; P ✕ & V ⬧) This popular restaurant and bar, set in a rustically authentic adobe, features live music nightly. It's really all about chef James Campbell Caruso's tapas, however. Come to sample small dishes like *espinaca con casas* (spinach, piñon, garlic, raisins; $6), *ceviche de mariscos* ($7) and *puerco asado* (pork tenderloin with figs and port; $8). Consider making reservations to enjoy the flamenco dinner show ($60 at 8pm on some Wednesdays.

Guadalupe St Area
BUDGET
MarketPlace (☎ 984-2852; 913 W Alameda; ⊙ 7:30am-9pm Mon-Sat, 9am-8pm Sun; P ✕ & V ⬧) Enjoy your choice of local and organic foods at this natural grocery – fresh and deli style. Along with main dishes (featuring the likes of tempeh, tofu and falafel), you can pick up smoothies and juices, baked goods, coffee, fine cheeses, and a wide range of organic fruits and vegetables.

Santa Fe Farmers Market (Map pp64-5; ☎ 983-4098; cnr Cerrillos Rd & Guadalupe St; ⊙ 7am-noon Sat & Tue Apr-Nov; P ✕ & V ⬧) Local produce, much of it heirloom and organic, is on sale in the refurbished Santa Fe Railyard

alongside homemade goodies, inexpensive food, natural body care and herbal products, and a fair number of arts and crafts.

Winter Market (Map pp64-5; ☎ 1614 Paseo de Peralta; ⊙ 9am-1pm Sat Nov-Apr; P ✕ & V ⬧) This is held at nearby El Museo Cultural de Santa Fe.

Cleopatra Cafe (Map pp64-5; ☎ 820-7381; 418 Cerrillos Rd; dishes $4-9; ⊙ 11am-9pm Mon-Sat; P ✕ & V ⬧) Hidden away in the Design Center, this Mediterranean eatery has great food, including two types of falafel (Egyptian, with favas, or Lebanese, using more common chickpeas) and a great chicken kabob ($6).

Bumble Bee's Baja Grill (Map pp64-5; ☎ 820-2862; 301 Jefferson; dishes $5-10; ⊙ 11am-9pm; P ✕ & V ⬧) Drop by this fun spot for healthy, bargain-priced food. Fresh fish tacos ($8 for two), chalupa bowls ($9) and asparagus burritos ($7) are made all the finer with a dash of the smoky roasted tomato salsa, which is a house special. Groove to live jazz on Saturday nights (6pm to 9pm).

Bert's La Taqueria (Map pp64-5; ☎ 988-5991; 416 Agua Fria St; dishes $5-12; ⊙ 11am-2pm & 5-10pm Mon-Sat; P ✕ & V ⬧) Long-time local favorite Bert's recently moved into a big new location closer to the center of town. Thank goodness that affordable food is still the norm, but

---

DOÑA TULES: CARDSHARK AND KINGMAKER

According to legend, Maria Gertrudis Barcelό was born the peon (indentured servant) of a wealthy Taos family in the early 1800s. After a short marriage to a local miner, the red-haired, cigar-smoking beauty found herself broke and on her own in Santa Fe. She may have sold soap on the plaza, or perhaps La Tules (her nickname, 'The Reed') capitalized on her historically notable assets as a consort to wealthy politicos. No one knows.

This much *is* known, though: the popular fashion plate (remembered for her heavy jewelry and plunging necklines) opened a gambling hall on Palace Ave, where she dealt 40-card monte and entertained an opulent clientele. Among her regulars was Governor Armijo, known for good looks, high taxes and blatant corruption during the chaotic decades of Mexican rule. The two were romantically linked, but his alleged affections did not compromise her political savvy.

Already friendly with Anglos who frequented her *sala* (salon), she was contacted in 1846 by US General Stephen Kearny, on his mission of Manifest Destiny: the Americans were coming. Irritated by Armijo's mistreatment of the poor – the class she had risen from – Doña Tules threw in her lot with the USA, loaning Kearny money and even warning him of subterfuge that threatened his tenuous occupation.

Upon her death in 1852, her will requested an elaborate funeral, more appropriate for nobility than a somewhat scandalous former servant. But the church opened its doors to Santa Fe's hostess with the mostest, and the eulogy may well have been given by the bishop himself.

To learn more of Doña Tules' story, or just get a sense of bodice-ripping old Santa Fe, check out *The Wind Leaves No Shadow*, by Ruth Laughlin. Or just stop by **Palace Restaurant** (142 W Palace Ave), on the site of Tules' old *sala*, for a toast.

now you can also choose between a large outdoor patio near the aromatic open-air grill and colorful indoor areas.

Santa Fe Chile Company (Map pp64-5; ☎ 995-9667; 500 Sandoval St; dishes $6-13; 🕙 11am-5:30pm Tue-Sat; ✗ ⑤ Ⓥ ♿) This combined salsa factory, grille and gift store offers fresh finds including meals of Southwest barbecue ($13) and gifts of New Mexico spice mixes, cactus-inspired tableware and piñon candles. Have lunch and shop in one quick stop.

MIDRANGE

Saveur (Map pp64-5; ☎ 989-4200; 204 Montezuma Ave; dishes per pound $10; 🕙 7:45am-3:45pm Mon-Sat; Ⓟ ✗ ⑤ Ⓥ ♿) Basically a foodie's dream salad bar, this innovative eatery serves everything from mixed greens to steamed fish and noodle salads, buffet style. Bonus: for takeout beginning at 3:15pm, soups and salads go for 30% off, and 50% off at 3:30pm.

Tomasita's (Map pp64-5; ☎ 983-5721; 500 S Guadalupe St; dishes $6-12; 🕙 11am-10pm Mon-Sat; Ⓟ ✗ ⑤ Ⓥ ♿) Locals hate to admit it, but they love this tourist standby for its outstanding green chile, served atop excellent burritos, enchiladas and on weekdays huge $10 blue-plate specials (set meals served at a reduced price). It's raucous – perfect for families hauling exuberant kids.

Zia Diner (Map pp64-5; ☎ 988-7008; 366 S Guadalupe St; dishes $6-14; 🕙 11am-10pm; Ⓟ ✗ ⑤ Ⓥ ♿) This cozy diner offers generous portions of something for everyone, from buffalo burgers with sweet-potato fries ($11) to grilled portabella sandwiches with onion rings ($10). Have a beer and watch pierced hipsters and graying progressives coo over their blue-plate specials (weekdays only). The banana splits ($6) are a local fave.

Guadalupe Cafe (Map pp64-5; ☎ 982-9762; 422 Old Santa Fe Trail; breakfast & lunch $5-12, dinner $7-15; 🕙 7am-2pm Tue-Fri, 8am-2pm Sat & Sun, 5:30-9 Tue-Sat; Ⓟ ✗ ⑤ Ⓥ ♿) A great place for hearty appetites, the café offers generous servings of burritos and cheese-stuffed chiles as well as comfort foods like meatloaf and burgers. Those accustomed to leaner fare can choose among the many salads.

Thai Café (Map pp64-5; ☎ 982-3886; 329 W San Francisco St; dishes $9-12; 🕙 11am-2:30pm & 4-9pm; Ⓟ ✗ ⑤ Ⓥ) Santa Feans and tourists done with the green chile thing can enjoy flavorful Thai cuisine here. You can't go wrong with the curries or the seafood.

Cowgirl Hall of Fame (Map pp64-5; ☎ 982-2565; 319 S Guadalupe St; dishes $8-13; 🕙 11am-midnight Mon-Fri, 8:30am-midnight Sat, 8:30am-11pm Sun, bar until 2am Mon-Sat, until midnight Sun; Ⓟ ✗ ⑤ Ⓥ) A fun place for all ages, thanks to the great playground outside and live music after 9pm, this place has fabulous food, too. Try the salmon tacos ($11), butternut-squash casserole ($9) or any mesquite-grilled specialty – all served with Texas caviar (black-eyed pea salsa) and wacky Western-style feminist flair.

Santa Fe Railyard Restaurant & Saloon (Map pp64-5; ☎ 989-3300; 530 S Guadalupe St; dishes $8-23; 🕙 11:30am-2:30pm Mon-Sat, 5:30-9:30pm daily; Ⓟ ✗ ⑤ Ⓥ) Housed in a corrugated-tin warehouse in the up-and-coming, gritty-artsy Railroad District, this conventional steaks-and-chops house also offers pastas, sandwiches and a bar menu.

Santa Fe Bar & Grill (Map pp64-5; ☎ 982-3033; 187 Paseo de Peralta; breakfast & lunch $7-10, dinner $11-20; 🕙 11am-3pm & 5-10pm; Ⓟ ✗ ⑤ Ⓥ ♿) OK, so it's not in a historic adobe, but it is located at the convenient DeVargas Center (p112). The patio, which overlooks a parking lot, and the sleek interior are packed with folks grooving on live acoustic guitar on weekends and grubbing on Southwestern-style salads ($8 to $9), piles of nachos with homemade chorizo ($7) and big plates of ribs ($14).

Andiamo! (Map pp64-5; ☎ 995-9595; 322 Garfield St; dishes $12-20; 🕙 5:30-10pm; ✗ Ⓥ) Everyone from hipsters to hippies will tell you that this is more than just another restaurant with an extensive, award-winning wine list, fabulous antipasti ($9), penne with spicy lamb sausage ($15) and a roster of authentic Italian desserts. Yeah, yeah, yeah...It's also *really* an excuse to see and be seen. You're likely to face a packed house, so make reservations.

Café San Estevan (Map pp64-5; ☎ 995-1995; 428 Agua Fria St; brunch $8-12, dinner $13-29; 🕙 5:30-9pm daily & 10am-2pm Sunday; ✗ Ⓥ) Settle in at a humble wooden table in this cozy dining room with a stone kiva fireplace. And then start enjoying burgers, steaks, salads and New Mexican favorites prepared by Franciscan monk Estevan Garcia.

Pranzo Italian Grill (Map pp64-5; ☎ 984-2645; 540 Montezuma Ave; lunch $6-10, dinner $18-22; 🕙 11:30am-3pm Mon-Sat, 1-9:30pm Sun, 5-9:30pm daily, lounge until 11pm Mon-Sat; Ⓟ ✗ ⑤ Ⓥ ♿) From thin-crust seafood pizzas to garlicky pastas to hearty grilled steaks, Italian flavors rule here. Stop by for a major meal, a romantic glass of wine on the rooftop terrace, or cool jazz Friday and Saturday nights after 9pm ($5 cover).

TOP END

Shohko Cafe (Map pp64-5; ☎ 982-9708; 321 Johnson St; lunch $4-17, dinner $9-25; ⏱ 11:30am-2pm Mon-Fri, 5:30-9pm Mon-Sat; Ⓟ Ⓧ ☒ Ⓥ ☒) Did you expect anything less? Even sushi comes Santa Fe–style – try the cream cheese and green chile roll. They also serve bento boxes at lunch and teriyaki dishes for folks who don't do raw fish.

Amaya (Map pp64-5; ☎ 800-825-9876; www.ho telsantafe.com; 1501 Paseo de Peralta; breakfast & lunch $7-10, dinner $19-27; ⏱ 7-10:30am, 11am-2pm & 5-9pm; Ⓟ Ⓧ ☒ Ⓥ) Within colorful Hotel Santa Fe, owned by the people of the 800-year-old-plus Picuris Pueblo, diners feast on authentic, contemporary Native American cuisine. Muse (and let your mouth water) on marinated elk tenderloin, mint-crusted lamb chop, buffalo sausage, and orange ginger duck breast with garlic herb demi glaze ($27).

Old House Restaurant (Map pp64-5; ☎ 995-4530; www.eldoradohotel.com; 309 W San Francisco St; lunch $11-14, dinner $24-38; ⏱ 11:30am-2pm & 5:30-10pm; Ⓟ Ⓧ ☒ Ⓥ) Dine by the fireplace at the El Dorado Hotel's (p94) award-winning restaurant where executive chef Paul Wade combines organic and artisan food in innovative dishes like coffee-crusted red deer loin with root vegetables and black cherry stew ($32). Each is accompanied by a much-heralded wine list, as you might expect.

Vanessie of Santa Fe (Map pp64-5; ☎ 982-9966; www.nmrestaurants.com/vanessie; 434 W San Francisco St; dishes $15-35; ⏱ 5:30-9:30pm, bar until midnight; Ⓟ Ⓧ ☒ Ⓥ ☒) You don't really come to Vanessie for the food, though it's fine. The attraction here is the piano bar, where Doug Montgomery and Charles Tichenor have been delighting crowds with cabaret and show tunes for 20 and 10 years, respectively.

Ristra (Map pp64-5; ☎ 982-8608; www.ristra restaurant.com; 548 Agua Fria St; dinner $18-34; ⏱ 5:30-9:30pm; Ⓟ Ⓧ ☒ Ⓥ) Savor your stroll up the wisteria-lined brick walkway and then savor French-inspired creations that have found a home inspired by Southwestern flavors – like the sumptuous achiote elk tenderloin in red wine sauce ($34).

Cerrillos Rd
BUDGET

Baja Tacos (Map p62; ☎ 471-8762; 2621 Cerrillos Rd; dishes $4-8; ⏱ 7am-9pm Mon-Sat, 8am-8pm Sun; Ⓟ Ⓧ ☒ Ⓥ ☒) Nosh on New Mexican classics – including an extensive vegetarian menu and good *carne adovada* – inside the cramped interior or at the drive-through. And here's a bonus: the amazing mural outside, *Her Story is a Part of Our History*, by noted area artists Julia Coyne and Amberleigh, uniquely depicts Santa Fe's cultural heritage, showing San Ildefonso potter Maria Martinez (p119), flamenco maestra Maria Benitez (p107) and painter Georgia O'Keeffe (p125).

Tecolote Café (Map p62; ☎ 988-1362; 1203 Cerrillos Rd; dishes $4-8; ⏱ 7am-2pm Tue-Sun; Ⓟ Ⓧ ☒ Ⓥ ☒) It's all here – any enormous combination you want to dream up of eggs, potatoes, tortillas, beans, salsas and the best Hollandaise sauce in town – at the finest, oldest hole-in-the-wall on the strip.

Santa Fe Baking Company & Café (Map p62; ☎ 988-4292; 504 W Cordova Rd; dishes $4-9; ⏱ 6am-8pm Mon-Sat, 6am-6pm Sun; Ⓟ Ⓧ ☒ Ⓥ ☒) This lively spot serves breakfast all day (as well as salads and sandwiches) and offers up live Irish music on Saturday mornings. Live it up with a New Mexico favorite, the Fritos pie ($5.50; p53).

Maria's New Mexican Kitchen (Map p62; ☎ 983-7929; 555 W Cordova Rd; dishes $6-11 ⏱ 11am-10pm Mon-Fri, noon-10pm Sat & Sun; Ⓟ Ⓧ ☒ Ⓥ ☒) Huge portions of New Mexico standards, like the steak and *chile rellenos* combo topped with green chile, would make this 1952 Santa Fe standby a winner anyway. But with more than 100 margaritas ($5.50 to $45), it's a must.

Saigon Cafe (Map p62; ☎ 988-4951; 501 W Cordova Rd; dishes $7-10; ⏱ 11am-9pm Mon-Sat; Ⓟ Ⓧ ☒ Ⓥ ☒) Tasty options include huge portions of hot Vietnamese soups; crispy, garlicky salads; and a variety of fried-noodle dishes.

MIDRANGE

Cloud Cliff Bakery (Map p62; ☎ 983-6254; 1805 2nd St; dishes $7-11; ⏱ 8am-2:30pm, café until 4:30pm; Ⓟ Ⓧ ☒ Ⓥ ☒) Slip on some Birkenstocks and drop by for a stack of groovy blue corn pancakes ($6). Rainbow trout wraps ($9), organic lamb and quinoa ($9), and soups and sandwiches are served alongside organic wines and microbrews. As for side helpings, look for lefty commentary, live music, poetry or lectures.

India House (Map p62; ☎ 471-2651; 2501 Cerrillos Rd; dishes $7-13; ☘ 11:30am-2:30pm Mon-Fri, 5-10pm daily; Ⓟ Ⓧ Ⓥ) Curries, naan and everything vindaloo are fabulous here, as is the abundant lunch buffet ($7). In fact, it's one of the best deals in town.

Mariscos 'La Playa' (Map p62; ☎ 982-2790; 537 Cordova Rd; ☎ 473-4594; 2875 Cerrillos Rd; dishes $8-16; ☘ 11am-9pm Wed-Mon; Ⓟ Ⓧ Ⓖ Ⓥ Ⓖ) Mexican-style seafood, including caldo 'El Mejor' ($10 to $12) – a tomato-based soup with shrimp, octopus, scallops, clams, crab and calamari – goes well with an agave wine margarita ($5).

Mudu Noodles (Map p62; ☎ 983-1411; 1494 Cerrillos Rd; dishes $12-22; ☘ 5:30-8pm Tue-Sat; Ⓟ Ⓧ Ⓖ Ⓥ Ⓖ) Pan-Asian, often organic delights like salmon dumplings, Vietnamese spring rolls and Malaysian laksa inspire throngs to line up out the door. The noodles (of course) and specials are always recommended, and almost everything has a vegan version.

Metropolitan Santa Fe
BUDGET
Museum Hill Café (Map p62; ☎ 820-1776; 720 Camino Lejo; dishes $6-9; ☘ 11am-3pm Tue-Sun; Ⓟ Ⓧ Ⓖ Ⓥ Ⓖ) Despite having a captive audience on Museum Hill (p67), the café serves excellent salmon en papillote ($9), New Mexico and Navajo-inspired fare.

Chocolate Maven (Map p62; ☎ 984-1980; 821 W San Mateo; dishes $6-11; ☘ 7am-5:30pm Mon-Fri, 9am-4pm Sat & Sun; Ⓟ Ⓧ Ⓖ Ⓥ Ⓖ) Sit down to white tablecloths and stemware, and watch as bakers work while you enjoy their incredible pastries, crème brûlée French toast ($7) or gourmet sandwiches.

MIDRANGE
Harry's Roadhouse (Map p116; ☎ 989-4629; 96B Old Las Vegas Hwy; breakfast & lunch $5-9, dinner $8-15; ☘ 7am-10pm; Ⓟ Ⓧ Ⓖ Ⓥ Ⓖ) The attractive setting and elegant cuisine far surpass the prices, and dishes like Moroccan vegetable stew over couscous ($9) and turkey meatloaf ($9) are overshadowed only by the barbecues and the specials. Excellent stuff.

Tesuque Village Market (☎ 988-8848; cnr Bishops Lodge Rd & NM 591; breakfast & lunch $4-9, dinner $8-15; ☘ 7am-9pm; Ⓟ Ⓧ Ⓖ Ⓥ Ⓖ) In the wooded, horsy, upscale village of Tesuque, grab gourmet groceries or an excellent lunch – from subtle cheeses to various fajitas – and enjoy them on the pleasant outdoor porch.

Bobcat Bite (Map p116; ☎ 983-5319; 420 Old Las Vegas Hwy; dishes $5-20; ☘ 11am-7:50pm Wed-Sat; Ⓟ Ⓧ Ⓖ Ⓥ Ⓖ) Often voted as serving the Best Burger in Santa Fe by locals, this relaxed roadhouse beneath the neon really does serve an outstanding green chile cheeseburger ($7). The steaks are pretty darn good too.

Gabriel's (☎ 455-7000; US 84/285; lunch $6-8, dinner $9-18; ☘ 11am-9pm; Ⓟ Ⓧ Ⓖ Ⓥ) The beautiful interior (hung with art by Miguel Martinez) and tree-shaded patio (featuring fountains and sweeping vistas) are fabulous spots to indulge in fresh guacamole, made to order right at your table. Enjoy the excellent New Mexican cuisine or the best ribs ever. Plan to stop if you're headed to the opera, Tesuque Pueblo flea market or points north.

Blue Heron Restaurant (Map p116; ☎ 428-3600; 242 Los Pinos Ave; dishes $16-26; ☘ 7:30-10am, 11am-2pm & 5:30-9pm Wed-Sun; Ⓟ Ⓧ Ⓖ Ⓥ) Join a yoga and meditation crowd at Sunrise Springs Inn where natural and organic cooking is the hallmark. Vegetarians and carnivores alike will enjoy portobello ravioli with seasonal vegetables in saffron cream ($16); meat and poultry – often organic – are on the menu as well. It's all served overlooking a spring-fed pond.

ENTERTAINMENT
To really sample the local Santa Fe, check out Spanish music, two-step and salsa dancing, wacky local performance art and the world-class Santa Fe Opera. Don't expect many options for staying out late, though – this city rolls up the sidewalks early. Live music and dancing start as early as 5pm at some locales and only one real dance club is still standing. But many pubs, restaurants and cafés offer live music and dancing in the (early) evenings. Check the *Reporter* or *Pasatiempo* for weekly listings.

Bars & Pubs
Dragon Room Bar (Map pp64-5; ☎ 983-7712; www .thepinkadobe.com; 406 Old Santa Fe Trail; pub grub $8-16; ☘ 5pm-midnight) This 300-year-old adobe is a consistent top fave for locals and Hollywood-famous visitors alike. Drop by for

---

STATE-WIDE QUEST FOR THE BEST MARGARITA

Nothing goes better with New Mexican cuisine than a good margarita, but who mixes the best? In an effort to answer this critically important question, Museum of New Mexico docents and margarita connoisseurs Mike and Anita Stevenson laboriously compiled this list of top tipples while testing the Shed's (p99) outstanding runner-up for the title. Someone has to do it (while still making deadlines). Be sure to ask if the bartender squeezes his or her own limejuice – for many this is a prerequisite for a great margarita.

La Fonda (p94) High-quality entry; gets extra points for the people-watching.

Maria's New Mexican Kitchen (p103) With more than 100 varieties, you can test these lemon-juice-only, all-agave concoctions all night long – or until you pass out.

Rancho de Chimayó (p126) Great margaritas, or try a Chimayó cocktail, with homegrown apple cider and crème de cassis.

Adobe Bar (p153) Top off your Taos adventure with live music and the perfect margarita.

Sadie's (p186) A cavernous place with great food and a long-enough menu of margaritas.

---

a signature Black Dragon margarita – after 9pm on Tuesday, Thursday or Saturday if you want it served with live music (flamenco guitar, Latin jazz and the like).

Santa Fe Brewing Company (Map pp64-5; ☎ 424-3333; www.santafebrewing.com; 27 Fire Pl; pub grub $4-8, cover $3-5; ☺ 7am-9pm Sun-Thu, 7am-10pm Fri & Sat) Sample the indigenous Santa Fe Ale at this often crowded, always fun pub adjacent to the brewery and tasting room (open 10:30am to 6:30pm Tuesday to Friday, 11:30am to 2pm Saturday; guided tours Saturday at noon). You can also rock to blue grass, Western rock, funk, jazz or some mix of them all. Dancing is encouraged!

Blue Corn Café & Brewery (Cerrillos Rd Map pp64-5; ☎ 438-1800; www.bluecorncafe.com, 4056 Cerrillos Rd; dishes $8-14; ☺ 11am-10pm Sun-Thu, until 11pm Fri & Sat; Plaza Mercado Map pp64-5; ☎ 984-1800; 133 Water St; ☺ 11am-9pm Sun-Thu, until 10pm Fri & Sat) This friendly brewpub wins awards for its Atomic Blonde Ale, High Altitude Pale Ale and others, served alongside burgers ($8), carne asada ($14) and Chuy's chalupas ($8). You'll find the same good food and great brews (but no live music) at the cavernous Plaza Mercado location.

Evangelo's (Map pp64-5; ☎ 982-9014; 200 W San Francisco St; ☺ 11:30am-2am) Everyone is welcome in this casual, rowdy joint owned by the Klonis family since 1971 (ask owner/bartender Nick about his father's unusual fame). Drop in, put on some Patsy Cline and grab a draft beer – it's the perfect escape from Plaza culture.

Second Street Brewery (Map p62; ☎ 982-3030; www.secondstreetbrewery.com; 1814 Second St; dishes $7-13; ☺ 11am-10pm Mon-Thu, 11am-11pm Fri & Sat,

noon-10pm Sun) After a hard day hiking (or just shopping for hiking equipment), stop by this microbrewery to pair a Cream Stout or Extra Special Bitter with fish and chips ($9) or beer-poached salmon salad ($8). There's often live music Thursday through Saturday evenings.

Belltower Bar (Map pp64-5; ☎ 982-5511; 100 E San Francisco St; ☺ 4pm-sunset Mon-Thu, 2pm-sunset Fri-Sun May-Oct) Why bag a peak when you can catch a picture-perfect view of a fiery Southwest sunset here, atop the La Fonda hotel, the tallest building in town, with a cold beer or killer margarita. The hotel's lobby La Fiesta Lounge (dishes $10 to $22, open 11am to 10pm) serves the same great margaritas alongside good New Mexican cuisine, including a popular lunch buffet ($10), and features live music and dancing almost nightly. No mountain views though.

Live Music

The ambitious **Mitch's New Mexico Music Portal** (www.nmmusic.com), with links to mp3s and profiles of local artists who play everything from country and mariachi to funk and punk, gives you an idea of what's happening on the New Mexico scene. Then check the *Reporter* and *Pasatiempo* to see what's going down when you're actually in town.

WilLee's Blues Bar (Map pp64-5; ☎ 982-0117; www.willees.com; 401 S Guadalupe St; cover from $5 Wed-Sat; ☺ 11:30am-2am Mon-Sat, until midnight Sun, shows at 9pm) This club is the real deal, drawing the likes of John Lee Hooker Jr, Leon Russell and Rockin' Jake to perform. Large portions of Italian food and burgers satisfy (dishes $8 to $14), but not like the blues do.

CHICANOBUILT

In the mood for some Latino hip hop and wild thumping mixes that really work the crowd? Want to dance all night long? Then check out ChicanoBuilt, featuring some of the most popular DJs in town: DJ Rockwell, Automatic and Carlitos, as well as Joe Ray Sandoval, a poet and performance artist who foments **Poetry Allowed**, with slam-style readings for la Raza. And la Raza packs venues all over Aztlán when this eclectic collection of lyrical mix masters takes the stage. Dress to impress and get ready to jump.

Log onto www.chicanobuilt.com to download mp3s and check out the events calendar. When you get to town, head over to **Chilacas Cantina** (Map p62; ☎ 984-2272; 2239 Old Pecos Trail; cover $45 after 8pm; 🕑 until 2am) on Saturday nights.

El Farol (Map p70; ☎ 983-9912; www.elfarolsf.com; 808 Canyon Rd; cover $7 Fri & Sat) This offers Spanish guitar, jazz, international music and flamenco a few nights a week (flamenco show with dinner on Wednesday is $60) – and outstanding food always (p101).

¡Chispas! (Map pp64-5; ☎ 983-6756; www.elmeson -santafe.com; 213 Washington Ave; cover $8; 🕑 8pm 1st Sat of the month; P ⊠ 🚫 V 🍴) Part of the El Mesón (p99), ¡Chispas! offers a tantalizing mix of good food and flamenco – much the same as El Farol does.

Cowgirl Hall of Fame (Map pp64-5; ☎ 982-2565; 319 S Guadalupe St; cover $1-5; 🕑 11am-midnight Mon-Fri, 8:30am-midnight Sat, 8:30am-11pm Sun, bar until 2am Mon-Sat, until midnight Sun; P ⊠ 🚫 V) Equal parts hip and rustic, this venue packs 'em in for live shows (despite the name, rarely country), and also serves microbrews and creative food (p102).

El Paseo Bar & Grill (Map pp64-5; ☎ 992-2848; www.elpaseobar.com; 208 Galisteo St; pub grub $4-8; 🕑 11:30am-1:30am Mon-Sat, 11:30am-midnight Sun, kitchen closes at 11pm) This wood-paneled pub has microbrews and green chile cheese steak sandwiches on offer. El Paseo is another primo place to catch a show or dance to a live DJ.

Catamount (Map pp64-5; ☎ 988-7222; 125 E Water St; 🕑 downstairs until 11pm Mon-Sat, upstairs until 2am, upstairs & downstairs until midnight Sun) It's got pool tables, a young crowd, a nice dark bar and nicer brighter patio, and live music a few nights a week.

Warehouse 21 (Map pp64-5; ☎ 989-4423; www .warehouse21.org; 1614 Paseo de Peralta; cover $1-8) This all-ages club and arts center, catering to the under-21 crowd in a 3500-sq-ft warehouse, is the perfect alcohol-free venue for catching cutting-edge local and touring bands and for comparing new piercings and tattoos.

Dance Clubs

Swig (Map pp64-5; ☎ 955-0400; 135 W Palace Ave; sushi & dishes $8-13; 🕑 5pm-2am Fri & Sat, closes earlier other nights) The closest any club in New Mexico comes to matching a South Beach or LA venue, this hot dance club actually waits until 9:30pm to set its trendy clientele loose on the dance floor with a live DJ spinning house, club and hip hop in the Orange Bar.

Bert's La Taqueria (Map pp64-5; ☎ 988-5991; 416 Agua Fria St; 🕑 5pm-late Mon-Sat) Bert's has a spirited indoor/outdoor location close to the center of town with a live DJ; dancing starts most summer nights at 5pm.

Café San Estevan (Map pp64-5; cover $7; 🕑 from 10pm Fri & Sat) This place sheds its quiet dining persona (p102), sometimes featuring wildly popular, predominantly gay dance nights. They come complete with celebrity DJs or offer up fabulous live-music parties for all.

Performing Arts

Santa Fe is solely an arts vacation for many visitors; the spectacular surrounding scenery becomes a stunning backdrop but not a destination in itself. Patrons from the world's most glittering cities are drawn to Santa Fe in July and August because of opera, chamber music, performance and visual arts, an area in which Santa Fe matches anywhere on the globe. The opera may be the belle of the ball – clad in sparkling denim – but it would be a shame to bypass other offerings unaware. Let the searchable, exhaustive **What's Happening in Santa Fe** (www.santafeartsandculture .org) calendar, with links to online advance ticket sales, become your new best friend because on many nights Santa Fe ranks right up there with Paris and Manhattan in another way – the crunch to get tickets and

SANTA FE

parking spaces. Plan ahead to score coveted seats, lodging and gourmet meals.

Santa Fe Opera (Map p116; ☎ 986-5900, 800-280-4654; www.santafeopera.org; standing room $10, seats $25-160; ☯ late Jun-late Aug) Many come to Santa Fe for this and this alone: the theater is an architectural marvel, with nearly 360-degree views of wind-carved sandstone wilderness crowned with sunsets and moonrises, and at center stage the world's finest talent performs Western civilization's masterworks. It's still the Wild West, though; you can even wear jeans – just try *that* in New York City.

Gala festivities begin two hours before the curtain rises. The ritual tailgate party is rendered glamorous in true Santa Fe style right in the parking lot. Bring your own caviar and Brie, make reservations for the buffet dinner and lecture ($45) or a picnic dinner ($30), or have your own private caterer – several customize the menu to the opera's theme – pour the champagne. Prelude Talks, free to ticket holders, are offered in Stieren Orchestra Hall one hour and two hours before curtain to accommodate various dining schedules. Shuttles run to and from the event for $16 from Santa Fe and $30 from Albuquerque; reserve through the opera box office.

While the 2128 seats come equipped with translations in English and Spanish on the back of the seat in front of you, the 106 patrons in standing room are on their own. Youth Night at the Opera (one adult and two children $32, two adults and three children

$56, each additional child $8) offers families a chance to watch dress rehearsals a few nights each summer – one precedes the run of each of the season's operas – with brief talks aimed at audience members ages six to 22. Backstage tours (adult/child $5/free; 1pm Monday to Saturday June to August) offer opportunities to poke around the sets, costume and storage areas.

Santa Fe Chamber Music Festival (☎ 982-1890; www.sfcmf.org; tickets $16-54, students $10; ☯ Jul-Aug) This big cultural event fills elegant venues like the Lensic and the stunning St Francis Auditorium with Brahms, Mozart and other classic masters. It's not just world-class acts like violinist Pinchas Zukerman and pianist Yuja Wang defining the season; top-notch jazz, world music and New Music virtuosos round out the menu, also available for lunch during popular weekly noon performances and at weekly youth concerts aimed at five- to 12-year-olds.

Maria Benitez Teatro Flamenco (☎ 982-1237; www.mariabenitez.com; tickets $28-50; ☯ 8:30pm Wed-Mon) One of the most revered flamenco artists in North America, Maria Benitez stopped performing in 2004 but still directs this outstanding troupe of protégées. She occasionally joins for a solo. These intensely focused and festively garbed performers have earned every accolade for their impressive Spanish dance and perform June through September at the Lodge (Map p62; ☎ 992-5800; 750 N St Francis Dr).

GAY & LESBIAN SANTA FE

Visitors familiar with Santa Fe's reputation as one of the most gay- and lesbian-friendly US destinations might be surprised to find that there are no real gay clubs and no gay neighborhood – not much at all to serve the high proportion of gay and lesbian residents, who by some estimations make up 25% of the city's population. But there's simply no reason to segregate.

'Santa Fe is very open, very accepting – the best thing is that you can just come here and be yourself,' explains Inn of the Turquoise Bear (p97) co-owner Ralph Bolton. 'There's no gay area because nothing's gay, and nothing's straight.'

There is a fabulous parade, the **Gay/Lesbian/Bisexual/Transgender Pride on the Plaza** (p91). Sometimes clubs like Swig (opposite) are labeled gay, though in reality they cater to people of every taste. The tourist board has never even bothered to market Santa Fe to gays and lesbians for a reason – they just don't think about it. Perhaps this is why Santa Fe is home to Rainbow Vision, one of the nation's most exciting assisted living/retirement communities for 'graying gays.'

Long before Witter Bynner and domestic partner Robert Hunt were hosting foreign dignitaries and movie stars at their opulent bashes, Santa Fe was a place where folks from the surrounding communities could come to be themselves; something that's even truer today. What all this adds up to is an absolutely normal vacation – your visit will be much like anyone else's. And, depending on where you're from, that might be the biggest attraction of all.

LANNAN FOUNDATION – AN OASIS

It's tough to imagine the world without the Lannan Foundation, and it's really tough to imagine Santa Fe without this progressive group sponsoring the annual Readings & Conversations (below), an excellent series for thirsty arts devotees in the desert. Established in 1960 and located in Santa Fe since 1997, this family foundation awards hundreds of thousands of dollars in grants annually to writers and artists challenging the historical status quo in favor of a more just and more diverse future.

Devoted to 'cultural freedom, diversity and creativity,' Lannan supports an impressive roster of contemporary artists and writers as well as 'inspired Native activists in rural indigenous communities.' And when they say support, they really mean support. For example, Dr Cornel West, the brilliant, forthright, hard-charging, world-renowned Princeton philosopher and African American Studies professor, received $350,000 as winner of Lannan's 2005 Prize for Cultural Freedom.

Don't worry that you've been left out, though. Lannan has a gift for you, too: hundreds of free audio downloads, dialogues from Readings & Conversations and other public events are available on the foundation's website (www.lannan.org). Listen to Edwidge Danticat, Leslie Marmon Silko, Noam Chomsky and the late avant-garde writer Gilbert Sorrentino, winner (just before his death in 2006) of Lannan's Lifetime Achievement Award.

Can't get enough flamenco? El Farol (p101) stages performances on some Wednesdays, while El Mesón (p99) has flamenco on the first Saturday of each month.

Santa Fe Desert Chorale (☎ 988-2282, 800-244-4011; www.desertchorale.org; tickets $15-50, some free events) Twenty lauded professional singers from around the country come together in July, August and the winter holidays to perform everything from Gregorian chants and gospel to Renaissance madrigals and modern love songs at venues like St Francis Cathedral and Loretto Chapel.

Santa Fe Symphony & Chorus (☎ 983-3530, 800-480-1319; www.sf-symphony.org; tickets $15-55) From September to May, a number of top musicians heat up venues like the Lensic with classical performances.

VENUES

Lensic Performing Arts Center (Map pp64-5; ☎ 988-1234; www.lensic.com; 211 W San Francisco St) This 1931 Moorish-revival movie house is an intimate 850-seat venue. It hosts the New Mexico Jazz Festival in July, the Santa Fe Chamber Music Festival and the Santa Fe Symphony, as well as lectures, theatre and dance.

Lannan Readings & Conversations (☎ 986-8160; www.lannan.org; adult/student $6/3) These staged readings, which tend to focus on cultural and progressive issues, by local and internationally renowned poets and authors take place on various Wednesday evenings throughout the year.

Site Santa Fe (Map pp64-5; ☎ 989-1199; www.sitesantafe.org; 1606 Paseo de Peralta; adult/student $8/4, free tours 6pm Fri & 2pm Sat & Sun; ☼ 10am-5pm Wed-Thu & Sat, 10am-7pm Fri, noon-5pm Sun) This nonprofit contemporary arts organization housed in a dramatic, minimalist space hosts a heralded annual International Biennial (July to December) featuring painting, photography, performance art, soundscapes, video and sculpture. It also welcomes innovative and experimental artists for lectures, performances and exhibits throughout the year; see also p83.

Center for Contemporary Arts (CCA; Map p62; ☎ 982-1338; www.ccasantafe.org; 1050 Old Pecos Trail; adult/child $8/5) CCA screens independent and artsy films and hosts annual African, gay and lesbian, and Native American film festivals. Weekends bring art openings and live performances.

Santa Fe Playhouse (Map p62; ☎ 988-4262; www.santafeplayhouse.org; 142 E DeVargas St; tickets $8-20; ☼ 8pm Thu-Sat, 2pm Sun) Local actors have been putting on plays, including the annual *Fiesta Melodrama* (in late August with audience participation!), in this historic adobe since 1922. Sunday matinees are 'pay what you wish.' The theater also hosts several other troupes, including the Southwest Children's Theatre (www.southwestchildrenstheatre.com; adult/child $10/5) featuring daytime plays for and by kids (plus a few childlike adults).

James A Little Theatre (Map p62; ☎ 827-6760; 1060 Cerrillos Rd) At the New Mexico School for the

Deaf, this unpretentious venue hosts community arts performances as well as the Santa Fe Institute's Public Lecture Series (☎ 984-8800; www.santafe.edu; admission free). Your neurons will fire faster listening to internationally prominent scientists discuss mass extinctions, evolution, natural disasters and genetically modified foods.

Armory for the Arts (Map p62; ☎ 984-1370; http://sfperformingarts.org/armory-theater.html; 1050 Old Pecos Trail; tickets $7-20) Primarily a place where community players and local teens stage favorites like *Fame,* this spot also hosts much bigger events. Theater Grottesco (☎ 474-8400; www.theatergrottesco.org; tickets $5-20), a highly recommended avant-garde troupe, performs here and nationwide.

Cinemas

Santa Fe is awash in art flicks, foreign films and indie offerings, though films here open a bit later than in major cities.

Santa Fe Film Center at Cinemacafé (Map p62; ☎ 988-7414; www.santafefilmfestival.com; 1616 St Michael's Dr; adult/student $8/7; ⌚ Tue-Sun) Home of the annual December Santa Fe Film Festival, this art house is known for the Tuesday-night New Mexico Showcase and Thursday-night gay and lesbian films. The best of independent cinema is screened the rest of the week.

Screen (Map p62; ☎ 473-6494; www.thescreen .csf.edu; 1600 St Michael's Dr; adult/child under 12/student $8.50/6.50/7) Only challenging and artsy independent films are shown at this small College of Santa Fe theater.

The Center for Contemporary Arts (opposite) also shows independent and artsy films. Conveniently located at DeVargas Center (p112), **UA DeVargas 6** (Map p62; ☎ 988-2775; 562 N Guadalupe St; adult/child/student $8.50/6/7.50, matinee $6.50) shows mainstream movies and a few artsy offerings. **UA North 6** (☎ 471-3377; 4250 Cerrillos Rd) and **UA South 6** (☎ 471-6066; 4250 Cerrillos Rd) – on the north and south sides of Santa Fe Place (p112) – screen a similar cinematic selection.

SHOPPING

Many venues are gallery-and-shop combos. Regardless of whether you can afford the wares – the $225,000 Native American artifact, the $30,000 painting or even the $4500 concho belt – you're welcome to browse, learning a lot in the process. The focus is mainly art, from Native American jewelry to wild contemporary paintings in this, one of the top three markets in the USA (after New York City and Los Angeles in terms of total annual sales).

The most famous strip of galleries lies on Canyon Rd (p70), and downtown is packed with fine art as well. The two biggest shopping extravaganzas are the juried shows of Spanish Market (p91) and Indian Market (p91), but the award-winning artisans – many of them driving buses and waiting tables, lest you think their pieces are overpriced – also exhibit their art in galleries throughout the year.

Contemporary & Fine Art

With far bigger budgets than many museums, collectors have helped concentrate some of the world's finest art into Santa Fe's strollable adobes. Gallery owners know they won't make much money off the casually clad tourists – they send photos of their wares directly to serious investors – so don't worry about a hard sell. Top galleries are more like storage depots, or advertising, and a public service for the rest of us. Wander the streets, checking out galleries with street appeal. Or plot your attack by picking up free copies of *The* magazine, a monthly black-and-white newsprint magazine for the arts, and the *Collectors Guide* with full color photos.

Chiaroscuro (Map p70; ☎ 992-1100; www.chiaro scurosantafe.com; 558 Canyon Rd) This contemporary art and photography gallery is all the rage with its new large location and new works by Udo Noger, devotee of light and translucence. Dealers balance this airy work with Magdalena Abakanowicz's sculptures in bronze, iron and stainless steel, and Jun Kaneko's modern takes on Japan's traditional art of ceramics.

Gerald Peters Gallery (Map p70; ☎ 954-5700; www.gpgallery.com; 1011 Paseo de Peralta) Santa Fe's preeminent restaurant and real-estate tycoon, Gerald Peters began dealing art in college and parlayed his hobby (helping artsy friends survive) into an empire: La Casa Sena and Blue Corn Café are just a few of his properties. And this gallery, two blocks from Canyon Rd, carries a collection of fine art that few museums can touch, with all the Southwest masters: Nicolai Fechin, Charles Russell, Edward Borein, Woody

Gwyn and many, many more. The back room has treasures the Museum of Fine Arts can't even afford, so check it out.

Andrew Smith Gallery (Map pp64-5; ☎ 984-1234; www.andrewsmithgallery.com; 203 W San Francisco St) There are few finer photography galleries in the country. That's right, in the country. Walking through these doors is like walking into a time capsule of the most transcendent and illuminating gelatin-silver and platinum printers who have ever lived. Contemporary photographers are not slighted, though, in favor of dead (er…classical) ones.

Nedra Matteucci Galleries (Map p70; ☎ 982-4631; www.matteucci.com; 1075 Paseo de Peralta) The Taos Society is on display at this top gallery, which shows the best work of Joseph Henry Sharp, Ernest Blumenschein and the rest of the gang. Don't miss the beautiful garden out back, which has monumental sculptures in stone and bronze, including work by *Vietnam Women's Memorial* designer Glenna Goodacre.

Shidoni (Map p116; ☎ 988-8001; www.shidoni.com; 1510 Bishops Lodge Rd; ☺ 10am-sunset Mon-Sat) One of Santa Fe's true wonders, these two enormous gardens are alive with figurative and abstract sculptures – some kinetic, some colorful, and all awe-inspiring – in every medium. A foundry demonstrates the art of pouring bronze four times on Saturday.

Tesuque Glassworks (Map p116; ☎ 988-2165) Next door to Shidoni; has open studios where you can watch artisans blowing glass – magic.

Native American Art

Several galleries specializing in Native arts are listed on p70. For jewelry, the top spot fronts the Palace of the Governors (p68). These following galleries, though, feature fine offerings you won't find anywhere else:

Shush Yaz Trading Company (Map p70; ☎ 992-0441; www.shushyaz.com; 1048 Paseo de Peralta) If you can't get to Gallup (p216), come here for fine silver and turquoise jewelry. Top artists include sculptor Cliff Fragua, painter Marvin Toddy and many tribal basket weavers. À la the PBS TV show *Antiques Roadshow*, gallery experts are also willing to examine old Indian blankets, turquoise jewelry or other artifacts you bring from home.

Robert Nichols Gallery (Map p70; ☎ 982-2145; www.robertnicholsgallery.com; 419 Canyon Rd) Contemporary Native American ceramicists with a serious sense of humor meld old-school techniques with modern sensibilities: Bruce Gilbert's languid pots, Kathleen Nez' interpretations of classic pottery designs and Diego Romero's unique combination of Liechtenstein-style cartoon irony with hand-built pueblo pottery are just some of the appealing offerings.

Morning Star Gallery (Map p70; ☎ 982-8187; www.morningstargallery.com; 513 Canyon Rd) Of all the Canyon Rd shops dealing Indian antiquities, this remains the best: weavings, jewelry, beadwork, kachina dolls and even a few original ledger drawings are just some of the stars at this stunning gallery, which specializes in pre-WWII Plains Indian ephemera. Some artifacts here are finer than those in most museums – like the 1775 Powhoge ceramic storage jar that sold for $225,000 and the 1860 Nez Perce war shirt that went for $220,000.

Clothes

That elegant if sometimes overwrought Santa Fe style doesn't come cheap – unless you're willing to buy used.

Back at the Ranch (Map pp64-5; ☎ 989-8110; www.backattheranch.com; 209 E Marcy) You'll get a kick out of high-style boots that go for up to $4000 – definitely more art than craft. That's when that pair of basic black ones ($895) starts seeming like a bargain.

James Reid Ltd (Map pp64-5; ☎ 988-1147; www.jrltd.com; 114 E Palace Ave) Maybe that $4500 concho belt really does make your waist look thinner? This renowned workshop offers Western and contemporary belts, cufflinks and bolo ties.

Montecristi (Map pp64-5; ☎ 983-9598; www.montecristihats.com; 322 McKenzie St) The classic Santa Fean hat is a steal at $550 but maybe you're more of a Trail Boss, a bad boy/bad girl hat for $1200. But you're not really outfitted until you've chosen just the right sterling-silver concho hatband (starting at $125).

Nathalie (Map p70; ☎ 992-1440; www.nathaliesantafe.com; 503 Canyon Rd) Come here for the finest cowboy and cowgirl gear, including gemstone-studded gun holsters, handmade leather, denim couture, and lingerie for that saloon girl with a heart of gold.

Sangre de Cristo Mountain Works (Map pp64-5; ☎ 984-8221; www.sdcmountainworks.com; 328 S Guadalupe St) When you're not wearing cowboy boots, you should be wearing biking or hiking shoes to make an impression in

WEAVING: SPANISH HISTORY AND MODERN ART

James Koehler of Santa Fe

Contemporary weavers like **James Koehler** (www.jameskoehler.com) use weaving like painting to create works that challenge the limits of two dimensions. Starting, for example, with a vibrant red or blue, Koehler adds elements of shadow, texture and motion that take weaving beyond what you thought it could do. Like traditional weavers, Koehler dyes his own wools to get the bold colors he envisions. And like other New Mexico artists, he credits the 'extraordinary landscape' and unique cultures of the state with shaping his work. Uniquely, however, he also acknowledges the 10 years he spent weaving in a Northern New Mexico Benedictine monastery as a force behind his art. 'I continue to be influenced by…certain aspects of the monastic aesthetic – simplicity, purity, seeking and portraying only what is essential,' he says. Perhaps for these reasons, James has a steady stream of apprentices seeking him out. One of them, Susan Matthew, says, 'James taught me that I need two things to be a successful tapestry weaver: consistency and concentration. As it turns out, these are keys to success in the rest of my life too.' Koehler also believes that weaving can teach you about life, if you can listen. The same can be said for looking at his work, if you can see.

You can see his fine, fine work at the **Jane Sauer Thirteen Moons Gallery** (Map p70; ☎ 995-8513; www.thirteenmoonsgallery.com; 652 Canyon Rd; ☼ 10am-5:30pm Mon-Sat, 11am-5pm Sun).

The Ortega and Trujillo families of Chimayó

Thank goodness for modern-day weavers who keep alive the patterns and traditions of the original weavers of 'New Spain,' Spanish settlers in New Mexico in the 1600s and 1700s, now known through the Rio Grande and Chimayó styles. Using wool from local sheep – often from the elegant, silky Churros – and using hand dyeing and spinning methods, today's weavers still incorporate the traditional graphic elements of the six-pointed Vallero star, the Tree of Life and serrated Saltillo squares.

Chimayó (p126) is a center of Hispanic weaving in the state, anchored by the Ortega family, whose members have been weaving in New Mexico for nine generations, and the Trujillo family, weaving in New Mexico since 1765. Their shops (Ortega's Weaving Shop, p126, and Centinela Traditional Arts, p126) offer an inspiring look at authentic techniques and styles combined with a dazzling modern aesthetic.

Bring your wallet, since a hand-woven, traditional Chimayó coat runs just over $500, a blanket anywhere from $10 to $525, a pillow about $80 and a small wall hanging perhaps $25, while a large one can easily cost $2000. Remember, too, that these pieces of art are investments to last a lifetime – this hardy wool doesn't easily wear out. Perhaps it'll even be handed down nine generations.

Santa Fe. Shop here for anything high-end outdoorsy – you know, a GPS unit, Gore-Tex and fleece.

Dust in the Wind (Map pp64-5; ☎ 986-1155; 131 E Palace Ave) Taking care of fashionable locals *and* trendy tourists, this boutique stocks the bright, the bold and the unique.

Cowboy Legends (Map pp64-5; ☎ 989-1554; www .cowboylegendsofsantafe.com; 227 Don Gaspar Rd) Vintage Western wear, including lots of broken-in boots for cowgirls as well, make this a must for the rhinestone cowperson on a budget.

Double Take at the Ranch (Map pp64-5; ☎ 820-7775; 321 S Guadalupe St) Vintage cowboy shirts, conversation-piece jewelry and other funky finds come secondhand but first-class.

Gifts

Five & Dime General Store (Map pp64-5; ☎ 992-1800; 58 E San Francisco St) Not just a convenient spot for snow globes, this souvenir shop also sells Southwest trinkets, postcards, T-shirts and, yes, old-fashioned Frito pies ($4) – hearty red chili and shredded cheese poured over corn chips still in the bag.

Jackalope (Map p62; ☎ 471-8539; www.jackalope santafe.com; 2820 Cerrillos Rd) Essential pieces of Southwest decor can be yours for a song. Start with a cow skull like Georgia O'Keeffe made famous, snap up a kiva ladder, add some colorful pottery and you'll be set. Don't leave without watching authentic prairie dogs frolic in their piñon enclosure.

Chavez Fine Jewelers (Map pp64-5; ☎ 988-8009; 171 Paseo de Peralta) Expert jewelers at this independent, family-owned store at DeVargas Center can craft the piece of your dreams in precious metals and gemstones.

Garcia Street Books (Map p70; ☎ 986-0151; www .garciastreetbooks.com; 376 Garcia St) Scavengers are rewarded with excellent bargains as well as the town's best selection of art books, including such rarities as a deluxe limited edition of Elias Rivera's paintings ($4200).

Artisan Santa Fe (Map p62; ☎ 954-4179; www .artisan-santafe.com; 2601 Cerrillos Rd) Since this art-supply shop's selection of oils, pastels and watercolors is good enough for the world-class artists of Santa Fe, it's probably good enough for you – buy yourself a present.

Nambé Foundry Store (W San Francisco St Map pp64-5; ☎ 988-3574; www.nambe.com; 104 W San Francisco St; Paseo de Peralta Map p70; ☎ 988-5528; 924 Paseo de Peralta) Gleaming and elegant, Nambé's signature sand-cast, mysterious-metal-alloy tableware, vases, jewelry and other lifestyle accoutrements have been winning design awards since 1951. This deliciously heavy stuff is the consummate commitment ceremony present.

Furnishings

Fans of Pueblo Revival architecture and Santa Fe style come here to snatch up home furnishings not found anywhere else. It's worth a look even if you're not having the manse redecorated. What, don't know how to get that new 200-year-old front door or those peeling pillars home? Details, details. Most stores will ship your treasures anywhere in the world.

Rainbow Gate (Map pp64-5; ☎ 983-8892; www .rainbowgate.com; 310 Johnson St) One-of-a-kind ceramic dinnerware and handmade tiles feature all the colors of the New Mexico sky – from soft pastel sunrise through midday cerulean blue to fiery sunset oranges, pinks and purples. Color and texture share the space with fruits, fish, horses and birds on too many lyrical tiles to count.

La Puerta, Inc (Map p62; ☎ 984-8164; www .lapuertaoriginals.com; 4523 State Rd, Hwy 14) Master mill workers and woodworkers welcome observers at this 4-acre architectural salvage yard. An on-site design center demonstrates ways to use these antiques – doors, windows, decorative trim – from 14 countries as rustic home furnishings.

Packard's on the Plaza (Map pp64-5; ☎ 983-9241; www.packards-santafe.com; 61 Old Santa Fe Trail) This combination gallery and store proffers exquisite contemporary and historic Native American arts and crafts, including Navajo rugs, Pueblo weavings and beautiful old pottery.

Packard's West (Map pp64-5; ☎ 986-6089; 125 W San Francisco St) Offers more of the same.

Markets & Malls

If you tire of traipsing along beautiful, historic, adobe-lined streets, all the wonders of the modern mall – and a few notable exceptions – await.

Tesuque Flea Market (Map p116; ☎ 670-2599; www.tesuquepuebloflreamarket.com; US 84/285; ◯ 8am-5pm Fri-Sun Mar-Dec) There aren't many fleas at this tony outdoor market a few minutes north of Santa Fe at Tesuque Pueblo. But high-quality rugs, jewelry, art and clothing definitely cost significantly less than in town. Just don't expect to score an old microwave for $5; it's not that kind of place.

Plaza Mercado (Map pp64-5; 112 W San Francisco St) Found just steps from the plaza, this swish spot is packed with art galleries, restaurants, antique stores, Santa Fe–style clothing and the famous Santa Fe School of Cooking (p58).

DeVargas Center (Map pp64-5; ☎ 982-2655; www .devargascenter.com; 564 N Guadalupe St) The most useful mall in town has a supermarket, the DeVargas 6 movie theater (p109), a post office and a slew of practical stores.

Santa Fe Place (Map p62; ☎ 473-4253; www.shop santafeplace.com; 4250 Cerrillos Rd) Surrounded by family-style restaurant chains and anchored by four department stores, this 570,000-sq-ft mall with 80-plus shops could be anywhere – except for that adobe color.

Santa Fe Outlets (Map p116; ☎ 474-4000; www .santafeoutlets.com; 8380 Cerrillos Rd) Vacations generally don't require corporate wear, but in planning for the return back home, duck into Jones New York, London Fog, Coach and several others of that ilk.

GETTING THERE & AWAY
Air

The tiny **Santa Fe Municipal Airport** (SAF; ☎ 955-2908; Airport Rd near NM 599), which is primarily a landing strip for private planes, is served only by **Great Lakes Aviation** (☎ 474-5300, 800-554-5111; www.greatlakesav.com), which offers four flights a day to Denver ($336 to $645 round-trip).

Albuquerque International Sunport (☎ 244-7700; www.cabq.gov/airport; 2200 Sunport Blvd), the region's major commercial hub, offers shuttles between the Sunport and Santa Fe several times daily; see the Transport chapter (p237) for more information.

Bus

Greyhound (Map p62; ☎ 471-0008; www.greyhound .com; 858 St Michael's Dr; ☒ 7-10am, 12:30-3:30pm & 7:30-8:30pm Mon-Fri, from 9am Sat & Sun) runs three buses daily to Albuquerque ($15) – some stopping at the Sunport – Denver ($78) and Los Angeles ($78). There are two buses daily to Taos ($17) and El Paso ($28 to $66). The Santa Fe Trails (right) bus 5 runs nearby.

Faust Transportation (☎ 758-3410, 888-830-3410; www.newmexiconet.com/trans/faust/faust.html; ☒ 7am-9pm) also runs between Santa Fe and the Albuquerque Sunport ($20), Taos ($40 to $45), Taos Ski Valley ($50), Angel Fire ($55) and Red River ($60). It's a favorite of hikers and bikers who need drop-off service; reservations required.

Car & Motorcycle

Santa Fe is about an hour from Albuquerque on I-25, which also connects the city to El Paso, Texas; and Denver, Colorado. There are two other routes between Santa Fe and Albuquerque: via the Turquoise Trail, which circumvents Sandia Crest from the east for a 1½-hour trip; or the much longer Jemez Scenic Byway, which takes you via Jemez Springs, Bandelier and Los Alamos – definitely the scenic route.

St Francis Rd becomes US 285/84 north of town, connecting Santa Fe to Los Alamos and Española, which serves as the hub for roads to Abiquiú, Ojo Caliente and the High and Low Roads to Taos. The Low Road is the fastest, taking about 1½ hours; the High Road will take at least three hours.

Train

Lamy Amtrak Station (☎ 466-4511, 800-872-7245; ☒ 9am-5pm), 18 miles southeast of Santa Fe, is the closest stop for the *Southwest Chief*, which runs between Chicago and Los Angeles daily. **Lamy Shuttle** (☎ 982-8829; ticket $16) runs between Santa Fe and Lamy with prior reservations.

GETTING AROUND
To/From the Airport

Santa Fe Trails (below) runs bus 1 between Santa Fe Municipal Airport (SAF) and the plaza every half hour.

Roadrunner Shuttle (☎ 424-3367; one way/round-trip $15/26) meets every incoming flight to SAF.

Sandia Shuttle Express (☎ 474-5696, 888-775-5696; www.sandiashuttle.com; one way/round-trip $25/45; ☒ 7am-9pm) offers service from the plaza and Santa Fe hotels (with confirmed reservations) 13 times daily to the Sunport and the University of New Mexico area.

Santa Fe Shuttle (☎ 243-2300, 888-833-2300; one way/round-trip $21/38, children $11/11; ☒ 8am-8pm) provides eight trips a day service to and from the Sunport. Reservations recommended.

Bicycle

Santa Fe is relatively flat – perfect for two-wheeling around or exploring the myriad trails. A couple of caveats: altitude and heat conspire to fell unprepared newbies. Drink plenty of water and don't overexert yourself. Bike lanes are rare and drivers notoriously distracted. Be careful out there!

Santa Fe city ordinances states that bicycles must have a license plate, an attached bell or horn and a front-mounted lamp when riding at night. Cyclists must follow the same traffic laws as automobile drivers. To find out about getting a license, good for one year, call ☎ 955-5751.

In addition to renting bikes ($9/hour shopping bike, $45/day mountain bike) and trailers for the kids, **Mellow Velo Bicycles** (Map pp64-5; ☎ 982-8986; www.sunmountain bikeco.com; 102 E Water St; ☒ 9:30am-5pm Mon-Sat, 10am-4pm Sun) will drop you off at trailheads throughout Northern New Mexico (up to $50) and can organize bicycle tours with advance notice.

Bus

Santa Fe Trails (Map pp64-5; ☎ 955-2001; www .santafenm.gov; cnr Sheridan St & Palace Ave; one way adult/child $1/0.50, day pass $2/1; ☒ 6am-11pm Mon-Fri, 8am-8pm Sat, 10am-7:45pm Sun with limited service) offers nine routes covering the city, with downloadable (and easy to find around town) maps, bicycle racks and access for wheelchair users. There's also curb-to-curb, on-demand transit for folks with ADA-certified disabilities and anyone older than 60.

However, buses run only from every 15 minutes to every hour, depending on the route. Monthly passes are affordable (adult/child $20/10), and kids under five ride free. The M-Line connects the plaza and Museum Hill via the city's historic districts.

Car

Though the winding streets close to downtown can be confusing, most of Santa Fe is fairly car friendly. One-way and unpaved roads are common in historic neighborhoods, particularly those east of the plaza. Note that using a cell phone while driving will get you a $60 ticket within city limits.

There are several rental-car places, most of which are closed Saturday afternoons and Sundays:

Avis (☎ 471-5892, 800-230-4898; www.avis.com; Airport Rd)

Budget Rent-a-Car (Map p62; ☎ 984-1596, 800-527-0700; www.budget.com; 1946 Cerrillos Rd)

Enterprise Rent-a-Car (☎ 986-1414, 800-736-8222; www.enterprise.com; 1611 St Michael's Drive) There's also a convenient, part-time location at the Hilton Hotel (☎ 989-8859; 100 Sandoval St).

Hertz (☎ 471-7189, 800-654-3131; www.hertz.com; Airport Rd) In addition to the airport location, there's another Hertz at the Hilton (Map pp64-5; ☎ 982-1844; 100 Sandoval St).

PARKING

Parking is a nightmare during high season, with a paltry 1100 spaces available in overpacked public lots around the plaza, running as high as $6 an hour. A better plan is to park several blocks from the plaza and hoof it. Parking tickets run $15 for an expired meter, $35 for parking in a loading zone and $100 for parking in a handicap spot. Folks with handicap placards, however, can park for free. You have 15 days to pay your tickets, after which fees double and a warrant is issued.

Walking

Walking is the quickest, easiest way to get around downtown. But, though the city was designed for pedestrians, and city officials have flirted with the idea of making the plaza pedestrian-only, drivers still dominate the roads. Santa Fe has one of the highest rates of traffic deaths in the country, and outside the main tourist area, a crosswalk does not legally give you the right of way. Make eye contact with drivers and yield to cars.

Taxi

Capitol City Cab (☎ 438-0000), Santa Fe's only cab company, operates around the clock. Flagfall is $2.50 (50¢ extra for every minute kept waiting), $1.50 for each extra person and $2.25 per mile.

AROUND SANTA FE

Leaving opulent art galleries and modern restaurants behind, a traveler departing Santa Fe has many choices. Many Americans have heart-breaking amnesia about this country's origins and its people. Thanks to the generous descendents of New Mexico's Indian pueblos, visitors who have forgotten – or never knew – can begin to remember, and new-found memories will be followed closely by respect.

Visit small, private villages where Spanish is preferred over English and the Catholic faith runs strong. Refugees from urban life, and those who never bothered, fill artists' hamlets and rustic towns whose main diversions are renovating old houses and soaking in hot springs. In one high-tech, futuristic hamlet lies the birthplace of the atom bomb, a massive laboratory complex pregnant with possibilities and possibly with the end of them all.

It's the ethereal landscape of mesas and canyons, however – floating yet anchored against the world's bluest sky – that has been the enduring attraction here since nearly the beginning of time.

NEARBY PUEBLOS

A quick glance at any map reveals the region north of Santa Fe to be the heart of Pueblo Indian lands. The **Eight Northern Pueblos** (which come together as the Eight Northern Indian Pueblos Council, based at Ohkay Owingeh – formerly San Juan Pueblo) all lie within 40 miles of Española, some of which is actually on long-term lease from Santa Clara Pueblo. The eight tribes are connected linguistically – the six listed below speak Tewa, while Taos (p156) and Picuris (p128) use somewhat similar Tiwa. Together they publish the excellent free *Eight Northern Indian Pueblos Visitors Guide*, available at any area visitors center.

Each pueblo is independently governed and unique. From isolated Picuris Pueblo's

VISITING NATIVE AMERICAN PUEBLOS

Imagine, for a minute, that your neighborhood is a rare example of a culture all but destroyed and now globally respected for its art, architecture and spirituality. Your suburban split-level ranch home, your grandmother's souvenir spoon collection and your macaroni-and-cheese dinner are all objects of mystery and intrigue.

Take it further. Packs of sunburned tourists parade across your lawn, asking what that plastic Santa Claus on your roof is all about, peeking in your windows and taking pictures of your kids. Welcome to life at the pueblo in high tourist season.

Pueblo Indians have opened up their world to visitors in a way that not many people would be willing to do – it's sort of the opposite of the gated-community mentality. You're a welcome guest, but don't wear it out. Courtesy, respect and a little knowledge go a long way, as does keeping your kids off the walls. Here are a few tips on how not to be a touron:

- You must buy a permit, usually at the Governor's Office, to take photos, sketch pictures or use a video camera, all of which are generally forbidden inside churches and on feast days – always ask before you photograph a person.

- Remember that these are sovereign nations and usually forbid alcohol. Give tribal police the same respect you would any other law enforcement officer (technically, they have broader powers), and obey all posted driving and parking rules.

- Never ever go into kivas or cemeteries, and don't wander into churches or people's homes uninvited.

- Don't pester folks about their religion and traditions.

- A ceremonial dance is a prayer, not a performance: turn off your cell phone and remain silent and respectful throughout, give the dancers and singers their space and don't clap afterward, which is about as appropriate as applause after Mass.

- Most businesses, including gas stations and galleries, are closed on that pueblo's feast days.

- If a guided tour is available, take it. If not, stick to obviously public areas and businesses.

- Pueblos can and will close with just a few hours' notice for religious purposes, and even calling ahead can't guarantee access.

magnificent scenery and Nambé's outdoor recreation to Pojoaque's casino and strip, the tribes have developed their resources and tourist infrastructure quite differently.

Many operate casinos, usually several miles from the main pueblo, which are generally open 8am to 4am Monday through Thursday, then stay open 24 hours through Sunday. Slots, craps, poker, shows and endless buffet tables are the big draws, but unlike casinos in Las Vegas, Nevada, there's usually a gift shop selling high-quality pottery and other work by local artisans.

The pueblos themselves aren't really tourist attractions – they're towns, with schools, modern houses, post offices and whatnot. But they are a must-see, as you'll learn (or unlearn) a lot about Native culture. And area artists in particular appreciate the traffic. Just respect the residents as they go about their day.

Begin by purchasing the required camera permits from either the visitors center, if there is one, or the Governor's Office, where staff may be able to point you toward galleries, guided tours and other areas of interest if they aren't too busy. **Ancient Storyteller Tours** (☎ 747-6710; www.ancientstorytellers .com; PO Box 1979, Española, NM 87532) provides customized tours of the pueblos. The Northern Indian Pueblos five-day tour includes a traditional meal and a pottery demonstration. The five-day Navajoland tour includes storytelling, traditional dancing and cooking, and sweat lodges.

Tesuque Pueblo
☎ 505 / pop 450 / elev 6000ft

A temporary encampment since at least AD 700, Tesuque Pueblo was probably founded as a permanent village in the early 1200s by settlers from abandoned Chaco Canyon. By 1541 the city-state comprised six towns and

SANTA FE

SANTA FE & AROUND

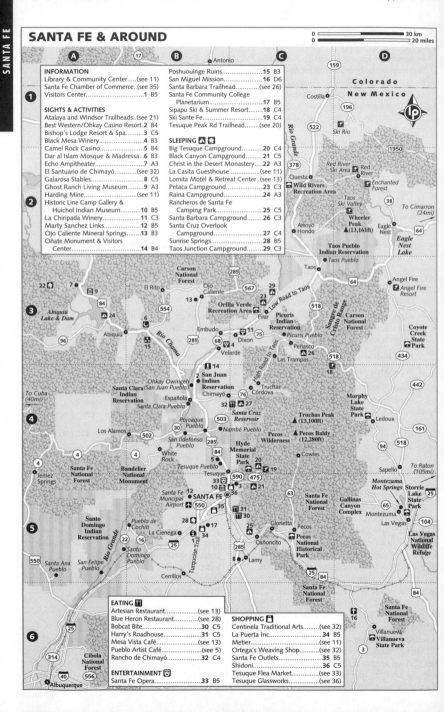

0 ____ 30 km
0 ____ 20 miles

INFORMATION
Library & Community Center.....(see 11)
Santa Fe Chamber of Commerce..(see 35)
Visitors Center.................................1 B5

SIGHTS & ACTIVITIES
Atalaya and Windsor Trailheads..(see 21)
Best Western/Ohkay Casino Resort.2 B4
Bishop's Lodge Resort & Spa.........3 C5
Black Mesa Winery........................4 B3
Camel Rock Casino.......................5 B4
Dar al Islam Mosque & Madressa..6 B3
Echo Ampitheatre..........................7 A3
El Santuario de Chimayó............(see 32)
Galarosa Stables............................8 C5
Ghost Ranch Living Museum.........9 A3
Harding Mine.............................(see 11)
Historic Line Camp Gallery &
  Huichol Indian Museum...........10 B5
La Chiripada Winery....................11 C3
Marty Sanchez Links....................12 B5
Ojo Caliente Mineral Springs.......13 B3
Oñate Monument & Visitors
  Center.....................................14 B4

Poshuouinge Ruins.......................15 B3
San Miguel Mission......................16 D6
Santa Barbara Trailhead............(see 26)
Santa Fe Community College
  Planetarium.............................17 B5
Sipapu Ski & Summer Resort.......18 C4
Ski Sante Fe................................19 C4
Tesuque Peak Rd Trailhead........(see 20)

SLEEPING
Big Tesuque Campground............20 C4
Black Canyon Campground..........21 C5
Christ in the Desert Monastery......22 A3
La Casita Guesthouse................(see 11)
Lomita Motel & Retreat Center..(see 13)
Petaca Campground.....................23 C3
Raina Campground......................24 A3
Rancheros de Santa Fe
  Camping Park.........................25 C5
Santa Barbara Campground.........26 C3
Santa Cruz Overlook
  Campground...........................27 C4
Sunrise Springs..........................28 B5
Taos Junction Campground.........29 C3

Colorado
New Mexico

Costilla

159
196
522   Ski Rio
378   Red River
       Ski Area   Red
Questa   River
       Wild Rivers   Enchanted
       Recreation Area   Forest
       Taos
Arroyo   Ski Valley   38   To Cimarron
Hondo   Wheeler   (24mi)
       Taos Pueblo   Peak   Eagle
       Indian Reservation   ▲(13,161ft)   Nest   64
              • Taos Pueblo   Eagle
       Taos   Nest
                    64   Lake

Carson
National   Angel Fire
Forest   Angel Fire
El Rito   Ojo   29   Resort
           Caliente   23
13 •   567   Low Road to Taos
       Orilla Verde   518   Carson
       Recreation Area   National   Coyote
Abiquiú   84   Pilar   Picuris   Forest   Creek
Lake & Dam 554   Indian   State
       24   Reservation   434   Park
96   6   Embudo   • Picuris Pueblo
       Abiquiú 285   11   75
              68   4   Peñasco
       Río Chama   Dixon   26   518
                    Velarde   Las Trampas
       14   18
To Cuba   2 San Juan   High Road to Taos
(40mi)   Indian
       Ohkay Owingeh   Reservation   Truchas   Morphy
       (San Juan Pueblo)   Chimayó   Córdova   Lake   442
Santa Clara   76   State
Indian   Española   Truchas Peak   Park
Reservation   ▲(13,100ft)   • Ledoux
       Santa Clara Pueblo 32   27
              Santa Cruz   ▲ Pecos Baldy   161
       Pojoaque   Reservoir   (12,280ft)
       Pueblo   503   Pecos   94   518
Los Alamos   30   • Nambé Pueblo   Wilderness
       502   San Ildefonso   • Cowles   To Raton
              Pueblo   285   84   (105mi)
       White   Hyde   Montezuma
       Rock   Memorial   Hot Springs   Storrie
Santa Fe   Tesuque Pueblo   State   20   Lake
National   Bandelier   Park   19   Gallinas   State
Forest   National   5   590   475   63   Canyon   Park
Jemez   Monument   Tesuque   33   21   Santa Fe   Complex   104
Springs   4   10   3   National   Montezuma   65
              SANTA FE   36   Forest   Las Vegas
       Santa Fe   12   Las Vegas
       Municipal   35   National
       Airport   550   31   Glorieta   Wildlife
       28   30   Refuge
Santo   Pecos
Domingo   17   25   National
Indian   La Cienega 34   Historical   Santa Fe
Reservation   22   16   285   Cañoncito   Park   National
       Santo   Forest   84
550   Santa Ana   Domingo   Cerrillos   8   • Lamy   25   84
Pueblo   San Felipe   Pueblo
       Pueblo   Santa Fe   Santa Fe
                           National   National
                           Forest   Forest   84
25   16
314   Cibola   Villanueva
       National   Villanueva
       Forest 556   State Park
40   Albuquerque   3

EATING
Artesian Restaurant.................(see 13)
Blue Heron Restaurant.............(see 28)
Bobcat Bite.................................30 C5
Harry's Roadhouse......................31 C5
Mesa Vista Café.......................(see 13)
Pueblo Artist Café....................(see 5)
Rancho de Chimayó....................32 C4

ENTERTAINMENT
Santa Fe Opera...........................33 B5

SHOPPING
Centinela Traditional Arts.........(see 32)
La Puerta Inc..............................34 B5
Metier.......................................(see 11)
Ortega's Weaving Shop............(see 32)
Santa Fe Outlets.........................35 B5
Shidoni......................................36 C5
Tesuque Flea Market................(see 33)
Tesuque Glassworks................(see 36)

welcomed Coronado on his quest for gold. Spanish–Tesuque relations deteriorated, however, as Catholic priests began punishing, with increasing severity, those who continued practicing Native religions.

Shortly before the Pueblo Revolt of 1680, the Spanish captured two Tesuque messengers. Elders, suspecting a security breach, ordered the assassination of a priest, a diversion that successfully convinced Spanish strategists to misdirect their troops. The war was won, but at great cost, in large part because of this extreme tactic. When DeVargas returned in 1692 with promises of peace, residents wisely abandoned their homes for two years.

Like most area tribes, heavy taxes, European diseases, and poverty resulting from lost lands and resources continued to devastate the Tesuque population until WWII. Since then they've been slowly rebuilding their culture and infrastructure.

In addition to famed **Camel Rock**, an odd and aptly named geological formation right off US 84/285, encircled by a short trail, the pueblo operates the Tesuque Flea Market (p112), Camel Rock Suites (p96) and **Camel Rock Casino** (Map p116; ☎ 984-8414, 800-462-2635; www.camelrockcasino.com; US 84/285), a swanky spot featuring the recommended **Pueblo Artist Café** (Map p116; buffet adult/child $9/6; ☺ 7am-9pm Mon-Fri, 7am-10pm Sat, 8am-9pm Sun; Ⓟ ♿ ♨), with a topnotch buffet serving Native and New Mexico foods. There's also an intimate, if not opulent, venue that hosts fun B-list acts like Pat Benatar and Paul Casey with his *Elvis – the Musical*. A **free shuttle** (☺ noon-9pm) runs from the plaza in Santa Fe – just call and it'll pick you up within 30 minutes.

Though a few art studios open for tours in the summer, there's not much to see in the pueblo itself. Visitors are asked to stay in the plaza area, site of the **Church of San Diego**, completed in 2004 after the original 1888 building burned down a few years before. Call the **Governor's Office** (☎ 993-2667; Tesuque Plaza; ☺ 9am-5pm Mon-Fri) for more information.

Pojoaque Pueblo
☎ 505 / pop 350 / elev 7000ft
Pojoaque has been the site of permanent habitation since about AD 500 and was a bustling commercial center of several villages by the time Coronado cruised through. Between the Pueblo Revolt and Reconquista, however, the once-populous tribe was reduced to a handful of families.

That was just the beginning: after resettlement, water shortages and disease, including the smallpox epidemic of 1890, decimated the tribe. In 1915 the pueblo was temporarily abandoned, and in 1933 reinstated with just 40 members and 12,000 acres, making it the smallest in the Eight Northern Indian Pueblos Council (ENIPC).

Since then, however, the tribe has taken full advantage of its location at a crossroads between Santa Fe, Los Alamos and Española to rebuild its former prominence – not to mention political pull. In the late 1990s former Governor Jacob Villareal jumped into traffic and threatened to shut down US 285/84, on Pojoaque land, if the state legislature didn't ratify certain gaming contracts. The contracts were ratified rather quickly.

A business park, buffalo-reintroduction program and **Poeh Cultural Center** (☎ 455-3334; www.poehcenter.com; 78 Cities of Gold Rd; ☺ 8am-4pm Mon-Sat), with a noted arts school for Native Americans, have been joined by a huge strip of tax-free businesses, including a fun **Sports Bar** (☎ 455-3984; Cities of Gold Rd; ☺ 8am-4am Sun-Wed, 24hr Thu-Sat) with video slots and gambling on horse and dog races.

The cultural center houses the **Poeh Museum**, an imposing adobe housing a huge collection of contemporary art and historical artifacts, mainly from the six Tewa speaking tribes. It features frequent arts demonstrations and occasional ceremonial dances.

The **visitors center** (☎ 455-3460; 96 Cities of Gold Rd; ☺ 9am-5pm Mon-Sat, 10am-4pm Sun) has a great selection of pottery, arts and crafts, and flyers and information about **Towa Golf Resort** (☎ 455-9000; www.towagolf.com; green fees $29-50, plus cart fee $15), which has greens known for their great views.

Cities of Gold Casino (☎ 455-3313, 800-455-3313; www.citiesofgold.com; Cities of Gold Rd; r $89) is a huge place with plenty of razzle-dazzle. There's also a free shuttle (☎ 455-4253), running from 8:30am to 10:30pm, to Santa Fe, plus the obligatory buffet and rooms that need remodeling.

Skip the buffet (unless it's seafood Sunday; adult/child $14/10) and cross the highway to **Roadrunner Cafe** (☎ 455-3012; US 284/85; dishes $3-8; ☺ 6am-9pm; Ⓟ ✗ ♿ Ⓥ ♨), beloved by its devoted trucker clientele for enchiladas, stuffed *sopapillas* and big breakfasts.

SANTA FE

The **Governor's Office** (☎ 455-3901; 17746 US 285/84; ☺ 8am-5pm Mon-Fri) has been actively spearheading a cultural revival since 1973, including Tewa-language programs and reviving several dances long unpracticed, including those on the December 12 **Virgen de Guadalupe Feast Day**.

San Ildefonso Pueblo
☎ 505 / pop 650 / elev 6000ft

Founded in the 1300s by settlers who had abandoned Bandelier in the wake of a long-term drought, San Ildefonso is perhaps the easiest and most interesting of the pueblos to explore independently. Black Mesa, a stronghold successfully used during the Reconquista to negotiate for better peace treaty terms with DeVargas, rises resolutely in the distance and is off-limits.

The helpful **visitors center** (☎ 455-3549; NM 502; admission per vehicle $5, photo/video/sketching permits $10/20/25; ☺ 8am-5pm), with a few small displays of tribal art and artifacts, has maps outlining a walking tour through the compact plaza, which features an attractive church and kiva, plus several excellent art studios.

San Ildefonso has been at the forefront of the Native American pottery and arts revival for half a century. The most famous artisan was Maria Martinez; a few pieces of her coveted black-on-black pottery are at the **Maria Poveka Martinez Museum** (admission free; ☺ 8am-4pm Mon-Fri), along with work by other pueblo artists. For a preview, check out former governor and artist John Gonzalez' website: www.sanildefonso.com.

During WWII three-quarters of San Ildefonso land was appropriated for the Manhattan Project (p129). The tribe is currently working with Los Alamos and the Department of Energy (DOE) to preserve historic sites that may be open for tours one day. Visitors are welcome to come to the January 23 **Feast Day** and **corn dances** held throughout the summer. For information not directly related to tourism, contact the **Governor's Office** (☎ 455-2273).

Nambé Pueblo
☎ 505 / pop 600 / elev 6200ft

Just the drive into the Pueblo of Nambé, through dramatically sculpted, multihued sandstone, is fantastic. NM 503, which leaves US 285/84 just north of Pojoaque to head into hills speckled with piñon, makes for a scenic addition to the High Road to Taos.

Perhaps because of the isolated location (or inspirational geology), Nambé has long been a spiritual center for the Tewa-speaking tribes, a distinction that attracted the cruel attentions of Spanish priests intent on conversion by any means. After the Pueblo Revolt and Reconquista wound down, Spanish settlers annexed much of the land.

Nambé's remaining lands, however, have some big attractions; the loveliest are two 20-minute hikes to **Nambé Falls** (day use $5, photo permits $5). The steep upper hike has a photogenic overlook of the falls, while the easier lower hike along the river takes in ancient petroglyphs.

The most popular attraction, however, is **Lake Nambé** (☎ 455-2304; Hwy 101; day use $10; ☺ 6am-8pm Fri-Mon Nov-Mar, 8am-8pm Tue-Thu Apr-Oct), created in 1974 when the US dammed the Rio Nambé, flooding historic ruins but creating an important reservoir that attracts boaters and trout lovers.

The **Governor's Office** (☎ 455-2036; NM 503; photo/video permits $10/20; ☺ 8am-5pm Mon-Fri) is right on the attractive plaza, but the ranger station is better equipped for visitors. The pueblo has several excellent artists who sell from their homes; the most famed Nambé potter is Lonnie Vigil, coauthor of *All That Glitters: The Emergence of Native American Micaceous Art Pottery in Northern New Mexico*, with Duane Anderson.

Public events include the October 4 **San Francisco de Asis Feast Day** and the December 24 **Catholic Mass** and **Buffalo Dance**.

You can **camp** (tent/RV $24/35) in the shady valley at the trailheads, or head up NM 503 to **Santa Cruz Lake Overlook Campground** (Map p116; ☎ 758-8851; NM 503; sites $7; ☺ Apr-Oct), which isn't shady but has a lovely view and some nice trails. Or, continue past Cundiyo to **Santa Cruz Lakeside Campground** (Map p116; ☎ 758-8851; NM 503; sites $9; ☺ Apr-Oct), with lake access and 6 miles of trails.

Santa Clara Pueblo
☎ 505 / pop 2600 / elev 6800ft

The ancestors of this bustling pueblo probably arrived in the area around 1200, along with those of Jemez Pueblo (p192), building a permanent settlement on the shores of the Rio Grande in the 1300s. They had an elaborate agricultural economy and

MARIA MARTINEZ: A RENAISSANCE IN BLACK

The pride of San Ildefonso Pueblo and probably the USA's most famous potter, Maria Antonia Montoya (1887–1980) was born into a time when Native pottery was a dying art, the lovely but labor-intensive ceramics increasingly abandoned for inexpensive, mass-produced cookware. As a child, however, Maria carefully studied the work of her aunts, master potters Martina Montoya and Nicolasa Peña Montoya. She soon became adept at creating smooth and utilitarian vessels, which were then generally traded for food or labor.

In 1909 her husband, Julian Martinez, was hired to help excavate nearby ruins. Archaeologist Dr Edgar Lee Hewitt asked Maria to reproduce some of the effects on found pottery shards there. After much experimentation, she and Julian were able to adapt techniques used in Santa Clara Pueblo's black pottery, creating matte-on-gloss designs that depicted ancient symbols like the *avanyu* (horned water serpent).

The unique pieces won multiple awards at the first Santa Fe Indian Market in 1922. After the Otowi Bridge connected the pueblo to Santa Fe in 1924, folks from all over the country started coming to San Ildefonso to shop, transforming the subsistence-economy pueblo into a vibrant arts center. When her vessels earned accolades at the 1934 Chicago Worlds Fair, Maria became world famous. Today work by Maria and Julian, their son Popovi Da, and other family members can command tens of thousands of dollars.

Maria, by Richard L Spivey, is a lavishly illustrated chronicle of her life and art, and *Maria Montoya Martinez: Master Potter*, by Maria's close friend Elsie Karr Kreischer, tells the ceramicist's story for children.

welcomed the Spanish settlers – at first. Later, one of the heroes of the 1680 Pueblo Revolt, Domingo Naranjo, would hail from Santa Clara. After the Reconquista, the tribe abandoned the pueblo for several years.

Today the tribe is business savvy and operates the Big Rock Casino in Española (p120); the tribe also opened the **Black Mesa Golf Course** (☎ 747-8946; green tees Mon-Thu $77, Fri-Sun $82) a couple of years ago. Its real claim to fame, though, is the pottery – luminous red and black vessels prized by collectors, particularly those of Santa Clara's three major matriarchs: Christina Naranjo, Mary Esther Archuleta and Margaret Tofoya, the last considered the most important pueblo potter after Maria Martinez.

The **Governor's Office** (☎ 753-7330, NM 30; ☻ 8am-4:30pm Mon-Fri) issues photo permits ($5). The sprawling village has a huge number of shops and studios selling the pueblo's renowned pottery, including **Toni Roller's Studio & Gallery** (☎ 753-3003; NM 30; ☻ 10am-5pm Mon-Sat), owned by Margaret Tofoya's daughter, and a 1918 church. Public events include the June 13 **San Antonio Feast Day** and the August 12 **Santa Clara Feast Day**.

The pueblo's famed **Puyé Cliff Dwellings**, a remarkably well-preserved and massive complex of ruins, has been closed indefinitely since the 2000 Cerro Grandé fire.

Check with the Governor's Office to see if a reopening has been scheduled.

Española Transit (p122) has services to the pueblo.

Ohkay Owingeh (formerly San Juan Pueblo)

☎ 505 / pop 6750 / elev 5600ft

Now known as 'Place of the Strong People,' or Ohkay Owingeh, this pueblo probably was founded in the late 1100s by the people who abandoned Chaco Canyon. It has been an important government seat for at least 700 years, possibly representing an unbroken line of pan-pueblo leadership back to Chaco's heyday.

For centuries it has been the only place where a pan-pueblo war could legally be declared, and then only by a Yunque-Owingeh (San Juan native). Most famously, local priest Popé stood here and called for the Pueblo Revolt of 1680 in response to the torture of Indian religious leaders. The Spanish were driven back to El Paso for 12 years before being allowed to return peacefully after agreeing to the pueblos' freedom of religion.

Ohkay Owingeh continues to function as a political center and is the seat of the Eight Northern Indian Pueblos Council. The **Eight Northern Pueblos Council Visitors Center**

SANTA FE

(www.eightnorthernpueblos.com) offers insight into the formation and function of the council and presents various Native arts.

Visitors can tour **Bison Park** and the excellent **Oke Oweenge Crafts Cooperative**, which sells the pueblo's renowned and very collectible carved red pottery, as well as jewelry, handicrafts and pottery from all the northern pueblos. Other attractions include the attractive 1889 **Nuestra Señora de Lourdes chapel** and brick 1913 **San Juan Bautista Church**; most other historic buildings are off-limits, and photography permits must be arranged with the **Governor's Office** (☎ 852-4400; NM 74).

Best Western/Ohkay Casino Resort (Map p116; ☎ 747-1668, 877-829-2865; www.ohkay.com; NM 68; d $70-100; P ⊠ ⬜ ⬛) fulfills all your gambling needs, including spacious rooms to crash in if you can't stay awake all weekend.

The on-site Silver Eagle Lounge serves alcohol and has live music four nights a week, while the **Harvest Cafe** (dishes $1-12, buffet $6-9; ⊠ 6:30am-midnight Sun-Thu, 6:30am-1am Fri & Sat) has a great salad bar and $1 breakfast specials. **Ohkay RV Park** (☎ 753-5067; 2016 N Riverside Dr; campsite/RV $10/21) is conveniently located near **San Juan Lakes** (adult/child $8/5).

Public events include the January **Basket Dance**, the February **Deer Dance**, the June 13 **Corn Dance**, the June 24 **San Juan Feast Day**, the July 8 **Northern Indian Pueblos Arts & Crafts Show**, and a series of Catholic and traditional dances and ceremonies from December 24 to 26.

ESPAÑOLA

☎ 505 / pop 9700 / elev 5578ft

Founded by Don Juan de Oñate in 1598 as the first state capital, Española today is sort of the anti-Santa Fe: for many here it's a hard-scrabble life and the drug overdose rate is the highest in the nation. The setting is stunning, framed by the Jemez Mountains and Truchas Peak, yet tragic – one in five people here live in poverty.

This town is designed for commerce, anchored north and south by two casinos; lodging is inexpensive, restaurants are authentic and adobes are real. It's also home to many proud and optimistic people. Farmers market organizers are purchasing a site with highly coveted water rights where a kids' demonstration garden and friendly gathering spot will water the soul of the community. Town celebrity Monica Lovato, a champion super flyweight boxer highly ranked by the World Boxing Council, brings hope and a great example to kids coming up behind her.

Española is rural, Chicano, all-American life.

Orientation

Española is the all-but-unavoidable gateway to Northern New Mexico. It's at the crossroads of several major highways: NM 30 (Los Alamos Ave) runs southwest to Santa Clara Pueblo, Los Alamos and Bandelier; US 84 (Oñate St) heads northwest to Abiquiú and Ghost Ranch; NM 76

THE ARTISTIC VISION OF MICHAEL NARANJO

Despite being the son of Rose Naranjo, a noted Santa Clara potter, Michael Naranjo wasn't particularly interested in making art as a young man. Besides, there was a war to fight in Vietnam. He went, as so many Native Americans did. And, like so many Americans, the 22-year-old did not come back physically whole: a grenade blinded him and all but destroyed his right hand.

While he was recuperating, a volunteer asked if she could get him anything. He wanted clay. She brought some in, and he began massaging it into forms he'd seen in nature. 'I knew then I could do it,' he told *Veterans Advantage*. 'It was exhilarating.'

When he returned home he told his family that he was moving to Santa Fe to launch a career as an artist. Though worried, they acceded. He learned to survive on his own and developed a sculptural style with clear roots in Native traditions, fluid and elegant forms reminiscent of Santa Clara's finest pottery, all built by hand. He cast- bronze figures danced, prayed and thrived – all without eyes. He was soon recognized as one of New Mexico's finest artists.

His powerful work is now on display at the Museum of Fine Arts in Santa Fe (p68) and the Albuquerque Museum's sculpture garden, as well as in the Vatican, White House and elsewhere. You can appreciate the beauty of his sculptures with your eyes, but close them for a moment and touch the pieces. For it is only through your hands that you will truly understand the artistic vision of Michael Naranjo.

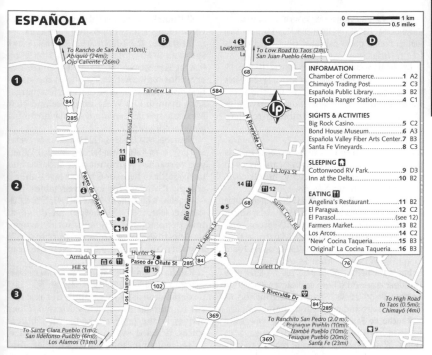

ESPAÑOLA

(Santa Cruz Rd; High Road to Taos) is the back road to Taos through Chimayó and Peñasco; N Riverside Dr/NM 68 heads north out of town as the Low Road to Taos; and S Riverside Dr/US 84/285 heads southeast to Santa Fe.

The city sprawls, with two major settlements located on either side of the Rio Grande, traversed by two bridges (at Oñate St and Santa Clara Bridge Rd). The western, older part of the city has a small historic district and most community services; the east side has more commercial development.

Information

Chamber of Commerce (☎ 753-2831; www.espanola nmchamber.com; 710 Paseo de Oñate; ⏰ 9am-5pm Mon-Fri) Pick up maps and flyers here.

Chimayó Trading Post (☎ 753-9414; Riverside Dr; ⏰ 9am-4pm Mon-Fri) This is on the National Register of Historic Places. It has flyers and maps, and sells pueblo pottery, Navajo rugs, Chimayó weavings and lots more.

Española Public Library (☎ 747-6087; 313 Paseo de Oñate; ⏰ 9am-6pm Mon-Thu, 9am-5pm Fri, 9am-3pm Sat) Free internet access.

Española Ranger Station (☎ 753-7331; 1710 N Riverside Dr; ⏰ 8:30am-4:30pm Mon-Fri) Has information on area trails and campsites.

Rio Grande Sun (www.riograndesun.com) The weekly paper has community events listings.

Sights & Activities

Española's not what you'd call a tourist trap.

An enormous 1880 adobe with Victorian airs, **Bond House Museum** (☎ 747-8535; 706 Bond St; admission by donation) is a newish museum with displays about Española's days as a frontier mercantile community, era antiques and art exhibitions.

Big Rock Casino (☎ 747-0059; 460-A Riverside Dr; ⏰ 8am-4am Mon-Thu, 24hr Fri-Sun) is right downtown, has a decent restaurant and features a **bowling alley** (games $2-4; ⏰ 10am-midnight) to amuse the kids while you gamble their college money.

Española Valley Fiber Arts Center (☎ 747-3577; www.la-tierra.com/evfac; 325 Paseo de Oñate; admission free; ⏰ 9am-4pm Mon-Sat) houses lots of beautiful antique looms and offers classes in weaving, spinning and natural dyes.

Santa Fe Vineyards (☎ 753-8100; www.santafe vineyards.com; US 285; ☯ 10am-5pm Mon-Sat, noon-5pm Sun) makes a good cab and port, and offers free tastings.

Oñate Monument & Visitors Center (Map p116; ☎ 852-4639; www.rioarribanm.com; NM 68; ☯ 8am-5pm Mon-Fri) is north of town: look for the great statue by artist Reynaldo 'Sonny' Rivera of Don Juan de Oñate in full military regalia.

Sleeping

Lodging – with one notable exception – is inexpensive, and hardy souls can go even cheaper at several semisketchy motels clustered in town along NM 68.

Cottonwood RV Park (☎ 231-2334; www.cotton woodrv.com; US 84/285; tent/RV $14/21; P) Just south of town, park your tent or RV here, and enjoy a margarita at nearby Martini'z Restaurant & Lounge (☎ 231-2334, open 10am to 4pm), with dishes from $4 to $11.

Inn at the Delta (☎ 753-9466, 800-995-8599; www .innatthedelta.net; 243 N Paseo de Oñate; r $100-150 incl breakfast; P ✕ ☷ ▯) Stylish, spacious rooms offer local art and adobe-toned ambiance.

Rancho de San Juan (☎ 753-6818; www.rancho desanjuan.com; 34020 US 285; r $275-375, casitas $450; P ✕ ☷ ▯) Casitas are one reason to stay here, then there's the world-class luxury, four-star cuisine, a tip-top wine list and pampered desert solitude. Every creature comfort is provided for, and area tours can be arranged. A cathedral-like sandstone shrine carved into a nearby mesa provides the only reasons to venture off premises.

Ranchito San Pedro (☎ 753-0583; www.janhart .com; SR 581; r $289; P ✕ ☷ ▯) Call for directions to the two cabins at this adobe 'art dude ranch.'

Eating

If you want lard-free Nouveau Mexican tapas, stick to Santa Fe. But when you're hankering for hearty family recipes perfected over 400 years of working with ingredients grown right here, come on up to Española.

Farmers Market (☎ 685-4842; 1027 N Railroad Ave; ☯ noon-5pm Mon Jun-Oct) Colorful fruits and vegetables from local growers, often matched by equally colorful entertainment, are a treat. But the real prize will be a planned new park with shade trees, permanent canopies, community gathering space and a teaching garden. (Watch for the new site three doors down.)

El Parasol (☎ 753-8852; dishes $2-8) This revered taco stand is opposite El Paragua.

El Paragua (☎ 753-3211, 800-929-8226; NM 76; lunch $6-9, dinner $9-20; ☯ 11am-9pm Mon-Thu, 11am-9:30pm Fri & Sat, 11am-8pm Sun; P ✕ ☷ Ⓥ) Make reservations on weekends for one of the state's best restaurants. Because of its perfect margaritas, Spanish Old West ambiance and New Mexican specialties, you'll be daydreaming about it for years.

Shanghai (☎ 753-8543; 1226 N Railroad Ave; dishes $6-11; ☯ 11am-8:30pm Mon-Sat; ✕ Ⓥ ☷) When you've reached your limit of enchiladas and tacos, settle in here for Chinese fare – they'll comply if you ask for extra vegetables.

Angelina's Restaurant (☎ 753-8543; 1226 N Railroad Ave; dishes $6-11; ☯ 7am-9pm) Sit down at this popular and delicious local favorite for the finest organic lamb burritos ($7) anywhere or any of the other New Mexican specialties.

Rancho de San Juan (☎ 753-6818; www.ranchode sanjuan.com; 34020 US 285; dishes $35; P ✕) Little details consistently catapult this restaurant to number one in New Mexico. Duck arrives at the table cooked with Chinese spices, drizzled with a blood orange glaze, served with pineapple and rice pilaf. Add an impressive wine list and a Chocolate Oblivion Tart ($10) for one heavenly meal.

'Original' La Cocina Taqueria (☎ 753-3486; 310 Los Alamos Ave; dishes $3-9; ☯ 7am-1:30pm Mon-Fri; ✕ ☷ Ⓥ ☷) is a beloved hole-in-the-wall that makes legendary stuffed *sopapillas*, while the **'New' Cocina y Cantina** (☎ 753-3016; 415 Santa Clara Bridge Rd; dishes $6-15; ☯ 11am-9pm; ✕ ☷ Ⓥ ☷) has nicer digs and a bigger menu, including the recommended fajita salad ($8). Related **Los Arcos** (☎ 753-3015; 819 N Riverside Dr; dishes $6-20; ☯ 11am-9pm Mon-Sat) has seafood and steaks.

Getting There & Around

The closest Greyhound station is in Santa Fe. **Española Transit** (☎ 753-4111; one way $1; ☯ 7am-6:30pm) covers the city, has service to Ohkay Owengeh and Santa Clara Pueblo, and connections with Los Alamos Bus System (p133).

ABIQUIÚ

☎ 505 / pop 550 / elev 6800ft

Abiquiú quietly answers the oft-asked question about how Georgia O'Keeffe could have left city life behind to live in seclusion.

By the time you depart, you'll realize how much easier it could be to stay than leave.

While O'Keeffe's paintings may have seemed like strong, quiet hyperbole, visitors to this ethereal realm come to understand the famed painter was actually under-reporting what she saw. Red rock desert, with brown, gold, pink and green striations; mesa silhouettes stark in the midday sun and soft and comforting at sunset – it's all here, just as the paintings of Rio Chama and flat-topped Pedernal Mountain intimated.

Come see for yourself, and consider staying the night.

Orientation & Information

Abiquiú stretches for about 20 peaceful miles along US 84, from the intersection with NM 554 (18 miles north of Española) to Ghost Ranch. There's no city center (although Bode's Mercantile serves the purpose), no public transportation and no chamber of commerce, though you can download information at www.digitalabiq uiu.com.

Sights & Activities

Make reservations in advance to take the **Georgia O'Keeffe House & Studio Tour** (☎ 685-4539; www.okeeffemuseum.org; admission $25; ☷ Tue, Thu & Fri Apr-Nov) of the home and studios of the artist who illuminated Abiquiú's quiet beauty with her own intensity of color and form. Fans will recognize the house (where she lived from 1945 to 1984) and the views from it, which have been enshrined in her master-pieces; just about all of them are available in poster and book form at the Abiquiú Inn.

NEW MEXICO'S LOWRIDING TRADITION

In some circles, Española is more famous for its fine arts tradition than either Taos or Santa Fe. That's right: lowriders as art. In fact, the entire state of New Mexico has long boasted some of the finest automobile customizers in the world.

The Lowrider Movement began in East Los Angeles during the 1930s, when young Chicanos gave up on assimilation and instead started dressing in zoot suits and customizing their cars quite differently from the racing crowd. 'We lowered the springs in the back,' explained César Chávez. 'Fender skirts. Two sidepipes.' The look was sleek – low-slung sedans, clean and chromed and later customized with wild paint and extravagant interiors. And always: pure class.

The first New Mexico lowriders began cruising the Española Valley in the 1950s, and during the 1960s, when laws against lowered suspensions swept the country, clever cruisers adapted hydraulic pumps that would lift their rides to legal height at the flick of a switch. Soon villages like Chimayó, Truchas, Peñasco and Hernandez were sporting some of the finest lowriders anywhere, and Española was at the center of it all.

Española's Viejitos car club organized one of the first lowrider shows anywhere in 1975; by this time, lowriding was a statewide phenomenon. The Smithsonian's only lowrider hails from Chimayó – David and Irene Jaramillo's 1969 Ford LTD, 'Dave's Dream.' And in 1993 (much to the consternation of East Los Angelenos) MTV announced the title Española had been claiming for years, 'Lowrider Capital of the World.'

Riding that wave, Albuquerque hydraulics entrepreneur Orlie Coca founded *Orlie's Lowriding* magazine, with readers in some 20 countries – including car-crazy Japan, which in the mid-1990s was enjoying a powerful yen and new adoration for old Detroit cruisers, including lowriders. Brokers soon began buying up clean rides from all over the country, and Española's cultural cache proved irresistible to Japanese collectors. By some accounts, Orlie alone was shipping almost 100 cars eastward every month at the peak of the trend.

Today, lowriding fans feel a little disappointed cruising the Rio Grande Valley, as newly built customs are often compact cruisers, beautiful but perhaps less impressive than the old Impalas and Monte Carlos lost to Yokohama. But you'll still see classic rides (that folks simply refused to sell) cruising on Friday nights and Sunday afternoons, not just in Española but also on Central Ave in Albuquerque, Alameda in Santa Fe and all over the northern part of the state.

Check out some of the most sparkling examples of classic cruisers in *Low 'N Slow: Lowriding in New Mexico,* by Carmella Padilla, or try to catch one of the region's many shows, which take place in parks, parking lots, stadiums and casinos throughout the state, usually on Sunday afternoons.

SANTA FE

DETOUR: OJO CALIENTE

Ojo Caliente means 'hot eye' in Spanish, a reference to the geothermal springs bubbling up throughout the region. **Ojo Caliente Mineral Springs** (☎ 583-2233, 800-222-9162; www.ojocalientespa .com; 50 Los Baños Dr; r $99-109, cottages $142-179; P ☒ ☒), 18 miles north of Española, has five of them, plus a charming, family-owned resort with pleasant if not luxurious rooms and casitas (the latter have been newly remodeled). The on-site **Artesian Restaurant** (mains $5-15; ☉ 7:30am-10:30am, 11:30am-2:30pm & 5-9:30pm; P ☒ ☒ V) prepares organic and local ingredients with aplomb, including fresh trout encrusted with pine nuts in a cilantro-jalapeño butter.

The springs, considered sacred by Pueblo Indians, are an unusual trick of hydrogeology: each of the beautiful pools is fed by a different water source with different mineral contents. The Lithia spring has a kick – bring a bottle so you can take some home. Drop by for a visit (weekday/ weekend $16/22) and consider indulging in a massage or spa treatment ($10 to $85), or one of four private pools (with kiva fireplaces) available for $40 (50 minutes) or $120 (four hours), or a hike along one of their trails.

Other accommodations within walking distance include the **Lomita Motel & Retreat Center** (☎ 583-2109, 800-480-7197; US 285; without/with kitchenette $49/69; P ☒), a New Agey place with sweat lodges, tepees and spacious, relaxing rooms that come with porches, but are a bit dingy. There are also a couple of restaurants in town, including the **Mesa Vista Cafe** (☎ 583-2245; US 285; mains $2-7; ☉ 8am-9pm; P ☒ ☒ V ☒), serving New Mexico diner food with lots of veggie options and a recommended red chile cheeseburger.

Ghost Ranch Living Museum (Map p116; ☎ 685-4333; www.ghostranch.org; US 84) was founded amidst the colorful canyonlands as the former 1766 Serrano Land Grant and later dubbed Rancho de los Brujos (Ranch of the Witches) because of reported eerie supernatural activity. The Presbyterian retreat offers lodging, classes and other activities for folks of any or no faith. Much of the movie *City Slickers* was filmed here.

There are two small museums: the **Ellis Museum of Anthropology** (admission by donation; ☉ 8am-5pm Tue-Sat, 11am-1pm Sun), outlining 12,000 years of human habitation in the area, and the **Ruth Hall Museum of Paleontology** (admission by donation; ☉ 8am-5pm Tue-Sat, 11am-1pm Sun), a cool collection of fossils excavated on the ranch, including a skeleton of Coelophysis, New Mexico's state fossil, which was discovered here. Take the recommended 4-mile round-trip trek into **Box Canyon** or the popular 3-mile round-trip to **Chimney Rock**, which has views of the Piedra Lumbre basin.

For a little insight into Islam, drop into the graceful adobe **Dar al Islam Mosque & Madressa** (Map p116; ☎ 685-4515; www.daralislam.org; NM 155; admission free; ☉ 8am-4pm Mon-Fri), which conducts classes and an outreach program for non-Muslims interested in broadening their horizons. The mosque once served a community of Muslim immigrants, most of whom have since moved away. A small

staff still offers teacher trainings and youth camps. Take NM 554 north from US 84 toward El Rito, cross the Rio Chama, make your first left onto NM 155 and follow it for 3 miles.

Every fall you can visit more than 30 local artists' studios and galleries by taking the **Annual Studio Tour** (☎ 685-4454; www.abiquiu studiotour.org; ☉ Oct), including the **Armando Lopez Studio** (☎ 685-4585; 21275 NM 84), known for fine painting and sculpture.

Scenic **Abiquiú Lake & Dam** (☎ 685-4371) is popular among boaters, campers and fishers. Ten miles north, you can experience the acoustically impressive **Echo Amphitheater** (Map p116; day use per car $2), a majestic natural cavern worn into the sandstone, and take to the trailhead for a couple of short hikes. Two miles south of town, an easy 1-mile-round-trip hike to the **Poshuouinge Ruins** (Map p116) offers a bird's-eye view of the Chama Valley and remains of a 700-room pueblo founded at least 600 years ago. The ruins themselves are off-limits.

Sleeping & Eating

Featuring phenomenal camping and other unusual accommodations, Abiquiú is best appreciated as an overnight destination. Many lodging operators offer meals as part of the package, a good idea considering the dearth of dining options.

SANTA FE

Raina Campground (Map p116; ☎ 685-4371, reservations 877-444-6667; tent/RV $5/14; **P**) With views of Abiquiú Lake and a nice 1-mile hiking trail, this is a fine place to stay overnight.

Ghost Ranch (Map p116; ☎ 685-4333; www.ghost ranch.org; US 84; tents $16, dm with shared bath $45-73, dm with private bath $83, all incl 3 meals; **P** **X** **🛏** **V**) When space is available (seminar participants get first dibs), you can get a dorm bed here, including cafeteria-style meals made with locally raised meat and organic veggies grown on the ranch farm.

Christ in the Desert Monastery (Map p116; fax 419-831-9113; www.christdesert.org; FS 151; s $50-70, d $85-125; **P** **X** **V**) When you want to get away from it all, head west from US 84 onto the rough dirt Forest Service Rd 151, then follow it along the meandering Rio Chama for 13 inspirational miles to this isolated Benedictine Monastery. Simple rooms, outrageous trails, and peace and quiet that includes vegetarian meals served without conversation. Prices include three meals; two-night minimum.

Abiquiú Inn (☎ 685-4378, 888-735-2902; US 84; www.abiquiuinn.com; RV $18, r $139, 4-person casitas $199; **P** **X** **🐾** **🖥**) An area institution, this sprawling collection of shaded adobes is peaceful and lovely, and some spacious rooms have kitchenettes. No tent sites are available. The very professional staff also run the onsite Abiquiú Cafe (dishes $6 to $20; open 7:30am to 9pm). Stick to the Middle Eastern menu –

falafel, dolmas and gyros are all winners – and you can't go wrong.

Las Parras de Abiquiú B&B (☎ 685-4200, 800-817-5955; www.lasparras.com; US 84; d $145 incl breakfast; **P** **X** **🐾**) Primarily a 5½-acre organic vineyard, Las Parras also features two luxuriously appointed rooms with outstanding art, fireplaces, an outdoor hot tub and lots of little amenities. It's top notch.

Independent eateries are in short supply, but **Bode's** (☎ 685-4422; US 84; dishes $2-7; 🕑 7am-8pm), a small grocery store and gas station, has a good deli (open 7am to 5pm), while **El Farolito** (☎ 581-9509; NM 554, El Rito; dishes $3-12; **X** **&** **V** **♿**), about 10 miles north of Abiquiú on NM 554, serves excellent New Mexican cuisine topped with award-winning green chile.

HIGH ROAD TO TAOS

Cruising by the 13,000ft peaks along the famed 'High Road to Taos' fills visitors with yet another kind of spaciousness. Here, the pine forests of Carson National Forest yield panoramas across sprawling farmlands and high mesas – quite a change from the cactus-covered environs of Albuquerque and Santa Fe.

In wintertime, the white of the snow-capped Sangre de Cristos Mountains intensifies against impossibly blue skies. You can feel the air cooling as you head to

---

GEORGIA O'KEEFFE *Bridgette Wagner*

Although classically trained as a painter at art institutes in Chicago and New York, 21-year-old Georgia O'Keeffe was always uncomfortable with traditional European style. For four years after finishing school, she did not paint, and instead taught drawing and did graphic design.

However, after studying with Arthur Wesley Dow, who shared her distaste for the provincial, O'Keeffe began developing her own style. She drew abstract shapes with charcoal, representing dreams and visions, and eventually returned to oils and watercolors. These first works caught the eye of her future husband and patron, photographer Alfred Steiglitz, in 1916.

In 1929 she visited Taos' Mabel Dodge Luhan Ranch and returned to paint *The Lawrence Tree*, still presiding over DH Lawrence Ranch (p161). O'Keeffe tackled the subject of the Ranchos de Taos Church, painted by so many artists before her, in a way that had never been considered: only a fragment of the mission wall, contrasted against the blue of the sky.

It was no wonder she loved New Mexico's expansive skies, so similar to her paintings' negative spaces. As she spent more time here, landscapes and fields of blue permeated her paintings. During desert treks, she collected smooth white bones of animals, subjects placed against that sky in some of her most identifiable New Mexico works.

Telltale scrub marks and bristle impressions divulge how O'Keeffe blended and mixed her vibrant colors on the canvas itself. This is in direct contrast to photographs of her work, which convey a false, airbrush-like smoothness. At the Georgia O'Keeffe Museum (p69), you can experience her work firsthand.

Taos, where fast-flowing rivers and powder-covered ski areas remind you that you're far, far above sea level.

The small villages along this route, settled more than 400 years ago, until very recently were known for keeping their isolated Spanish-colonial character pristine. In recent years new artists have moved into these rugged mountains, opening their own studios alongside those famed for Spanish artistic traditions.

The drive from Santa Fe to Taos takes more than two hours without stopping – but you'll want to linger, drinking in vast alpine splendor, churches and studios.

Head north on St Francis Dr from Santa Fe, where it becomes US 285/84, continuing north past Pojoaque. You can either make a right onto NM 503 toward Nambé Pueblo to begin your trek, or continue north to Española. In Española, make a right onto NM 76, at the sign to Chimayó, heading east toward the Santuario.

Chimayó
☎ 505 / pop 4400 / elev 6200ft
The village of Chimayó, folded into a lush valley surrounded by dramatically sculpted high desert, is striking from above and seems welcoming as you meander its shady streets. Though it has much to recommend it – a famed santuario and a 400-year-old tradition of fine weaving – Chimayó also has a love-hate relationship with the 300,000 camera-snapping tourists who roll through each year. Show respect, and lock your car.

Collectors come for woven wool tapestries, a tradition of craftsmanship passed down unbroken through generations of families who have raised sheep and grown the plants to make natural dyes. The original storefront is the century-old **Ortega's Weaving Shop** (☎ 351-4215; NM 76; ⏰ 8:30am-5pm Mon-Sat); see p111.

There are several other spots in town for finding that perfect weave, including **Centinela Traditional Arts** (☎ 351-2180; www.chimayoweavers.com; NM 76; ⏰ 9am-6pm Mon-Sat, 10am-5pm Sun), which has 100-year-old looms and great information on Rio Grande weaving online; see also p111.

Learn more about Chimayó's history at tiny **Chimayó Museum** (☎ 351-0945; www.chimayomuseum.org; cnr NM 76 & NM 502; ⏰ 11am-3pm Tue-Sat), on historic Plaza del Cerró, still fortified by

protective adobe structures that now house shops. It has exhibits by local artists and a permanent collection of old photos.

The most famous place for dinner is **Rancho de Chimayó** (Map p116; ☎ 351-4444; www.ranchodechimayo.com; NM 76; dishes $10-17; ⏰ 11:30am-9pm, closed Mon Nov-Apr; P ⊠ ⅁ V), serving classic New Mexican cuisine, courtesy of the Jaramillo family's famed recipes, and perfect margaritas ($5). It's the location and old school ambiance that packs 'em in. You can also find accommodation (doubles $98 to $105) here.

Excellent, authentic and ultra-festive **Chimayó Holy Chile Mercadito Milagroso** (☎ 351-4824; NM 76; dishes $2-7; ⏰ 10am-5pm; P ⊠ ⅁ V ⅁), across from the Santuario, is easier on your budget, serving great chicken tamales ($5) and a selection of tacos ($2 to $4), exactly what you need after that long pilgrimage.

From the Santuario, NM 76 rises 3000ft as it passes the villages of Córdova, Truchas and Peñasco.

Córdova
☎ 505 / pop 400 / elev 800ft
Just off NM 76, carpenters founded Córdova in the 1700s near the site of old Pueblo Qemado. The community of woodworkers established a tradition of carved and unpainted retablos and bultos. These were created from strikingly grained woods, including juniper, aspen, ash and cedar, carefully pieced together for an unusual effect.

'Córdova-style' pieces, pioneered by masters like José Rafael Oregón and Jose Dolores Lopéz, are now collected by the Smithsonian and other museums. You can find small animals and angels for around $10 (much cheaper than in Santa Fe), while larger and more complex museum-quality pieces – saints and the Tree of Life are the classic subjects – run well over $1000.

Operated by Terry Enseñat Mulert, who carves graceful, traditional bultos in the style of legendary carver Patrociño Barela (p38), and Paula Castillo, who shows contemporary acrylic paintings and imposing steel sculptures, the unusual **Castillo Gallery** (☎ 351-4067; www.castillogallery.com; Main Rd; ⏰ 9am-6pm) also organizes poetry festivals and other events.

More traditional carvings are sold at the homes of *santeras* **Gloria López** (☎ 351-4487; Main Rd; ⏰ 9am-5pm, but call first), who has perfected her techniques over 54 years of carving, and **Sabanita Lopéz Ortiz** (☎ 351-4572; Main Rd; ⏰ 8am-4pm, but call first), great-granddaughter of Jose Dolores Lopéz.

Truchas
☎ 505 / pop 950 / elev 8400ft

A case study in rural gentrification (or, more precisely, gallerification), Truchas has become something of an arts center in recent years. A dozen studios now grace the dramatic set of Robert Redford's movie *The Milagro Beanfield War*, chosen after camerashy Chimayó turned down the actor.

Once you come here – and it is a fine detour – you'll understand why creative spirits congregate atop this mesa: picturesque farms, ancient traditions, and stunning views of 13,100ft Truchas Peak and the wide Española Valley conspire to inspire.

The village still operates according to the bylaws of its 1754 Spanish land grant, forcing lowrider cars to compete with livestock for the narrow road connecting galleries like **Cordovas Handweaving Workshop** (☎ 689-1124; Main Truchas Rd; ⏰ 8am-4pm Mon-Sat), which boasts unique weavings, and **Hand Arts Gallery** (☎ 689-2443; Main Truchas Rd; ⏰ 8am-5pm Mon-Sat),

featuring work from area artisans, much of it displayed in the outdoor sculpture garden.

Continue to the end of Main Truchas Rd to the Truchas Peak trailhead (though most hikers begin at Cowles, north of Pecos), where an alpine meadow beneath that granite peak will take your breath away.

Rancho Arriba B&B (☎ 689-2374; www.ranchoarriba .com; Main Truchas Rd; s/d with shared bath $50/70, d with private bath $85 incl breakfast; P ⏰ ⏰ ⏰ ⏰), in a rustic adobe farmhouse where the owner/homesteader has been creating a haven over the past 40 years on the edge of Pecos Wilderness, has horses and wood stoves, and will arrange to cook you dinner in advance.

Truchas Farmhouse (☎ 689-2245; Main Truchas Rd; d $50-90; P ⏰ ⏰) is simpler but still nice.

There are no restaurants, but you can grab snacks and beer at **Tofoya's General Store** (☎ 689-2418; Main Truchas Rd; ⏰ 8am-7pm Mon-Sat, 11am-4pm Sun; P), serving Truchas since 1915.

Las Trampas
The tiny adobe village of Las Trampas is most famous for outstanding Spanish-colonial architecture, particularly the restored 1760 **San José de Garcia Church** (⏰ noon mass 1st & 3rd Sun, no mass Jul), considered among

---

SANTUARIO DE CHIMAYÓ

In the days leading up to Good Friday, it seems that all roads leading to **El Santuario de Chimayó** (☎ 351-4889; NM 76; admission free; ⏰ 8am-6pm; mass 11am Mon-Sat, 10:30am, noon & 4:30pm Sun) are lined with pilgrims, many barefoot, some dragging crosses and all in a state of spiritual self-discovery (read: drive carefully).

According to legend, it was during Holy Week in 1810 that Bernardo Abeyto, a Penitente, saw a light shining forth from the earth. When he went to investigate, he found a crucifix bearing the image of Our Lord of Esquipulas, aka the Black Christ, patron saint of a Guatemalan village known for its own healing sanctuary.

Abeyto took the cross to Santa Cruz, where it promptly disappeared, rematerializing back in Chimayó. A second long procession proved just as maddeningly miraculous. Abeyto finally gave up and built a shrine at the *santo*'s chosen spot, where the Santuario stands today.

Other tales tell of hot springs sacred to the Tewa tribes. Now dry, the springs' healing powers remained in the loose earth upon which the Santuario was constructed. Which is really why you're here: sure, it's a beautiful place, graceful and venerable, with five outstanding reredos and a famed bulto of El Señor Santiago, but most folks come for the dirt, known for its healing powers.

Walk past *santos* of every design, from traditional wooden carvings to black velvet airbrushed paintings, and enter a small room behind the altar. There a modest pit of sand lies open, allegedly on the very spot where the crucifix was found. If you so desire, kneel down and scoop some sand into your own container (none are supplied), then add it to your bath, rub it onto the worn-out parts of your body, even mix it with water and drink it – but don't treat this miracle lightly. Too many prayers have been answered here, too many wounds healed and good deeds done by whatever power is working through this crowded shrine to consider this place just another roadside attraction.

the loveliest in the country. Original carvings and paintings remain in excellent condition, and bloodstains from the Los Hermanos Penitentes are still visible.

There are few services in town, but you can pitch a tent at Trampas Diamante or **Trampas Trailhead** (☎ 842-3292; CR 207; campsites $7), about 5 and 8 miles, respectively, south of NM 76 from the El Valle turnoff, along a rough dirt road.

Peñasco

☎ 505 / pop 650 / elev 7452ft

This 250-year-old community of farmers and ranchers is a gateway to the Carson National Forest. Stop into the **Camino Real Ranger Station** (☎ 587-2255; 15160 NM 75; ☼ 8am-4:30pm Mon-Fri) for information on camping, hiking and cross-country skiing.

Sipapú Ski & Summer Resort (Map p116; ☎ 587-2240, 800-587-2240; www.sipapunm.com; NM 518; lift tickets adult/child $33/25; **P**) is a cozy, family-operated ski resort, 10 miles south of Peñasco on NM 518, with 65 acres of powder, 31 trails, a 1055ft vertical drop, and some of the shortest lines and best deals on downhill skiing in New Mexico. Makes a great overnight (tents $9, doubles $29 to $84, RVs $14 to $39).

Serious hikers may attempt the 23-mile-round-trip **Santa Barbara Trail** to Truchas Peak, which begins at **Santa Barbara Campground** (Map p116; ☎ 587-2255; FR 116), about 9 miles south of Peñasco on a good dirt road. In town, the colorful **Sugar Nymphs Bistro** (☎ 587-0311; NM 75; dishes $9-12; ☼ 11:30am-3pm & 5:30-7:30pm Mon-Sat, 11am-2pm Sun, Thu-Sat winter; **P** ✗ & **V**) offers creative and healthful diner food, sinful desserts and sometimes live performances.

From Peñasco, you can head west on NM 75 to Picuris Pueblo and Dixon; or east on NM 518, which will take you to Las Vegas; or north, continuing along the High Road, topping out at 8500ft on US Hill. Continue on to Rancho de Taos, where you join NM 68, the Low Road to Taos, for the short final leg of your journey.

Picuris Pueblo

☎ 505 / pop 350 / elev 7500ft

This pueblo was once among the largest and most powerful. The Pikuri tribe built adobe cities at least seven stories tall, and the pueblo boasted a population approaching 3000. After the Pueblo Revolt and Reconquista, when many retreated to Kansas rather than

face DeVargas' wrath, the returning tribe numbered only 500. Between the Spanish and Comanche raids, that number continued to dwindle.

The tribe has chosen not to open a casino and instead owns and operates the popular Hotel Santa Fe (p95) and runs a successful bison program on pueblo land that began with one cow in 1992 and today nears 100 creatures. The tribe sells buffalo meat at the Santa Fe Farmers Market (p101) and to restaurants in Santa Fe and beyond.

One of the smallest and most remote pueblos, Picuris is well off the beaten tourist trail. The **Governor's Office** (☎ 587-2519; photo/video permits $6/10; ☼ 8am-5pm Mon-Fri) can, with advance notice, arrange guided pueblo tours, including the small buffalo herd, organic gardens, ruins from the old pueblo site and the exquisite 1770 **San Lorenzo de Picuris Church**. The unique tower kiva is off-limits to visitors but makes quite an impression even from the outside.

Picuris is best known for its micaceous pottery, golden-hued, unglazed vessels flecked with gleaming mica that New Mexicans swear are the best pots for simmering beans. Anthony Duran is probably the best-known Picuris potter, but other well-regarded artists include Margaret Archuleta and Diane Sign. Most artisans open their studios on weekends.

Public events include the **Tri-Cultural Arts & Crafts Fair**, in late August, and the popular **San Lorenzo Feast Days**, August 9 and 10, which feature food and crafts booths, dances, races and pole climbs.

LOW ROAD TO TAOS

If you don't have all day to make the trip between Española and Taos, your best bet is NM 68, a speedy 40-mile trek that would be famous for its views of deeply cut Rio Grande Gorge if it didn't have to suffer comparisons with the spectacular High Road.

Velarde

About 15 minutes north of Española, Velarde has a few produce stands and **Black Mesa Winery** (Map p116; ☎ 852-2820, 800-852-6372; www.blackmesawinery.com; 1502 NM 68; ☼ 10am-6pm Mon-Sat, noon-6pm Sun), where you can enjoy a free seven-vintage flight, including the excellent signature Coyote Red and best-selling Black Beauty, a red wine with chocolate flavoring.

Embudo

☎ 505 / pop 725 / elev 5815ft

Plan your trip around lunch at New Mexico's first brewpub, **Embudo Station** (☎ 852-4707; www.embudostation.com; NM 68; dishes $6-20; ☪ 11:30am-9pm Tue-Sun, closed mid-Dec–Apr; Ⓟ ⊠ ⊠). An idyllic riverside patio sits alongside a particularly lovely stretch of the Rio Grande – *embudo*, Spanish for 'funnel,' refers to the narrow pass. Come for New Mexico wines and microbrews (try the green chile ale) that accompany Southwestern cuisine made with local produce and meats smoked on the premises. The station also rents a nice cabin (double cabin $100 including breakfast) and arranges leisurely two-hour rafting trips ($35).

Just up the road, the **Classical Gas Museum** (☎ 852-2995; NM 68; admission by donation) has no regular hours, but if the gate's open, stop in to see an enormous collection of antique pumps, advertisements, oil cans and more – it's a must, especially for photographers. Seriously. Donations support the Dixon Animal Shelter.

Pilar

☎ 505 / pop 100 / elev 6400ft

Populated by a small but dedicated community of nature lovers and river rats, Pilar is the gateway to outdoor adventures, most famously white-water rafting. 'The Box,' with Class VI+ rapids, is best appreciated in May and June (though the season runs April through October) when the water level is higher. Mellower floats are available from a variety of area outfitters. Because of a recent (and longstanding) drought, the Box and other venues may not be running consistently; call ahead.

Big River Raft Trips (☎ 758-9711, 800-748-3746; www.bigriverrafts.com; cnr NM 68 & CR 570) offers floats, from an all-day experience in the Box ($108) to half-day trips on the Class III Racecourse ($60) and Class III Lower Gorge ($60).

Far Flung Adventures (☎ 758-2628, 800-359-2627; www.farflung.com) offers similar trips as well as those combining rafting with horseback riding ($145), a three-day 'gourmet river trip' ($845) replete with chef-prepared meals, and various kayak trips. Most leave from the **Pilar Yacht Club & Café** (☎ 758-9072; cnr NM 68 & CR 570), which also sells sandwiches and burritos.

BLM-administrated **Orilla Verde Recreation Area** (☎ 758-8851; www.nm.blm.gov/recreation/taos; CR 570; day use $3, sites with/without shelter $7/5) operates nine campgrounds in the same area with some sites along the river; Petaca (Map p116) is the nicest for tent campers, while Taos Junction (Map p116), just across the Taos Junction Bridge, is best for RVs.

The **Rio Grande Gorge Visitors Center** (☎ 751-4899; NM 68; ☪ 8:30am-4:30pm summer) has information on campsites and area hikes, including the 2-mile **La Vista Verde Trail**, with great gorge views and petroglyphs, and the less-developed 9-mile **West Rim Trail**, popular with mountain bikers. Both begin just past Taos Junction Bridge.

You can continue up NM 68 into Taos, or follow CR 570 across the Taos Junction Bridge, which becomes a steep dirt road to CR 567 for about three tortuous miles, then intersects a very nice, paved shortcut directly to Ojo Caliente.

LOS ALAMOS

☎ 505 / pop 18,365 / elev 7355ft

Los Alamos is to science what Aspen is to skiers – an upscale, world-class destination. Some of the world's top minds live in this stunning gateway to the Jemez Mountains, and they work in the world's most sophisticated weapons lab.

Perhaps surprisingly, Los Alamos is one of the wealthiest towns in the country, with the highest number of millionaires per capita in the US. (One in five of the 8000 households here is worth more than $1 million – and that's excluding home values!) Who says science doesn't pay?

Studded with WWII-era military-grade architecture, all centered on secretive Los Alamos National Laboratory (LANL), this town isn't a tourist attraction, it's a scientific experiment. Still, the Bradbury Science Museum and the Los Alamos Historical Museum are worth a look, especially if you're too young to remember exactly what happened in August 1945 in Japan.

Then hit the local trails or head out to spectacular Bandelier to resume your desert wanderings and digest what you just saw.

History

The secret city was founded by federal order in 1943 in its isolated mesa-top location. Here, General Leslie Groves and physicist Robert Oppenheimer assembled an army of top scientists and engineers, furnished them with every possible resource and gave

SANTA FE

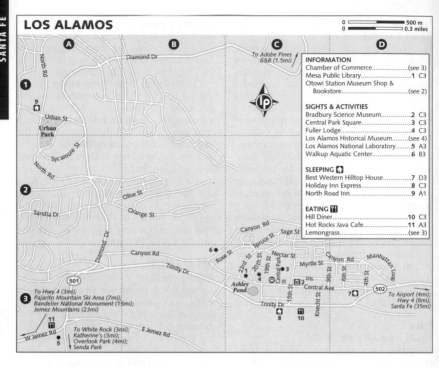

LOS ALAMOS

0 — 500 m
0 — 0.3 miles

INFORMATION
Chamber of Commerce..................(see 3)
Mesa Public Library........................**1** C3
Otowi Station Museum Shop &
  Bookstore.................................(see 2)

SIGHTS & ACTIVITIES
Bradbury Science Museum...............**2** C3
Central Park Square.........................**3** C3
Fuller Lodge...................................**4** C3
Los Alamos Historical Museum........(see 4)
Los Alamos National Laboratory.......**5** A3
Walkup Aquatic Center...................**6** B3

SLEEPING
Best Western Hilltop House...............**7** D3
Holiday Inn Express.........................**8** C3
North Road Inn...............................**9** A1

EATING
Hill Diner......................................**10** C3
Hot Rocks Java Cafe.......................**11** A3
Lemongrass...................................(see 3)

them a single mission: to build an atomic bomb before Nazi Germany did.

Brainpower recruited from across the world reported to 109 Palace St in Santa Fe, where they were whisked out the back door and shuttled past guard towers keeping watch over the code-named Manhattan Project. Housing was flimsy, water was scarce and security was tight.

Schoolchildren did not use their last names, scientists did not discuss work with their families and all correspondence was heavily censored. Information was given on a need-to-know basis; few on the project knew exactly how their creation would manifest.

The weapon was a blinding success. On July 16, 1945, the world's first nuclear device detonated at White Sands, a luminous inferno that prompted Oppenheimer to quote the *Bhagavad Gita:* 'I am become death, the destroyer of worlds.'

A month later Hiroshima and Nagasaki were hit hard by the new technology: at least 120,000 civilians were killed instantly, more in the following days, prompting Japan to surrender and end WWII. The

USA became a world power, the word 'fallout' entered the dictionary, and in 1949 the USSR tested its own nuclear device, getting the Cold War started with a bang.

Los Alamos remained federally owned and operated after the war, restricting visitors and keeping close tabs on residents, including Communist Party members Ethel and Julius Rosenberg, who were executed in 1953 for espionage. Finally, in 1957 Los Alamos was opened to the public, just like a normal city. Sure.

LANL is the region's top employer, with a $2.2-billion annual budget and 9000 workers, but it's not just for WMDs anymore: supercomputers, genome decryption and nuclear safety are pursued. Constant federal supervision and high-level worries about security lapses, however, make it clear there's more going on than just cutting-edge medical research.

Orientation

Built atop a series of slender mesas, Los Alamos would be difficult to navigate even if it hadn't been designed as a military facility.

Luckily most attractions are well signed and located along Central Ave (NM 502) between 9th and 20th Sts. The suburb of White Rock is just south of Los Alamos on NM 4.

Information

Chamber of Commerce (☎ 662-8105, 800-444-0707; www.visit.losalamos.com; 109 Central Park Sq; ☷ 9am-5pm Mon-Fri, 9am-3pm Sat & Sun) Has a free map, accommodations listings and pamphlets.

Los Alamos Monitor (www.lamonitor.com) The daily paper.

Mesa Public Library (☎ 662-8240; 2400 Central Ave; ☷ 10am-9pm Mon-Thu, 10am-6pm Fri, 10am-5pm Sat, noon-5pm Sun) Offers free internet access.

Otowi Station Museum Shop & Bookstore (☎ 662-9589; www.otowistation.com; 1350 Central Ave) Has a wide selection of scientific and historic tomes.

White Rock Chamber of Commerce (☎ 672-2183; Rover Rd; ☷ 8am-4pm) Just off NM 4, this branch of the chamber of commerce is more convenient if you want to head directly into the forest.

Sights & Activities

Los Alamos itself is a sight to behold: chosen for its isolation among mountains and steep canyons, it enjoys stunning views best appreciated at **Overlook Park** in White Rock; they form an impressive backdrop to the military-efficient architecture. WWII buffs may appreciate the almost Soviet-style

aesthetic with which this town was thrown together. **Buffalo Tours** (☎ 662-5711; adult/child $15/7; ☷ 1:30pm, but call ahead) begin at the Bradbury Science Museum for 1½-hour tours of Los Alamos' and LANL's history, science and geology. Those with a hankering for the wet stuff can visit **Walkup Aquatic Center** (☎ 662-8170; 2760 Canyon Rd; adult/child $3/2), which has showers and an Olympic-sized pool.

BRADBURY SCIENCE MUSEUM

The outstanding **Bradbury Science Museum** (☎ 667-4444; www.lanl.gov/museum; cnr 15th St & Central Ave; admission free; ☷ 10am-5pm Tue-Sat, 1-5pm Sun & Mon) is LANL's public face, offering insight into the political and scientific challenges the lab faces in its primary mission of 'ensuring the safety and reliability of America's nuclear weapons.' Well-designed exhibits offer serious, thought-provoking examination of the nuclear age.

Historical exhibits focus on the Manhattan Project, and the defense gallery stockpile includes a W80 warhead, cruise missiles and a Fat Man casing (identical to the bomb dropped on Nagasaki).

LOS ALAMOS HISTORICAL MUSEUM

For an introspective examination of the world's reaction to the Atomic Age, visit the **Los Alamos Historical Museum** (☎ 662-4493;

DETOUR: DIXON

Snuggled almost invisibly between two beaten paths, Dixon's not a destination many folks take the time to seek out. Which is a shame, considering the potential for relaxation in this community of artisans, organic farmers and other folks who appreciate the solitude. Stop by the **Library & Community Center** (☎ 579-9181; NM 75; ☷ 10am-5pm Mon-Tue, noon-6pm Wed-Thu, noon-5pm Fri, 10am-5pm Sat) for free internet access, maps and information about area studios and farm tours.

The big draw is **La Chiripada Winery** (Map p116; ☎ 579-4437, 800-528-7801; www.lachiripada.com; NM 75; ☷ 10am-6pm), which makes many of New Mexico's top-rated wines, including an award-winning Riesling and Embudo Blanco, as well as a highly regarded cabernet sauvignon.

Pick up locally made food products – think wild cherry-red chile jam – to go with your chosen vintage at the distinctive **Metier** (☎ 579-4111; NM 75; ☷ 10am-5pm Tue-Sun), an artists' and growers' cooperative representing some 60 area craftspeople. Look for the historic rock house on the west end of town and you will have found it.

If you find yourself more interested in rocks than art, **Harding Mine** (☎ 277-4204; epswww.unm .edu), a mile north of town and a place of geological extremes, may be for you. Owned by UNM, it's open to rockhounds – if you've secured a permit in advance. Check the website for specifics. Since you can only reach the mine by crossing private lands, you should ask permission to do so (even after you've gotten the permit from UNM).

There are a few B&Bs scattered throughout town, including **La Casita Guesthouse** (Map p116; ☎ 579-4297; www.cyberrentals.com/nm/millenm.html; r $85 incl breakfast, 2 night minimum; ℗ ☒ ☒ ▣ ☙), a peaceful spot lost in another time behind the vineyards of La Chiripada.

NUTS FOR NUKES? LEARN MORE

You may opt to continue worrying rather than learn to love the bomb, but Dr Strangelove himself (the real-life Edward Teller) shows up in most of these books and websites designed to illuminate both the humanity and technology of the nuclear age.

■ *'Surely You're Joking, Mr Feynman!,'* by Richard P Feynman. A witty Nobel Prize–winning physicist remembers the Manhattan Project and the minds that made it all happen.

■ *The House at Otowi Bridge,* by Peggy Pond Church. The story of Edith Warner's tearoom, where scientists mingled with San Ildefonso Indians.

■ *The Making of the Atomic Bomb,* by Richard Rhodes. The best-written, best-researched history of the bomb yet.

■ *My Country Versus Me,* by Wen Ho Lee. Dr Lee's side of the story that alleged that he, while working at Los Alamos Labs, gave information about the US nuclear program to China. Turns out not to be true – the story, that is. The *New York Times,* which first ran the story in 1999, and the government later apologized. But between then and then (278 days to be exact), Lee was kept in solitary confinement in chains. Lee received a settlement of $1.6 million from media agencies and the US government in 2006 for violating his privacy.

■ Los Alamos National Laboratories (www.lanl.gov). The official LANL website.

■ Los Alamos Study Group (www.lasg.org). All the news you can use (and hair you could lose) from folks on the other side of the fence.

www.losalamoshistory.org; 1921 Juniper St; admission free; ⊗ 9:30am-4:30pm Mon-Sat, 1-4pm Sun). This museum provides a wrenching 360-degree photo of Hiroshima the morning after the US launched the world's first atomic bomb attack. Exhibits also include overviews of local geology, Native American culture and early homesteading.

The outstanding LANL monthly public lecture series takes place next door at **Fuller Lodge** (☎ 662-9331; 2132 Central Ave, Los Alamos), and the museum bookshop sells a wealth of interesting related tomes.

PAJARITO MOUNTAIN SKI AREA

Cold fusion still eludes them, but frustrated physicists strap on their skis and get inspired at this small **resort** (☎ 662-5725; www .skipajarito.com; 397 Camp May; lift tickets adult $43, child $28-34; ⊗ 9am-4pm Fri-Sun Dec-Apr), operated by the nonprofit Los Alamos Ski Club. It's got short lines for five lifts, 37 trails and 1400ft of vertical drop, all topped with 125in of snow annually – but no snow machines.

HIKING

The city's dramatic location above several finger canyons means Los Alamos has more than its fair share of hiking. Favorites include the steep, 2-mile-round-trip **Blue Dot Trail**, descending 70ft into White Rock

Canyon from Overlook Park, and the similarly steep, 3-mile-round-trip, petroglyph-lined **Red Dot Trail**, beginning at La Senda Park. For more options, check out www .losalamos.com/hiking.

Sleeping

Most visitors are government employees with tight expense accounts and low expectations, and rooms tend to be both threadbare and overpriced, with bargains on the weekends.

North Road Inn (☎ 662-3678, 800-279-2898; www .northroadinn.com; 2127 North Rd; r $75; P ⊠ ▢) One of several B&Bs in Los Alamos, this is a businesslike affair serving continental breakfasts. Probably the best deal in town.

Holiday Inn Express (☎ 661-1110; 2455 Trinity Dr; d weekdays/weekends incl breakfast $90/75; P ⊠ ⊠ ▢) Arguably the nicest chain offering in town. Add $10 to prices for suites.

Adobe Pines B&B (☎ 661-8828; www.losalamos lodging.com; 2101 Loma Linda; r $90; P ⊠ ▢) Nicer than many, a pretty adobe overlooking a canyon.

Best Western Hilltop House (☎ 662-2441, 800-464-0936; 400 Trinity Dr; d weekends $115, weekdays $85-100; P ⊠ ⊠ ▢ ▣) Not far behind Holiday Inn as the best chain accommodation in Los Alamos.

Eating

When asked about their favorite spot for an inexpensive meal, residents invariably reply, 'Española.' But there are a few gems on the hill.

Hot Rocks Java Cafe (☎ 663-5282; 4200 Jemez Rd at Research Park near TA-3; dishes $4-8; ☒ 6am-6pm Mon-Fri; P ☒ ☒ V ☒) Grab sandwiches, daily hot specials and other quick and convenient fare while rubbing shoulders with scientists from the many private-sector players like Sun Microsystems and Motorola who are linked with LANL.

Hill Diner (☎ 662-9745; 1315 Trinity Dr; dishes $7-9; ☒ 11am-9pm, 11am-8pm winter; P ☒ ☒ V ☒) Physicists and flunkies alike flock to this restaurant decorated with photos of old scientists. They come for all-American comfort foods, including several species of barbecue, and downright Midwestern mashed potatoes on the side.

Katherine's (☎ 672-9661; 121 Longview Dr, White Rock; lunch $7-10, dinner $12-24; ☒ 11:30am-1:30pm Tue-Fri, 5:30-9pm Tue-Sat; P ☒ ☒ V) This White Rock restaurant, featuring fresh and hearty European gourmet standards in style – anything Italian is a sure bet – is the most elegant place in town.

Lemongrass (☎ 661-4221; 160 Central Park Sq; dishes $7-11; ☒ 11am-2pm Mon-Fri, 5-9pm Mon-Sat; P ☒ ☒ V ☒) This strip-mall entry serves authentic Vietnamese fare and sugary iced coffee.

Getting There & Around

You can get here by car from several directions: from Santa Fe and Pojoaque Pueblo on NM 502, and from Española and Santa Clara Pueblo along NM 30, which joins NM 502 for the last stretch up the hill into downtown. White Rock, Bandelier and the museums are all well signed from this road. The most scenic route, from Albuquerque, is through the Jemez Mountains (p192).

The **Los Alamos Bus System** (☎ 662-2080; www .labus.org; $1-3; ☒ 6am-6pm Mon-Fri) runs buses every 15 minutes throughout the limited Los Alamos downtown area. Roadrunner Shuttle offers an on-demand service (advance reservations required) from the Santa Fe Municipal Airport ($50 one way) and the Albuquerque Sunport ($75 one way) but often does not provide service after 6pm.

BANDELIER NATIONAL MONUMENT

The reason why **Bandelier** (☎ 672-3861; www .nps.gov/band; car for 7 days $12; ☒ 8am-dusk) is so expensive and crowded – some 350,000 people visit the park annually – is because it's incredible. Pale and pockmarked canyon walls plunging into lush, narrow valleys would have marked this land for preservation even without the beautiful and well-preserved Puebloan Indian ruins, occupied between 1150 and 1550. Show up early on weekends to beat the crowds.

More than 70 miles of trails traverse almost 33,000 acres of pine forest. Standouts include the easy 1.4-mile **Main Loop Trail**, which runs past petroglyphs and the Frijoles Ruins, with a worthwhile 2-mile round-trip spur out to the skyscraping **Ceremonial Cave**, otherwise known as the Alcove House. (The 150ft of ladders at the Alcove House may not be suitable for smaller kids but climbing into these actual, ancient dwellings is a remarkable experience for everyone else.) **Falls Trail** offers a 3-mile round-trip to the Upper Falls, and a steep and recommended 5-mile round-trip past the Lower Falls to the Rio Grande. In an unattached segment of the park 13 miles north on NM 4, 2-mile **Tsankawi Trail** threads along a path so ancient that it's literally worn into the mesa bedrock.

Hard-core hikers should consider taking the three-day, 28-mile walkabout to **Stone Lion Shrine**, near the ruins of Yapashi Pueblo, an ancestral home of the Chochiti tribe. This is still a sacred site of pilgrimage, so please respect the two ancient carvings of lions, which probably predate Pueblo culture. A free backcountry permit is required for overnight hikes.

Juniper Campground (tent/RV $12) is close to the visitors center, which has maps, guidebooks and historical artifacts on display.

The park is located on NM 4, 12 miles from Los Alamos, and can also be accessed from Jemez Springs.

Taos

You can almost hear the tugging of your own heartstrings when you lay eyes on Taos; your senses register sage in the air, silver conch decorating belts and saddles, that sweep of mesa as it rises suddenly to crest at Taos Mountain. The same wayward wind that tousles your hair has been stirring souls for centuries as it sifts through canyons and down dusty byways.

A lucky breakdown stranded a couple of artists here on the cusp of the 20th century, giving rise to an artists' enclave. Eons of wanderers and explorers have fallen under the spell of the place as well. Taos has gathered the most remarkable collection of people to its scenic breast and nurtured them to magnificence far beyond what one would expect from a small mountain village. It's a haven where refugees from the modern world – whether the 16th or 21st century – have collected themselves and made homes.

Tourists come here, most certainly, to challenge themselves at one of the nation's top ski resorts, just the tip of a mountain of attractions. Art collectors, movie stars and the merely curious wander galleries and museums, but Taos doesn't consciously cater to them – which is a bit shocking after a few days in Santa Fe. Then it's a relief.

Taos is its own world, welcoming those willing to accept its own strange terms.

HIGHLIGHTS

- Revitalize your soul at the deeply spiritual **Taos Pueblo** (p156)
- Indulge your taste for the arts at the **Millicent Rogers Museum** (p139)
- Visit the historic adobe church **San Francisco de Asis** (p141)
- Saddle up for horseback tours in the **Blue Lakes Wilderness** (p157)
- Exercise your wallet and your eyes at the shops and galleries on **Ledoux St** (p154)
- Savor the **Taos Ski Valley** (p158), remarkable in any season
- Drive behind the scenes on the **back roads** (p160)
- Fight off vertigo at **Rio Grande Gorge Bridge** (p141) as you take in the rising and setting sun
- Get off the grid at **Earthships** (p142)
- Feast your eyes on the art at the **Harwood Foundation Museum** (p139)

| ■ TELEPHONE CODE: 505 | ■ POPULATION: 4700 | ■ ELEVATION: 6950FT |

TAOS IN...

ONE DAY

Get up early in Santa Fe and take the **Low Road to Taos** (p128), making a quick detour to **San Francisco de Asis** (p141). In Taos, chow down at **Mante's Chow Cart** (p151) or **Caffe Tazza** (p151). Pop into galleries and shops on **Ledoux St** before visiting the **Harwood Foundation Museum** (p139). Visit **La Fonda** (p151) for a peek at **DH Lawrence's Forbidden Art** before heading to **Taos Pueblo** (p156). Enjoy an early dinner at **Lambert's** (p153), leaving time to watch the sunset at **Rio Grande Gorge Bridge** (p141). Listen to some music and down a margarita (just one!) at **Adobe Bar** (p153) before returning to Santa Fe.

TWO DAYS

Take the **Low Road to Taos**, stopping at **Embudo Station** (p129) on the way and then **San Francisco de Asis**. Check into your hotel and make a bee-line for **Taos Pueblo**. Visit the **Blumenschein** (p140) today and the **Harwood** tomorrow. Drink margaritas. Watch the sunrise over the **Rio Grande Gorge** and tour an **earthship** (p142). Return via the **Millicent Rogers Museum** (p139) and have a lunchtime burrito at **Orlando's** (p152). Then it's the **High Road** (p125) south, with stops at **La Chiripada Winery** (p131), galleries in **Truchas** (p127) and the **Santuario de Chimayó** (p127). Relax at **Rancho de Chimayó** (p126) for dinner before heading back to Santa Fe.

FIVE DAYS

Follow the two-day itinerary, but instead of taking the High Road, stop into **La Hacienda Martinez** (p140) then head north, lunching in **Arroyo Seco** (p157) and hiking at **Taos Ski Valley** (p158). Watch the sun set, have a late dinner, then relax in hot springs or a hot tub. Wake early to drive the **Enchanted Circle** (p160), paying respects at the **DH Lawrence Memorial** (p161) and hiking or driving the **Wild Rivers Recreation Area** (p163). Sleep in **Red River** (p163). Continue in the morning with more hiking or fishing and visit the **Vietnam Veterans Memorial** (p167). After a long shower in your Taos hotel room, scope out the live music scene – at **Eske's** (p154)? The **Alley Cantina** (p154)? The Adobe Bar again? Wake up late, grab some breakfast and poke around the galleries before hitting the High Road back to Santa Fe.

ORIENTATION

Downtown Taos is at the northern terminus of NM 68, called Paseo del Pueblo Sur (roughly, 'South Pueblo Rd') as it enters the village, and is centered on the intersection of US 64 (called Kit Carson Rd as it heads southeast toward Angel Fire) and Paseo del Pueblo Norte ('North Pueblo Rd'). Together, the paseos are often referred to as Main St.

As you hit Taos coming north from Santa Fe on NM 68, Paseo del Pueblo Sur is lined with budget hotels, chain stores and restaurants. Continue north a couple more increasingly gridlocked miles on Paseo del Pueblo Sur into downtown.

One mile north of town, Paseo del Pueblo Norte forks: to the northeast it becomes Camino del Pueblo and heads toward Taos Pueblo; to the northwest, US 64 continues to the intersection of Taos Ski Valley Rd (NM 150), NM 522 to Questa and, after making a hard left at the stoplight, to the

Rio Grande Gorge Bridge. Though just a normal stoplight now, this intersection was once marked by the 'blinking light' and is still sometimes referred to as such.

Maps

Taos is small enough to navigate using the maps provided in this book, but Rand McNally's *Santa Fe/Taos Local Street Detail* folding map, available at most gas stations, has more detail. Real wanderers will want to pick up a copy of the *New Mexico Road & Recreation Atlas*. Native Sons Adventures (p142) and Cottam's (p144) both carry large selections of maps, including USGS topos.

INFORMATION
Bookshops

Taos is still served well by a lively enclave of independent booksellers.

Brodsky Bookshop (Map p138; ☎ 758-9468; 226B Paseo del Pueblo Norte; 10am-6pm Mon-Sat) A treasure

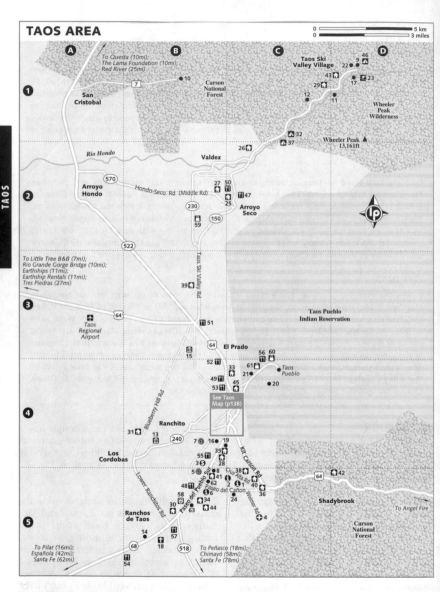

TAOS AREA

hunt of a layout, with contemporary and classic literature, a nice children's selection (a favorite hang-out of fluffy, black Simone de Beauvoir, a tome of a cat in her own right), fiction, Southwest and Native American titles, as well as used books.

Lucille's Book Exchange (Map p138; cnr Camino de la Placita & Ledoux St) A book-lover's dream, with heaps of used paperbacks.

Moby Dickens (Map p138; ☎ 758-3050, 999-442-9980; www.mobydickens.com; 124A Bent St; ⏱ 10am-6pm Mon-Thu, 10am-8pm Fri & Sat) It's always interesting to poke around this collection of new, used, rare and really rare classics.

Mystery Ink Bookshop (Map p138; ☎ 751-1092; 121 Camino de la Placita; 10am-5pm Mon-Fri, 11am-5pm Sat) Mystery lovers flock here to linger over the latest offerings, chilling classics and some kids' books, too.

(Chile Relleno Nogado)
Antonio's - Mexican Food

TAOS

Emergency

Fire, Police, Ambulance Immediate Dispatch (☎ 911)

Holy Cross Hospital Emergency Room (Map p136; ☎ 758-8883; 1397 Weimer Rd)

Police (Map p138; ☎ 758-2216; 107 Civic Plaza Dr)

Internet Access

Magic Circle Bagels Cyber Cafe (Map p136; ☎ 758-0045; 710 Paseo del Pueblo Sur; per hr $6; ⏰ 6:30am-3pm Mon-Fri, 7am-2pm Sat, 7am-noon Sun) Three fairly fast computers go well with lattes, soups and 19 different bagels (snacks $3 to $6). In the Raley's shopping center.

Taos Plaza Sit at a bench and flip your laptop open anywhere on the plaza and start surfing for free.

Taos Public Library (Map p138; ☎ 758-3063; 402 Camino de la Placita; ⏰ noon-6pm Mon, 10am-6pm Tue-Fri, 10am-5pm Sat) Internet access costs $1 per half hour (one hour maximum) without a library card. A temporary (four-month) card without residency costs a buck plus a $25 refundable deposit and grants you full library access.

Wired CyberCafe (Map p136; ☎ 751-9473; 705 Felicidad Lane; ⏰ 7am-7pm Mon-Fri, 8am-7pm Sat & Sun, 7am-5pm daily Oct-Mar) Internet access costs you nothing if you BYO laptop; otherwise $2 buys you 15 minutes ($7 per hour) if you rent one of the café's rigs. Enjoy high-speed java drinks and fabulous munchies in this atmospheric hang-out.

Internet Resources

Destination Taos (www.destinationtaos.com) The chamber of commerce posts events listings and tourism and relocation information online.

Taos Guide (www.taosguide.com) Click for an exhaustive list of easy-to-navigate links.

Taos Is Art Online (www.taosis.com) Check the schedule of art openings and studio tours, plus links and articles on local galleries.

Taos Link (www.taoslink.com) Busy-looking, but loaded with links to every website even remotely associated with Taos.

Taos Webb (www.taoswebb.com) Access links and information, including sites covering north-central New Mexico.

Media
PUBLICATIONS

To get the lowdown on what's going on where, check out the following:

Horse Fly (www.horseflyonline.com) A fat, free, monthly journal of politics and arts that includes at least three inspired rants about sometimes-Taos-resident Donald Rumsfeld in each edition.

Taos News (www.taosnews.com) This award-winning daily updates its website every Friday, when it also publishes the weekly arts and entertainment pullout *Tempo*, with events listings.

TAOS

0 _____ 300 m
0 _____ 0.2 miles

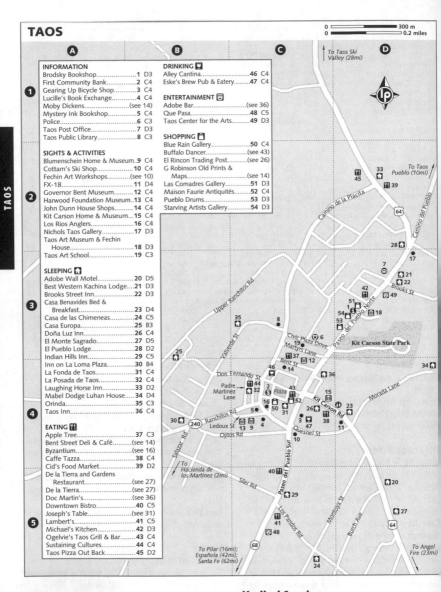

INFORMATION
Brodsky Bookshop.....................**1** D3
First Community Bank...............**2** C4
Gearing Up Bicycle Shop...........**3** C4
Lucille's Book Exchange............**4** C4
Moby Dickens......................(see 14)
Mystery Ink Bookshop..............**5** C4
Police.................................**6** C3
Taos Post Office....................**7** D3
Taos Public Library.................**8** C3

SIGHTS & ACTIVITIES
Blumenschein Home & Museum..**9** D3
Cottam's Ski Shop...................**10** C4
Fechin Art Workshops...........(see 10)
FX-18.................................**11** D4
Governor Bent Museum...........**12** C4
Harwood Foundation Museum..**13** C4
John Dunn House Shops..........**14** C4
Kit Carson Home & Museum.....**15** C4
Los Rios Anglers....................**16** C4
Nichols Taos Gallery...............**17** D3
Taos Art Museum & Fechin
  House..............................**18** D3
Taos Art School.....................**19** C3

SLEEPING
Adobe Wall Motel..................**20** D5
Best Western Kachina Lodge....**21** D3
Brooks Street Inn....................**22** D3
Casa Benavides Bed &
  Breakfast..........................**23** D4
Casa de las Chimeneas............**24** C5
Casa Europa.........................**25** B3
Doña Luz Inn........................**26** C4
El Monte Sagrado..................**27** D5
El Pueblo Lodge....................**28** D2
Indian Hills Inn.....................**29** C5
Inn on La Loma Plaza..............**30** B4
La Fonda de Taos...................**31** C4
La Posada de Taos..................**32** C4
Laughing Horse Inn.................**33** D2
Mabel Dodge Luhan House......**34** D4
Orinda................................**35** C3
Taos Inn...............................**36** C4

EATING
Apple Tree............................**37** C3
Bent Street Deli & Café.........(see 14)
Byzantium........................(see 16)
Caffe Tazza...........................**38** C4
Cid's Food Market..................**39** D2
De la Tierra and Gardens
  Restaurant........................(see 27)
De la Tierra........................(see 27)
Doc Martin's.....................(see 36)
Downtown Bistro...................**40** C5
Joseph's Table...................(see 31)
Lambert's............................**41** C5
Michael's Kitchen...................**42** D3
Ogelvie's Taos Grill & Bar........**43** C4
Sustaining Cultures.................**44** C4
Taos Pizza Out Back...............**45** D2

DRINKING
Alley Cantina........................**46** C4
Eske's Brew Pub & Eatery.......**47** C4

ENTERTAINMENT
Adobe Bar..........................(see 36)
Que Pasa.............................**48** C5
Taos Center for the Arts........**49** D3

SHOPPING
Blue Rain Gallery...................**50** C4
Buffalo Dancer....................(see 43)
El Rincon Trading Post..........(see 26)
G Robinson Old Prints &
  Maps...............................(see 14)
Las Comadres Gallery............**51** D3
Maison Faurie Antiquités.........**52** C4
Pueblo Drums.......................**53** D3
Starving Artists Gallery............**54** D3

RADIO & TELEVISION

All TV stations and most radio stations are based in Santa Fe and Albuquerque, with a few exceptions. National Public Radio (NPR) is on KRZA 88.7 FM and 91.9 FM, while KXMT 99.1 FM is Spanish-language public radio. KTAO 101.9 FM (p143) is a local station that broadcasts using solar power.

Medical Services

Holy Cross Hospital (Map p136; ☎ 758-8883; www .taoshospital.com; 1397 Weimer Rd) Southeast of town; make a right onto Weimer Rd off Paseo del Cañon E.
Raley's Supermarket (Map p136; ☎ 758-1203; 1100 Paseo del Pueblo Sur; ⏰ 9am-7:30pm Mon-Fri, 9am-4:30pm Sat, 9am-2:30pm Sun) There's a pharmacy here.

Money

There is nowhere in town to exchange foreign currency.

Centinel Bank (Map p136; ☎ 758-6700; 512 Paseo del Pueblo Sur) Has drive-through ATMs, but it's worth going inside to see the rotating and permanent collections of Southwest art, including some impressive work from heavy-hitters of the art world.

First Community Bank (Map p138; ☎ 758-6600; 120 W Plaza) Conveniently located downtown; has an ATM.

Post

Taos Post Office (Map p138; ☎ 758-2081; 318 Paseo del Pueblo Norte) The main post office is just north of the plaza.

Tourist Offices

Bureau of Land Management (BLM; Map p136; ☎ 758-8851; www.nm.blm.gov; 226 Cruz Alta Rd; 7:30am-4:30pm Mon-Fri) This office has information about recreational activities on public lands.

Carson National Forest Supervisor's Office (Map p136; ☎ 758-6200; www.fs.fed.us/r3/carson; 208 Cruz Alta Rd; 8am-4:30pm Mon-Fri) Just down the road from BLM, this office has information on hiking, camping, rafting and everything else about this forest.

Taos Visitors Center (Map p136; ☎ 758-3873; www.taoschamber.com; cnr Paseo del Pueblo Sur & Paseo del Cañon; 9am-5pm Mon-Sat, 9am-5pm Sun in summer) Stop here for flyers, a small museum on Taos Pueblo, and Historic Taos Trolley Tours (p146). This center also has free wireless internet available as well as two hard-wired computers for visitors to use.

SIGHTS

For a village that gets as much tourist traffic as Taos, there aren't many sights. **Downtown** is a collection of ancient and irregularly shaped adobes centered on the picturesque **plaza**, threaded through by historic **Ledoux St** – at least one bar dates to the 16th century.

The **Museum Association of Taos** (www.taosmuseums.org) offers a $20 pass to five area museums (a $35 value). All the museums have different hours, themes and single-entry prices.

The area's two top attractions, **Taos Pueblo** and **Taos Ski Valley**, are covered in their own sections later in this chapter.

Harwood Foundation Museum

With a grand Pueblo Revival exterior, the **Harwood Foundation Museum** (Map p138; ☎ 758-9826; www.harwoodmuseum.org; 238 Ledoux St; adult/child under 12 $7/free; 10am-5pm Tue-Sat, noon-5pm Sun),

the second-oldest in New Mexico, is about as world-class as it gets in a town this size. It houses the largest collection of works from the original Taos Society of Arts (TSA) and a sprawling array of fine cultural expression spanning the past couple of centuries – from one of John Gaw Meem's earliest works to touring exhibitions such as a Jasper Johns retrospective.

Anyone with a passing interest in New Mexico art will recognize pieces like John Ward Lockwood's *Portrait of Clyde Lockwood*, Irving Couse's *Cacique* and the largest public collection of bultos carved by Patrociño Barela anywhere.

If you're over the TSA theme, check out the white-on-white work of internationally acclaimed artist and long-time Taos resident Agnes Martin. Upstairs you'll find work of many Hispanic Works Progress Administration (WPA) artists, with an emphasis on santos, reredos and other sacred art.

Millicent Rogers Museum

See what a top-quality squashblossom necklace is supposed to look like at the jam-packed **Millicent Rogers Museum** (Map p136; ☎ 758-2462; www.millicentrogers.org; 1504 Millicent Rogers Rd; adult/child $8/2; 10am-5pm, closed Mon Nov-Mar), showcasing the collection of oil heiress, fashion designer and Native arts aficionado Millicent Rogers, who possessed a Lauren Bacall–style glamour and lots of fantastic jewelry.

The 'Best Dressed List' alumna spent the 1940s and '50s defining Santa Fe style – velvet Navajo shirts and flowing skirts cinched with concha belts, accented with heavy silver bracelets and draped with those necklaces – and she made it work. Then everybody else tried it.

You can see her smashing outfits and endless assortment of accessories here, along with one of the best collections of pueblo pottery in existence. The museum showcases the gleaming Martinez (as in Maria; p119) family collection, plus work by all the important matriarchs: Santa Clara's Margaret Tofoya, Christina Naranjo and Mary Esther Archuleta; Cochiti's Helen Cordero; and many more.

Spanish artists are also well represented. The largest Spanish-Colonial hide painting (c 1700), showing Christ washing the feet of the disciples, is one of five in existence. You'll also see many Virgens, santos and retablos.

La Hacienda de los Martinez

Built to protect the community from the Comanche raids of the 18th century, the 21-room adobe fortress **La Hacienda de los Martinez** (Map p136; ☎ 758-1000; Ranchitos Rd (NM 240); adult/child $7/3; ☺ 10am-5pm Mon-Sat, noon-5pm Sun) has fun, tactile displays that engage the kids. Adults who take time to read the fine print will come away with a sense of history glossed over elsewhere.

Don Antonio Severino Martinez purchased the property in 1804 and raised six children here, including Padre Antonio Martinez, owner of the region's first printing press. Padre Martinez is remembered best for friction with Archbishop Lamy. *Death Comes for the Archbishop* presents one side of the story – that Martinez and his pals were corrupt – but historians note that Martinez encouraged locals to educate themselves on US property laws, so they wouldn't lose their Spanish land grants.

Displays at the hacienda present a series of obsessively accurate representations of Spanish colonial life: the walls are whitewashed with *tierra blanca,* a mixture of wheat paste and micaceous clay; the churro wool hangings are colored with vegetable dyes; and quilters (on Fridays) and weavers (on Mondays) talk about their craft as it has spanned the eras.

Kit Carson Home & Museum

Tour this recently spiffed-up 1825 adobe spread (Map p138; ☎ 758-4945; 113 Kit Carson Rd; adult/child $5/3; ☺ 9am-6pm, shorter winter hr) with old man Kit himself – or a reasonable facsimile thereof. The duded-up docent will tell you he bought the place in 1843 for his 14-year-old bride, Josefa Jaramillo-Vigil. He also might give you more reasons to remember him than his shooting skills: turns out he was quite the diplomat. Mainly thought of as an 'Indian killer' (though, according to exhibits, only in self-defense), he was also an accomplished linguist, fluent in Spanish, English and at least 10 Native tongues, and could facilitate communication in the Southwest's regular Tower of Babel as he scouted the trail ahead.

Kit was also a staunch supporter of the US government's efforts to annex the territory. Taos is one of only a few places in the USA where the flag can fly at night, as he and his pals guarded it around the clock during the Mexican-American War.

Blumenschein Home & Museum

A fine example of a 200-year-old adobe house, the **Blumenschein Home & Museum** (Map p138; ☎ 758-0505; 222 Ledoux St; adult/child $7/3; ☺ 10am-5pm Mon-Sat, noon-5pm Sun, shorter winter hr) was recently restored and is packed with spectacular artworks by the founder of the Taos art scene. Painter Ernest Blumenschein and fellow artist Bert Phillips broke a wagon wheel 20 miles north of town one fateful September afternoon in 1898. They flipped a coin to see who would go get it fixed. 'Blumy' lost the toss and made his muddy, miserable way into Taos. Then the clouds parted over Taos Pueblo and its awesome backdrop, and that was that.

Phillips relocated to Taos almost immediately, while Blumenschein returned several times to paint the scene, finally moving here for good in 1919. He had to convince his wife and fellow painter, Mary Shepherd Greene, that Taos really wasn't a backwater per se and founded the Taos Society of Artists (opposite) to drive home the point.

Works by all six of the original TSA artists are joined by Mary's detailed illustrations, pieces by their daughter Helen, as well as work by later Taos painters: Elmer Turner, Jozef G Bazos, Leon Gaspard, Gene Kloss and many others.

Taos Art Museum & Fechin House

A fascinating alliance of art museum and historic home, the **Taos Art Museum & Fechin House** (Map p138; ☎ 758-2690; www.taosartmuseum .org; 227 Paseo del Pueblo Norte; admission $4; ☺ 10am-5pm Tue-Sun) is a repository for some of the finest art to arise in Taos. Though he didn't get here until 1927, the year the TSA disbanded, Nicolai Fechin was among the finest artists Taos has ever inspired. Much of his work still hangs at his former home. His paintings, drawings and sculptures are in museums and collections worldwide, but this may be the only place you can see his hand-built furniture, carved with a distinctly Russian intent.

Fechin transformed the adobe structure with trompe l'oeil archways and massive architectural elements. Upstairs, his remarkable oil paintings will soon be joined by the collection of Duane Van Vechten, formerly housed at the Van Vechtin-Lineberry Taos Art Museum. The work of these two impressive talents shares space with Fechin's

TAOS

THE TAOS SOCIETY OF ARTISTS *Bridgette Wagner*

On the cusp of the 20th century, the magnetism of color, light, landscape and the lifestyle of the Wild West drew artists to visit this region. Those who fell under its spell stayed.

In 1893 Joseph Henry Sharp began spreading the word of this mystical spot. Artists Ernest Blumenschein and Bert Phillips were famously halted in their journey to Mexico by a fortuitous breakdown. Others followed, and by 1912 the Taos Society of Artists (TSA) was formed to market their work, with Oscar Berninghaus, Eanger Irving Couse and Herbert Donton fleshing out the ranks of the original six members.

Early TSA paintings were inspired by the backdrop of the Sangre de Cristo Mountains as well as the buildings and people of Taos Pueblo. Set against the tonal shapes and neutral colors of earth, human figures act as anchors of color seen nowhere else in the desert. Pueblo architecture, with its golden clusters of block shapes, organic and sculptural, reflecting the high desert light, also appealed to the Taos painters' artistic sensibilities.

The artists' styles were as diverse and experimental as the many philosophies of painting that defined the first half of the 20th century. From Sharp's illustrative and realistic approach and Blumenschein's impressionistic treatment of Southwestern themes to the moody art-deco spirit of Dunton's landscapes, the TSA portrayed the same subjects in infinite ways.

Larger collections of these influential works can be viewed in Taos at the Harwood Foundation (p139) and Blumenschein (opposite) museums. In Santa Fe, look to the Museum of Fine Arts (p68) as well as the Gerald Peters (p109) and Nedra Matteucci (p110) galleries.

---

private collection, including lots of Asian art. The lovely adobe also hosts occasional chamber music events.

Governor Bent Museum

Alongside the eclectic artifacts in **Governor Bent Museum** (Map p138; ☎ 758-2376; 117-A Bent St; adult/child $2/1; ☾ 10am-5pm, shorter winter hr) swirls a fascinating matrix of speculation concerning the uprising of January 19, 1847. Even if you linger only to see the hole in the adobe wall through which the wives of Governor Charles Bent and Kit Carson escaped during the uprising, this place is worth a stop.

When the USA annexed New Mexico in 1846, Bent became the first US territorial governor and clearly had no idea what he was getting into. Though locals didn't organize regular troops to resist the incursion, a group of guerillas (or drunks, depending on which historian you talk to) loyal to former Governor Armijo allied with several Indians from Taos Pueblo, although it's unclear if they were acting with the pueblo government's blessing. The details of the attack remain shrouded in history, but while his family escaped Bent was scalped, touching off yet another bloody episode in European-Native relations.

In addition to the hole in the wall, the museum features lots of animal skulls, stuffed guanas, mastodon tusks, a collection of beer steins, and all sorts of Indian, Aleutian,

Spanish and Anglo artifacts not necessarily hailing from the Governor Bent period.

San Francisco de Asis Church

An authentic adobe structure 4 miles south of Taos, this Ranchos de Taos church has an unusual grace that inspires artists to capture its slow and beautiful dance with ever-changing sunlight. Built in the mid-18th century and opened in 1815, **San Francisco de Asis Church** (Map p136; ☎ 758-2754; St Francis Plaza; donations appreciated; ☾ 9am-4pm, closed for masses at 7am, 9am & 11:30am) once served as a refuge from attack – hence the fortress-like walls.

Inside the church *The Shadow of the Cross*, a painting by Henri Ault, is a miracle that you too can witness firsthand ($3; last showing 4pm). Step into the side room where you'll watch a video, after which the room goes entirely dark. Above Christ's left shoulder, the luminous silhouette of a cross (some folks also see a boat) appears. Neither scientists nor Ault himself have been able to explain the apparition.

Rio Grande Gorge Bridge

The most magical time to visit this vertigo-inducing bridge (Map p162) is in the early-morning hours, when you might catch a hot-air balloon wafting above or below this lofty 650ft perch. Located on US 64 about 12 miles northwest of Taos, this is the second-highest suspension bridge in the USA. A walkway runs along the entire 1272ft span. When it was built in 1965 it was called the 'Bridge to Nowhere' because funding ran out before the road could be continued when it reached the other side. The second-most magical time might be at night, when the ghost of a young woman has reportedly appeared near the center of the bridge before vanishing. There's always magic in the western views over the empty Taos Plateau and down into the jagged walls of the Rio Grande.

Earthships

About 2 miles past the Rio Grande Gorge the world's premier sustainable, self-sufficient community of spaceships – er, Earthships – rises from the planet like a scene from your favorite B-movie. Go ahead, take the **Solar Survival Tour** (Map p162; ☎ 751-0462; http://earthship.com; US 64; tour $5; ☻ 10am-4pm) and you might just decide to build your own pod sweet pod.

The brainchild of architect Mike Reynolds, sometimes described as one-third visionary, one-third entrepreneur and one-third cult leader, earthships are a form of biotecture (biology + architecture = buildings based on biological systems of resource use and conservation) that maximizes available resources so that you'll never have to be on the grid again.

Walls made of old tires are laid out for appropriate passive solar use, packed with tamped earth, then buried on three sides for maximum insulation. The structures are outfitted with photovoltaic cells and an elaborate gray-water system that collects rain and snow, which filters through several cycles that begin in the kitchen and end in the garden.

Though Taos is their homeworld, earthships have landed in Japan, Bolivia, Scotland, Mexico and beyond, often organized into little communities, and more are being built using available kits. Buy one already built, starting at $150,000. You can tour a deluxe version or even stay overnight; if you've come as far as the bridge, at least drive by.

ACTIVITIES

Tucked as it is into the mountains, wrapped as it is by canyons and rivers, it doesn't take long to get from Taos to an endless variety of outdoor activities, from llama trekking and Nordic skiing to hot-air balloon rides. **Taos Outdoor Recreation** (www.taosoutdoorrecreation.com) has an online rundown of all your options.

Native Sons Adventures (Map p136; ☎ 758-9342, 800-753-7559; www.nativesonsadventures.com; 1033 Paseo del Pueblo Sur; ☻ 7:30am-7pm winter, 7:30am-5pm summer) is a one-stop adventure-tour shop: take a guided bike tour ($25 per hour) or just have guides shuttle you to a trail ($25 per person, $80 minimum). You might also try a 3½-hour guided ATV tour ($85), a guided hike ($110) or a white-water rafting trip (half/full day/two days $50/99/325). In winter you can rent skis, snowmobiles and other equipment. The store also sells just about everything you'd need to strike out on your own, including USGS maps and guidebooks. If Native Sons can't get enough people together to make shuttles to hiking and biking trails cost-effective, contact Faust Transportation (p155), which may be able to get you there for less.

The huge **Taos Mountain Outfitters** (Map p138; ☎ 758-9292; www.taosmountainoutfitters.com; 114 S Plaza) has everything – including guides, maps and gear – you need to get out and play: sleeping bags, tents, backpacks, cross-country ski packages and more. The staff can point you toward top spots or guides who can show you the ropes.

Hiking

For a rundown of backwoods adventure options, you'll find a wealth of information at the Carson National Forest Supervisor's Office (p139) or BLM (p139).

You'll find excursions beyond Taos in other sections of this book, including Taos Ski Valley (p158), with several spectacular and difficult climbs, including the challenging trail to Wheeler Peak; Wild Rivers Recreation Area (p163), with a plethora of short hikes into and along the scenic canyon; Orilla Verde Recreation Area (p129), with great views of the Rio Grande Gorge, and Red River (p163), worth the drive for access to alpine lakes and the longer, prettier trail to Wheeler Peak.

Oso Negro (☎ 776-1628), in San Cristobal, offers guided hikes into the wilderness and teaches outdoor skills. Prices start at half/full day $50/75. Native Sons Adventures (above) can hook you up with others.

If you enjoy **hiking with llamas** (who'll carry all the water), you're in luck: two

GOOD DAY SUNSHINE

Those within 40 miles of Taos will get their sunshine from more than just the sky: it'll come beaming from their radios in the form of KTAO 101.9 FM, broadcasting from Taos and powered entirely with sunshine. Programming covers every conceivable permutation of music, as well as interviews with the famous, infamous, and others who normally live their lives below the radar.

Station owner Brad Hockmeyer installed 500,000 watts worth of photovoltaic cells atop Mt Picuris in 1991 and beams those radio waves throughout the region.

Of all the events the station sponsors, nothing rivals the **Solar Music Festival** (p147), held the last weekend in June as a benefit for the **New Mexico Solar Energy Association** (www.nmsea .org). Talent like Ani DiFranco show up here to plug into the sun and fill the air with music.

A free Solar Village sets up outside the gates, showcasing everything from the Los Alamos National Laboratory's solar-powered supercomputer to homemade solar cookers. Grab a cup of solar-percolated coffee and chat up the fine folks from the **Taos Earthship Community** (opposite) and alternative-energy lovers pitching straw-bale construction, solar cars and passive solar design ('used at Taos Pueblo for a thousand years!').

Long renowned for its quality of light – though the artists who extolled that virtue probably didn't have anything like this in mind – Taos is on the crest of a trend, and indie radio stations and private homeowners nationwide come here to learn more about harnessing all that free sunshine, then dance the night away.

outfitters, **El Paseo Llama Expeditions** (☎ 800-455-2627; www.elpaseollama.com; half/full day $64/84, 2- to 8-day overnights per day $125) and **Wild Earth Llama Adventures** (☎ 800-758-5262; www.llamaadventures .com; day/overnight $89/299) offer 'Take a Llama to Lunch' day hikes and multiday excursions near Taos and Santa Fe, with guides strong in the nature-knowledge department. Note that El Paseo lets your tots ride the beasts, while Wild Earth does not.

Fishing

Taos is ringed with stocked streams and lakes that draw adventuresome anglers (some choice spots require a rigorous hike to reach) happy hooking trout, cutthroat and German brown. Many sites are within steps of your car door; some spots are fully handicapped-accessible.

Red River (p163) and the Rio Grande generally have the best fishing September through April, while Cimarron Canyon State Park (p166) and area lakes (some stocked with salmon) are best between May and September. You must have a license to take advantage of all those fish; contact **New Mexico Game & Fish** (☎ 505-476-8000 in Santa Fe, 222-4700 in Albuquerque; www.wildlife.state.nm.us).

Los Rios Anglers (Map p138; ☎ 758-2798, 800-748-1707; www.losrios.com; 126 W Plaza Dr) specializes in elite guided fly-fishing trips (one/two persons half day $175/200, one/two persons full day $250/300) onto unspoiled private

lands threaded with secret sparkling streams. Make reservations 48 hours in advance. Or do it yourself – they've got all the tackle you could possibly need.

Taos High Mountain Angler (☎ 770-1419; www .highmountainangler.com) leads evening fishing trips ($145) and guided day trips (half day one/two persons $185/210, full day one/two persons $275/300) to areas such as Ville Vidal, Rio Costilla, Red River and the Rio Grande. They also rent rods and tackle ($12) and waders ($12), and produce a line of custom hand-built rods. In addition to organizing custom fly-fishing trips, **Ed Adams** (☎ 586-1512; www.edadamsflyfishing.com), in nearby Questa, runs trips (half/full day $200/275) while maintaining a river schedule and fishing reports online.

Rafting

The froth in Taos Box drops 90ft per mile, making it one of the wildest rides in the West. Mellower Class III Rio Grande Gorge attracts a flurry of sunburned and screaming tourists to the put-in at Pilar. The best time to go is May and June, when snowmelt (usually) keeps the rivers rapid, but it's warm enough to enjoy the splash. If you know what you're doing, the **BLM** (www.nm.blm.gov) has information for independent river rats.

Los Rios River Runners (Map p136; ☎ 776-8854, 800-544-1181; www.losriosriverrunners.com; 4003 S NM 68 at mile-marker 40) can take you on a variety of full-day trips including the Box (adult/child $109/95), Lower Gorge ($89/79) and an ultramellow half-day float fine for little kids at Orilla Verde Recreation Area ($48/39). Racecourse is the most popular section of the Rio Grande, and Los Rios will take you right to it (adult/child $48/39). The company also offers multiday camping and rafting trips on the Rio Grande (adults only, $289 to $450) and the Rio Chama (adult/child $450/350). Native Sons Adventures (p142) can set you up as well.

Pilar offers more opportunities for getting wet, while there's an opportunity for dinner floats at Embudo Station (p129).

Horseback Riding
A number of stables offer horseback rides nearby, including Taos Indian Horse Ranch (p157).

From July through September, **Rio Grande Stables** (Map p136; ☎ 776-5913; www.lajitasstables .com/taos.htm; near the Ski Valley) offers one- to four-hour trips ($40 to $80), all-day jaunts (including to the top of Wheeler Peak for $140) and half-day trots with lunch ($85). Attend a Cowboy Clinic and brush up on those roping skills at **Bobcat Pass Wilderness Adventures** (Map p162; ☎ 754-2769; www.bobcatspass .com; Red River), or hop on a horse for an hour ($30) or a full day ($125). Lose yourself in September foliage on a five- or seven-day pack trip ($225 per day).

Mountain Biking
Where else are you going to find biking this good, this close to the sky? Why bother looking elsewhere when an enormous network of mountain-bike and multiuse trails cover the region of the Carson National Forest between Taos, Angel Fire and Picuris Peak? Pick up maps and information at the Carson National Forest Supervisor's Office (p139).

Standouts include the 9-mile **West Rim Trail** at Orilla Verde Recreation Area, suitable for strong beginners and intermediate cyclists who enjoy views of Rio Grande Gorge; and storied **South Boundary Trail**, considered one of the best mountain-bike trails in the nation – a 28-mile ride for experienced bikers, with maps and more specific information; talk to Native Sons (p142).

Check Red River (p165) for more mountain-biking opportunities, including downhill runs from the top of the chairlift.

The 84-mile **Enchanted Circle** loop makes a fine road-bike circuit, once you've acclimated to the altitude.

In addition to Native Sons, **Gearing Up Bicycle Shop** (Map p138; ☎ 751-0365; www.gearingup bikeshop.com; 129 Paseo del Pueblo Sur; ☼ 9am-6:30pm) rents mountain and hybrid bikes (per hour/day/week $10/35/123), full-suspension bikes ($50 per day) and road bikes ($45 per day).

Skiing
When there's snow, Taos Ski Valley (p158) is as spectacular as ever – and is still one of a handful of ski areas in the country that bans snowboards. If this doesn't suit, check out other nearby ski resorts including Angel Fire (p167), which has opened its slopes to shredders, providing some awesome board runs and a 400ft half-pipe. Red River (p164) overlooks a friendly resort town and boasts fantastic beginner and intermediate skiing. Enchanted Forest (p164) has 25 miles of groomed Nordic trails while Sipapú (p128) is a small family-owned resort.

Carson National Forest maintains crosscountry ski trails, and you can pick up the free guide, *Where to Go in the Snow*, at the Supervisor's Office (p139). Most trails are concentrated near Questa, Red River and Valle Vidal, but 15 minutes from town on NM 518 the three **Amole Loop Trails** (cnr NM 518 & Amole Canyon Rd) offer 15 miles of powder to beginning and experienced Nordic skiers.

Cottam's Ski Shop (Map p138; ☎ 758-2822, 800-322-8267; www.cottamsskishops.com; 207-A Paseo del Pueblo Sur; ☼ 7am-6pm, shorter summer hr) rents ski packages ranging from ancient skis and boots from the late 1990s ($15) to modern equipment ($20 to $25) to the high-performance stuff ($35 to $40). It also sells anything else you might need and has other shops in Taos Ski Valley and Angel Fire. **Adventure Ski Shops** (Map p136; ☎ 758-1167, 800-433-1321; 1033 Paseo del Pueblo Sur; ☼ 7am-7pm) rents backcountry skis ($12 per day), snowshoes ($15 per day), snowboards ($24 per day), and alpine skis ($13 to $23 per day).

Other Activities
Fly through the Rio Grande Gorge in early-morning light with **Pueblo Balloon** (☎ 751-9877; www.puebloballoon.com; flight $225), just one of the area's hot-air balloon operators who'll send you up softly, then bring you back down for champagne and brunch.

'Are those clouds going to keep us from seeing the stars?' **Night Sky Adventures** (☎ 754-2941; www.nightskyadventures.com; fees vary) gets asked that all the time. Um, that's actually the Milky Way Galaxy. This roving observatory can be found in state parks and at ranches and festivals…You name it. Check out the website schedule and follow it wherever it roams – you'll thank your lucky stars.

Mountain Skills Rock Climbing Adventures (☎ 776-2222; www.climbingschoolusa.com) offers full-day private instruction and guided climbs for $230 per person, with rates dropping dramatically for couples and groups. A Red Rocks multipitch day starts at $275 for a novice excursion, $200 for intermediate and $350 for advanced pitches.

TAOS WALKING TOUR

Start the walking tour by indulging in a coffee or a snack at **Caffe Tazza** (**1**; p151) and drop into the **Kit Carson Home & Museum** (**2**; p140) across the street. Then head southeast on Kit Carson Rd and make a left onto unpaved Morada Lane to the **Mabel Dodge Luhan House** (**3**, p149). Take the self guided tour (ask first). Then head back down Morada Lane, cross Kit Carson Rd

WALK FACTS

Distance About 2 miles
Duration Two to three hours

and follow Quesnel St past galleries and antique adobes galore.

Cross Paseo del Pueblo Sur and make a quick detour into **Blue Rain Gallery** (**4**; p154) for a peek at the finest in Native arts, then continue west on Camino de la Placita. Take a left on Ledoux St, stopping at the **Blumenschein** (**5**; p140) and **Harwood** (**6**; p139) museums. Poke around fine galleries and bookshops along the way.

Make a right onto Ranchitos Rd, then a left on Doña Luz St; if you need to rest your feet, grab a snack at **Sustaining Cultures** (**7**; p152), where you might also indulge in a tarot-card reading. Alternatively, continue north, making a right on Don Fernando St and left onto Camino Placita, and a quick right to the village's oldest building, now **Alley Cantina** (**8**; p154).

Wander to the plaza, perhaps stopping for a while in **La Fonda de Taos** (**9**; p151) to take in the Forbidden Art, or perhaps purchasing a Taos snow globe at one of the souvenir shops. Then make your way through the maze of adobe to the John Dunn House Shops, searching out **G Gordon Robinson Old Prints & Maps (10)** and **Moby Dickens** (**11**; p136). Turn right onto Bent St, stopping at the **Governor Bent Museum** (**12**; p141) to see Taos' most famous hole in the wall.

Continue down Bent St, cross Paseo del Pueblo Sur and finish with a well-deserved break (and margarita) at **Adobe Bar** (**13**; p153).

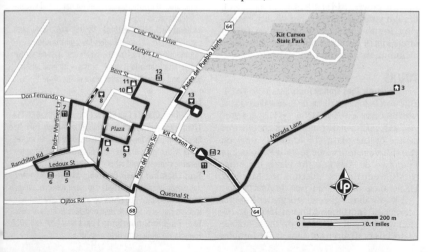

COURSES

Inspired? That's what Taos is all about. Creative souls are catered to by several schools.

Fechin Art Workshops (☎ 776-2622; www.fechin .com; $475-700) offers five days of instruction at Donner Ranch, 18 miles north of Taos, focusing on oil painting and landscapes. Rustic accommodations, with buffet-style meals.

Taos Art School (☎ 758-0350; www.taosartschool .org; $300-700) has weekend and week-long classes covering everything from painting New Mexico's churches to making micaceous pottery. There's even a Navajo weaving class held right on the reservation, where you'll stay in a hogan, herd sheep and cart wool before even prepping the loom.

Nichols Taos Gallery (Map p138; ☎ 758-2475; www.nicholsgallery.com; 403 Paseo del Pueblo Norte; 3hr of instruction $195) makes available on-demand teaching with area artists, who will teach you everything from abstract watercolor to glassblowing, pottery to metal sculpture.

TAOS FOR CHILDREN

Tiempo has a 'For Kids' calendar with listings of events and activities.

The **Taos Youth & Family Center** (Map p136; ☎ 758-4160; www.taosyouth.org; 407 Paseo del Cañon E; ☼ 9am-8pm Mon-Sat, 10am-7pm Sun) has a skate park (admission free), pool (adult/child $3/1) as well as big-screen TV and arcade games.

La Hacienda de los Martinez (p140) and the Harwood Foundation Museum (p139) are both designed with kids in mind. Llama hikes (p142) cater to kids, while Los Rios River Runners (p143) offers an all-ages float, though your teenagers will probably be begging for the Box. Taos Ski Valley (p158) offers lots of resources during the ski season, including day care and full-day lessons.

TOURS

With **Historic Taos Trolley Tours** (Map p136; ☎ 751-0366; www.taostrolleytours.com; cnr Paseo del Pueblo Sur & Paseo del Cañon; adult/child $33/10; ☼ 10:30am & 2pm) you can take a red trolley from the visitors center or the plaza (15 minutes later) on two different tours: one to Taos Pueblo, San Francisco de Asis and the plaza; the other to Millicent Rogers Museum, the Martinez Hacienda and San Francisco de Asis.

'I know all the ghosts,' storyteller Roberta Meyers of **Enchantment Dreams Tours** (☎ 776-2562) will tell you. She takes on the character of dozens of denizens of Taos as she rambles with you through town on foot or in your vehicle. She'll customize your tour to your interests – be that history, art or the ghosts themselves. Reservations required.

In addition to brewing up more than 400 herbal concoctions, including Yerba de la Negrita shampoo, a medicinal herbalist from **Taos Herb Company** (Map p136; ☎ 800-353-1991; www .taosherb.com; 710 Paseo del Pueblo Sur; hike $40) leads day hikes into the mountains, where you'll learn the lore and uses of medicinal plants.

FESTIVALS & EVENTS

The Taos visitors center (p139) publishes comprehensive listings, while *Tiempo* keeps tabs on current events.

January

Taos Pueblo Turtle Dance (☎ 758-1028; www.taos pueblo.com) January 1.

Taos Winter Wine Festival (☎ 776-2233; www.ski taos.org; Taos Ski Valley) In mid- to late January, learn about wines from around the world at seminars, tastings, chef demos and dinners at area restaurants.

March

Ernie Blake Celebration & Beer Festival (☎ 776-2233; www.taosskivalley.com) In mid-March, celebrate the Taos Ski Valley founder's big day with music, a treasure hunt and buckets of suds; there's a torchlight parade and fireworks display too.

May

Taos Spring Arts Festival (☎ 758-3873, 800-732-8267; www.taoschamber.org) All through May, art in all its forms around town – culinary, performance and visual – is celebrated.

Annual Folk Life Festival (☎ 758-2462; www.milli centrogers.org; Millicent Rogers Museum) This free community event has traditional art and craft demos by Native American and Hispanic artists; with food, music, dance and storytelling. Takes place in late May.

June

Red River Classic Car Show (☎ 754-1708, 877-754-1708; www.redrivernewmex.com; Brandenburg Park, Red River) This early-June show features all years and makes, along with night parades, hula-hoop and bubble-gum-blowing contests, and other down-home fun.

Taos Chamber Music Festival (☎ 776-2388; www .taosschoolofmusic.com) Listen to three weeks of concerts and seminars by a rich roster of talent and amazing student concerts as well. Held mid-June to early August.

Taos Pueblo San Antonio Feast Day (☎ 758-1028; www.taospueblo.com) Held mid-June.

Solar Music Festival (☎ 800-732-8267; www.solar
musicfest.com; Kit Carson Park; 1/3 days $40/85, child
under 10 free) This three-day festival held in late June
features exhibits, camping and a solar-powered stage
packed with performers like Michelle Shocked, Los Lobos
and Harry Belafonte. See also p143.

Annual Rodeo de Taos (☎ 758-9374, 800-732-8267)
Come for barrel-racin', calf-ropin' and bull-ropin' fun in
late June.

San Juan Feast Day (Taos Pueblo; www.taospueblo
.com) Highlights include a sunrise mass at San
Geronimo church and traditional corn dance. In late June.

July

Independence Day Sparks fly over Taos Ski Area, Santa
Rosa, Angel Fire and Eagle Nest Lake on July 4.

Taos Pueblo Powwow (☎ 758-1028; www.taos
pueblopowwow.com; Taos Pueblo Rd) On the second week
of the month, this centuries-old gathering of Indian
nations, which includes traditional song and dance
competitions, takes place.

Angel Fire Balloon Rally (☎ 263-0254, 800-446-
8117; www.angelfirechamber.org) About 40 balloons come
to play, and some may take you along for the ride.

Fiestas de Taos (☎ 800-856-1516; www.fiestasdetaos
.com) Taking place on the last weekend of the month, this
fiesta has been passed down through the generations and
celebrates the explorers, Indians, trappers, mountain men
and others who helped make Taos ever so Taos.

August

Taos County Fair (☎ 758-3982; www.taoscountyfair
.com) This weekend of agricultural feats includes arts and
crafts derring-do, livestock competitions and the fruits of
the labors and talents of Taoseños. Don't miss the pie-
eating contest. Held in late August.

Autumn Run Car Show (☎ 758-1405, 800-732-8267;
www.taoschamber.com/calendar) Check out classic cars,
street dancing, barbecue and general family-style fun here
in late August.

September

**Enchanted Circle Century Bike Tour, Top of the
World Mountain Bike Race, Bobcat Pass Hill
Climb** (☎ 348-6444; www.redrivernm.com/chamber
/biking) The Sangre de Cristo Mountains never felt so high
as when going up – or down – them on two wheels. Held
in mid-September.

Art along El Camino Real Norte (☎ 751-3220;
www.taosartretreat.com) Travel the original trade route to
Mexico and visit artists in their studios, as well as historic
sites and artful happenings along the way. Mid-September.

High Road Studio Tour (☎ 866-343-5381; www.high
roadnewmexico.com) Tour the heart of the art community
on the High Road from Taos to Santa Fe. Mid-September.

Old Taos Trade Fair (☎ 758-0505; Hacienda de los
Martinez) Historic traditions come to life in this cultural
celebration in late September. Food, music, art, mountain-
man encampment, competitions, dancing – dancing with
mountain men? Give it a try!

Taos Fall Arts Festival (☎ 758-5015; www.taosfall
arts.com) In late September to mid-October, hundreds of
the finest artists in Taos County show up with their work.

San Geronimo Day (Taos Pueblo; www.taospueblo
.com) This centuries-old trading event includes traditional
ceremonial activities. Held late September.

October

Taos Wool Festival (☎ 888-909-9665; www.taos
woolfestival.org) Wool comes from sheep, goats, rabbits,
alpacas and llamas, and you'll see the ways it has been
made into textiles for nearly a half century – and get a
chance to try it yourself. Takes place in early October.

Taos Mountain Film Festival (☎ 758-3873, 800-732-
8367; www.taosmountainfilm.net) Along with readings,
exhibits and symposia, this early-October festival features
films of adventure, wildlife, culture, the environment and
human rights.

Taos Story Telling Festival (☎ 758-0081, 877-758-
7343; www.somostaos.org) Tale tellers come for three days
of yarn-spinning in late October.

Taos Mountain Balloon Festival (☎ 839-9485;
www.taosballoonrally.com) The air fills with bubbles of
helium during late October, while on the ground you'll find
parades, balloon glows and mass ascensions.

November

Yuletide in Taos (☎ 758-3873, 800-732-8267; www
.taoschamber.com) In late November to December, come to
see adobe buildings lighted with luminarias, a tree-
lighting ceremony, and artists decking the hills with a
Taoseño-style holiday spirit.

December

Festival of Trees (☎ 758-2241; www.taoschamber
.org; Fechin Inn) An early-December holiday party and
silent auction benefits 40 Taos area nonprofits. Bid on
uniquely decorated holiday trees and wreaths.

Christmas Holidays The holidays burst with dances at
Taos Pueblo; mass and Las Posadas at San Francisco de Asis
Church; Christmas carolers and *biscochitos* all over down-
town; and *farolitos* everywhere keeping spirits bright.

**Christmas Eve Procession of the Virgin at Taos
Pueblo** (☎ 758-1028; www.taospueblo.com) This
beautiful pageant showcases community, ancient culture
and awe-inspiring images.

Luminaria Tour (☎ 754-2374, 800-966-9381; www
.enchantedforestxc.com; Enchanted Forest Cross-Country
Ski Area) Take a ski and snowshoe tour by candlelight on
Christmas day.

TAOS

SLEEPING

An array of accommodations await, but plan well ahead during two high periods: ski season (Thanksgiving through March with lulls in early December and mid-January) and summer (late May through October), when the rest of the Southwest is unbearably hot. Christmas holidays see a real spike in prices. Don't worry if a place doesn't have air-conditioning: the elevation and thick adobe-style walls usually mean temperatures remain comfortable.

Taos has more B&Bs than anywhere in New Mexico, and the **Association of Taos Bed & Breakfast Inns** (www.taos-bandb-inns.com) lists many.

If you're having trouble deciding, these reservation services have a bead on additional lodging, not to mention scores of available vacation homes:

Accommodations Taos (☎ 800-257-7720; www
.accommodationstaos.com) B&Bs, hotels, cabins and lodges in Taos, Red River and Angel Fire.

Premiere Properties (☎ 800-987-8423; www
.premiereproperties.com) Private residences, second homes, vacation rentals and condos.

Taos Vacation Rentals & Property Management
(☎ 758-7150, 800-480-7150; www.taosproperty
management.com) Even more vacation homes, with much better weekly and monthly rates.

Ski Central Reservations (☎ 776-9550, 800-238-2829; www.taosskicentral.com) Lodging in the Ski Valley and Taos.

Budget

The strip south of town along Paseo del Pueblo Sur is lined with budget hotels and chains. Rooms are clean and basic, breakfast is continental and decor can run to either extreme of the palatability scale. In-town camping is fine but nothing to write home about, especially considering the wealth of verdant options an hour's drive from Taos.

Enchanted Moon Campground (Map p162; ☎ 758-3338; www.emooncampground.com; US 64; tent/RV $15/20; P) Located between Taos and Angel Fire, this tree-shaded spot has a lodge, a playground, hot showers and a trout pond, plus a sense of being in the middle of nowhere.

Taos Valley RV Park & Campground (Map p136; ☎ 758-4469, 800-999-9571; 120 Estes Rd; www7.taos net.com/rv/; tent/RV $22/36; P) Park your RV or snuggle your tent into the chamisa just five minutes from the plaza. Free wireless internet access.

Hacienda Inn (Map p136; ☎ 758-8610, 800-257-7720; www.haciendainntaos.com; 1321 Paseo del Pueblo Sur; r $49-79; P) This family-owned and operated place has spacious rooms arranged around a nice enough courtyard, with views of the mountains. It's been voted cleanest motel by the *Taos Valley Times*.

Adobe Wall Motel (Map p138; ☎ 758-3972; 227 Kit Carson Rd; r $56-66; P X) For almost 100 years this shady courtyard motel has been setting up travelers in big, slightly tattered rooms, some with wonderful fireplaces.

Indian Hills Inn (Map p138; ☎ 758-4293, 800-444-2346; 233 Paseo del Pueblo Sur; r $62-119; P X ☐ ☎) This inexpensive and independently run option offers pleasant, fairly basic rooms within walking distance of the plaza.

Budget Host Inn (Map p136; ☎ 758-2524, 800-323-6009; www.taosbudgethost.com; 1798 Paseo del Pueblo Sur; r $64; P X) Much better rooms than you'd expect judging from the exterior of this somewhat inconveniently located but super-clean hotel. Wireless internet access.

Sun God Lodge (Map p136; ☎ 758-3162, 800-821-2437; www.sungodlodge.com; 919 Paseo del Pueblo Sur; r $85; P) Recently refurbished with hand-made furniture, this old travel lodge is independently owned, with nice-enough, quaint adobe rooms arranged around a courtyard.

El Pueblo Lodge (Map p138; ☎ 758-8700, 800-433-9612; www.elpueblolodge.com; 412 Paseo del Pueblo Norte; r $95 incl breakfast; P ☎) Right downtown, this place has big, clean rooms with fridges; some have kitchenettes and/or fireplaces.

Midrange

Enjoy a spacious, modern room on Paseo del Pueblo Sur or something more historic (read: nice but cramped) downtown. Folks who don't usually like B&Bs should note that many in Taos have private entrances and baths, which give you the same privacy as a hotel.

Inn on the Rio (Map p136; ☎ 758-7199, 800-859-6752; www.innontherio.com; 910 Kit Carson Rd; r $85-129; P X ☎) This whimsical spot is part 250-year-old adobe, part 1950s addition. It has floral murals, pretty Southwestern-style rooms with private entrances and excellent *biscochitos*. The owners are happy to hook you up with restaurants and activities. Wireless internet access in lobby.

Old Taos Guesthouse (Map p136; ☎ 758-5448, 800-758-5448; www.oldtaos.com; 1028 Witt Rd; r $85-165; P ⊠ 🖵) This atmospheric treasure features spacious, old-world adobe rooms with undulating walls (just try to find a right angle here) and hand-carved wood furnishings and doors. Hidden away in a quiet residential neighborhood, the shady lawn and gardens beckon with inviting hammocks and 60-mile sunset views. The proprietors are seasoned adventurers and can point you toward great excursions.

American Artists Gallery House B&B (Map p136; ☎ 758-4446, 800-532-2041; www.taosbedandbreakfast.com; 132 Frontier Lane; r $95-195; P ⊠ 🖵) Art flows here in ever-changing shows drawn from local galleries. George the peacock and lots of cats will be your inn-mates, while Jacuzzi rooms will blow your mind. All rooms have wood-burning fireplaces. Creative breakfasts are legendary.

Earthship Rentals (Map p162; ☎ 751-0462; US 64; d/f $100/150; P) Want to experience life off the grid, forgoing TV and phone? Stay in a 100% solar-powered earthship (p142), with a gray-water system, beautifully biotectured interior and reduced rates for multiple night stays. If you plan on using the kitchen, BYO eats and drinks.

Mabel Dodge Luhan House (Map p138; ☎ 751-9686, 800-846-2235; www.mabeldodgeluhan.com; 240 Morada Lane; r $95-225; P ⊠) Every inch of this place exudes an elegant yet rustic beauty. The 'Patroness of Taos,' Mabel Dodge Luhan (by equal measures graceful and grand, scandalous and unbearable) built this fabulous mansion to welcome everyone from Emma Goldman and Margaret Sanger to Carl Jung for a nice chat. You can sleep in rooms where Georgia O'Keeffe, Ansel Adams or Willa Cather once laid their heads, or where DH Lawrence added artful touches.

Holiday Inn Don Fernando de Taos (Map p136; ☎ 758-4444, 800-759-2736; www.donfernandodetaos.com; 1005 Paseo del Pueblo Sur; r $114; P ⊠ 🖵) This chain hotel offers tennis courts, an enclosed pool and a shuttle to the plaza. Suites (sleeping six with a fireplace and fridge) will soon be joined by the reopened restaurant and wireless internet access.

Inn on La Loma Plaza (Map p138; ☎ 758-1717, 800-530-3040; www.vacationtaos.com; 315 Ranchitos Rd; r $125-300; P ⊠ 🖵) Although these plush rooms are smallish, this rambling 200-year-old hacienda pays high-end attention to detail. Full breakfast, afternoon appetizers, evening cookies and turn-down service make this an ahhhhh-some spot. Guests can enjoy tennis and gym privileges at two nearby resorts.

Best Western Kachina Lodge (Map p138; ☎ 758-2275, 800-522-4462; www.kachinalodge.com; 413 Paseo del Pueblo Norte; r $149; P ⊠ 🖵) Handmade furnishings and nightly, firelit Native American dances (May to October) lend this chain a local sensibility. It also offers free wireless internet, a yoga center and an art gallery. Kids under 17 stay free with parents.

Brooks Street Inn (Map p138; ☎ 758-1489, 800-758-1489; www.brooksstreetinn.com; 119 Brooks St; r $149; P ⊠) The delight is in the details here: fresh flowers in rooms, thoughtfully placed amenities and gourmet goodies with an earthy Southwestern flair. A graceful Japanese-style arch leads to a peaceful garden buzzing with hummingbirds, while the sky-lit casitas have kiva fireplaces.

San Geronimo Lodge (Map p136; ☎ 751-3776, 800-894-4119; www.sangeronimolodge.com; 1101 Witt Rd; r $150; P ⊠ 🖵) This grand old lodge looks out on Taos Mountain and Carson National Forest and exudes tranquility. Fireplaces everywhere warm your spirit; hearty breakfasts feed your soul; a chile-pepper-shaped pool supplies the fun factor. Hand-built furniture and artwork by local artisans fill out the picture.

Comfort Suites (Map p136; ☎ 751-1555, 888-751-1555; www.choicehotels.com; 1500 Paseo del Pueblo Sur; ste $159 incl breakfast; P) All accommodations sleep four and have two TVs – suite! Wireless access in lobby, DSL in rooms.

Hacienda del Sol (Map p136; ☎ 758-0287, 866-333-4459; www.taoshaciendadelsol.com; US 64; r $160; P ⊠) Mountain views, fireplaces and Jacuzzis make this 200-year-old foothills retreat (where Mabel Dodge and beau Tony Luhan first shacked up) one of the most romantic spots in town. A steam room, health-club privileges and yoga classes offer other distractions.

Laughing Horse Inn (Map p138; ☎ 758-8350, 800-776-0161; www.laughinghorseinn.com; 729 Paseo del Pueblo Norte; r $160; P ⊠) Explore this interesting inn and you'll find 113 years of successive additions and treasures. Narrow adobe rooms (most with shared bathrooms) are furnished with chile-shaped Christmas lights, piñon incense and hand-hewn furniture – it's how Taoseños actually live! A communal atmosphere continues with a hot tub under the stars and a huge penthouse. Each room captures the quirk of old Taos. Organic breakfast foods are available all day. Guests cook their own meals, which can sometimes turn into a delightful culinary mosaic of everyone's offerings. Free wireless internet access.

Orinda (Map p138; ☎ 758-8581, 800-847-1837; www.orindabb.com; 461 Valverde St; r $160; P ⊠ 🖳) This chef-owned adobe estate is a font of quietude, yet is only a two-minute walk from the plaza. French-style breakfasts are as spectacular as the views. Swing in a hammock under a cottonwood tree and you'll never want to get up again.

Casa Europa (Map p136; ☎ 758-9798, 888-758-9798; www.casaeuropanm.com; 840 Upper Ranchitos Rd; r $175; P ⊠) Cool breezes provide the air-conditioning at this stunning 18th-century estate. Views of pastures and mountains are sublime. Euro-style antiques mix artfully with Southwestern-style pieces. Offers an elaborate breakfast and afternoon treats in summer, evening hors d'oeuvres in winter. Comfort, light and air define this welcoming spot. Free wireless internet access.

Top End

Taos' finest options are in a quirky class by themselves and satisfy even the most pampered souls with style to spare. These luxurious retreats include exquisite antiques, evening wine tastings, multicourse breakfasts and all the saltillo-tiled elegance you'd want.

Casa de las Chimeneas (Map p138; ☎ 758-4777, 877-758-4777; www.visit-taos.com; 405 Cordoba Rd; r $165-325; P ⊠ 🖳) This lavish B&B is surrounded by well-tended flower gardens and their immaculate Southwest-style rooms go way, *way* beyond saltillos and vigas. Managers play concierge for excursions including golfing, hot-air balloon rides, white-water rafting and three-hour beautification regimes at the on-site spa. Linger over breakfast or the complimentary 'light buffet' dinner while you plan, then get ready to relax.

Little Tree B&B (Map p162; ☎ 776-8467, 800-334-8467; www.littletreebandb.com; 226 County Rd; r $185; P ⊠) With 70-mile sunset views, a garden filled with hundreds of hummingbirds and an adobe structure made the traditional way (with annual remudding by experts from the Taos Pueblo), this is one of the more intriguing places to stay. Of the four

TONY LUHAN: UNLIKELY AMBASSADOR OF PUEBLO CULTURE

Taos was well on its way to becoming an artists' enclave by the time Mabel Dodge and her third husband moved here in 1916. Mabel was entranced by prominent Pueblo Indian Antonio Luhan and his spiritual connection to nature.

The courtship was brief and intense – despite their respective spouses – and in 1918 the two lovebirds, one a worldly heiress and the other a prominent Taos Pueblo Indian, moved in together; neither came from a culture particularly comfortable with such a romance. While the thrice-married Dodge sniffed unconcerned at the gossips, Tony would spend the rest of his life working overtime as an ambassador between his own Native culture and the eclectic collection of artists and writers he and Mabel would host.

Ansel Adams, Carl Jung, Aldous Huxley, DH Lawrence and others were introduced to Northern New Mexico through the prism of Tiwa philosophy. Luhan's wagon rides and introspective air inspired author Willa Cather to create the character of Eusabio, friend of Lamy in *Death Comes for the Archbishop*. With Georgia O'Keeffe, Luhan formed a special bond, joining her well away from the sometimes hectic salon while she painted in peace.

And in 1922, when federal legislation threatened Taos Pueblo's sovereignty and land, Luhan called in favors. He led his pack of famous friends to battle the bill, which was subsequently struck down in Congress.

Between trips to New York City and Washington, DC, Luhan would return to Taos Pueblo for prayer and rituals that remained more important than any urban enticement beyond the kiva walls. And through 40 years of marriage to his unlikely love, he managed to engender an understanding and respect for Pueblo Indian culture and wisdom among those influential newcomers and their audiences around the world.

rooms, be sure to get the one with the private garden with an outdoor hot tub. They also breed big, fluffy, friendly BraveHeart dogs here, which frolic freely. Free wireless internet access.

Doña Luz Inn (Map p138; ☎ 758-4874, 800-758-9187; www.stayintaos.com; 114 Kit Carson Rd; r $204; P ⊠ 🐕 🖳) Your world will be framed only by the horizons at this 200-year-old inn. Rooms with adobe fireplaces, patios, kitchenettes and hot tubs range from the tiny La Luz to the three-level Rainbow Room suite, with a hot tub on the rooftop sundeck. All are decorated in colorful Spanish-colonial style, a cheerful clutter of Native American and Spanish colonial antiques, artifacts and art – lots of it sacred and all of it beautiful.

La Posada de Taos (Map p138; ☎ 758-8164, 800-645-4803; www.laposadadetaos.com; 309 Juanita Lane; r $219; P ⊠) This quiet, 100-year-old adobe oasis offers blissful quietude. All rooms have mountain or courtyard views and a kiva-style fireplace. Hearty breakfast will keep you going, but gardens filled with wildflowers and a certain rustic elegance may make you want to stay put.

La Fonda de Taos (Map p138; ☎ 758-2211, 800-833-2211; www.hotellafonda.com; 108 S Plaza; r $239; P ⊠ 🐕 🖳) This upscale hotel, formerly owned by notorious playboy Saki Karavas, just can't shake its sexy vibe – even the kiva gas fireplaces in the smallish, sensually angled suites seem like they're up to illuminate no good. Perhaps it's the Forbidden Art of DH Lawrence (p161), banned in 1929 Europe and displayed here to consenting adults, depicting, and perhaps inspiring, all sorts of sinful fun. No children under 13.

Taos Inn (Map p138; ☎ 758-2233, 800-826-7466; www.taosinn.com; 125 Paseo del Pueblo Norte; r $250; P ⊠ 🐕) Parts of this National Register of Historic Places landmark date to the 17th century, which explains why it's not exactly the plushest place in town. But it's still fabulous, despite the gradually settling adobe architecture. Perhaps it's the cozy lobby, heavy wood furniture and the sunken fireplace. Or the classic restaurant Doc Martin's (p152) and lots of live local music at its famed Adobe Bar (p153).

Casa Benavides Bed & Breakfast (Map p138; ☎ 758-1772, 800-552-1772; www.taos-casabenavides .com; 137 Kit Carson Rd; r $300; P ⊠ 🐕 🖳) This romantic spot spans five buildings, and has lots of fireplaces, patios, balconies and gardens. Furniture is mostly antique and handmade, and shares space with artful treasures. Some rooms have kitchens.

Touchstone Inn (Map p136; ☎ 758-0192, 800-758-0192; www.touchstoneinn.com; 110 Mabel Dodge Lane; r $350; P ⊠) Considered sacred medicine land by its Pueblo neighbors, this is indeed a powerful spot. Rooms are named after famous literary figures and the whole place is artfully scattered with iconic objects: a saddle here, a skull there, cowhide throws, a baby grand piano. Inventive breakfasts are served on a glassed-in patio. Kids are welcome in certain rooms.

ourpick El Monte Sagrado (Map p138; ☎ 758-3502, 800-828-8267; www.elmontesagrado.com; 317 Kit Carson Rd; r $199-699; ⊠ 🐕 🖳 🐾) A lush oasis in the high desert, this lavishly decorated eco-resort has bright and cozy suites whimsically decorated with Native American, Mexican, Moroccan and Egyptian cultures in mind, all arranged around a flourishing courtyard irrigated with a gray-water system. It has an on-site spa, wireless internet access and plenty of package deals with the ski valley.

EATING

Although there are some quality options around the plaza, that old rule of thumb still applies: the further you get from the tourist epicenter, the better the food – or at least, the better the deal.

Budget

Cid's Food Market (Map p138; ☎ 758-1148; 623 Paseo del Pueblo Norte; ⏲ 7:30am-7pm Mon-Sat) If it's local, organic, holistic or just plain tasty, you'll find it at this fabulous natural-foods emporium, with a meat department specializing in elk and other game.

Caffe Tazza (Map p138; ☎ 758-8706; 122 Kit Carson Rd; goodies $2-6; ⏲ 7am-7pm, until 9pm for events; P ⊠ ♿ V 🐾) Tazza is more than just coffee drinks, Taos Cow rBGH-free ice cream, healthy soups (go for the vegan green chili), homemade sandwiches, burritos and vegan desserts. This place packs its patio and cozy art-lined interior with crunchy-hipster Taoseños, who also participate in live music, open mics and readings.

Mante's Chow Cart (Map p136; ☎ 758-3632; 402 Paseo del Pueblo Sur; dishes $2-7; ⏲ 7am-10pm; P ⊠ ♿ V 🐾) Drive through this independently owned joint and get your 'Trujillo' on the go. Great breakfast burritos will keep you going all day. Some dishes are available as meal deals with fries and a large drink.

Taos Wrappers (Map p136; ☎ 751-9727; 616 Paseo del Pueblo Sur; dishes $2-7; 🕑 11am-3pm Mon-Sat; P ✖ V ♿) A local favorite, this is the spot to grab fresh, tasty eats. Don't pass up the pesto chicken wrap ($6) or weekend breakfasts.

Bean (Map p136; ☎ 758-5123; 1033J Paseo del Pueblo Sur; dishes $4-8; 🕑 7am-2pm for meals, until 4pm for drinks & baked goodies; P ✖ ♿ V ♿) *Huevos rancheros* ($7) never tasted so good, particularly when paired with the best lattes in town.

Sustaining Cultures (Map p138; ☎ 751-0959; 114 Doña Luz St; dishes $5-8; 🕑 9:30am-5:30pm Mon-Sat; P ✖ ♿ V ♿) Some people can't start their day without a Wheatgrass Hopper from this New Agey outpost. Although known for the best salad bar in town (open 11am to 3pm), should your Cancer moon ache for the avocado and cheese sandwich or your Taurus ascendant insist on the tempeh burger glazed with peanut sauce, there's still hope: tarot-card readers ($1 per minute) are usually available to assist you in these and other decisions.

Orlando's (Map p136; ☎ 751-1450; US 64; dishes $7-11; 🕑 11am-3pm & 5-10pm; P ✖ ♿ V ♿) This is it: the best New Mexican food in town, period. Although 2 miles out of town, that doesn't stop the crowds from coming here for *los colores* ($9.75) with three meats and three chiles.

Midrange

Bent Street Deli & Café (Map p138; ☎ 758-5787; 120M Bent St; breakfast & lunch $3-10, dinner $11-20; 🕑 8am-4pm Mon-Wed, 8am-9pm Thu-Sat, 10am-3pm Sun; ✖ ♿ V ♿) All three meals (and in-between snacks) are tasty, whether you're building your own sandwich or choosing one of 21 recommended combos and an array of irresistible sides. Dinner revolves around gourmet comfort food, while the rotating brunch menu is over the top.

Taos Pizza Out Back (Map p138; ☎ 758-3112; 712 Paseo del Pueblo Norte; slices $4-6, medium pies $18-23; 🕑 11am-9pm; P ✖ ♿ V ♿) Pizza dreams come true with every possible ingredient under the sun. (For example, the recommended Vera Cruz has chicken breast and veggies marinated in a honey-chipotle sauce.) Slices are enormous, and crusts are

made with organic flour. Out Back will also bake dough balls for kids, and has a great back patio.

Guadalajara Grille (Map p136; ☎ 751-0063; 1384 Paseo del Pueblo Norte; lunch $4-8, dinner $6-13; 🕑 10:30am-9pm; P ✖ ♿ V ♿) This find serves true Mexican (*not* New Mexican) eats. Try the Mazatlan shrimp and fresh oysters, basic but bombastic burritos and white wine sangria on the side!

Doc Martin's (Map p138; ☎ 758-1977; www.taosinn.com; 125 Paseo del Pueblo Norte; breakfast & lunch $5-15, dinner $12-35; 🕑 7:30-11am, 11:30am-2:30pm & 5:30-9pm; P ✖ ♿ V ♿) Hang out where Bert Philips (the Doc's bro-in-law) and Ernest Blumenschein cooked up the idea of the Taos Society of Artists. Sit by the kiva fireplace, pop a cork on one of their award-winning wines, dive into the *chile relleno* ($12) and you'll be inspired to great things as well. Reservations recommended.

Sheva Cafe (Map p136; ☎ 737-9290; 1405 Paseo del Pueblo Norte, El Prado; dishes $5-30; 🕑 9am-9pm; P ✖ V) Unusual Middle Eastern and Central European delicacies are served up alongside hummus, baba ganoush and the other usual suspects in friendly, hippie-Israeli style. Sample the Israeli coffees, one of the 26 varieties of bread or, better still, one of the 18 desserts.

Apple Tree (Map p138; ☎ 758-1900; 123 Bent St; lunch $6-10, dinner $13-28; 🕑 11:30am-3pm & 5-9pm Mon-Sat, 10am-3pm & 5-9pm Sun; ✖ ♿ V ♿) Whether a simple but elegant lunch or a gourmet twist on an old New Mexican classic (mango chicken enchilada), you'll want to savor your meal on the patio. The fancy surroundings in this historic adobe blend well with fine art, candles and a huge wine list. At lunch an abbreviated to-go menu wraps up simpler, but still stunning fare for a few dollars less than you'd pay to eat inside.

Bravo (Map p136; ☎ 758-8100; 1353-A Paseo del Pueblo Sur; lunch $6-11, dinner $9-19; 🕑 11am-9pm Mon-Sat; P ✖ ♿ V ♿) This easy-going spot, where specials (and suds) have an international spin, also has an on-site package store. The all-around fave is the roast chicken ($11).

Byzantium (Map p138; ☎ 751-0805; Ledoux St at La Placita; 🕑 5-9pm Thu-Mon; P ✖ ♿ V) One cook, one waiter, seven tables. Byzantium has been at it for 20 years and that experience shines through with smooth service and artful dishes. Ask for the lobstertail cocktail ($18).

Trading Post Café (Map p136; ☎ 758-5089; cnr NM 68 & NM 518; lunch $6-12, dinner $7-22; 🕑 11am-9:30pm Tue-Sun; P ✕ ♿ V) You'll be hard-pressed to keep your eyes on your plate, or even your mate, with the incredible art that fills this place. White tablecloths and stemware complete the fine ambiance, improved only by the *penne arrabbiata* ($13.50).

Michael's Kitchen (Map p138; ☎ 758-4178; 304C Paseo del Pueblo Norte; dishes $8-13; 🕑 7am-8:30pm; P ✕ ♿ V 🍴) OK, so it's a little touristy, but it's still an old local favorite, in part because the energy is witty and entertaining, the food pretty darn good and the in-house bakery produces goodies that fly out the door.

Downtown Bistro (Map p138; ☎ 737-5060; Pueblo Alegre Mall, 223 Paseo del Pueblo Sur; lunch $9-12, dinner $13-28; 🕑 11am-2:30pm Mon & Wed-Fri, 5-9pm Mon & Wed-Sun; P ♿ V 🍴) Rosey adobe walls, a kiva fireplace and intimate lighting create the perfect atmosphere for savoring this bistro-style menu. Don't leave without at least thinking about ordering spicy Cajun pasta ($16).

Top End

Ogelvie's Taos Grill & Bar (Map p138; ☎ 758-8866; 103 E Plaza; lunch $8-11, dinner $10-26; 🕑 11am-9pm; ✕ ♿ V 🍴) There's no place like the second-floor patio for surveying the scene on the plaza. And there's nothing like the chicken mole for lunch ($11) or the garlic and black pepper ribeye ($25).

De la Tierra & Gardens Restaurant (Map p138; ☎ 758-3502; www.elmontesagrado.com; 317 Kit Carson Rd; breakfast & lunch $8-13, dinner $27-39; 🕑 7am-11am, 11:30am-2:30pm & 6-10pm; P ✕ ♿ V 🍴) The name means 'from the earth,' and that's where much of the ingredients hail – from the El Monte gardens and as local as possible otherwise. The Gardens is an Edenic spot to begin your day: an atrium filled with tropical plants and trees, with a 1200-gallon saltwater fishtank and two rock waterfalls. Formal dinners are served in De la Tierra, where the elk chop ($30) is absolutely superb.

Joseph's Table (Map p138; ☎ 751-4512; La Fonda Hotel, 108 S Plaza; lunch $4-16, dinner $10-30; 🕑 11:30am-2:30pm Mon-Sat, 5:30-10pm daily; ✕ V 🍴) The food here is inventive, with a tantalizing three-course gourmet prix fixe lunch ($16), and indigenous recipes from around the planet, including a fine representation from right here in the Southwest. The decor is ebullient,

with the Butterfly Bar seemingly aflutter with hand-painted butterflies, and the dining room walls decked out in giant flowers.

Old Blinking Light (Map p136; ☎ 776-8787; Taos Ski Valley Rd, El Prado; dinner $10-27; 🕑 5-10pm; P ✕ ♿ V 🍴) Dine within a walled garden with amazing mountain views on a full roster of steaks, ribs, fajitas, seafood, margaritas and their famous green chile cheeseburger ($10). Live music livens the place on Monday and Friday nights.

Stakeout Grill & Bar (Map p136; ☎ 758-2042; 101 Stakeout Dr, Rancho de Taos; dinner $16-28; 🕑 5-10pm; P ♿ V 🍴) Steak and seafood prepared with a continental flair draw folks 8 miles south of town off NM 68. Patrons also come for the great wine list and the stellar sunset views of the Rio Grande Gorge from atop Outlaw Hill. (Yes, there were outlaws here at one point.)

Lambert's (Map p138; ☎ 758-1009; www.lambert softaos.com; 309 Paseo del Pueblo Sur; dishes $20-35; 🕑 5-9pm; P ✕ ♿ V 🍴) Lambert's bar is a cozy local hang-out, with patrons sinking deeply into sofas and conversation for hours on end. Lace curtains and subtle elegance make this atmospheric eatery a fine experience, whether you're digging into caribou, buffalo or the pepper-crusted lamb loin ($34).

ENTERTAINMENT

Considering the variety of venues around town, start your search at **Que Pasa** (Map p138; ☎ 758-7344; www.taosnews.com/TTN/Calendar; 338 Paseo del Pueblo Sur; 🕑 10am-6pm Mon-Sat, noon-5pm Sun), a music store that maintains an exhaustive calendar of area events. *Tiempo* also has listings, and tickets are available in a variety of venues, depending on the event.

Pubs, Bars & Live Music

You can often catch live music at restaurants, including acoustic and poetic offerings at Caffe Tazza (p151) and eclectic selections at the Old Blinking Light (above).

Adobe Bar (Map p138; ☎ 758-2233; www.taosinn .com; 125 Paseo del Pueblo Norte; 🕑 last call at 10:30pm; P) Known as 'the living room of Taos,' this packed, streetside patio is adjacent to the Taos Inn and has some of the state's (yes, the state's!) finest margaritas and an eclectic lineup of great live music such as flamenco, bluegrass, gospel, Celtic and Native folk. There's almost never a cover.

TAOS

Alley Cantina (Map p138; ☎ 758-2121; www .alleycantina.com; 121 Terracina Lane; pub grub $4-14; ☺ 11:30am-1am Mon-Sat, 11:30am-11pm Sun; ℗) Built in the 1500s by forward-thinking Native capitalists as the Taos Pueblo Trading Post, the Alley Cantina is now a laid-back bar where you can catch live music ranging from zydeco to rock and jazz almost nightly. Don't miss the local fave, the Cullen Winter Blues band.

Eske's Brew Pub & Eatery (Map p138; ☎ 758-1517; www.eskesbrewpub.com; 106 Des Georges Lane; pub grub $6-11; ☺ 11:30am-10pm; ℗ ⊠ ⟨ ⟩ ⓥ) This crowded hang-out rotates more than 25 microbrewed ales (from Taos Green Chile to Doobie Rock Heller Bock) that complement hearty bowls of Wanda's green chile stew ($8) and sushi on Tuesday. Live local music, from acoustic guitar to jazz, is usually free but national acts might charge a cover.

Sagebrush Inn (Map p136; ☎ 758-2254; 1508 Paseo del Pueblo Sur; ☺ 3-10pm Sun-Tue, 3pm-midnight Wed-Sat; ℗ ⟨ ⟩ ⓥ) Live, usually danceable music almost nightly. Focuses on classic rock and country. No kids under 21 are allowed after dark.

Fernando's Hideaway Lounge (Map p136; ☎ 758-4444; 1005 Paseo del Pueblo Sur; pub grub $5-13; ☺ 4-10pm Mon-Thu, 4-11pm Fri & Sat; ℗ ⟨ ⟩ ⓥ) Just because it's a hotel bar (at the Holiday Inn) doesn't keep crowds away from the renowned happy hour, the DJs spinning all kinds of music and live performances. Best of all? There's no cover.

Performing Arts

Taos Center for the Arts (TCA; Map p138; ☎ 758-2052; www.taoscenterforthearts.org; 133 Paseo del Pueblo Norte) Located in a remodeled 1890s adobe mansion, the TCA stages local and international performances of everything from chamber music to belly dancing to theater.

Taos Chamber Music Group (☎ 758-0150; http://taoswebb.com/tcmg; adult/child $15/8, at door $17) Look out for classical and jazz music at venues located throughout the region, including at the Taos Center for the Arts and Harwood Foundation Museum. Performances usually start at around 7pm, sometimes opening with a speaker. Local restaurants often offer dinner discounts when you show your ticket; this option makes a great date-night out.

Cinemas

Storyteller Cinema (Map p136; ☎ 758-9715; 110 Old Talpa Cañon Rd; adult/child $7.50/5, matinee adult/child $5.75/5) You'll find current blockbusters along with lots of artsy ones here, right off Paseo del Pueblo Sur.

SHOPPING

Everything you'll need (Wal-Mart, supermarkets, liquor stores) can be found on Paseo del Pueblo Sur, south of downtown. But everything you'll want is by the plaza.

Art

Most international artists who maintain New Mexico galleries stick to Santa Fe, where they'll get the most foot traffic. But Taos is just far enough off the beaten path that most work you see here was actually done here. The best spot for good-quality Native American jewelry, crafts and art on any budget is at Taos Pueblo, where you can peruse local work after your tour.

Lumina Gallery (Map p138; ☎ 776-0123; www .luminagallery.com; 11 NM 230) The gallery spills out the doors of this old hacienda onto 3 acres of Japanese gardens liberally sprinkled with some of the finest sculpture around. Breath-defying views compete for your eyeballs. This place changes your inner climate in astonishing ways.

Las Comadres Gallery (Map p138; ☎ 737-5323; www.lascomadresgallery.com; 228A Paseo del Pueblo Norte) Tin, glass, fabric, paper, paint, photography – this women's collective of local artists has made mind-blowing art from just about every material imaginable. Some of these high-octane artists have pieces in the Smithsonian and other large museums.

Pueblo Drums (Map p138; ☎ 758-7929; www .pueblodrums.com; 110 Paseo del Pueblo Norte) Stop in for handmade drums and drum-related gadgets by Phillip Martinez.

Starving Artists Gallery (Map p138; ☎ 758-0166; 216C Paseo del Pueblo Norte) Emerging artists and unknown geniuses are given elbow room here, where you can emerge with fine art at nonstratospheric prices.

Blue Rain Gallery (Map p138; ☎ 751-0066; www .blueraingallery.com; 117 S Taos Plaza) This gallery, with an exquisite collection of museum-quality contemporary Pueblo Indian and other Native art, has high-end paintings, jewelry and baskets – some traditional, some not.

Jewelry

El Rincon Trading Post (Map p138; ☎ 758-9188; 114 Kit Carson Rd) Owner Estevan Castillo is the third generation of the same family that began this shop in 1908. They shun imported jewelry, and encourage Native youths to contribute jewelry and artwork, selling it right alongside the elders' treasures. The selection is as wide-ranging as it is stunning. Check out the free museum in the back with photos, clothing, pipes and beadwork from Taos Pueblo.

FX-18 (Map p138; ☎ 758-8590; www.fx18.com; 140 Kit Carson Rd) Wry, edgy and artful all at once, FX-18 has everything from fine jewelry (including bracelets worn by Taos' sweetheart, Julia Roberts, in *The Mexican*) to Jesus action figures and cliché-busting local jewelry.

Buffalo Dancer (Map p138; ☎ 758-8718; 103A E Plaza) The oldest outlet for Native American jewelry on the plaza, this place features the work of Rodney Concha and Lawrance Archulita, plus other work in silver and semiprecious stones, and antiques.

Gifts

Taos Gems & Minerals (Map p136; ☎ 758-3910; 637 Paseo del Pueblo Sur) For 44 years old-timers have come here for a selection of gems, minerals, fossils and jewelry, while New Agers stop by for particularly effective crystals. Rockhounds all over the state consider this a top shop.

G Robinson Old Prints & Maps (Map p138; ☎ 758-2278; Dunn House Shops, 124D Bent St) This trove of original maps of the American West, including railroad, geological and army surveys, is a find. It boasts collectable cartography from all over the world, dating back to the 1500s.

Maison Faurie Antiquités (Map p138; ☎ 758-8545; 1 McCarthy Plaza) A fantasy shop of unusual finds, rare treasures and arbitrary artwork, this unusual collection includes medical objects, US military memorabilia and art-deco lamps. And it's all crammed into this fine spot for poking around.

GETTING THERE & AWAY

Air

Tiny **Taos Regional Airport** (☎ 758-4995; US 64) has no commercial service at the moment, though **Wild Blue Yonder** (866-288-2399; www.wild-blue-yonder.net) will get you there from almost anywhere in their twin-prop C-90 seven-seater. Call for a quote. The airport primarily serves as a landing strip for personal, charter and occasional shuttle planes. Most people fly in to Albuquerque or Santa Fe and rent a car.

Bus

Greyhound (Map p136; ☎ 758-1144, 800-231-2222; www.greyhound.com; 1386 Paseo del Pueblo Sur) buses leave the station next to Rosita's at 6:25pm daily for Santa Fe ($18 to $20, 1½ hours) and Albuquerque ($30 to $32, 2¼ hours). There's also direct service to Denver. Buy your ticket seven days in advance and save up to 40%; all transactions are cash only.

Twin Hearts Shuttle (☎ 800-654-9456) runs between Taos and the Albuquerque Sunport ($45), Santa Fe ($20), Española ($35), Red River ($55) and Questa ($50) daily. Shuttles also serve southern Colorado. Make reservations in advance.

Faust Transportation (☎ 758-3410, 888-830-3410; www.newmexiconet.com/trans/faust/faust.html) offers similar services and similar prices, and it's the favorite of hikers and bikers who need drop-off service. It also offers a private car and driver for up to four passengers.

Car

Taos is about 90 minutes from Santa Fe via the Low Road and about three hours on the more scenic High Road (though with recommended stops it could easily take all day). It's about three hours to Las Vegas, NM, on NM 518.

GETTING AROUND

Though downtown Taos is easily explored on foot, and the Chile Line serves many major sites including Taos Pueblo, exploring the greater area will require a car.

Bicycle

Mountain bikes, road bikes and bike racks can be rented through Gearing Up Bicycle Shop (p144) and Native Sons Adventures (p142) for about $35 to $50 daily, with discounts for long-term rental.

Bus

The **Chile Line** (☎ 751-4459; www.taosgov.com/transportation; one way 50¢, 7-day pass $5; ⏰ 7am-7pm Mon-Sat, 8am-5pm Sun) runs north–south along NM 68 between the Rancho de Taos post office and Taos Pueblo every 30 minutes, hourly on Sunday, connecting to Greyhound buses. In winter, the Chile Line also serves the Ski Valley and Arroyo Seco. Buses are handicap-accessible and have bike racks. Purchase passes at the chamber of commerce.

Car
Enterprise Rent-a-Car (Map p136; ☎ 758-5553; 1350 Paseo del Pueblo Sur; ☼ 8am-6pm Mon-Fri) is just south of downtown.

Taxi
Faust Transportation (☎ 758-3410; ☼ 8am-8pm or by appointment) provides taxi service around town.

AROUND TAOS

TAOS PUEBLO
☎ 505 / pop 1264 / elev 7100ft
The only Native American community designated both as a Unesco World Heritage Site and a National Historic Landmark, **Taos Pueblo** (☎ tourism office 758-1028, Governor's Office 758-9593; www.taospueblo.com; Taos Pueblo Rd; adult/child over 13 $10/5, photography or video permit $5; ☼ 8am-4pm, closed for 10 weeks around Feb & Mar & for certain tribal rituals) is perhaps the most awe-inspiring mélange of history, art, architecture and mystery in all New Mexico.

The city's traditional adobe architecture – two five-story complexes in ancient adobe: Who-ma on the north side of red-willow-lined Rio Pueblo, and Whoa-quima to the south – has also made it among the most visited and stunningly photographed spots in the state. Which may explain why residents are so tourist-savvy (or in some cases, tourist-weary).

It's easy to find as you follow the signs to the main gate, where you'll get hooked up with passes and permits, then pointed toward the 1850 **San Geronimo Chapel**, home to a lovely Virgin regularly decked out in colors and symbols that reflect the changing seasons. There, guides will begin the tale of Taos Pueblo.

History
A wall of privacy surrounds the most intimate aspects of religion and daily life, including many details of the pueblo's history. What we do know is that construction began sometime between AD 1000 and 1450 with Hlauuma (north house) and Hlaukwima (south house) being the oldest. The pueblo has long served as a trade and cultural center where Pueblo and Plains Indians could come together.

Captain Fernando Alvarado believed he had found the lost city of Cibola when he first visited Taos in 1540. By 1619 Spanish arrivals had completed the original San Geronimo Chapel, using forced Native labor, of course. Everyone got a new Spanish surname and the Catholic religion, harshly enforced, did not go over well. So when Popé declared a pan-pueblo war at Santa Clara, Taos was ready to roll.

Military strategists led by Popé, who quickly moved operations to remote and heavily fortified Taos Pueblo, were clever: using Spanish to communicate with linguistically diverse tribes, and yucca cords with knots untied each morning in a universal countdown, they coordinated the only successful indigenous revolt in North America. And though DeVargas resettled Santa Fe in 1692, Taos held out for four more years.

While periods of civil unrest and sporadic violence followed the reoccupation, it was not until 1847 that political tensions again exploded. Territorial Governor Charles Bent, representing the new US government, was assassinated by a coalition of Spanish and Indian guerillas almost certainly acting independently of the pueblo government.

Bent was scalped, Taos was blamed and the US Army decided to teach the pueblo a lesson. Some 150 women, children and elders (most soldiers were not there) were burned alive as they huddled inside that first chapel. Today nothing remains but the slowly dissolving bell tower.

Unbowed, Taos remained a political force, spearheading resistance to legislation that would have compromised Indian sovereignty throughout the USA in 1922, and successfully lobbying for the reintegration of Blue Lake, an important and sacred watershed, which was returned to the tribe in 1970 by order of President Nixon. Today many members live outside the village walls and enjoy modern conveniences, and occupy their homes within the pueblo when observing ceremonies, forgoing running water and electricity in order to maintain the city's integrity. Many residents speak not only Tiwa but English and Spanish as well.

Sights & Activities

The only smoke-free casino in the country, and considerably less razzle-dazzle than some, the cozy alcohol-free **Taos Mountain Casino** (Map p136; ☎ 737-0777, 888-946-8267; www .taosmountaincasino.com; Taos Pueblo Rd; ⏱ 8am-1am Sun-Wed, 8am-2am Thu-Sat) is one of the nicest places around to blow your cash on one-cent machines, blackjack tables, video poker and Keno. Tuck into prime rib ($8) at the surprisingly good Lucky 777s Cafe (Map p136; dishes $3 to $15), open from 8am to 10pm.

Several craftspeople sell fine jewelry, micaceous pottery and other arts and crafts at the main pueblo, which you can peruse after your tour. You can also grab tacos, chewy horno bread and other snacks ($3 to $5). **Summer Rain Gift Shop** (Map p136; ⏱ 10am-4pm), on the northwest side within Pueblo, was begun 14 years ago by Debbie Lujan and her mother Shirley from inside their ancestral home. In addition to Shirley's traditional mica pottery, the shop specializes in hand-coiled pottery and contemporary and traditional jewelry by regional artisans. It may also be the only place in the pueblo that sells cameras, batteries and snacks. **Tony Reyna Indian Shop** (Map p136; ☎ 758-3835; 915 Veteran Rd; ⏱ 8:30am-4:30pm), just outside the main pueblo, has a vast collection of Kachina dolls, drums, sculpture, pottery, and arts and crafts from Taos and other tribes.

Taos Pueblo's vast **Blue Lakes Wilderness** is off-limits to visitors – unless you go on horseback with **Taos Indian Horse Ranch** (Map p136; ☎ 758-3212, 800-659-3210; www.homestead.com; 340 Little Deerhorn Rd; 1½hr easy rider $45/85; 2/4hr high-country excursions for experienced riders $121/237). This unusual outfitter, located on the reservation, combines basic and challenging rides through sacred lands with cultural and historical information. Of the many activities offered, the best are a sunset ride (6pm to 8pm, $121); a two-hour seminar in the hills with an artist (rates vary); and a two-day paddle-and-saddle trip that includes kayaking an easy stretch of the Box (minimum four people, $385 per person). Reservations are highly recommended for all.

Eating

Tewa Kitchen (Map p136; Taos Pueblo Rd; dishes $6-15; ⏱ 11am-5pm Wed-Mon, until 7pm in summer; ⓟ ⓖ Ⓥ) This is one of the few places in the state where you can sit down to a plate of Native treats like *phien-ty* (blue corn fry bread stuffed with buffalo meat), *twa chull* (grilled buffalo) or a bowl of heirloom green chile grown on pueblo grounds.

ARROYO SECO

☎ 505 / pop 1149 / elev 7100ft

Over the years, a historic uneasiness between locals and hipsters has settled into a comfortable vibe. Ever since urban creep consumed El Prado, it's been up to Arroyo Seco to maintain that hip edge and unprocessed local flavor. And it does, with a groovy plaza, growing art scene and one big hurdle to anyone looking to capitalize on it all: despite the name, it's not the lack of water limiting development, but a high water table that makes wastewater treatment a real pain in the derriere.

So, while anyone hoping to build a big resort is smack out of luck, the rest of us get to enjoy pure, unadulterated high-desert lounging of the very finest sort. There's not much to do right in town, and plenty of ways not to do it.

Sleeping

There's no middle ground in Arroyo Seco, nor are there any bad options.

Abominable Snowmansion HI Hostel (Map p136; ☎ 776-8298; www.snowmansion.com; 476 Taos Ski Valley Rd/NM 150; dm $18-20, s/d campsite $12/16, teepee or cabin $32-33, d $38-45, discount to members $3; ⓟ ⓧ ▯) Who needs an on-site pool when you've got the Rio Grande and hot springs nearby? Or air-conditioning when you've got the altitude and mountain breezes to cool things down? This HI hostel has a cozy lodge, clean (if slightly threadbare) private rooms (some with private bathrooms), a campground with an outdoor kitchen, and, best of all, teepees! The communal area centers around a warm gas fireplace and big kitchen; a pool table and piano keep the party going. There's no lockout, lots of room to store your ski equipment, and a complimentary breakfast in the winter months. It's served by Chile Line buses in winter only.

Quail Ridge Inn Resort (Map p136; ☎ 758-1811, 800-987-8423; www.premiereproperties.com; Taos Ski Valley Rd/NM 150; studio $75-175, 2-bedroom $125-325; ⓟ ⓧ Ⓢ) The two-bedroom units can be transformed into three-bedroom/three-bath units, sleeping up to eight people, while

TAOS

CEREMONIAL DANCES OPEN TO THE PUBLIC

Each pueblo invites visitors to some of its dances and events (www.santaana.org/calendar.htm has a complete schedule). With the exception of the powwow, these are religious observances, and proper respect is requested.

Turtle Dance January 1.

Deer or Buffalo Dance January 6.

Closed to public visitation March through April.

Santa Cruz Dance Footraces on May 3 in the morning and young people dancing.

San Antonio Feast Corn Dance June 13.

San Juan Day Corn Dance June 24.

Taos Pueblo Powwow On the second weekend in July, the Plains and the Pueblos meet for the biggest bash this side of Albuquerque, and you can even take photos.

Santiago Day Corn Dance July 25.

Santa Ana Day Corn Dance July 26.

San Geronimo Feast Days Vespers on September 29, dancing and pole climbing on the day following.

Procession of the Virgin Early-evening bonfire procession and traditional dances on December 24.

Deer or Matachines Dance Spanish-influenced traditional dances on December 25.

---

studios hold four people. Big draws include a fireplace in every unit, patios and decks, and full kitchens. Guests are also drawn to year-round tennis with the on-site pro.

Adobe and Stars B&B (Map p136; ☎ 776-2776, 800-211-7076; www.taosadobe.com; Taos Ski Valley Rd/ NM 150; r $120-190 incl breakfast; P ✕) This great B&B has amazing rooms with real fireplaces and private entrances, fabulous mountain views through huge windows, decks for hanging out or enjoying the delicious full breakfast, and simply wonderful vibes. It sits smack in the middle of skiing, hiking, fishing, golfing, horseback-riding, biking and everything-outdoors territory. Free wireless internet access.

Alma de Monte (Map p136; ☎ 776-2721, 800-273-7203; www.almaspirit.com; 372 Hondo-Seco Rd; r $165-255 incl breakfast; P ✕) A gorgeous place that will take your breath away if the altitude hasn't done so already, Alma de Monte is a flawlessly decorated hacienda with spacious rooms, amazing mountain views, fireplaces and antiques everywhere, a three-course breakfast and hammocks in the courtyards.

Eating

Once again, you'll be enjoying life on the cheap or on the credit card; either way you'll be on cloud nine.

Abe's Cantina y Cocina (Map p136; ☎ 776-8516; Taos Ski Valley Rd/NM 150; dishes $3-8; ✆ 7am-6pm Mon-Fri, 7am-2pm Sat, cantina 10am-close; P V ☝) Locals grab their grub here and sit at tables vying for space with the groceries. This small

grocery store and deli predates the hipsters by a decade or three, and is renowned for its tamales and cantina. It's a good place to throw one back and chat up folks.

Gypsy 360° (Map p136; ☎ 776-3166; dishes $3-11; ✆ 8am-4pm Mon-Sat, 9am-3pm Sunday brunch; P ✕ ☝ V ☝) Located in 'downtown' Arroyo Seco, this caters to the traveler in everyone with foods and suds from around the world – but what really gets patrons salivating is the acclaimed giant hamburger with spicy chipotle mayo ($9.50).

TAOS SKI VALLEY

☎ 505 / pop 56 / elev 9200ft

First settled in the 1800s by a group of adventurous miners as the rough-and-tumble town of Twining, this area's natural charms later became a mecca for outdoor enthusiasts of all stripes. Skiers will find one of the USA's most challenging mountains, which gets folks from Colorado – heck, even Switzerland – all excited. And jealous. 'It's like looking at a wall when you stand at the bottom,' says one ski bunny, but don't let that stop you. Well, unless you're one of those crazy snowboarders, in which case you're headed to Angel Fire, as they don't appreciate yer kind around here.

Summer visitors to the village will find an alpine wilderness with great hiking and mountain biking, and cheap lodging but no public transportation during the off season ('off' being any time the slopes aren't skiable).

Skiing

With more than 300in of all-natural powder annually, a peak elevation of 11,819ft and a 2612ft vertical drop, seasoned skiers will be stoked that more than half of the ski area's 72 trails are ranked experienced.

The valley's **chamber of commerce** (☎ 776-2291, 800-992-7669; www.taosskivalley.com; Village Office, Firehouse Rd; ☺ 8am-4pm Mon-Thu, 8am-noon Fri) offers lots of skiing-lodging-dining-lessons packages. Rates for basic lift tickets vary throughout the season (adult $28 to $57, child $22 to $45). Week-long ski packages, including room, board, lessons and lift tickets, average $1800 per person.

You can rent equipment (adult $26 to $45, child $16) at the Ski Valley, or stop at **Cottam's Ski Shop** (Map p136; ☎ 776-8719, 800-322-8267; www.cottamsskishops.com; 101 Sutton Pl; packages $15-40; ☺ 7am-6pm, shorter summer hr). Cottam's rents ski packages ranging from ancient skis and boots from the 1990s ($15) to modern equipment ($20 to $25) to the high-performance stuff ($35 to $40). Not surprisingly, it'll also sell you anything else you need.

Hiking

This is the high country and special considerations should be taken before attempting any of the longer hikes. The Questa Ranger Station (p163) and Carson National Forest Supervisor's Office (p139), in Taos, both have maps and other information. Water is generally available year-round but must be treated. Many trails have some risk of avalanche, particularly in the early spring.

If you just want to romp, get tickets for the **chairlift** (adult/child $7/5; ☺ 10am-4:30pm Thu-Mon late Jun-Sep) at **Taos Ski & Boot Company** (Map p136; ☎ 776-2292, 888-285-8920; Taos Ski Valley Rd), at the base of Chairlift #1 in the village, then walk on down the mountain along any of the super scenic and well-marked trails.

Twining Campground is the trailhead for two hikes: the excellent 8-mile round-trip to scenic **Williams Lake**, with opportunities for rock climbing; and the granddaddy of all area hikes, summiting 13,161ft **Wheeler Peak** – this is the short-and-steep route (for the longer trail beginning near Red River, see p165). It's a 16-mile round-trip; you could do it in a day, but consider camping overnight.

Gavilan Trail follows pretty Gavilan Creek for a steep hike (2000ft elevation gain) that opens up into a gorgeous alpine meadow,

for a total 7-mile round-trip. It connects into a trail system accessing Lobo Peak, Flag Mountain and Gold Hill trails.

Italianos Canyon Trail starts next to Columbine Inn and follows the canyon up a newly rebuilt trail that's popular with llama trekkers.

Sleeping

The conspicuously quaint village of Taos Ski Valley, a clutch of Tudor-style lodges with rooms sleeping six and cutesy names that unsubtly refer to the actual Alps, operates the **Taos Valley Resort Association** (☎ 800-776-1111; skitaos.org), which can reserve rooms year-round.

Most rooms have hot tubs, fireplaces and kitchenettes, which will save you cash if you bring food from Taos. Rates are 50% to 65% lower in the summer.

Austing Haus B&B (Map p136; ☎ 776-2649, 800-748-2932; 1282 NM 150; r incl breakfast $210; Ⓟ ▣) Two miles from the slope, this claims to be the tallest wood-framed structure in the USA, with views to match. The dining room is a great vantage point, and the breakfast buffet includes a fun, make-your-own waffle rig.

Snakedance Condominiums & Spa (Map p136; ☎ 776-2277, 800-322-9815; www.snakedancecondos.com; 110 Sutton Pl; r incl breakfast $225; Ⓟ ✕ ▣) This huge condo-hotel at the bottom of the lifts has a restaurant, a bar, in-room massages and lots of other amenities, including a hot tub, a sauna and in-room kitchens.

Taos Mountain Lodge (Map p136; ☎ 776-2229, 866-320-8267; www.taosmountainlodge.com; 1346 NM 150; r $280; Ⓟ ✕) A mile from the bustle of the ski area, this lodge offers quietude and privacy. Kiva-style fireplaces in the deluxe units, and kitchens (or kitchenettes) in all the units, contribute to a sense of self-contained respite. The outdoor hot tub and sundeck overlook the forest.

Summer visitors, particularly those with fishing poles, should check out three tiny **Carson National Forest campgrounds** (☎ 758-6200; www.fs.fed.us; no fee; May-Oct), none of which have running water. Twining Campground (Map p136), 19.7 miles north of Taos on NM 150, is near good fishing at Rio Hondo, sits at 9400ft (so can get chilly) and has trails that take off for Wheeler Peak and Columbine Hondo. Tents share the few spots with RVs here. Sites are shady at Cuchilla del Medio

Campground (Map p136), while Lower Hondo Campground (Map p136) is sunnier, with the easiest RV access; both are 12 to 13 miles north of Taos on NM 230. Trails are a few miles northeast on NM 230.

Eating

The Snakedance Condominiums & Spa (p159) has a quality sit-down restaurant with gourmet dinners, good burgers and high-energy snacks.

Tim's Stray Dog Cantina (Map p136; ☎ 776-2894; 105 Sutton Pl; breakfast & lunch $5-10, dinner $8-22; ⏱ 8am-9pm; P ☒ V ☖) Perfect for budget skiers, this place has beer and Southwest grub, not to mention a mean breakfast burrito ($9). Breakfast is served on an irregular schedule.

Bavarian (Map p136; ☎ 776-8020; www.the bavarian.com; lunch $10-17, dinner $12-35; ⏱ 11:30am-4:30pm daily, 5:30-9pm Thu-Sun; P ☒ ☖ V ☖) Located mid-mountain at the bottom of Chairlift #4 (call for directions), this eatery boasts the best selection of brats, wursts and krauts in the West, as well as servers dressed in traditional Bavarian attire pouring plenty of European suds and wines. Enter through 300-year-old castle doors and head straight for the sun porch if the weather favors outdoor noshing. Dig into the popular wiener schnitzel ($26) and top it off with apple strudel ($9), and you'll yodel all the way back down the mountain.

Getting There & Away

Take US 64 north from Taos to the stoplight and veer right on NM 150. The beautiful winding drive follows the Rio Hondo about 20 miles to the village. The Chile Line (p155), Faust Transportation (p155) and Twin Hearts Express (p155) make runs to Taos, Santa Fe and Albuquerque daily in winter, but only by prior arrangement in summer.

ENCHANTED CIRCLE

There's a reason for the name, and you'll know it when you see it. This 84-mile stretch of highway, comprising NM 522, NM 38 and US 64, travels through alpine highlands that rise to 13,161ft Wheeler Peak, and past crystalline lakes, pine forests scenically draped with feldspar and rolling steppes carpeted with windswept meadows. You're in marmot and elk country.

Most towns on the circuit (with the notable exception of Questa) are relatively young, founded in the 1880s gold rush by mostly Anglo settlers looking for the mother lode. It never quite panned out, however, and the abandoned mines and ghost towns are highlights of the trip.

Those settlers who remained turned to tourism, opening major ski resorts at Red River and Angel Fire; knickknack shops and adventure tours are probably the other

---

EXPLORING THE HIGH COUNTRY

Even in New Mexico, this is considered high altitude, with most of the Enchanted Circle at well over 7500ft. The oft-repeated advice to acclimate goes double here – the high altitude and cool temps mask the dryness of the air; a ration of 7 quarts (8 liters) of water per day is not extraordinary.

Unlike in the rest of the state, water is rarely a problem, although it has to be treated. Within the general seasonal weather patterns there are wild, unpredictable variations. Snow melts by June at even the highest developed campgrounds, but tent sites and trails higher than 9000ft may have drifts for another month. Early summer's dry heat yields to monsoons in July and August. Prepare for nighttime temperatures to drop into the 40s, and for occurrences of hail and snow, even in July. Before setting out, seek in-depth advice on what you'll need and heed it.

You will likely be sharing the trails with horses, hunters and livestock. Be sure to leave gates how you found them: open or closed, and check with the ranger station for hunting activity information.

Summer-afternoon thunderstorms can be dangerous, and not just because of the potential for hypothermia – you're likely the tallest thing around. You'll probably be able to see storms rolling in from quite a distance, but they move fast – get below the tree line ASAP, even if you only *feel* one coming let alone see one. Pick up appropriate USGS maps and get a basic understanding of how to use a compass. Then grab a backcountry permit and register your itinerary at either the Questa Ranger Station (p163) or the Carson National Forest Supervisor's Office in Taos (p139).

two major employers. If you just do this as a drive, you may be a bit disappointed – folks around here are more likely to compare their rare world to the Bermuda Triangle than the tourist bureau's more evocative moniker. But take time to explore, and it will be one of the highlights of your trip.

Taos Net (www.enchantedcircle.org) has links to all area visitors centers; these links in turn link to outfitters, hotels and restaurants. **Taos Vacation Guide** (www/taosvacationguide .com) has a quick guide to sights along the way. Fill your gas tank in Taos, where it's cheaper, and allow at least a full day to make the journey. Better yet, spend the night along the way.

DH Lawrence Ranch & Memorial

In 1924 Mabel Dodge Luhan gave DH Lawrence's wife Frieda this 160-acre ranch (Map p136; ☎ 776-2245; www.unm.edu/~taosconf/links /lawrence.htm; admission free; ☼ sunrise-sunset), now administered by UNM, where the Lawrence-obsessed can pay their respects to the famed author of such classics as *Lady Chatterley's Lover*. While you are free to wander the grounds, you can't go into the cabins.

Lawrence and Frieda lived here for only a few months from 1924 to '25, along with artist Dorothy Brett, who accepted Lawrence's invitation to create 'Rananim,' a utopian society. Lawrence spent his time repairing the cabins, chopping wood, hiking the trails and (with the help of his wife, Frieda) fighting off the attentions of Dorothy and patron Mabel Dodge Luhan. He also managed to complete the novella *St Mawr*, his biblical drama *David*, parts of *The Plumed Serpent* and other works in between. Relax beneath the **Lawrence Tree**, which brings in the O'Keeffe fans (yep, it looks just like her painting) and contemplate what he called 'the greatest experience I ever had from the outside world.'

Lawrence returned to Europe in 1925 and succumbed to tuberculosis in 1930. After Frieda moved back to Taos in 1934, she ordered his body exhumed and cremated, and had the ashes brought here. Luhan and Brett both showed up uninvited to help scatter said ashes, which, according to legend, prompted Frieda to finally dump the remains into a wheelbarrow full of wet cement, saying, 'Let's see them try to steal this!' According to one story, the cement was used to make the memorial's altar –

ironic, as his personal symbol, the phoenix, rises therefrom.

Ascend the meandering paved walkway to the memorial, designed by Frieda's third husband, where the lump of concrete has been inscribed with DHL's initials and green leaves and yellow flowers. It's heartwarming, with a scandalous giggle, just like Lawrence would have wanted.

Lama Foundation

A spiritual retreat, the **Lama Foundation** (Map p162; ☎ 586-1269; www.lamafoundation.org; sliding-scale donation includes meals $25-55; May-Sep; ☻), off NH 522, near San Cristobal, offers several simple summertime shelters – yurts, dorm space – and tent sites, available by donation or trade for work. There are also two private hermitages for 'rustic seclusion.' The foundation also offers an ever-changing variety of classes based on a range of traditions. Call in advance for directions and reservations.

Questa & Around

☎ 505 / pop 1864 / elev 7670ft

The Spanish word *cuesta* means 'cliff, large hill.' Thanks to a misspelling when the town was founded in 1842, it's now Questa. But its roots go much deeper. This was once the northernmost settlement in the Americas when Spain held sway here. This wonderfully un-'themed' community is primarily a mining town (the last vestige being the nearby molybdenum mine – the stuff used to help harden steel), though a growing enclave of artists, subsistence farmers and other organic types live here. Everyone appreciates the view: an alpine bowl glittering with lakes (you can rent ice-skates downtown during winter) and bright wildflowers, and spectacularly torn by the great chasm just north.

The **Artesanos de Questa & Visitors Center** (Map p162; ☎ 586-0443; 41 NM 38), open irregular hours, sells work by local artists, can recommend B&Bs, and will point you toward pretty **St Anthony's Church** and local artists' studios. The artisans also hold **Cambalache** (early October) nearby, an arts-and-crafts festival culminating with the burning of *el cucui* (the bogeyman).

Kachina Motel (Map p162; ☎ 586-0640; 2306 NM 522; d $80; ☻ ☒) is cute, clean and pretty basic but located right on the fish-filled Red River.

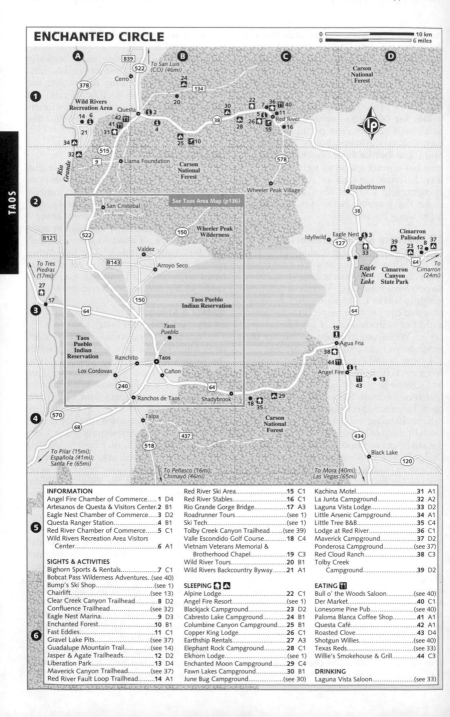

ENCHANTED CIRCLE

Grab a bite at the **Questa Café** (Map p162; ☎ 586-9631; 2422 NM 522; dishes $3-9; ☻ 6am-10pm Mon-Sat, 6am-3pm Sun; ⓟ), an expansive diner beloved for its Frito pie, chile-cheese fries (go for red) and homemade desserts. **Paloma Blanca Coffee Shop** (Map p162; ☎ 586-2261; 2322 NM 522; snacks $1-5; ☻ 7am-6pm Mon-Sat; ⓟ) has lattes, pastries, burritos, ice cream, lemon squares and the beloved Cloud Nine cake ($2.50).

Questa Ranger Station (Map p162; ☎ 586-0520; 184 NM 38; ☻ 8am-4:30pm Mon-Fri), about a mile east of Questa, has info on where the wild things are and other alerts about the area wilderness. Folks headed for the Valle Vidal Loop in particular should stop by for up-to-date road and camping conditions. This is also where backpackers should leave their itineraries.

After making the detour to Wild Rivers Recreation Area, you'll leave Questa and enter the **Carson National Forest** on NM 38. The road follows Red River past a string of beautiful **campgrounds** (fee $15; May-Oct) with fishing access and some wheelchair-accessible sites:

Cabresto Lake This top fishing and camping spot, just east of Questa on rough FR 134 (make a left just after NM 38 begins and follow the signs for about 10 gravelly miles), has running water and a trailhead for scenic Lake Fork Trail to 11,500ft Heart Lake, where you could also pitch a tent.

Columbine Canyon This one does have potable water plus access to short, steep Columbine Trail, through canyons and over four bridges. You can also access the 11-mile Rio Hondo & Red River Canyon Trail to Rio Hondo Bridge.

Elephant Rock Fish in both the river and nearby Fawn Lakes, and enjoy running water too.

Fawn Lakes At 8500ft, it's the highest of the bunch, with running water, fishing and pull-through sites.

June Bug This pretty spot has river fishing and running water.

Wild Rivers Recreation Area

It seems every state has its own 'Grand Canyon' equivalent, and among the strong candidates in New Mexico is the 800ft-deep Rio Grande Gorge, carved into volcanic ash and surrounded by piñon-studded plugs of the ancient volcanoes that wrought this lonely place. Here the Rio Grande and the Red River, protected as 'Wild and Scenic' by Congress, merge. The Wild Rivers Recreation area provides access to the rim and to inside the gorge itself, offering Grand Canyon–style views, but without the crush of people. Just try finding this sort of peace on the rim of Arizona's claim to fame.

The **visitors center** (Map p162; ☎ 770-6600; NM 378; day use $3; ☻ 10am-4pm Fri-Sun, Memorial Day–Labor Day) has information about the park's five hike-in **sites** (s/d $7/10), none with running water, and the five hiking trails that drop 800ft from each campsite into the gorge below. **La Junta** has the best view, but **Little Arsenic** is the most coveted, with shade and fresh spring water that should be treated.

Trails descend into another world, perceptibly moister and cooler, and the vegetation around you erupts into lush green. At the bottom, these trails are connected by the **Confluence Trail**, running from La Junta along the Rio Grande through the cottonwood to Little Arsenic; a rim trail runs along the top. You can camp at the bottom with a permit.

Other, less shady trails investigate the volcanoes, including the 2-mile **Red River Fault Loop** and the steep but rewarding 4-mile round-trip **Guadalupe Mountain Trail**, accessible by a turnoff 2 miles north of the visitors center.

Even if you don't feel like a hike, just driving the scenic 13-mile **Wild Rivers Backcountry Byway** loop allows an impressive and visceral experience. La Junta provides the perfect spot for a picnic, overlooking the confluence of the twin gorges.

Wild River Tours (Map p162; ☎ 586-1189; www.tournewmexico.net; 195 Cerro Rd) arranges area guided hikes (adult/child $60/30) and driving tours (adult/child $120/60), as well as group camping and expeditions to abandoned area gold mines, birding tours, women's adventure weekends, and more.

Red River

☎ 505 / pop 484 / elev 8750ft

The cusp of the 19th and 20th centuries saw a pretty wild populace of gold miners and mountain men, with saloons and brothels lining Red River's muddy thoroughfares. The cusp of the latest century finds mountain men, and women as well, only this time tricked out in Gore-Tex instead of skins, and looking for a whole different kind of extracurricular activity – for the most part. When the hard-drinking miners' hopes were crushed by the difficulty of processing the ore, those who stayed realized that their outdoor paradise might appeal to flatlanders with income. Indeed.

TAOS

The town appears as a cluster of cheerfully painted shops and chalets, gleaming in the high desert sun. Red River, ski resort for the masses, decked out in German-peasant style with an Old West theme – you would think it wouldn't work, but it does.

Six historic buildings, and lots of dilapidated mines, have since been joined by a ski resort, adventure outfitters, ticky-tacky shops galore and, this being New Mexico, art galleries.

ORIENTATION & INFORMATION

The main drag is NM 38, which forks south at the western end of town to NM 578, and ends at the trailhead for Wheeler Peak, or forks north to continue the Enchanted Circle. The entire town is within three blocks of the highway.

The **chamber of commerce** (Map p162; ☎ 754-2366, 800-348-6444; www.redrivernewmex.com; 100 E Main St; ☼ 8am-5pm Mon-Fri) publishes a comprehensive visitors guide, which contains great information about the surrounding wilderness. There is even a trolley, the **Red River Miners' Transit** (☎ 770-5959; 50¢; ☼ 7:30am-5pm Sun-Thu, 7:30am-11pm Fri & Sat), which runs from one end of town to the other on NM 38.

WINTER ACTIVITIES

Red River Ski Area (Map p162; ☎ 754-2223, 800-331-7669; www.redriverskiarea.com; lift tickets adult//teen/child $53/47/38; ☼ 9am-4pm Nov-Mar) caters to families and newbies with packages that include lessons and equipment rental. Deals on multiday stays include accommodations at more than 30 area lodges, and your fourth day is usually free. The basic package includes a lesson, lift ticket and all your gear; kids get supervised lessons and games all day while you ski your buns off. Snowboarders and skiers alike want to visit the terrain park complete with boxes and rails, specifically designed to lure you east from Angel Fire.

At **Enchanted Forest** (Map p162; ☎ 754-2374, 800-966-9381; www.enchantedforestxc.com; NM 38; adult/teen/child $12/9/5; ☼ 9am-4:30pm Nov-Mar) you can ski with your dog on a 5km trail, or schuss with the humans on more than 34km of groomed trails near 9820ft Bobcat Pass at New Mexico's premier Nordic ski area. The views are spectacular and snowshoeing is encouraged. Special events include the illuminated Christmas Luminaria Tour, Moonlight Ski Tours (the Saturday before a full moon) and Just Desserts Eat & Ski (late February), when you'll ski from stand to stand as area restaurants showcase their sweet stuff.

DETOUR: VALLE VIDAL LOOP

In the mood for a longer drive through the highlands? Try the 173-mile Valle Vidal Loop, which departs the Enchanted Circle in Questa, heading north past the Wild Rivers Recreation Area on NM 522 and rejoining the road more traveled in Eagle Nest via US 64.

The bulk of the route is impassable during winter, and the washboard gravel road of FR 1950 is no picnic at the best of times – bring a spare tire. The northern gate to FR 1950 is closed April 1 to early June for elk calving season, while the southern gate closes January through March to let them winter in peace. The estimated 1800 elk are a major attraction the rest of the year and are best seen in the morning and evening.

Take NM 522 north past the El Rito turnoff, which accesses the elk-infested **Latir Peak Wilderness**, with mesas at 12,000ft and higher, administrated by the Questa Ranger District. Privately owned **Latir Lakes** (☎ 586-0542 for permits), eight alpine gems set into 12,700ft Latir Peak, are worth the hike that begins here.

Further north the **Urraca Wildlife Area** (☎ 476-8000; www.gmfsh.state.nm.us) has hiking and fishing. Just out of small town of Costilla, NM 196 loses its cement and heads into a wilderness – where elk, wildcats and bears roam – that's sometimes called 'New Mexico's Yellowstone.'

FR 1950 follows stocked Rio Costilla, a fly-fishers paradise and a great place to relax, and opens onto unlimited access to multiday backpacking adventures in the national forest.

Continue your journey into Carson National Forest, wending through meadows, forest, more elk, outstanding views of granite peaks and four developed **campgrounds**.

The route becomes blessedly paved again when you make a left onto US 64 for the drive through Cimarron Canyon State Park (p166) and into Eagle Nest, where you rejoin the Enchanted Circle.

At **Southwest Nordic Center** (Map p162; ☎ 758-4761; www.southwestnordiccenter.com; Mon-Thu per night $85, Fri & Sun per night $100, Sat $125) you can escape into the mountains on skis or snowshoes for a few days. Stay in the Bull of the Woods yurt, a 2-mile trek in, with plenty of terrain to explore once you get there, including adrenaline-inducing verticals and stunning scenery, with spring skiing at its best.

There are several places to rent skis and snowboards, including **Bighorn Sports & Rentals** (Map p162; ☎ 754-2721; 220 E Main St). For more adrenaline-pumping fun, rent a snowmobile at **Fast Eddie's** (Map p162; ☎ 754-3103; 619 E Main St), which offers tours ($45 to $100) of an extensive snowmobile trail system – ghost towns, mining encampments and other unusual stuff.

SUMMER ACTIVITIES

Frye's Old Town Shootout (Main St; admission free; ✆ 4pm Tue, Thu & Sat Jun-Sep) showcases the Second Amendment in all its ten-gallon-hatted, buckskin-jacketed glory, as good guys try to stop the bad guys from robbing a bank and end up in a faux showdown right in the center of town. From there, head out into the spectacular wilderness surrounding the strip.

The 2-mile **Red River Nature Trail**, beginning at the covered bridge in Brandenburg Park or the head of Goose Lake Rd, has interpretive plaques about the area's geology and ecosystems.

Take NM 578 into the heart of the **Wheeler Peak Wilderness** for more challenging options. **Horseshoe Lake Trail** leaves the Ditch Cabin Site for a 12-mile round-trip to the 11,950ft-high lake with good camping and fishing. **Wheeler Peak Trail** ascends the 13,161ft summit, beginning at 9400ft, via a 16-mile round-trip route, with options for a 19-mile total loop. Allow three days, and contact the Questa Ranger Station (p163) before attempting this one. **Lost Lakes** is 4 miles along the trail and makes a great overnight spot with ample fishing opportunities.

The **fishing** here is spectacular, with several lakes stocked with rainbow and German brown trout, as well as Red River itself. **Jeff Fagan** (☎ 754-2504; jefffagan25@hotmail.com; half/full day $150/200, each extra person $25) leads guided fly-fishing expeditions and supplies all your gear.

The **Summer Chairlift** (adult/child $11/7, day bicycle pass $15; ✆ 10am-3pm), which operates weekends from late May until mid-June, then daily until Labor Day, takes you to 10,350ft, where a restaurant, hiking trails and mountain-bike runs begin.

You could also bike the two rough **Jeep trails** into USFS land that access dozens of old mines in various states of collapse. Pick up interpretive flyers at the chamber of commerce, then hike, bike or drive (4WD recommended, particularly in wet weather) **Pioneer Canyon Trail**, along 4-mile FR 485, beginning at Pioneer Rd behind Arrowhead Lodge. Also hike the **Placer Creek Trail**, along 4-mile FR 486, just east, beginning at the stream crossing at the end of Goose Lake Rd and passing fishing ponds, mines and mills.

Or take a horseback ride with **Red River Stables** (Map p162; ☎ 754-1700; NM 38), just east of town.

SLEEPING

Red River has more than 50 RV parks, lodges, B&Bs and hotels, many of which offer package deals with local outfitters and the ski area. Once the snow melts, this is the best place on the Enchanted Circle to bargain for a great room.

Reservations Unlimited (☎ 754-6415, 800-545-6415; www.redriverreservations.com; (P) (X)) Arranges stays in vacation homes, cabins and condominiums.

Copper King Lodge (Map p162; ☎ 754-6210, 800-727-6210; www.copperkinglodge.com; 307 East River St; r $59-169; (P) (X)) Rough-hewn wood, rustic furnishings and a great backyard make these cabinlike apartments and condos with kitchenettes a great value. A hot tub next to the river seals the deal.

Alpine Lodge (Map p162; ☎ 754-2952, 800-252-2333; www.thealpinelodge.com; 417 Main St; r $80-160; (P) (X)) This comfortable chalet has rooms sleeping six or more plus two hot tubs. A private park has equipment for the kids, picnic tables and grills to cook what you catch in the Red River (which runs right through the property).

Lodge at Red River (Map p162; ☎ 754-6280, 800-915-6343; www.redrivernm.com/lodgeatrr; 400 E Main St; r $165; (P) (X)) This huge prefab resort hotel has some of the nicest knotty-pine-paneled rooms in town, plus an on-site bar and a restaurant that serves fresh trout all summer long.

TAOS

EATING

Even the grocery store has a Saxon theme: **Der Market** (Map p162; ☎ 754-2974; 307 W Main St; ⏱ 7am-7pm; P) is not only adorable, it's the best place to grab last-minute supplies for Enchanted Circle forays.

Shotgun Willies (Map p162; ☎ 754-6505; cnr Main St & Pioneer Rd; dishes $5-10; ⏱ 7am-7pm; P) has artery-clogging breakfast specials and barbecue by the pound, with an over-the-top brisket combo for $7.

Bobcat Pass Wilderness Adventures (Map p162; ☎ 754-2769; www.bobcatpass.com; 1660 NM 38 at Bobcat Pass; mid-Jun through Labor Day) has Cowboy Evenings ($40) at 6pm Tuesday, Thursday and Saturday, featuring a campfire, a chuck-wagon dinner, cowboy poetry and sing-alongs.

If you prefer a little line dancing with your barbecue, Red River is a favorite stop on the country-and-western music circuit. Catch live acts around town on weekends, including at **Bull o' the Woods Saloon** (Map p162; ☎ 754-2593; Main St; P) and **Lonesome Pine Pub** (Map p162; ☎ 754-2488; Main St; P).

Eagle Nest

☎ 505 / pop 306 / elev 8382ft

The first inhabitants came here to stock up on golden and bald eagle feathers – until the 1860s when prospectors came streaming in after gold in them thar hills. The town became a home base for miners; it's now a home base for those wishing to escape the tourist overkill of nearby hot spots. It doesn't have Red River's range of services, but the mile-long arts-and-crafts strip (US 64) makes for a nice stroll.

Ranchers Charles and Frank Springer built a dam, forming 2200-acre Eagle Nest Lake. Good fishing and the ideal getaway spot spurred anglers and tourists to join the cowboys in whooping it up. Shortly after statehood, the town found quicker ways to get rich: it became a gambling mecca in the 1920s, attracting winners and losers from Santa Fe en route to the Raton racetrack. Gambling eventually lost its allure, which is why you may be able to spot old slot machines at the bottom of Eagle Nest Lake.

The tiny **chamber of commerce** (Map p162; ☎ 377-2420, 800-494-9117; www.eaglenest.org; 54 Therma Dr; ⏱ 10am-2pm Mon-Fri) has piles of information for the Enchanted Circle, Cimarron Canyon State Park and the Valle Vidal Loop (p164), which begins here.

CIMARRON CANYON STATE PARK

Three miles north of Eagle Nest on US 38, this dramatic 8-mile stretch of scenic **Cimarron River** (☎ information 377-6271, reservations 877-664-7787; www.nmparks.com; entrance $5, campsite/RV $8/18), hued in pine greens and volcanic grays, encompasses Horseshoe Mine, beaver ponds, lots of wildlife and fishing, and plenty of hikes.

Three developed campgrounds have showers, running water and electrical hookups: **Tolby Creek** is the closest to Eagle Nest, with easy access to 14-mile Tolby Creek Canyon Trail along old logging roads that make for good mountain biking; Maverick Canyon abuts the gravel lake pits (prettier than they sound); and **Ponderosa** has access to 10-mile Maverick Canyon Trail.

There's also primitive, five-tent **Blackjack Campground**, with port-o-potties and no running water. It's closest to two of the prettiest hikes in the park: 4-mile-roundtrip **Jasper and Agate Trails**, popular among the horseback set, and lovely 7-mile round-trip **Clear Creek Canyon Trail**, which follows a mossy little stream punctuated with waterfalls and lined with aspen trees, which makes for a golden-hued hike come September.

Rock climbers can attempt the cliffs at **Cimarron Palisades** close to Palisades Picnic Area (permits required), or just take advantage of the photo op, while **Horseshoe Mine** is just a short walk from the day-use parking lot.

EAGLE NEST LAKE

Spreading across more than 2200 acres, the expansive Eagle Nest Lake is why most folks are here. Originally dammed by ranchers in 1918 – it's thought to be the largest privately constructed dam in the US – the lake is now stocked with trout, kokonee and koho salmon, and you can row around and admire the reflection of Wheeler Peak while attempting to catch dinner.

It's not what you'd call a pristine mountain experience, but it's certainly entertaining – especially on July 4, when Eagle Nest explodes a disproportionately large fireworks show over the lake. **Eagle Nest Marina** (Map p162; ☎ 377-6941; www.eaglenestmarina .com; 500 Eagle Nest Rd) rents 24ft pontoon boats ($165 per day) and gas.

SLEEPING & EATING

Laguna Vista Lodge (Map p162; ☎ 377-6522, 800-821-2093; www.lagunavistalodge.com; 51 Therma Dr; r $125; ℗) This place has spacious, beautiful rooms and amenities galore, including kitchenettes in the family suites and full kitchens in the lake-facing sportsmen's cabins. Texas Reds (Map p162), open from 5pm to 9pm, within Laguna Vista, serves steaks, lobster and burgers.

Laguna Vista Saloon (Map p162; 51 Therma Dr; ⊙ 11am-2am Mon-Sat, noon-midnight Sun; ℗) This neighboring saloon is worth checking out even if you don't go for the hard booze: it's rustic, has all kinds of neat old stuff, and the floors creak just like they did for the old-timers. The front doors of this 1880s-era building are among the most-photographed icons in the valley.

Vietnam Veterans Memorial & Brotherhood Chapel

This gracefully sculpted **memorial** (Map p162 ☎ 377-6900; www.angelfirememorial.com; NM 64; donations appreciated) overlooks the vast and lonely plains, inspiring all sorts of emotions with its soaring lines. It was the first monument built to honor US troops in Vietnam. The family of Victor David Westphall III built the shrine in the memory of their son, who died in battle in 1968.

The simple and genuinely moving **chapel**, open 'forever,' is a place where former soldiers have found solace since 1969. They still stream in and out, veterans of many wars, stopping to light a candle or study 12 portraits of fallen soldiers, changed monthly for photos donated by families across the country.

The **visitors center** (⊙ 9am-5pm late May-early Sep, 9am-7pm in winter) has become a museum, hung with the American and South Vietnamese flags, among others. It displays artifacts, exhibits and personal items that attempt to convey the experience of being a soldier, or family member, during that conflict. Doves should note that there's no glamorizing of war in this place. The message board, in fact, reveals quite the opposite.

Angel Fire

☎ 505 / pop 1048 / elev 8382ft

It's sort of like the lost suburb, centered on massive and media-savvy Angel Fire Resort, which boasts the closest slopes to Taos

where you can snowboard. It doubles in size when the snow machines start to hum, and summer attracts baked refugees from lower altitudes.

The **chamber of commerce** (Map p162; ☎ 377-6661, 800-446-8117; www.angelfirechamber.org; 3407 NM 434; ⊙ 9am-5pm Mon-Sat) has lots information on area businesses.

SKIING

As if the 2077ft vertical drop and 450 acres of trails weren't enough, **Angel Fire Resort** (Map p162; ☎ 377-6401, 800-633-7463; www.angelfireresort .com; NM 434; lift tickets 1-day adult/child $45/36, 5-day $221/176; ⊙ 9am-4pm Oct-Mar) recently underwent a massive $40-million retrofit, adding lifts, trails, snowbiking (on bikes with skis, $35), snowskating (on skateboards without wheels), snowshoeing ($12) and a ski park just for kids, making this one serious winter wonderland.

The resort takes full advantage of the Taos Ski Valley snowboard ban with **Liberation Park**, featuring the state's only half-pipe: a Chris Gunnarson–designed, 400ft-long, competition-quality monster, with a wicked 26% grade. You can, like, totally take advantage of all this with the Learn to Snowboard, Keep the Gear deal, including two days of lessons plus boots and board for $249. Snowboarding on your own: adult/child $32/28.

You may get better prices on rental equipment from **Bump's Ski Shop** (Map p162; ☎ 800-993-4754; NM 434) or **Ski Tech** (Map p162; ☎ 377-3213; NM 434).

OTHER ACTIVITIES

The resort offers guided **snowmobile tours**, or rent your own and pick up a map to trails at the chamber of commerce.

Valle Escondido Golf Course (Map p162; ☎ 758-3475; NM 64; Mon-Fri $14, Sat & Sun $16), open daily dawn to dusk, has the third-highest-altitude 18-hole course in the USA (your ball will fly). For nonmembers, cash only.

Roadrunner Tours (Map p162; ☎ 337-6416; www .rtours.com; NM 434; hr/day $25/185 incl lunch) offers horseback rides with add-ons including gold panning, breakfast or dinner by a campfire, riding lessons or even multiday pack trips and cattle drives ($200 to $600).

In summer Angel Fire Resort organizes lots of activities for kids (mostly geared to small children and preteens) including

TAOS

miniature golf, mountain biking, **chairlift rides** (all day adult/child $25/20, single ride $12/10, Jun-early Sep), fishing, tubing (tubes provided) and a 5200ft-long maze where you can lose your kids for hours. Not long enough? Childcare is also available.

Balloons in Professional Services (☎ 377-2477; www.bipsnm.com; per person $200) will take you closer to the sky to greet the dawn.

SLEEPING & EATING

For reservations at lodges, B&Bs and hotels, try **Angel Fire Central Reservations** (☎ 377-3072, 800-323-5793; www.angelfirenm.com/cenres/index.html).

Elkhorn Lodge (Map p162; ☎ 377-2811; 3377 NM 434; r $165; P) This place has a central location, decks off all rooms, and suites that sleep six and feature kitchenettes.

Red Cloud Ranch (Map p162; ☎ 751-0015; www.redcloudranch.com; NM 434; r $175; P) A cluster of rustic cabins made from trees right here on the 220-acre ranch with furniture made by locals, Red Cloud offers amenities like a giant hot tub, trout pond and four-course dinners ($40). Summertime rates include breakfast. It's also at the epicenter of a series of hiking and biking trails throughout adjacent Carson National Forest.

Angel Fire Resort (Map p162; ☎ 377-6401, 800-633-7463; www.angelfireresort.com; NM 434; r $209, ste $359; P ⊠ ✈ 💻 🏊) Comprehensive and self-contained, this resort's got three restaurants, package deals, childcare (☎ 377-4213; per day $50 to $60) and much more. Summer means empty rooms, so bargain. With all the activities for children, it's a good deal for families, especially if the kids need a break from being cooped up in the car.

Willie's Smokehouse & Grill (Map p162; ☎ 377-2765; Pinewood Plaza, 3453 Mountain View Blvd; dishes $9-12; 🕑 11am-8pm Mon-Sat; P) Head here for barbecued chicken, beef and pork, but if you want to do like the locals, order the burrito grande ($7). Why? 'It's just huge!'

Roasted Clove (Map p162; ☎ 377-0636; www.roastedclove.com; 48 N Angel Fire Rd; dishes $17-35; 🕑 5-9pm Wed-Mon; P ⊠ ♿) Everyone's favorite fine dining: chipotle roasted chicken, sautéed wild mushrooms and mesquite-grilled filet (or elk) are just a few of the gourmet dishes that you'll be pairing with a fine wine.

GETTING THERE & AROUND

Angel Fire is strung out along the northern terminus of NM 434, just south of the intersection with US 64. Continue on US 64 through the Carson National Forest back to Taos.

Faust Transportation (☎ 758-3410, 888-830-3410; www.newmexiconet.com/trans/faust/faust.html; 🕑 7am-8pm) offers shuttle service year-round.

Shadybrook & Carson National Forest

Just when the endless vistas of alpine meadows and sheer granite peaks start getting old, it's back into the forest as US 64 descends from the high plains.

Carson National Forest (Map p136; ☎ 758-6200; www.fs.fed.us/r3/carson) administrates most of the final 10 miles back to Taos, with several campsites (and some private cabins) along the way. Sites with drinking water run $6; others are otherwise free.

At **Taos Creek Cabins** (Map p136; ☎ 758-4715; www.taoscreekcabins.com; 26094 US 64; cabin $85/150; P) a stream runs by beautiful cabins with full kitchens, luxuriously rustic interiors, fireplaces, televisions and decks (but no phones), plus a short trail to a waterfall just outside (read: decadent retreat).

Albuquerque

It's far too easy to ignore Albuquerque. She suffers in the sybaritic shadow of Santa Fe and she doesn't engender the mystery of Taos. But ignore her at your loss if you want to understand New Mexico. For she will, if given half a chance, introduce you to the spirit of the place. She's far more than the sum of her strip malls and legendary sprawl.

Albuquerque exists at the crossroads of I-25 and I-40, where drought and the manufacture of computer chips converge. Albuquerque is a 'real' Western town with a New Mexico–style independence streak.

Albuquerque doesn't give up her charms quickly, but they're right there. Hike La Luz trail or venture out to Kasha-Katuwe Tent Rocks; take the tram to Sandia Crest or mountain bike in Elena Gallegos; walk along irrigation ditches or the Rio Grande bosque; shop for Western wear or Route 66 kitsch; decipher pueblos and Hispanic culture at the respective cultural centers. And above all, begin a life-long love affair with green chile.

HIGHLIGHTS

- Savor the art, history and great café at the **Indian Pueblo Cultural Center** (p177)
- Ride the tram up to **Sandia Crest** (p182) and enjoy the high-altitude trails and panoramic views
- Watch while hundreds of hot-air balloons hang like lanterns from heaven during the **Albuquerque International Balloon Fiesta** (p194)
- Motor along the neon-lit **Route 66** (p178)
- Work up a sweat on **Kasha-Katuwe Tent Rocks** (p193) hike, which boasts more scenery per calorie than any other hike around
- Hike and bike at **Elena Gallegos** (p178), where coyotes howl and people picnic against a twinkling city skyline

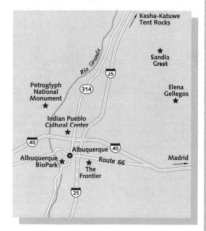

- Visit the zoo, botanical gardens, aquarium, nature center and little lakes along the bosque at the **Albuquerque BioPark** (p176)
- Memorize **Madrid** (p194), part of the Turquoise Trail and a town that time forgot
- Pay your respects to ancient rockers at **Petroglyph National Monument** (p177)
- Test your tastebuds on fiery green chile at the **Frontier** (p184)

| TELEPHONE CODE: 505 | POPULATION: 712,738 | ELEVATION: 5285FT |

METRO ALBUQUERQUE

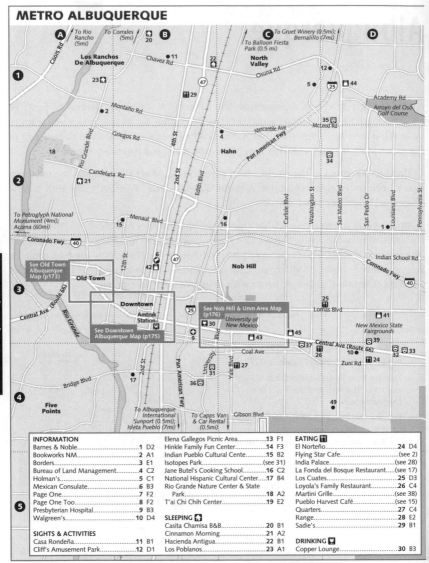

INFORMATION		
Barnes & Noble..................................	1	D2
Bookworks NM..................................	2	A1
Borders...	3	E1
Bureau of Land Management.........	4	C2
Holman's...	5	C1
Mexican Consulate...........................	6	B3
Page One...	7	F2
Page One Too....................................	8	F2
Presbyterian Hospital.......................	9	B3
Walgreen's..	10	D4

SIGHTS & ACTIVITIES		
Casa Rondeña....................................	11	B1
Cliff's Amusement Park....................	12	D1

Elena Gallegos Picnic Area..............	13	F1
Hinkle Family Fun Center................	14	F3
Indian Pueblo Cultural Cente........	15	B2
Isotopes Park................................(see 31)
Jane Butel's Cooking School...........	16	C2
National Hispanic Cultural Center....	17	B4
Rio Grande Nature Center & State		
Park..	18	A2
T'ai Chi Chih Center.........................	19	E2

SLEEPING		
Casita Chamisa B&B.........................	20	B1
Cinnamon Morning...........................	21	A2
Hacienda Antigua.............................	22	B1
Los Poblanos.....................................	23	A1

EATING		
El Norteño..	24	D4
Flying Star Cafe...........................(see 2)
India Palace..............................(see 28)
La Fonda del Bosque Restaurant....(see 17)
Los Cuates..	25	D3
Loyola's Family Restaurant..............	26	C4
Martini Grille............................(see 38)
Pueblo Harvest Café...................(see 15)
Quarters..	27	C4
Range..	28	E2
Sadie's...	29	B1

DRINKING		
Copper Lounge.................................	30	B3

ORIENTATION

Albuquerque sprawls over 224 sq miles. Locals give directions using compass points (north, south etc) rather than saying 'right' or 'left,' and drivers venturing much off the beaten path will finally understand why Bugs Bunny was always making that wrong left turn here.

Remember that Sandia Crest is to the east and most of the city is built on a grid, and you'll be fine.

The Rio Grande runs north–south through the city, just west of Old Town. Across the river, the volcanoes visible from almost anywhere in the city are now protected as a part of Petroglyph National Monument.

Central Ave (old Route 66, now NM 333) bisects the city running roughly east–west and connects most areas of interest: Nob Hill, the UNM area, downtown and Old Town.

Addresses are designated by their relationship to the point where Central Ave crosses the railroad tracks, just east of First St downtown: NW, SW, NE and SE.

Two major interstates cross just north of downtown. I-40 (east–west) connects the city to Tucumcari and Acoma Pueblo, while I-25 (north–south) runs between Santa Fe and El Paso, Texas.

The International Sunport (it's an airport, but sunny – get it?) is in the SE quadrant, off I-40; it can also be reached by Yale Blvd, which intersects Central Ave near the University of New Mexico (UNM). The Turquoise Trail (NM 14) begins as you leave town on I-40 East, at the Tijeras exit.

Maps

The maps in this book cover Albuquerque's major sights, but explorers should pick up a *Rand McNally* or *UniversalMap* folding map to the city.

The *Rand McNally Albuquerque, Santa Fe & Taos Streetfinder* ($18) may be useful if you plan to stay a while.

Online maps can be found at www.itsatrip.org. This site includes specialized maps for specialized interests, including sports and recreation, dining and self-guided tours. You could also head to Page One (below) and the UNM Bookstore (below), which also gives out a free, no-frills map of the city.

INFORMATION
Bookstores

Barnes & Noble (Map pp170-1; ☎ 883-8200; 6600 Menaul Blvd NE, Coronado Mall)

Bookworks NM (Map pp170-1; ☎ 344-8139; 4022 Rio Grande Blvd NW) A wide range of guides, maps and Southwestern literature.

Borders (Map pp170-1; ☎ 797-5681; 5901 Wyoming Blvd NE)

Newsland Bookstore (Map p176; ☎ 242-0694; 2112 Central Ave SE) Come for worldwide publications, especially newspapers and French, Italian and German magazines.

Page One (Map pp170-1; ☎ 294-2026; 11018 Montgomery Blvd NE) This store is huge, independent and comprehensive.

Page One Too (Map pp170-1; ☎ 294-5623; 11200 Montgomery Blvd NE) This used bookstore, opposite Page One, features a rare books and antiquarian department.

UNM Bookstore (Map p176; ☎ 277-5451; cnr Central Ave & Cornell St) Along with a good selection of guides, maps and Southwestern literature, there's free parking in the UNM parking structure with validation at the shop.

ALBUQUERQUE

ALBUQUERQUE IN...

One Day
Jump-start your belly with green chile from the **Frontier** (p184), then head over to the **Indian Pueblo Cultural Center** (p177), where you'll get a head start on a primo pueblo education. Pick your preferences at the **Albuquerque BioPark** (p176); it boasts a zoo, aquarium, botanical gardens and nature trails along the bosque. Dine outdoors in **Nob Hill** (p184), thick with eateries and the grooviest neighborhood in Albuquerque. Wander over to **Old Town** (opposite) and admire the **San Felipe de Neri Church** (p174) and ancient architecture. Splurge at the **Artichoke Café** (p184).

Two Days
Before it gets too hot, wander around the **Petroglyph National Monument** (p177) and follow it up with a cooling driving tour of **North Valley** (p177). (Forge along the back roads of Corrales.) Indulge in some rolled enchiladas from **Sadie's** (p186) at lunchtime, then target a few one-of-a-kind shops scattered around the city. Take a cool late-afternoon hike in **Elena Gallegos** (p178) before riding the **Sandia Peak Tramway** (opposite) at dusk to the crest. After having a late-ish dinner at **Flying Star** (p185), hang with the 20-somethings at a watering hole downtown. It's never too late to start searching for the state's best margaritas.

Emergency

Fire, Police, Ambulance Immediate Dispatch (☎ 911)
NM Poison Control Center Emergency (☎ 222-1222)
Police (Map p175; ☎ 242-2677; 400 Roma Ave NW)
UNM Hospital (Map p176; ☎ 272-2411; 2211 Lomas Blvd NE)

Internet Access

Albuquerque is wired. The Old Town Plaza, Sunport, downtown Civic Plaza, Aquarium and Botanic Gardens have free wireless internet, as do Rapid Ride buses.
Kinko's/FedEx (Map p176; ☎ 255-9673; 2706 Central Ave SE; per hr $12) Open 24 hours, and with several locations, Kinko's also has laptop internet hook-ups and wireless.
Main Library (Map p175; ☎ 768-5140; 501 Copper Ave NW) Free internet access after you purchase a $3 library card. For branch locations (most of which have free wireless), surf on over to www.cabq.gov/library.

Internet Resources

Albuquerque Online (www.abqonline.com) Look for exhaustive listings and links for Albuquerque businesses, as well as specifics on lodging, shopping, art and dining.
Albuquerque.com (www.albuquerque.com) Surf around for more information on attractions, hotels and restaurants.
City of Albuquerque (www.cabq.gov) The city's excellent site has information on public transport, area attractions and more.
Downtownabq.com (www.downtownabq.com) Dedicated to promoting this burgeoning neighborhood.

Media

ABQ Arts (www.abqarts.com) This free monthly covers the art and music scenes.
Albuquerque Journal (www.abqjournal.com) New Mexico's largest daily also publishes the evening *Tribune* and Friday's *Venue*, an arts and entertainment pullout.
Alibi (www.alibi.com) This fun, free weekly features entertainment listings and more.

Medical Services

Presbyterian Hospital (Map pp170-1; ☎ 841-1234, emergency 841-1111; 1100 Central Ave SE) This facility has shorter lines in the emergency room than UNM Hospital.
UNM Hospital (Map p176; ☎ 272-2111, emergency 272-2411; 2211 Lomas Blvd NE)
Walgreens (Map pp170-1; ☎ 265-1548, 800-925-4733; 6201 Central Ave NE; ◷ 24hrs) Call the toll-free number to find other all-night-pharmacy locations.

Post

Downtown (Map p175; ☎ 346-1256; 201 5th St SW; ◷ 9am-5pm Mon-Fri)
Old Town (Map p173; ☎ 242-5927; 2016 Central Ave SW; ◷ 10am-6pm Mon-Fri, noon-5am Sat)

Tourist Information

Albuquerque Convention & Visitors Bureau (Map p175; ☎ 842-9918, 800-284-2282; www.itsatrip.org; 401 2nd St NW; ◷ 9am-5pm Mon-Fri) On the 6th floor in the Galleria, this bureau has visitor information for all of New Mexico.
Bureau of Land Management (BLM; Map pp170-1; ☎ 761-8700; www.nm.blm.gov; 435 Montaño Rd NW; ◷ 7:45am-4:30pm Mon-Fri) Head here for recreation advice, maps and information on the surrounding wilderness.

Cibola National Forest Office (Map p175; ☎ 842-3292; www.fs.fed.us/r3/cibola; 333 Broadway SE; ⏰ 8am-4:30pm Mon-Fri) Head here for recreation advice.
Old Town Visitors Center (Map p173; ☎ 243-3215; www.itsatrip.org; Don Luis Plaza; ⏰ 9am-5pm) This has plenty of information on Albuquerque.

SIGHTS

Most of Albuquerque's top sites are concentrated in downtown and Old Town, down Central Ave from Nob Hill and UNM. Some of the best attractions though – including the Indian Pueblo Cultural Center, Petroglyph National Monument and Sandia Tramway – are more far flung and most easily accessible by car. Also consider a daytrip to Acoma Pueblo (p214) from Albuquerque.

Old Town

Old Town is best appreciated through a historical lens: these quaint adobe shops were not built 20 years ago to attract tourists – some have been here since 1706 when the first 15 Spanish families called the newly named Albuquerque their home. From its founding until the arrival of the railroad in 1880, Old Town Plaza was the hub of daily life. With many museums, galleries and original buildings within walking distance, this is the city's most popular tourist area. As you walk around, try to keep your mind's eye trained partly on the past. Imagine this area as it began, with a handful of hopeful families grateful to have survived a trek across hundreds of miles of desert wilderness.

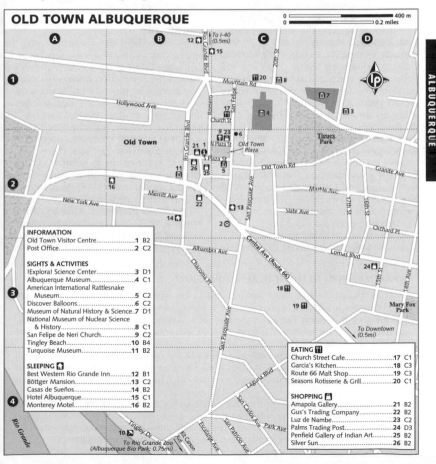

OLD TOWN ALBUQUERQUE

0 —————— 400 m
0 —————— 0.2 miles

INFORMATION
Old Town Visitor Centre.................1 B2
Post Office..2 C2

SIGHTS & ACTIVITIES
!Explora! Science Center.................3 D1
Albuquerque Museum.....................4 C1
American International Rattlesnake
  Museum...5 C2
Discover Balloons............................6 C2
Museum of Natural History & Science.7 D1
National Museum of Nuclear Science
  & History..8 C1
San Felipe de Neri Church..............9 C2
Tingley Beach..................................10 B4
Turquoise Museum..........................11 B2

SLEEPING
Best Western Rio Grande Inn.........12 B1
Böttger Mansion..............................13 C2
Casas de Sueños.............................14 B2
Hotel Albuquerque.........................15 C1
Monterey Motel...............................16 B2

EATING
Church Street Cafe.........................17 C1
Garcia's Kitchen..............................18 C3
Route 66 Malt Shop........................19 C3
Seasons Rotisserie & Grill..............20 C1

SHOPPING
Amapola Gallery..............................21 B2
Gus's Trading Company..................22 B2
Luz de Nambe..................................23 C2
Palms Trading Post..........................24 D3
Penfield Gallery of Indian Art........25 B2
Silver Sun..26 B2

ALBUQUERQUE

From mid-April to mid-November, the Albuquerque Museum (below) offers informative, free guided **Old Town walking tours** (🕐 11am Tue-Sun mid-Mar–mid-Dec). The museum's information center publishes *Old Town: A Walking Tour of History and Architecture*, guiding you to 17 historical structures.

San Felipe de Neri Church (Map p173; ☎ 243-4628; www.sanfelipedeneri.org; San Felipe Plaza; 🕐 7am-5:30pm daily, museum 10am-4pm Mon-Sat) dates from 1793 and is Old Town's most famous photo op. Mass is given daily at 7am; Sunday mass is at 7am, 10:15am and noon.

Turquoise Museum (Map p173; ☎ 247-8650; 2107 Central Ave NW; admission $4; 🕐 9:30am-3pm Mon-Sat) gives an enlightening crash course in determining which stones are high quality, or even real. Kids enjoy the hands-on activities.

More than just a place to get creeped out by slithering snakes, the **American International Rattlesnake Museum** (Map p173; ☎ 242-6569; www.rattlesnakes.com; 202 San Felipe St NW; adult/child $3.50/2.50; 🕐 10am-5pm Mon-Sat, 1-5pm Sun) will dispel myths, teach you about venom and convince you of the importance of rattlers to the ecosystem. Kids will enjoy the 'certificate of bravery' awarded to those who make it out the door (which is everyone).

Albuquerque Museum (Map p173; ☎ 242-4600; www.albuquerquemuseum.com; 2000 Mountain Rd NW; adult/child $4/1, 1st Wed of the month free; 🕐 9am-5pm Tue-Sun) is a fine museum that disseminates local history and features a great gallery of New Mexican artists. Family Art Workshops are offered on Saturdays at 2:30pm and gallery tours are given daily at 2pm.

Museum of Natural History & Science (Map p173; ☎ 841-2800; www.nmnaturalhistory.org; 1801 Mountain Rd

NW; adult/child $6/3; 🕐 9am-5pm, closed Mon Jan & Sep) includes the Lodestar Astronomy Center, Hall of Jurassic Supergiants and Dynatheater, a five-story IMAX screen. Call for feature films and show times. Hands-on activities for children make this a fun stop.

!Explora! Science Center (Map p173; ☎ 224-8300; www.explora.mus.nm.us; 1701 Mountain Rd NW; adult/child $7/3; 🕐 10am-6pm Mon-Sat, noon-6pm Sun) offers scientific fun for smaller kids; look for bubbles, tops, and arts and crafts.

National Museum of Atomic Nuclear Science & History (Map p173; ☎ 245-2137; www.atomicmuseum.com; 1905 Mountain Rd NW; adult/child $5/4; 🕐 9am-5pm) has something for all ages. It features an impressive collection of nuclear weapons, exhibits on nuclear energy and interactive activities for children.

Downtown

As in many US cities, downtown isn't the epicenter for action that it was some decades ago, when Route 66 was a novelty and reason enough to set out from either coast in a big '55 Chevy. City planners and business owners have done a good job in recent years, though, of restoring some of that fab '50s neon and encouraging trendy restaurants, galleries, clubs and a multiplex theater. Drive through downtown just after it gets dark to glimpse America's past, updated, and cruise through on Saturday night when Central Ave is jammed with 20-somethings cruising in lowriders to see and be seen.

New Mexico Holocaust & Intolerance Museum (Map p175; ☎ 247-0606; www.nmholocaustmuseum.org; 415 Central Ave NW; admission free; 🕐 11am-3:30pm Tue-Sat) emphasizes WWII exhibits, but there

---

WHAT HAPPENED TO THE 'R' IN ALBURQUERQUE?

Sly Don Francisco Cuervo y Valdez wanted to build a city on the Rio Grande, but in 1706 he still didn't have the required 30 families to do it. He knew, however, that the paperwork would be processed by one Viceroy Fernandez, the Duke of Alburquerque. In a shameless ploy to curry his favor, the new settlement – if approved – would be named to the Duke's eternal glory. And so Alburquerque was born.

After US annexation, English speakers poured into the Duke City, but found that first 'r' a bit difficult to pronounce. Besides, the sign at the new train station (this is a legend, perhaps) just wasn't long enough for that jumbled mouthful of letters. Somewhere along the way, that 'r' was lost forever.

Or perhaps not. Rudolfo Anaya, UNM professor emeritus and author of the seminal Chicano novel *Bless Me, Ultima*, in 1992 published the not-quite-as-revered (but better) *Alburquerque*, resurrecting the city's proper name. And oddly enough, through a mist of magical realism, he was able to invoke the essence of this strange city, along with that long forgotten 'r.'

DOWNTOWN ALBUQUERQUE

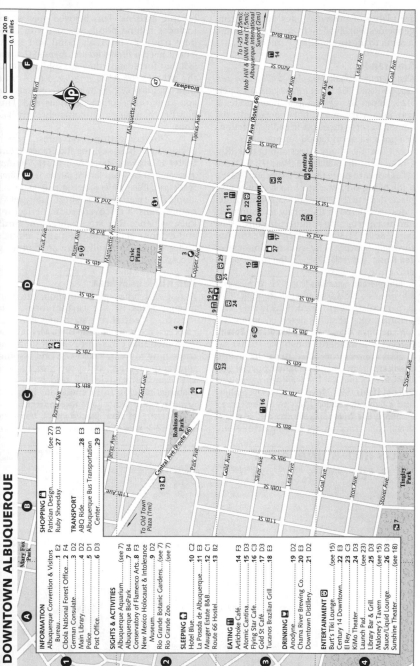

INFORMATION
Albuquerque Convention & Visitors Bureau	**1** E2
Cibola National Forest Office	**2** F4
German Consulate	**3** D2
Main Library	**4** D2
Police	**5** D1
Post Office	**6** D3

SIGHTS & ACTIVITIES
Albuquerque Aquarium	(see 7)
Albuquerque BioPark	**7** B4
Conservatory of Flamenco Arts	**8** F3
New Mexico Holocaust & Intolerance Museum	**9** D2
Rio Grande Botanic Gardens	(see 7)
Rio Grande Zoo	(see 7)

SLEEPING
Hotel Blue	**10** C2
La Posada de Albuquerque	**11** E3
Mauger Estate B&B	**12** C1
Route 66 Hostel	**13** B2

EATING
Artichoke Café	**14** F3
Atomic Cantina	**15** D3
Flying Star Cafe	**16** C3
Gold St Café	**17** D3
Tucanos Brazilian Grill	**18** E3

DRINKING
Anodyne	**19** D2
Chama River Brewing Co	**20** E3
Downtown Distillery	**21** D2

ENTERTAINMENT
Burt's Tiki Lounge	(see 15)
Century 14 Downtown	**22** E3
El Rey	**23** C3
KiMo Theater	**24** D2
Launch Pad	(see 23)
Library Bar & Grill	**25** D3
Maloney's Tavern	(see 15)
Sauce/Liquid Lounge	**26** D3
Sunshine Theater	(see 18)

SHOPPING
Patrician Design	(see 27)
Ruby Shoesday	**27** D3

TRANSPORT
ABQ Ride	**28** E3
Albuquerque Bus Transportation Center	**29** E3

ALBUQUERQUE

arc plenty of powerful ones documenting genocides worldwide – from close-to-home Acoma to all-too-familiar Armenia.

Rio Grande

Albuquerque BioPark (Map p175; ☎ 764-6200; www .cabq.gov/biopark; 903 10th St NW; adult/child for 3 parks $12/5, per park $7/3; ☺ 9am-5pm) incorporates a zoo, an aquarium and botanic gardens; the combo ticket to three kid-friendly attractions is a good value and good for one day.

Set on 60 shady acres along the Rio Grande, the **Rio Grande Zoo** (Map p175; 903 10th St SW) is home to more than 250 species. There's a lot going on here: sea lion feedings take place daily at 10:30am and 3:30pm; camel rides are offered in the spring and summer; and an entertaining summertime bird show happens at 11:30am and 2pm Wednesday through Sunday. The summertime series **Zoo Music** (adult/child $10/5; ☺ 7pm Fri Jun-Aug) is also quite popular.

Albuquerque Aquarium (Map p175; ☎ 903 10th St NW) boasts a 285,000-gallon shark tank. This is particularly well loved, which isn't surprising given the state's desert environment. On the flora side, visit the **Rio Grande Botanic Gardens** and wander through the 10,000-sq-ft glass conservatory filled to the brim with Mediterranean and desert fauna. Special gardens events include the walk-through show **River of Lights** (late November to December) and a **Butterfly Pavilion** (May to September).

Tingley Beach (Map p173; admission free; ☺ sunrise-sunset) is connected to the aquarium and botanic gardens. This beloved open space includes fishing ponds stocked with rainbow trout, a children's pond and trails. You'll need a **fishing license** (day pass $17, annual $35), but fortunately they are sold on-site at the **gift shop** (☎ 248-8522; ☺ 9am-5pm). A little **train** (adult/child $2/1; ☺ 10am-3pm) connects the zoo, aquarium/botanic gardens and Tingley Beach; it runs approximately every half hour.

A 270-acre cottonwood forest (which is called the bosque), the **Rio Grande Nature Center & State Park** (Map pp170-1; ☎ 344-7240; www .rngc.org; 2901 Candelaria Rd NW; parking $3; ☺ 8am-5pm for park, 10am-5pm for visitor center; P ☺) runs along the river and has short interpretive nature trails, a discovery room perfect for kids, wetlands that attract migrating birds and exhibits about bosque plants, animals and geology. The trails here are handicap accessible.

Nob Hill & UNM Area

A fun and funky place to shop, eat, rent foreign films or see current ones, this stretch of Central Ave starts at UNM and runs east to about Carlisle Blvd. Mall-averse 20-somethings can scour colorful shops for something to wear; artists will find inspiration and supplies; and people of all ages with innovative style will find home furnishings ranging from enormous Mexican armoires to delicate Japanese lanterns.

University of New Mexico (UNM; Map p176; ☎ 277-5813; www.unm.edu; Central Ave NE) is an

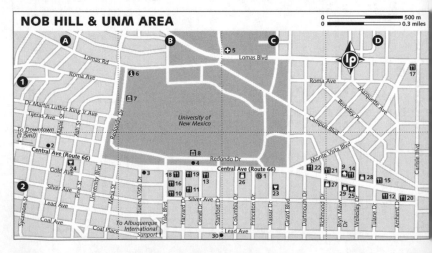

NOB HILL & UNM AREA

adobe wonderland with 13 museums and galleries and lots of public art, a perform-ing arts center and the **Tamarind Institute**, which single-handedly saved the art of lithography from extinction in the 1960s and '70s. The **UNM Welcome Center** (Map p176; ☎ 277-1989; Las Lomas Rd; ☉ 8am-5pm Mon-Fri) has information and maps.

Maxwell Museum of Anthropology (Map p176; ☎ 277-4405; Redondo Dr; ☉ 9am-4pm Tue-Fri, 10am-4pm Sat) will satisfy the cultural anthropolo-gist in you, so make a bee-line for permanent exhibits on people of the Southwest and on ancestors, but do check out traveling exhib-its and activities for children.

The **University Art Museum** (Map p176; ☎ 277-4001; Center for the Arts Bldg, cnr Redondo & Cornell Drs; ☉ 9am-4pm Tue-Fri, 5-8pm Tue, 1-4pm Sun) displays the largest fine-art collection in all of New Mexico.

Metropolitan Albuquerque

Operated by the All Indian Pueblo Council, **Indian Pueblo Cultural Center** (IPCC; Map pp170-1; ☎ 843-7270; www.indianpueblo.org; 2401 12th St NW; adult/child $6/3; ☉ 9am-5pm) is a must-see. Sure, history exhibits are fascinating, but the arts wing features the finest examples of each pueblo's work. Do your homework here before considering any major purchases. The IPCC also houses a large gift shop and retail gallery. The on-site restaurant (p185) has demos and great Native New Mexican cuisine.

Sandia Peak Tramway (Map p191; ☎ 856-7325; www.sandiapeak.com; Tramway Blvd; adult/child $15/10; ☉ 9am-9pm) is Albuquerque's most famous attraction (after the Indian Pueblo Cul-tural Center). At 2.7 miles, it's the world's longest aerial tram, rising from the desert floor to the top of 10,378ft Sandia Peak for spectacular views anytime. (But sunsets are particularly drop-dead brilliant.)

Located in the historic Barelas neigh-borhood, **National Hispanic Cultural Center** (Map pp170-1; ☎ 246-2261; www.nhccnm.org; 1701 4th St SW; adult/child $3/free, Sun free; ☉ 10am-5pm Tue-Sun) is a center for Hispanic visual, performing and literary arts. It has three galleries and the nation's premier Hispanic genealogy library. It is also home to the La Fonda del Bosque Restaurant (p186) and the Roy E Disney Center for the Performing Arts (p187).

Easily accessible off I-40, **Petroglyph Na-tional Monument** (Map p191; ☎ 899-0205; www.nps.gov/petr/home.htm; Unser Blvd; parking $2; ☉ 8am-5pm) is a field that has hiking trails and picnic areas scattered throughout five (nonactive) volcanic cones. Over 20,000 images have been sketched into shiny black volcanic rock by Native peoples and early Spanish settlers.

There's a surprising amount of fine wine being made in them thar hills, but there are two particular standouts. **Gruet Winery** (Map p191; ☎ 821-0055; 8400 Pan American Fwy NE; ☉ 10-5pm Mon-Fri, noon-5pm Sat) gives daily tours at 2pm and free tastings. **Casa Rondeña** (Map pp170-1; ☎ 344-5911; 733 Chavez Rd NW; ☉ 10am-6pm Wed-Sat, noon-6pm Sun) only gives tours during the July Lavender Festival and charges $3 for tastings.

South Valley and **North Valley** are traditional, agricultural areas near the Rio Grande char-acterized by open spaces, small ranches, farms, bosque (Spanish for 'woods') and acequia (historical irrigation ditches that also mark popular walking paths). Chickens and horses roam fields between historic adobe and wood-frame houses and newer commercial and housing developments. With a population nearly 80% Hispanic, the 39-sq-mile South Valley is bordered by I-25, I-40 and the West Mesa and volcanic cliffs.

North Valley is more mixed and upscale, with a reputation that's affluent, pastoral, quiet and determined to keep it that way. Although it measures just 7 miles from downtown Albuquerque, it's more like a world away. This 100-sq-mile area is roughly bordered by I-40, I-25, the Rio Grande and the Bernalillo/Sandoval County line. To refresh your mind, stop at exceptional and independent Bookworks NM (p171) and the adjacent Flying Star Café (see p185). If there is a Flying Star here, you know it must be a groovy neighborhood.

The village of **Corrales** (Map p191), just north of North Valley, was established by Spanish settlers in 1710, but it was home to Tiwa Indians for centuries before that – they were practicing irrigated agriculture here 1300 years ago. Even more rural than North Valley, Corrales offers splendid strolling through the bosque and along acequia. Take NM 448 north into the village and then drive or walk along any side roads – most are unpaved and will reward with earthy scents of farms and open fields, horses, scampering rabbits and quail criss-crossing your path among 200-year-old adobes and modern replicas.

ACTIVITIES

Sandia Crest (p182) is Albuquerque's playground, popular for skiing and hiking.

Elena Gallegos Picnic Area (Map pp170-1; ☎ 857-8334; Simms Park Rd; parking $2; ☺ 7am-7pm winter, 7am-9pm summer), in the foothills of the Sandias, is a popular jumping-off point for hiking, running and mountain-biking trails; some are handicap accessible. Go early in the day before the overhead sun gets too hot, or at dusk to take advantage of the panoramic western sunset views and watch the city lights begin twinkling below. Time your walk carefully, though, because darkness falls quickly after the sun sets and howling coyotes ring the park. They won't bother you, but if you're a full-fledged urbanite and unaccustomed to uninvited nighttime company, it might be unnerving.

Bicycling is a major sport in Albuquerque, for beginners and national-level competitors. Get outfitted at **Northeast Cyclery** (Map pp170-1; ☎ 299-1210; 8305 Menaul Blvd NE; rentals per day $25, bike racks available) and head out. Download a useful city map at www.cabq.gov/bike to find dedicated off-road tracks along arroyos. To ride along the Rio Grande, park at the Albuquerque BioPark (p176) and follow the riverside trail north or south (the smell of green chiles roasting at local factories is best appreciated if you head south in October; the path is less urban if you head north). You can also ride along acequia in North Valley (p177). A great track runs the entire length of Tramway Blvd, running past

---

ROUTE 66 IN ABQ

Albuquerque boasts one of the liveliest sections of Route 66. Although the historic route, known in these parts as Central Ave, is admittedly camouflaged by modern storefronts, the UNM campus and a country club, certain blocks and buildings are vintage Route 66.

Route 66 extends for 18 miles in Albuquerque, but the mother lode of the mother road is the stretch between the state fairgrounds (at Central Ave and Louisiana Blvd) and downtown (at Central Ave and 8th St).

Remember that Albuquerque has always been a humble city, and the historic buildings were built in the 1930s, '40s and '50s. The two best times to photograph the wackiest signs and most deco exteriors are mid-afternoon, when the sun is not directly overhead (but buildings and signs still seem pinned against a brilliant blue sky), and dusk, when the western sky is striated with sunset and the neon signs are just beginning to show themselves in all their faded glory.

Don't miss the astoundingly original **Aztec Motel** (3821 Central Ave). It was built in 1931 and is still in use, though mostly by folks who are maybe a little down on their luck. Motel directories from the mid-1950s listed about a hundred places to overnight along Central Ave, but only 30 still stand today. And of those, only 20 are still in business. Cap off your hunt at the **Route 66 Malt Shop** (p183) and crank your i-pod to the Rolling Stones' cover of *Route 66*.

ONE PERSON'S ART IS ANOTHER'S WEAPON OF MASS DESTRUCTION

From conventional bronze to salvaged, silvery aircraft parts, from ancient Pueblo pottery to modern bus stops, the range of public art in Albuquerque is difficult to describe. The best way to appreciate it? Keep your eyes peeled as you drive and walk around the city because you never know what you'll find.

The city began its Public Art Program in 1978 and was one of the first in the country to run one. They maintain a partial roster with photos on www.cabq.gov/publicart, but you're mostly on your own. Here's a wide-ranging list of pieces and locales to give you a start:

- Albuquerque Sunport and the I-40: Giant replicas of Pueblo Indian pottery vessels dot the medians as you enter/exit the airport or drive along the east–west artery through the city. These stunning 8ft-tall pieces dwarf your car and draw your eye – but not for too long, please, you're driving!
- South Valley: Lightning bolts add drama to the utilitarian concept of a bus stop at the intersection of Broadway and Avenida Cesar Chavez SE.
- Nob Hill: A large car atop a ceramic tile arch at the corner of San Mateo and Gibson Blvds in the UNM neighborhood underscores Route 66 history.
- Northeast Heights: A mother bear and two cubs cavort atop a granite boulder along the entry to Bear Arroyo (a great biking and walking path through desert scrub) on the west side of Tramway Blvd, just south of Spain Rd.
- I-40 E: A shimmering likeness of the native datil yucca plant borders the north side of the highway as you head east out of town. Salvaged aluminum fuel tanks from military aircraft form the retina-burning vertical leaves that reflect the sun and cause passersby to wonder whether they're looking at a replica of a plant or a weapon. Now you know: it's both.

the Prairie Dogs (p180) and turning east into Elena Gallegos (opposite). From late May to early September and during October's Balloon Fiesta, you can rent bikes at the top and purchase an all-day **chairlift pass** (adult/child $40/30) to bring you back up to the crest after biking down thousands of vertical feet.

Walking the **irrigation ditches** is a downright local thing to do. Get a decent city map and find the thin blue lines branching out in North Valley from the Rio Grande between Montaño Rd and Paseo del Norte and around Rio Grande Blvd. Acequia are bordered by walking paths, a gift to early-morning risers who value cool morning temps in the summer.

Take to the skies in a hot-air balloon with **Discover Balloons** (Map p173; ☎ 842-1111; www .discoverballoons.com; 205B San Felipe St NW; ride $150). Excursions include hotel pickup, a one-hour ride and a champagne brunch. Make reservations at least one month in advance during the summer.

If you're in the market for an authentic Latin experience, take a class at the **Conservatory of Flamenco Arts** (Map p175; ☎ 242-7600; www .nationalinstuteofflamenco.org; 214 Gold Ave SW; classes $10-15). Stomp and clap to rhythms of live guitar music and your Spanish instructors. Don't forget your flamenco shoes! You don't have any? Buying a pair at the conservatory will set you back about $100, but it could be the start of a lifelong passion. Class attire for men includes long pants and a fitted shirt, for women a full skirt and fitted top or leotard.

Who on earth would think about skating in the desert? Turns out, quite a few people. Fork over $6 to skate and $2 to rent a pair at **Outpost Ice Arena** (Map p191; ☎ 856-7595; 9530 Tramway Blvd NE; ☼ 1-3pm Mon-Sat) and enjoy every chilly moment. Just try not to bump into too many kids. Evening skate times change monthly.

ALBUQUERQUE FOR CHILDREN

Families will not want for diversions in this city. Learn about creepy-crawly snakes at the American International Rattlesnake Museum (p174); sharks and other deep-sea creatures at Albuquerque Aquarium (p176); birds that nest alongside easy trails at the Rio Grande Nature Center & State Park (p176); all sorts of age-appropriate science at !Explora! Science Center (p174); and native desert plants (as well as butterflies) at the Botanic Gardens (p176).

ALBUQUERQUE

ALBUQUERQUE

OH GIVE ME A HOME…WHERE THE PRAIRIE DOGS ROAM

Not to be confused with Puxatawney Phil in *Ground Hog Day* or the golf course gopher in *Caddyshack*, the Gunnison's prairie dogs of Albuquerque are in a league of their own.

Part wildlife habitat and part walking/biking path, the east side of Tramway Blvd between Indian School Rd and Menaul Blvd is home to thousands of 'city' prairie dogs.

No matter how cute, be forewarned: these *are* wild animals. Accustomed to human presence, though, they won't run away from you and will even creep toward you looking for handouts. Visitors needn't be afraid of them – in fact, walking among them is delightful – but don't feed, pet or handle them.

That said, you must pay them a visit! Arrive between 7am and 2pm to see wizened adults and cavalier juveniles at their most active. Park in the small commercial complex on Indian School Rd east of Tramway Blvd, across from Walgreen's, and walk about 50ft down to the path along Tramway. You really won't believe your eyes. Hundreds of little creatures will be frolicking, eating, chasing one another, napping and cautiously eyeing you. No cages, windows or bars separate you and them – you're on their turf. Hay for nesting and baby carrots, gifts of the caretakers (www.prairiedogpals.com), dot the otherwise pallid beige and green landscape.

Stand quietly among scores of burrows and let your eyes adjust to the active community. Hundred of pairs of beady little eyes have already checked you out, and a few responsible prairie dogs will issue squeaky warning calls (sounding rather like those squeezable dog toys).

These furry little denizens are oblivious to the busy four-lane boulevard beside them or the neon sign illuminating the 24-hour pharmacy above them. Their adaptability is a marvel. We should all be so fortunate.

The Museum of Natural History & Science (p174) introduces kids to meteorites and dinosaurs.

When the kids have had enough learning (or they're hot), **Cliff's Amusement Park** (Map pp170-1; ☎ 881-9373; www.cliffsamusementpark.com; 4800 Osuna NE; adult/child $22/19; ⏰ Apr-Sep) is a great reward. The park has about 25 rides, including a roller coaster, the Water Monkey, a play area and other traditional favorites.

Hinkle Family Fun Center (Map pp170-1; ☎ 299-3100; www.hinklefamilyfuncenter.com; 12931 Indian School Rd NE; 5hr pass $35 or per ride $6; ⏰ noon-10pm Mon-Thu, noon-midnight Fri & Sat, 10am-10pm Sun) keeps little ones amused with bumper cars, laser tag, mini-golf and a huge 'jungle play area' where kids can crawl and climb and slide around. Burn off some energy, especially if it's too hot or cold or wet to play outside.

TOURS

New Mexico native Christy Rojas runs **Aventura Artistica** (☎ 800-808-7352; www.newmexicotours.com), which specializes in three- to four-day tours of the Albuquerque–Santa Fe area.

The UNM Department of Continuing Education's **Story of New Mexico Program** (☎ 277-2527; www.dcereg.com) offers excellent lectures on all things New Mexico, as well as tours to Santa Fe like the Folk Art Market, Indian Market and Opera, and gallery tours along the High Road to Taos by top-notch guides like Sharon Niederman. Advance registration is required.

FESTIVALS & EVENTS

The Friday *Albuquerque Journal* and *Alibi* both have weekly events listings.

Gathering of Nations Powwow (☎ 836-2810; www.gatheringofnations.com) Held at the Pitt on the last full weekend of April, this is the single biggest event in Native America, with participants coming from all over the continent for dancing, drumming, art shows, a Miss Indian World pageant and the Indian Traders' Market.

Albuquerque Gay/Lesbian/Bisexual/Transgender Pride (☎ 873-8084; www.abqpride.com) While upwards of 10,000 parade participants and bystanders line Central Ave, 'Albuqueerque' will never be mistaken for Castro Street and San Francisco. But do come for the Pride Pet Parade, Pride Art Show, Pride Idol or just a gay ole good time. Gather around the Central Ave Starbucks on Nob Hill in mid-June.

Festival Flamenco Internacional de Alburquerque (☎ 277-1868; www.nationalinstututeofflamenco.org) This energetic, week-long celebration of flamenco brings Spanish performers to town for performances ($30 to $50), workshops ($50) and a competition. Events are held at Popejoy Hall (p187) and the National Hispanic Cultural Center (p177) in mid-June.

Summerfest (☎ 505-768-3556) Held at the Civic Center, this free weekly festival features food, music, arts and crafts, dance and plenty of family activities on Saturday evenings in June and July.

New Mexico State Fair (☎ 265-1791; www.exponm .com; tickets $5) Give into having fun with food, music, prize livestock, juried art shows, rodeos, shopping, evening concerts (mostly country) and creaky carnival rides. Held in late September.

International Balloon Fiesta (☎ 821-1000, 800-422-7277; www.aibf.org; adult/child per session $6/free) The very helpful website has launch-site maps, park and ride information, and exact dates for this early-October event, which features over 700 hot-air balloons! You just haven't lived until you've seen a three-story-tall Tony the Tiger land in your hotel courtyard, which is exactly the sort of thing that happens all over town during this two-week extravaganza. Yeah, everything's packed and parking is horrible, but being on the ground during Mass Ascension, with hundreds of colorful balloons fluttering and inflating all around you like living, breathing beings...it's so worth it. And being in the air? Even better! The Special Shape Rodeo, Night Magic and Balloon Glow are always well-deserved crowd pleasers. If you're coming from the south, vehicular access to the enormous Balloon Fiesta Park is off Alameda Blvd NE. If you're coming from Santa Fe, take I-25 Frontage Rd to the Balloon Fiesta Parkway.

SLEEPING

Although Albuquerque has about 150 hotels (all full during the International Balloon Fiesta and the Gathering of Nations), it's not exactly swimming in interesting nonmotel lodging. The Albuquerque Convention & Visitors Bureau (p172) has information, and links to more options, and many local B&Bs participate in the **New Mexico Central Reservations Line** (☎ 766-9770, 800-466-7829).

Old Town
BUDGET
Monterey Motel (Map p173; ☎ 243-3554; 2402 Central Ave SW; r $40; ⓟ ⊠ ⊠ ⊠) Close to downtown, these 15 perfectly acceptable nonsmoking rooms also have wireless internet.

Best Western Rio Grande Inn (Map p173; ☎ 843-9500, 800-959-4726; www.riogreandeinn.com; 1015 Rio Grande Blvd NW; r $90; ⓟ ⊠ ⊠ ⊠) South of I-40 and two blocks from Old Town, this place has 173 large, Southwestern-style rooms with handcrafted furniture and lots of little amenities like in-room internet hookups.

MIDRANGE
Casas de Sueños (Map p173; ☎ 247-4560; www.casas desuenos.com; 310 Rio Grande Blvd SW; r incl full breakfast $119-189; ⓟ ⊠ ⊠ ⊡) This lovely and peaceful place with luscious gardens and a pool has 21 adobe casitas featuring handcrafted

furniture and original artwork. Some casitas have a kitchenette, fireplace and/or private hot tub (a couple are even outside in a private garden).

Hotel Albuquerque (Map p173; ☎ 843-6300, 800-237-2133; www.hotelabq.com; 800 Rio Grande Blvd NW; r from $140 ⓟ ⊠ ⊠ ⊠) Formerly the Sheraton Old Town, this 188-room hotel has an Olympic-sized outdoor pool, a rose arbor, and a salon and day spa. There is a $5 charge for five days of wireless, and it's within walking distance of Old Town, the Museum of Natural History & Science and the Albuquerque Museum.

Böttger Mansion (Map p173; ☎ 243-3639, 800-758-3639; www.bottger.com; 110 San Felipe St NW; d incl breakfast $140-250; ⓟ ⊠ ⊠) The most deluxe of several Old Town area B&Bs, this huge Victorian built by German wool exporter Charles Bottger in 1905 has been a Buddhist colony and boarding house, but currently has eight elegant rooms, including one suite, and wireless internet.

Downtown
Route 66 Hostel (Map p175; ☎ 247-1813; 1012 Central Ave SW; dm $17, d $28; ⓟ ⊠ ⊠) With discounts for HI-AYH members, this 42-person hostel is clean, fun and conveniently located between downtown and Old Town. A kitchen and library are available for guest use.

Hotel Blue (Map p175; ☎ 924-2400; www.thehotel blue.com; 717 Central Ave NW; s/d $69/79; ⓟ ⊠ ⊠ ⊠) This art deco-style hotel has 135 rooms and fewer frills. But it is right downtown and offers internet hookups as well as breakfast.

La Posada de Albuquerque (Map p175; ☎ 242-9090, 800-777-5732; www.laposada-abq.com; 125 2nd St NW; r $80-160; ⓟ ⊠ ⊠) This 1939 downtown landmark offers fine rooms, a relaxed bar with weekend jazz, and a classic coffee shop. It was completely renovated during 2006.

Mauger Estate B&B (Map p175; ☎ 242-8755, 800-719-9189; www.maugerbb.com; 701 Roma Ave NW; r $89-179; ⓟ ⊠ ⊠ ⊡ ⊠) This restored Queen Anne house (Mauger is pronounced 'major'), whose eight rooms have stocked refrigerators and freshly cut flowers, attracts the likes of Linda Rondstadt and Martin Sheen, but as the hosts are proud of saying, 'every guest is treated like a celebrity.' The city's Rapid Ride transit, which stops at Nob Hill and the Albuquerque BioPark, also stops just a few blocks away from this B&B.

ALBUQUERQUE

DETOUR: SANDIA CREST

Albuquerqueans always know which way is east thanks to 10,678ft Sandia Crest, sacred to Sandia Pueblo and well named for both its wavelike silhouette and the glorious pink (*sandia* is Spanish for 'watermelon') its granite cliffs glow at sunset. There are three ways to the top.

Beautiful 8-mile (one way) **La Luz Trail** (FR 444; parking $3) is the most rewarding, rising 3800ft from the desert, past a small waterfall to pine forests and spectacular views. It gets hot.

Sandia Peak Tramway (p177) is the most extravagant route to the top; you can hike the La Luz up and take the tram down, trekking two more miles at the bottom on Tramway Trail to your car.

Finally you can drive, via NM 14, making a left onto Sandia Crest Rd (NM 165), stopping at Tinkertown Museum (p194). The road is lined with trailheads and picnic spots (a daily $3 parking fee covers all of them), and low-impact camping ($3) is allowed by permit throughout Cibola National Forest. The choices are endless, but don't skip the easy 1-mile round-trip to **Sandia Man Cave**, where the oldest human encampment in North America was discovered in 1936. Bring a flashlight.

At the top, the **Sandia Crest Visitors Center** (Map p191; ☎ 248-0190; NM 165; ☽ 8am-5pm, closed Sun in winter) offers nature programs daily; **Sandia Crest House** (Map p191; ☎ 243-0605; NM 165; dishes $3-7; ☽ 9:30am-sunset), in the same building, serves burgers and snacks. This is the jumping-off point for the exquisite **Sandia Crest Trail**, which heads 11 miles north and 16 miles south with incredible views; hike north along the ridgeline as long as you'd like to appreciate the best of them.

Take the trail 2 miles south, past **Kiwanis Cabin** rock house, to the tram terminal and **High Finance** (Map p191; ☎ 243-9742; lunch $8-12, dinner $16-42; ☽ 11am-9pm), which offers mediocre food and more fabulous views.

This is also the site of **Sandia Peak Ski Park** (☎ 242-9052; www.sandiapeak.com; lift tickets adult/child $41/31; ☽ 9am-4pm Dec-Mar & Jun-Sep), a smallish but scenic ski area. In summer, the park rents **mountain bikes** ($30/40 incl lift tickets) for blazing those downhill runs; note that bikes aren't allowed on the tram.

Nob Hill & UNM Area

Hiway House (Map p176; ☎ 268-3971; 3200 Central Ave SE; s/d $35/40; P ✕ ✕ ✕) Once part of a prolific Southwest hotel chain, this Hiway was the last one built in the 1950s. Perhaps that's why the staff can be less than friendly, a rarity in Albuquerque. Just beyond the heart of the UNM and Nob Hill neighborhood, it's a 60-room place with the original 1958 neon sign and colonial-style architecture, but has updated with wireless internet connections.

Metropolitan Albuquerque

BUDGET

Inexpensive motels line Central Ave, concentrated around the I-25 on-ramp and east of Nob Hill. You can score a room in the $35 to $45 range, but trust your gut instincts – some are pretty sleazy. The best bets for midrange accommodations are the endless chain motels that hug I-25 and I-40.

Albuquerque North Bernalillo KOA (Map p191; ☎ 867-5227, 800-562-3616; www.koa.com; 555 Hill Rd, Bernalillo; tent $21-33, RV $30-51, cabin $37-56; P ✕) Located about 15 miles north of the Albuquerque city limits, the better of the city's two KOAs has wireless internet and is within easy exploring distance of city attractions.

Casita Chamisa B&B (Map pp170-1; ☎ 897-4644; www.casitachamisa.com; 850 Chamisal Rd NW; r $80-95; P ✕ ✕ ✕ ✕) Accommodations here include a two-bedroom guesthouse equipped with a kitchenette and vibrant greenhouse, a large bedroom in the main house and a studio with a kitchenette. The friendly host, Arnold Sargeant, offers valuable advice about area offerings and the archeological site where the B&B is located.

MIDRANGE TO TOP END

Cinnamon Morning (Map pp170-1; ☎ 345-3541; www.cinnamonmorning.com; 2700 Rio Grande Blvd NW; r $90-180; P ✕ ✕) This B&B near Old Town has four rooms and a two-bedroom guesthouse, an outdoor hot tub and wireless internet. Southwest charm and enough common areas make this a relaxing and homey stay.

Hacienda Antigua (Map pp170-1; ☎ 345-5399, 800-201-2986; www.haciendantigua.com; 6708 Tierra Dr NW; r $99-229; P X X R) This eight-room inn is brimming with authentic New Mexican style. From the pale adobe walls to vigas (wooden roofing beams), your expectations of a Southwestern vacation will be met.

our pick Los Poblanos (Map pp170-1; ☎ 344-9297, 866-344-9297; www.lospoblanos.com; 4803 Rio Grande Blvd NW; r $145-250; P X X) This six-room B&B, surrounded by gardens, lavender fields (blooming mid-June through July) and an organic farm, is a registered National Historic Place. Los Poblanos is a five-minute drive from Old Town and is within walking distance of the Rio Grande and open space trails. Organic eggs and produce from the farm are served for breakfast, and rooms feature kiva fireplaces and internet hookups.

EATING

Albuquerque offers the region's widest variety of international cuisines while at the same time serving up some of the best New Mexican food found anywhere. However, it is not a foodie destination like Santa Fe, and many restaurants that are geared to tourists are less than outstanding. Instead, it's best to head to any of the modest, family-owned joints serving excellent and authentic local cuisine or to the cluster of colorful and (mostly) inexpensive restaurants centered on Nob Hill. Restaurants in Albuquerque are nonsmoking,

while bars not attached to restaurants still allow smoking.

Old Town

The plaza is surrounded with average eateries serving average food at premium prices (it's the cost of convenience). Consider walking a few blocks for a better selection.

BUDGET

Route 66 Malt Shop (Map p173; ☎ 242-7866; 1720 Central Ave SW; dishes $5; ☽ lunch & dinner Mon-Sat; P X & V) This nostalgic and friendly place only has one table, one booth and a tiny counter with four stools. But it serves great green-chile cheeseburgers, hot pastrami and other sandwiches.

Garcia's Kitchen (Map p173; ☎ 842-0273; 1736 Central Ave SW; dishes $5-9; ☽ 6:30am-10pm; P X & V) Homemade specialties – including excellent *carne adovada*, stuffed *sopapillas* and five-star breakfasts – make this an Albuquerque classic.

Church St Cafe (Map p173; ☎ 247-8522; 2111 Church St NW; dishes $7-12; ☽ 8am-4pm Sun-Wed, 8am-8pm Thu-Sat; P X & V) The food is delicious, and the café is historic and the exception to the plaza rule. Try the Albuquerque roast beef, and the French dip with green chile on a flour tortilla.

TOP END

Seasons Rotisserie & Grill (Map p173; ☎ 766-5100; www.seasonsonthenet.com; 2031 Mountain Rd NW; lunch $7-14, dinner $14-28; ☽ lunch & dinner Mon-Fri, dinner Sat & Sun; P X & V) Bright-yellow walls, high ceilings, fresh flowers and a creative

ALBUQUERQUE

HOME TO A SINGULAR MEDITATIVE MOVEMENT

The **T'ai Chi Chih Center** (Map pp170-1; ☎ 299-2095; www.taichichihassociation.com; 3107 Eubank Blvd NE, Scottsdale Village) is the only one of its kind in the country to teach T'ai Chi Chih, a moving meditation originated by Albuquerque resident Justin Stone in 1974. Not to be confused with T'ai Chi Chu'an, the ancient martial art with 108 poses, these movements focus on softness, continuity and circularity. Activating, balancing and circulating the Chi (or life force), the practice has a way of bringing into balance for each practitioner that which needs balancing. It's a tough concept to accept mentally until you try it for yourself. Over its relatively short life span, regular TCC practice has been shown to help all sorts of ailments, from arthritis and migraine headaches to osteoporosis and high blood pressure.

As Justin Stone says, 'Since most students feel the effects of the practice very quickly, it is not necessary to accept results as a matter of faith.' There are over 2200 teachers worldwide, and hundreds in the Albuquerque area. Maybe you'll get lucky and meet the originator, who often drops into the center to offer his wisdom.

YOU CAN RUN BUT YOU CAN'T HIDE

Albuquerque may lack the panache of Beverly Hills or the élan of Manhattan's Upper East Side, but this desert city has its fair share of the rich and famous nonetheless. You never know who may be standing behind you in line at Whole Foods.

Best-selling author, and one of New Mexico's wealthiest residents, Tony Hillerman, known for detective novels (set in the Four Corners area of New Mexico and Arizona) featuring Navajo main characters, taught at the University of New Mexico for 21 years. His latest novel, *The Shape Shifters*, was published in 2006.

Jeff Bezos, founder of Amazon.com, was born in Albuquerque in 1964 and spent most summers of his youth on the ranch of his grandfather, regional director of the US Atomic Energy Commission here.

Bill Gates, Microsoft co-founder and richest man in the world, was arrested in Albuquerque on December 13, 1977, for racing his Porsche 911 across the desert, according to the BBC.

Visionary architect Antoine Predock, 2005 winner of the American Institute of Architect's Gold Medal, lives here and has designed several buildings across the state and across the world, including Taiwan's National Palace Museum and Canada's Museum for Human Rights.

Popular TV and film actor Freddie Prinze, Jr, named one of *People* magazine's '50 Most Beautiful People in the World' in 2000 and star of the hit sitcom *Freddie* through 2006, grew up in Albuquerque and Puerto Rico.

menu; this place provides welcome relief from the usual Old Town atmosphere. Try the hearty red-chile-dusted chicken burgers or Baja tacos inside or on the rooftop cantina.

Downtown

Atomic Cantina (Map p175; ☎ 242-2200; 315 Gold Ave SW; dishes $5-11; ⌚ 4pm-midnight Tue-Sat, 4-11pm Sun; ⅏ Ⓥ) This live-music club features a popular local cook who runs the in-house Café Gee and prepares a mean line of Cuban sandwiches. Rock bands start tuning up most nights at 10pm.

Gold St Café (Map p175; ☎ 765-1633; 218 Gold Ave SW; dishes $6-15; ⌚ 7am-10pm Tue-Sat, 7am-2pm Sun & Mon; ⓧ ⅏ Ⓥ ⓐ) This pleasant café serves standard New Mexican and American cuisine and has above-average espresso drinks.

Tucanos Brazilian Grill (Map p175; ☎ 246-9900; www.tucanos.com; 110 Central Ave SW; lunch $11, dinner $17; ⌚ 11am-9pm Mon-Wed, to 10pm Thu & Sat, to 11pm Fri, to 8pm Sun; Ⓟ ⓧ ⅏ ⓐ) Tucanos serves an all-inclusive Brazilian-style BBQ with skewered meats and a comprehensive salad bar.

our pick **Artichoke Café** (Map p175; ☎ 243-0200; 424 Central Ave SE; dishes $17-30; ⌚ 11:30am-2:30pm Mon-Fri, 4:30-9:30pm Mon-Sat; Ⓟ ⓧ ⅏ Ⓥ) Elegant and unpretentious, this popular bistro does creative gourmet cuisine with panache and is high on foodies' lists of Albuquerque's best.

Nob Hill & UNM Area
In the grand tradition of university neighborhoods, this is the best area for cheap, healthy and vegetarian meals. You can also find a number of swanky places to nosh.

BUDGET
Irysh Mac's (Map p176; ☎ 265-5597; 110 Yale Blvd SE; snacks $4-10; ⌚ 7am-midnight Mon-Fri, 8am-midnight Sat, 9am-10pm Sun; Ⓟ ⓧ ⅏) Excellent lattes, pastries and other light snacks complemented with live local music around 8pm most nights – staff put a sign out front if there's a gig. As a bonus, it offers wireless internet.

Satellite Coffee (Map p176; ☎ 254-3800; 2300 Central Ave SE; snacks $1-5; ⌚ 6am-11pm Sun-Thu, until midnight Sat; ⓧ ⅏ Ⓥ ⓐ) Albuquerque's answer to Starbucks lies in these hip coffee shops, luring patrons in with free wireless internet. Owned by the same brilliant folks who started the fabu Flying Star, look for plenty of locations around town.

Frontier (Map p176; ☎ 266-0550; www.frontier restaurant.com; 2400 Central Ave SE; dishes $3-7; ⌚ 24hr; Ⓟ ⓧ ⅏ Ⓥ ⓐ) Get in line for enormous cinnamon rolls (made with, like, a stick of butter each!) and the best *huevos rancheros*. Period. The food, people-watching and Western art are all outstanding.

Anapurna (Map p176; ☎ 262-2424; 2201 Silver Ave SE; dishes $6-8; ⌚ 7am-8pm Mon-Sat, 10am-6pm Sun; Ⓟ ⓧ ⅏ Ⓥ ⓐ) This awesome vegetarian café has some of the best food in town, including delicately spiced ayurvedic delights that even carnivores love, plus *real* chai.

Model Pharmacy (Map p176; ☎ 255-8686; 3636 Monte Vista Blvd NE; dishes $5-8; ☺ 9am-6:30pm Mon-Fri, 9am-2pm Sat; P ⊠ ⅃ V ⅃) Stop by to sample fun perfumes, a grand selection of hair ornaments, souvenirs you actually want to buy and great soda-fountain fare at this charming retro spot.

La Montanita Co-op (Map p176; ☎ 265-4631; 3500 Central Ave SE; dishes $5-10; ☺ 7am-10pm; P ⊠ ⅃ V ⅃) Mainly a grocery store, the co-op also sells sandwiches, salads and lunch specials at the on-site deli.

El Patio (Map p176; ☎ 268-4245; 142 Harvard Dr SE; dishes $6-10; ☺ 11:30am-10pm; P ⊠ ⅃ V ⅃) Relax on the patio, where guitarists sometimes strum; tasty New Mexican dishes.

Olympia Cafe (Map p176; ☎ 266-5222; 2210 Central Ave SE; dishes $5-12; ☺ 11am-10pm Mon-Fri; P ⊠ ⅃ V ⅃) This isn't just the best Greek food in town – it may be the best Greek food anywhere (yes, including Greece).

II Vicino Pizzeria (Map p176; ☎ 266-7855; 3403 Central Ave NE; dishes $6-8; ☺ 11am-11pm; P ⊠ ⅃ V ⅃) Sure, you can come for simple traditional fare like wood-fired pizza, sandwiches and pasta. But the real bread and butter here is spectacular award-winning micro-brewed beer, including the Wet Mountain IPA and Slow Down Brown.

MIDRANGE

Flying Star Cafe (Map p176; ☎ 255-6633; www.flyingstarcafe.com; 3416 Central Ave SE; dishes $6-12; ☺ 6am-11:30pm; P ⊠ ⅃ V ⅃) This incredibly and deservedly popular local chain draws flocks with innovative mains (and homey fare like chicken pot pie, and fish and chips), an extensive breakfast menu, sumptuous desserts, free wireless internet and creative, vibrant decor. It's pushed over the top of the groovy scale with organic, free-range and antibiotic free ingredients. It's simply a must. And portions are humungous. There are additional locations at 4501 Juan Tabo Blvd (☎ 275-8311), 723 Silver Ave SW (Map p175; ☎ 244-8099), 8001 Menaul Blvd (☎ 293-6911) and 4026 Rio Grande Blvd NM (Map p170-1; ☎ 344-6714).

Zinc Wine Bar (Map p176; ☎ 254-9462; 3009 Central Ave NW; lunch $8-12, dinner $14-25; ☺ 11am-2:30pm Sun-Fri, 5-10pm Mon-Sat; P ⊠ V ⅃) Bistro-like spot in a renovated two-level bakery; rotisserie and locally produced meats and vegies.

Yanni's Mediterranean Bar & Grill (Map p176; ☎ 268-9250; 3109 Central Ave NE; lunch $11-25, dinner $12-30; ☺ 11am-10pm Mon-Sat, noon-9pm Sun; P ⊠ ⅃) A pleasant and bright place, Yanni's prepares perfect Atlantic salmon, parmesan-encrusted yellow fin sole and Albuquerque's best calamari. Start with a light lemon chicken or red lentil soup, but save room for a baklava sundae. It also has more traditional Greek platters.

Scalo (Map p176; ☎ 255-8781; 3500 Central Ave SE; lunch $5-10, dinner $12-30; ☺ lunch & dinner; P ⊠ ⅃ V ⅃) A northern-Italian grill and an Albuquerque staple, Scalo specializes in handmade gnocchi and grilled pork chops with raspberry mint sauce.

TOP END

Gruet Steakhouse at the Monte Vista (Map p176; ☎ 256-9463; www.gruetwinery.com; 3201 Central Ave NE; dishes $19-36; ☺ 5-10pm; P ⊠ ⅃) Ensconced in the former, historic Monte Vista Fire Station, this fine-dining establishment is owned by the Gruet Winery (p177). As a result, you'll enjoy a great wine-and-steak pairing here. Although you'll probably have something like steak salad, they also have a fair amount of seafood. Upstairs, the popular bar spills onto a balcony overlooking the nighttime scene.

Metropolitan Albuquerque

The most famous restaurant in town, High Finance (p182), requires a tram ride from the base of the Sandias; the following fine choices aren't quite that far off the beaten track, however.

BUDGET

Loyola's Family Restaurant (Map pp170-1; ☎ 268-6478; 4500 Central Ave SE; dishes $5-8; ☺ 6am-2pm Tue-Fri, 6am-1:30pm Sat, 7am-1:30pm Sun; P ⊠ ⅃ V ⅃) Pure Route 66 style, Loyola's has been serving fine, no-frills New Mexican fare since before there was even a song about the Mother Rd.

Pueblo Harvest Café (dishes $5-8; ☺ 8am-3pm Mon-Fri, 8am-5pm Sat & Sun; P ⊠ ⅃ V ⅃) Along with serving Native New Mexican cuisine, this place at the Indian Pueblo Cultural Center (p177) has weekend art demonstrations, bread-baking demos and dances. If Tewa Tacos, Navajo mutton stew or pumpkin piñon bread make your mouth water, head here.

El Norteño (Map pp170-1; ☎ 256-1431; 6416 Zuni Rd SE; dishes $6-10; 🕑 11am-9pm; P 🖂 ♿ V 🍴) Mexican – not New Mexican – cuisine is the thing here, with fantastic *pollo norteño*, chicken mole and *cabrito al horno* (oven-roasted goat).

Los Cuates (Map pp170-1; ☎ 255-5079; 5016B Lomas NE; dishes $7-10; 🕑 11am-9pm; P 🖂 ♿ V 🍴) Lines are often out the door for huge plates of high-quality New Mexican cuisine. Los Cuates changed ownership recently, but the food is still first-rate.

La Fonda del Bosque Restaurant (Map pp170-1; ☎ 247-9480) Located in the National Hispanic Cultural Center (p177).

MIDRANGE

Sadie's (Map pp170-1; ☎ 345-5339; 6230 4th St NW; dishes $6-13; 🕑 10am-10pm Mon-Sat, 10am-9pm Sun; P ♿ V 🍴) Massive place with a barnlike atmosphere (and big-screen TV in the bar). It's a local institution. This is our first stop in Albuquerque – bar none. Recite along with us: 'a carafe of grand gold margaritas, please, and the enchilada dinner with blue corn, rolled, chicken, green vegetarian, no onions and a side of guac. Great. Thanks.'

Quarters (Map pp170-1; ☎ 843-7505; 801 Yale Blvd SE; dishes $6-18; 🕑 11am-9pm; P ♿ V 🍴) The best barbecue in town is slow-roasted at this dark little place.

India Palace (Map pp170-1; ☎ 271-5009; 4410 Wyoming Blvd NE; dishes $8-14; 🕑 lunch & dinner; P 🖂 ♿ V 🍴) Locally favored for spicy East Indian cuisine, the tandooris, curries, seafood and vegetarian dishes are custom-made to suit anyone's heat tolerance.

Range (Map pp170-1; ☎ 293-2633; 4200 Wyoming Blvd NE; breakfast & lunch $4-9, dinner $9-20; 🕑 7:30am-10pm; P 🖂 ♿ V 🍴) Known for its *huevos rancheros* and enchiladas; also has omelets, waffles and other standard American fare.

ENTERTAINMENT

For a comprehensive list of Albuquerque's diverse nightspots and a detailed calendar of upcoming events, get **Alibi** (www.alibi.com), a free weekly published every Tuesday. The entertainment sections of Thursday-evening's *Albuquerque Tribune* and the Friday and Sunday *Albuquerque Journal* are helpful too.

Bars & Live Music

Downtown has a great bar scene, and Nob Hill's scene is good too because of UNM.

El Rey (Map p175; ☎ 242-2353; www.elreytheater.com; 624 Central Ave SW; 🕑 from 7pm) A fabulous venue for local and national rock, blues and country acts. Over the years, it's hosted such stars as Ella Fitzgerald, Etta James and Arlo Guthrie. Although the theater itself is nonsmoking, smoking is usually allowed in the attached bar, Puccini's Golden West Saloon.

Launch Pad (Map p175; ☎ 764-8887; www.launchpadrocks.com; 618 Central Ave SW; 🕑 from 7pm) This retro-modern place is the hottest stage for local live music, and allows smoking inside.

Sauce/Liquid Lounge/Raw (Map p175; ☎ 242-5839; 405 Central Ave NW) A three-bars-in-one combo deal, this place has dancing and DJs spinning house music most nights. But it's not so loud that you can't just hang and talk. Popular and trendy, Sauce primarily

---

GLBT VENUES

Albuquerque's gay, lesbian, bisexual and transgender communities thrive here. Reflecting the city's great diversity, thousands of multicultural revelers attend the Pride Parade (p180), though other than that it's hard to find gays in large numbers outside the clubs and the Zia Regional Rodeo (p188). Its part of the price we pay for acceptance into the social fabric: there's no real gay neighborhood. (Flying Star on Central, p185, serves as the unofficial hang-out of lesbians city-wide.) Find your people among the cowgirls and boys at Sidewinders, or mix it up with hip young dancers at Pulse/Blu. To keep loose tabs on the ever-changing scene, check out www.gayalbuquerque.com, www.planetout.com and www.gaybardirectory.com, all of which can be fallible.

Gay and lesbian nightclubs include the venerable **Albuquerque Mining Company** (Map pp170-1; ☎ 255-4022; www.albminingco.com; 7209 Central Ave NE; 🕑 from 6pm) and the hipper **Pulse/Blu** (Map pp170-1; ☎ 255-3334; www.pulseandblu.com; 4100 Central Ave SE; 🕑 from 9pm), a great place for dancing. **Renea's** (Map pp170-1; 6132 4th St NW) is the city's only lesbian bar. **Sidewinders** (Map pp170-1; ☎ 275-1616; 8900 Central Ave SE; 🕑 noon-2am Mon-Sat) offers country-and-western dance lessons (7pm to 9pm Thursday) and country-and-western dancing and leather nights (Friday and Saturday).

serves very tasty gourmet pizza. The funky lounge in the back is a busy spot to hang out with a late-night drink.

Caravan East (Map pp170-1; ☎ 265-7877; 7605 Central Ave NE; ☼ from 4:30pm) Perfect for practicin' your two-steppin'.

Midnight Rodeo (Map pp170-1; 4901 McLeod Rd NE; ☼ from 4pm) You can mix with rancheros and black-T-shirted indie-music fans alike here on the edge of town. It's home to Albuquerque's first and only all-female roller-derby league, the Duke City Derby, whose punky players compete here at 4pm ($5) one Saturday each month.

Library Bar & Grill (Map p175; ☎ 242-2992; www.thelibraryusa.com; 312 Central Ave SW; ☼ 11am-2am) DJs on Friday and Saturdays, and live music on some Wednesdays.

Burt's Tiki Lounge (Map p175; ☎ 247-2878; www.burtstikilounge.com; 313 Gold Ave SW; ☼ 8pm-2am Mon-Sat) This small venue hosts rock, indie, bluegrass, punk and hip-hop bands most days of the week. They never charge a cover. Never say never?

Maloney's Tavern (Map p175; ☎ 242-7422; 325 Central Ave NW; ☼ 11am-2am Mon-Sat, 11am-midnight Sun) After about 10pm, the tables are moved and everyone dances to a live DJ.

Graham Central Station (Map pp170-1; ☎ 883-3041; 4770 Montgomery Blvd NE; ☼ 6pm-2am Wed, 7pm-2am Thu, 5pm-2am Fri, 7pm-2am Sat) Here four different bars showcase different types of music, including hip hop, country, '70s and '80s, and karaoke. Free buffet on Fridays from 5pm to 7pm.

Drinking

Anodyne (Map p175; ☎ 244-1820; 409 Central Ave NW; ☼ 4pm-2am Mon-Sat) This is an excellent spot for a game of pool. Anodyne is a huge space with book-lined walls, wood ceilings, plenty of overstuffed chairs, more than 100 bottled beers and great people-watching on Central.

Martini Grille (Map pp170-1; ☎ 255-4111; 4200 Central Ave SE; ☼ 4pm-2am Mon-Sat) Often wins the vote for the 'Best Martinis and Margaritas' in town.

Kelly's Brewery (Map p176; ☎ 262-2739; 3226 Central Ave SE; ☼ 8am-midnight) Come here for patio dining, lots of local microbrews, slow service, lots of 20-somethings hanging out and live bands on weekends.

Carraro's (Map p176; ☎ 268-2300; 108 Vassar Dr SE; ☼ 11:30am-2am Mon-Sat, 2pm-midnight Sun) A

popular place to relax with brews, pool, pizza and pals.

Downtown Distillery (Map p175; ☎ 765-1534; 406 Central Ave SW; ☼ 4pm-2am Mon-Sat, 2pm-midnight Sun) The Distillery boasts a casual crowd, pool and a jukebox, so you can be your own DJ.

Copper Lounge (Map p176; ☎ 242-7490; 1504 Central Ave SE; ☼ 4pm-2am Mon-Sat, 2pm-midnight Sun) Recently voted one of the city's best 'ladies' night out' spots, the Copper Lounge plays host to a friendly, mixed crowd.

Chama River Brewing Co (Map p175; ☎ 842-8329; www.chamariverbrewery.com; 106 2nd St NW; ☼ 4pm-2am Mon-Sat, 2pm-midnight Sun) Features handcrafted lagers and ales, four large TV screens for watching sports, a cigar lounge and a popular restaurant serving steaks, seafood and other massive dinner dishes ($13 to $22).

Performing Arts

Popejoy Hall (Map p176; ☎ 277-3824; www.popejoyhall.com; cnr Central Ave & Cornell St) The largest of three theaters at the UNM Center for the Performing Arts, this 2000-seat theater welcomes national acts, and is the main venue of the New Mexico Symphony Orchestra (below).

KiMo Theater (Map p175; ☎ 768-3522; tickets 764-1700; www.cabq.gov/kimo; 423 Central Ave NW) A registered historic landmark downtown and built in the Pueblo-Deco style. Offers an interior graced with elaborate woodcarvings and paintings as well as performances.

Sunshine Theater (Map p175; ☎ 764-0249; www.sunshinetheaterlive.com; 120 Central Ave SW) This is an intimate venue staging a variety of smaller-name artists.

Roy E Disney Center for the Performing Arts (Map pp170-1; ☎ 724-4771; www.nhccnm.org; 1701 4th St SW) This stylized Mayan pyramid is at the National Hispanic Cultural Center. It cost $23 million, opened in late 2004 and hosts all manner of performing arts. Catch something here if you can.

New Mexico Symphony Orchestra (☎ 881-8999; www.nmso.org; tickets $10-50) The orchestra performs primarily at Popejoy Hall and the National Hispanic Cultural Center, but also mounts special concerts at the Albuquerque Zoo.

New Mexico Ballet Company (☎ 292-4245; www.nmballet.org; tickets $5-25) The ballet company performs from October to April.

Musical Theater Southwest (☎ 262-9301; www.musicaltheatersw.com; tickets $30) Stages between five and 10 musical productions annually.

ALBUQUERQUE

Pit (Map pp170-1; ☎ 925-5626; www.unmtickets .com) and **Tingley Coliseum** (Map pp170-1; ☎ 265-1791; 300 San Pedro NE) host hair bands and teen divas.

Cinema

Guild Cinema (Map p176; ☎ 255-1848; www.guildcine ma.com; 3405 Central Ave NE; tickets $7) The only independently owned, single-screen theater in town; has great indie, avant-garde, Hollywood fringe, political and international features. There are discussions following select films.

United Artist High Ridge (Map pp170-1; ☎ 326-3264; 12921 Indian School Rd NE; adult/child $9/$5.50) Although a bit out of the way, this theater is often the only place to see some foreign and independent films.

Century 14 Downtown (Map p175; ☎ 243-7469; 100 Central Ave SW; adult/child $8.75/5.25) Right in the thick of things downtown, this relatively new and conveniently located theater has plush seating and a good selection of popular flicks.

Spectator Sports

Albuquerque Isotopes (www.albuquerquebaseball .com) First of all: yes, the city's baseball team really was named for the *Simpson's* episode 'Hungry, Hungry Homer,' when America's favorite TV dad tried to keep his beloved Springfield Isotopes from moving to Albuquerque. It didn't work for Homer, and now the 'Topes sell more merchandise than any other minor-league team – and most major-league teams, for that matter. They sometimes even win, too. They play at Isotopes Park (☎ 924-2255; 1601 Avenida Cesar Chavez NE; berm seating tickets $5).

Albuquerque Scorpions (☎ 881-7825; www .scorpionshockey.com; tickets $10-28) This ice-hockey team will soon have its own stadium in Rio Rancho.

State Rodeo (☎ 265-1791; www.exponm.com; tickets $10-40) Held during the State Fair in September, this takes place at Tingley Coliseum (left).

UNM Lobos (☎ 277-4569; www.unm.edu) Football and men's and women's basketball have loyal followings, but it's men's soccer and women's volleyball teams that have been to national championships in the last few years. UNM home games are held either at the Pit (Map pp170–1; ☎ 925-5626; www .unmtickets.com; 1111 University Blvd SE) indoor arena or the adjacent outdoor stadium.

BROKEBACK MOUNTAIN WAS THE TIP OF THE ICEBERG

In New Mexico, those cute leather chaps aren't just a fashion statement like they are in San Francisco – they're actually rodeo wear. Yee haw! Saddle up that handsome horse and gallop on over to the **Zia Regional Rodeo**, held each August in Albuquerque and hosted by the New Mexico Gay Rodeo Association (NMGRA).

There's no better place to watch guys and gals compete in bareback bronc ridin', calf ropin', steer ridin' and barrel racin'. And there's no group that does these sports prouder than the Rainbow Nation, where animal welfare is at the top of their list of concerns.

For chute-doggin' (steer wrestling) Shery Lynn Fowler, 'Rodeo is about the connection between the horse and the rider – both have to be athletes, and both train closely together. Gay rodeo is also about connection, camaraderie. It's about being really me – this is part of who I am.' Fowler continues, 'Some people think I have a death wish, chute-doggin', but it just makes me feel really alive. When I do an event, it's like someone opens up the top of my head and pours in 10 gallons of adrenaline.'

Established in 1984, NMGRA has counterparts in several other states west of the Mississippi, including California, all of whom belong to the International Gay Rodeo Association. Between them, they hold 19 rodeos.

NMGRA is dedicated to 'fostering the western lifestyle within the gay community.' That means more than wearing a big silver belt buckle, though you do get extra credit in this crowd for doing so. NMGRA does a fair amount of charity fundraising, and rodeo profits have benefited New Mexico AIDS Services, New Mexico Breast Cancer Coalition, New Mexico Domestic Violence Hotline and People of Color AIDS Foundation, among others. So saddle on up, pay your entrance fee with a happy heart and enjoy the *trés* gay show.

SHOPPING
Old Town & Downtown
There are no two ways around it: shops clustered around plazas are geared toward visitors. Having said that, there are still a few places worth popping into.

Amapola Gallery (Map p173; ☎ 242-4311; 206 Romero St NW) A cooperative of 40 artists whose work includes painting, photography, weaving, jewelry and pottery.

Penfield Gallery of Indian Arts (Map p173; ☎ 242-9696; 2043 S Plaza NW) Has a large selection of Zuni fetishes and Hopi, Navajo and New Mexico pueblo pottery as well as sand paintings, rugs and baskets.

Luz de Nambé (Map p173; ☎ 242-5699; 328 San Felipe St NW) Sells discounted and famed Nambé ware.

Silver Sun (Map p173; ☎ 242-8265; 2042 South Plaza NW) is a reputable spot for turquoise. For a wide selection of Native American crafts, stop by the **Palms Trading Post** (Map p173; ☎ 247-8504; 1504 Lomas Blvd NW) or **Gus's Trading Company** (Map p173; ☎ 843-6381; 2026 Central Ave SW).

You'll find a nice but small selection of local boutiques downtown on Gold Ave between 1st and 4th Sts. Check out **Ruby Shoesday** (Map p175; ☎ 848-7829; 228 Gold Ave SW), arguably one of the best small shoe stores in the West, and **Patrician Design** (Map p175; ☎ 242-7646; 216A Gold Ave SW), a nice gallery-like place to buy artsy gifts.

Nob Hill & UNM Area
If you're feeling like some exercise, head to Nob Hill; it's a good spot to stroll and lacks the touristy feel of Old Town. Walk east from UNM along Central Ave to find an eclectic mix of shops (everything from a tattoo parlor to a herbal medicine shop to a toy store) until you reach the **Nob Hill Shopping Center** (Map p176; 3500 Central Ave SE) at Carlisle. Within this shopping center, look for Beeps, which has cards and wacky novelty items; Terra Firma, which has great clogs and sandals; and Papers, which sells you-can-guess-what.

Among the hip shops on Central Ave, pop into **Martha's Body Bueno** (Map pp170-1; ☎ 255-1122; 3901 Central Ave NE), which specializes in handmade beauty supplies and lingerie couture. **Masks y Mas** (Map p176; ☎ 256-4183; 3106 Central Ave SE) is filled with Mexican and New Mexican folk art. **Objects of Desire** (Map p176; ☎ 232-3088; 3300 Central Ave SE) has beautiful and unique home decorations. Whatever you do, don't miss **hey jhonny!** (Map p176; ☎ 256-9244; 3418B Central Ave SE), Albuquerque's most sophisticated home-furnishing store, offering Buddhas and Balinese art for every budget. **Sachs** (Map p176; ☎ 266-1661; 3112 Central Ave SE) caters to your leather and piercing needs. **International Market** (Map p176; ☎ 265-7001; 2622 Central Ave SE) is a spacious and cosmopolitan place, with aisles devoted to food from Asian countries such as Taiwan and Thailand.

Metropolitan Albuquerque
These places may seem far flung, but each offers something worth going out of the way for.

Jackalope (Map pp170-1; ☎ 349-0955; 6400 San Mateo Ave NE; www.jackalope.com) Here the Southwest meets the Orient. It's fun for small gifts as well as rugs, folk art, pottery and furniture from around the state and the eastern part of the globe. Bring home a cow (or rabbit) skull for your loved ones.

Strictly Southwestern (Map pp170-1; ☎ 292-7337; 1321 Eubank Blvd NE) Offers custom-made Southwestern furniture and lighting. Be the first in your town to have Kokopelli dancing across your outdoor wall lights.

Hillson's Western Wear (Map pp170-1; ☎ 268-5070; 8800 Central Ave SE) This store showcases a huge selection of hats, boots and other western wear. And staff know how a boot is supposed to fit.

Fleamarket (Map pp170-1; ☎ 265-1791; ☒ 7am Sat & Sun) Held most weekends on the north end of the State Fair Grounds, has over 1300 vendors.

Gertrude Zachary (Map pp170-1; ☎ 247-8452; 416 2nd St SW) Specializes in contemporary Southwest Native American jewelry, including turquoise and sterling silver.

Western Warehouse (Map pp170-1; ☎ 559-5100; 11205 Montgomery Blvd NE) This place can send you on your way decked out in boots, a Stetson, good-looking jeans or even a full rodeo outfit.

GETTING THERE & AWAY
Air
New Mexico's largest airport, the **Albuquerque International Sunport** (Map p191; ☎ 244-7700; www.cabq.gov/airport; 2200 Sunport Blvd) offers free wireless internet and is served by multiple airlines and car-rental companies, as

ALBUQUERQUE

well as private shuttles that run from the Sunport and downtown Albuquerque to Santa Fe and points north. See the Transportation chapter (p237) for more information on these.

Bus
The **Albuquerque Bus Transportation Center** (Map p175; 300 2nd St SW) is home to Greyhound and **TNM&O** (☎ 243-4435, 800-231-2222), which offers two morning buses to Santa Fe ($10.50) and Taos ($30).

Train
Amtrak's *Southwest Chief* stops at **Albuquerque Amtrak Station** (☎ 842-9650, 800-872-7245; 214 1st St SW; ☺ ticket office 10am-5pm), from which daily trains run between Chicago and Los Angeles, with stops in Lamy and Las Vegas, New Mexico.

GETTING AROUND
To/From the Sunport
The Sunport is served by bus 50 ABQ Ride. The **Airport Shuttle** (☎ 765-1234) and **Sunport Shuttle** (☎ 883-4966, 866-4966; www.sunportshuttle.com) both run 24 hours a day. Fares range from about $5 to $60, depending on where you are headed. Expect to pay around $14 one way to Old Town and $12 to downtown.

Bicycles
Contact **Parks & Recreation** (☎ 768-2680; www.cabq.gov/bike) for a free map of Albuquerque's elaborate system of bike trails, or alternatively visit the website. All of the ABQ Ride buses are equipped with front-loading bicycle racks.

Bus
ABQ Ride (Map175; ☎ 243-7433; www.cabq.gov/transit; 100 1st St SW; adult/child $1/35¢; ☺ 6am-8pm Mon-Thu, 6am-2:30am Fri & Sat, check website for Sunday routes) is a public bus system covering most of Albuquerque on weekdays and major tourist spots daily. Maps and schedules are available on the web; three-day passes ($4) are available at the main office. Exact change is required when buying tickets onboard. Rapid Ride buses (which run on hybrid diesel engines and have free wireless internet!) offer access to the BioPark, downtown, Nob Hill, the fairgrounds and Old Town.

Taxi
In general you must call for a taxi, though they do patrol the Sunport, Amtrak and bus station. Both companies charge about $5 for the first mile and $2.30 per mile thereafter.
Albuquerque Cab (☎ 883-4888)
Yellow Cab (☎ 247-8888, 800-657-6232)

Train
Railrunner Express (☎ 245-7245; www.nmrailrunner.com; trip $2, day pass $4) inaugurated service for commuters north of Albuquerque in July 2006; future plans were sketchy at press time, but there is talk of a possible link to Santa Fe by 2008. Fares are expected to change as routes increase.

ALBUQUERQUE TO SANTA FE

There are three main routes connecting New Mexico's two major cities: it takes a speedy hour along the semi-scenic I-25; at least 90 minutes on the much lovelier NM 14, the Turquoise Trail; or a day (or better, two) to meander through the stunning Jemez Mountains.

INTERSTATE 25
It is a one-hour straight shot through to Santa Fe, but it's easy to stretch out if you're on vacation.

Sandia Pueblo
Having opened one of the first casinos in New Mexico, **Sandia Pueblo** (☎ 867-3317; www.sandiapueblo.nsn.us; I-25 exit 234) subsequently used its wealth to successfully lobby for legislation preventing further development of Sandia Crest and their sacred lands. They also bought other large tracts of land scheduled for development.

Sandia Resort & Casino (☎ 796-7500, 800-526-9366; www.sandiacasino.com; 30 Rainbow Rd NE), one of the region's nicest, boasts the elegant Sandia Casino Amphitheater, hosting everything from symphonies to boxing and Bill Cosby. There's also an 18-hole golf course (☎ 798-3990; www.sandiagolf.com; $65 to $75), and the hotel (doubles $180) offers a pool, spa, salon and fitness center. Gamblers sensitive to smoke will enjoy the smoke-free gaming section of the casino.

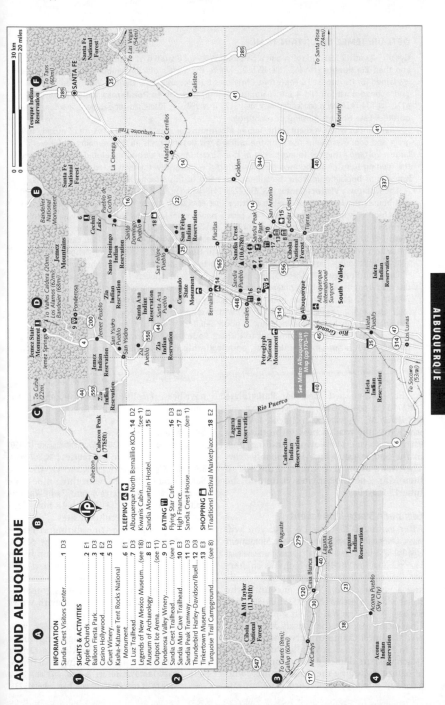

AROUND ALBUQUERQUE

30 km
20 miles

INFORMATION
Sandia Crest Visitors Center.................1 D3

SIGHTS & ACTIVITIES
Apple Orchards...............................2 E1
Balloon Fiesta Park..........................3 E1
Casino Hollywood............................4 E2
Gruet Winery..................................5 D3
Kasha-Katuwe Tent Rocks National
   Monument...................................6 E1
La Luz Trailhead..............................7 D3
Legends of New Mexico Museum.......(see 18)
Museum of Archaeology......................8 E3
Outpost Ice Arena...........................(see 11)
Ponderosa Valley Winery....................9 D1
Sandia Crest Trailhead....................(see 1)
Sandia Man Cave Trailhead...............10 E3
Sandia Peak Tramway.......................11 D3
Thunderbird Harley-Davidson/Buell...12 D3
Tinkertown Museum..........................13 E3
Turquoise Trail Campground.............(see 8)

SLEEPING
Albuquerque North Bernalillo KOA...14 D2
Kiwanis Cabin..............................(see 1)
Sandia Mountain Hostel....................15 E3

EATING
Flying Star Cafe.............................16 D3
High Finance.................................17 E3
Sandia Crest House........................(see 1)

SHOPPING
ITraditions! Festival Marketplace.........18 E2

ALBUQUERQUE

DETOUR: JEMEZ MOUNTAIN TRAIL

Get off I-25 at US 550 and roll along a passionless 25-mile stretch of scrub past Santa Ana Pueblo and then **Zia Pueblo** (☎ 867-3304; US 550), where the state's official symbol was first designed; it's famed for its August 15 Feast Day, Christmas Buffalo, and Crow Dances. When you reach San Ysidro, head north on NM 4 into paradise. Detour, perhaps, to **Ponderosa Valley Winery** (Map p191; ☎ 834-7487; www.ponderosawinery.com; 3171 Hwy 290; ☺ 10am-5pm Tue-Sat, noon-5pm Sun) for a bottle of Late Harvest Riesling or pinot noir.

That's about when you enter the **Jemez Mountains** proper. A ragged expanse of moody tufa grays and cool evergreens rise from the brilliant red desert; this is all that remains of the world's largest volcano – they've found pieces of it in Texas. Meander through sculpted formations and the melting ruins of abandoned pueblos along the Jemez River, which is fed by snowmelt and hot springs bubbling up from the still-molten heart of this strange and beautiful wilderness.

The **Walatowa Visitors Center** (☎ 834-7235; 7413 NM 4; ☺ 8am-5pm) at **Jemez Pueblo** is excellent and houses the **Museum of Pueblo Culture** (free admission). Across the road, **Jemez Red Rocks** hosts food stands on summer weekends, plus a powwow in late May. The pretty village of **Jemez Springs** was built around a cluster of springs, as was the ruined pueblo at **Jemez State Monument** (☎ 829-3530; NM 4; adult/child $3/free; ☺ 8:30am-5pm, closed Tue in winter). You can experience the waters yourself at rustic **Jemez Springs Bath House** (☎ 829-3303; www.jemezspringsbathhouse .com; 62 Jemez Springs Plaza; per hr $10-15; ☺ 10am-8pm), with private tubs, massages and more.

Giggling Springs (☎ 829-9175) lets you soak in private springs for $15 an hour. It's across the road from the **Laughing Lizard Inn** (☎ 829-3108; www.thelaughinglizard.com; NM 4; winter/summer $49/64; P ⊠ ⊠), which has great rooms and an attached **café** (dishes $5-11; ☺ 11am-8pm Tue-Sat, 11am-6pm Sun, ☺ limited hr in winter; P) with live music on weekends. There are a handful of restaurants in Jemez Springs, including a good deli.

Before leaving town, take time out to inspect **Soda Dam**, a warm waterfall that's enveloped boulders with bizarre mineral deposits, and **Battleship Rock**, a dramatic trailhead and fishing spot.

The Kiva-shaped **Bien Mur Marketplace** (☎ 821-5400, 800-365-5400; www.bienmur.com; 100 Bien Mur Dr NE; ☺ 9am-5:30pm Mon-Sat, 11am-5pm Sun) across the road claims to be the largest Native American–owned trading post in the Southwest, which is probably true. The tribe's bison herd grazes to the east of Bien Mur. The tribe invites visitors to the June 13 **Feast Day**.

Coronado State Monument

After exiting I-25 onto US 550, you will pass **Coronado Campground & State Monument** (☎ 980-8256; US 150; tent/RV $8/18, parking at monument $3; ☺ 8:30am-5pm Wed-Mon), which has shelters for shade, showers ($4), interpretive trails and a visitor center. You'll encounter the ruins of **Kuau'a Pueblo** (☎ 867-5351; US 150; admission free; ☺ 8am-5pm Wed-Sun). It's not exactly Chaco Canyon, but the murals are considered the finest example of precontact mural art in North America: various Pueblo gods (Kachinas) are depicted as personifications of nature, including the Corn Mother, who gave the Pueblo people corn. The murals

have been artfully restored inside the visitor center and underground kiva.

Santa Ana Pueblo

This **pueblo** (☎ 867-3301; www.santaana.org; US 150) is posh. It boasts two **golf courses** (☎ 867-9464, 800-851-9469; www.santaanagolf.com; $32-42): the Santa Ana Golf Club, with three nine-hole courses; and the extravagant **Twin Warriors Golf Club** (☎ 771-6155; $145), with 18 holes laid out among ancient cultural sites.

Nearby is premier fine dining at **Prairie Star** (☎ 867-3327; 288 Prairie Star Rd; dishes $17-34; ☺ 5-9pm; P ⊠ ☺), which dishes up bison tenderloin in foie gras butter and red chili mushroom enchiladas with truffle-scented cream corn. It's all served in a romantically appointed historic adobe, with views of sunsets over the Sandias.

Santa Ana Star Casino (☎ 867-0000; www .santaanastar.com; US 150) has a staggering buffet ($8 to $10), 36 lanes of bowling, a family arcade and over 1000 gaming machines. The **Hyatt Tamaya Resort & Spa** (☎ 867-1234; www.tamaya.hyatt.com; 1300 Tuyuna Trail; r from $235;

Ⓟ ⓧ ⓧ ⓧ), tucked into the desert landscape with expansive views, is an impressive place with three pools, three restaurants and a small spa.

The **Stables at Tamaya** (☎ 771-6037) offer 90-minute trail rides and lessons ($75 to $100) through the bosque – into which the pueblo has recently pumped millions of dollars for cleanup and restoration. And, lest you forget that this is not Beverly Hills west, there are **Corn Dances** on June 29 and July 26.

Legends of New Mexico Museum

The independent **!Traditions! Festival Marketplace** (Map p191; ☎ 867-8600; Budaghers exit-257 off I-25; adult/child $5/free; ☯ 10am-4pm Thu-Mon) museum spotlights the state's most famous visitors and residents – from Billy the Kid to Bill Gates, from the Roswell aliens to Popé and Smokey Bear. When they say it's a tribute to multiculturalism, they mean it. The marketplace itself features shops, galleries and a restaurant at which everything is either made in New Mexico or historically sold in the state.

San Felipe Pueblo

Though best known for the spectacular **San Felipe Feast Green Corn Dances** on May 1, this conservative Keres-speaking **pueblo** (☎ 867-3381; I-25 exit 252) also invites visitors to the June 29 **San Pedro Feast Day** and October **Arts & Crafts Fair**. Apart from these events, outsiders are not encouraged to visit the pueblo – and photography is forbidden. However, the following San Felipe attractions are open to the public.

Casino Hollywood (Map p191; ☎ 867-6700, 877-529-2946; www.sanfelipecasino.com; I-25 exit 252) isn't just for gambling, this themed venue pulls in acts like Los Lobos and Julio Iglesias.

The pueblo also runs **Hollywood Hills Speedway** (☎ 867-6700, 877-529-2946; www.hollywood hillsspeedway.com; I-25 exit 252; adult/child $10/free), a 0.37-mile clay track that hosts primarily sprints, plus a few stock-car races, monster-truck rallies, rodeos and powwows.

Santo Domingo Pueblo

Long a seat of Pueblo government, Santo Domingo Pueblo is the home of the tribe of which Catiti was a member. He was a hero of the Pueblo Revolt, who led the Keres-speaking pueblos to victory. The original city was later torched, twice, but survivors moved here, on NM 22 about 6 miles northwest of I-25, exit 259.

The nongaming **pueblo** (☎ 465-2214; NM 22; ☯ 8am-dusk) has a **cultural center**, small **museum** in the gas station and several **galleries** and **studios** at the pueblo itself, most fronting the plaza in front of the pretty 1886 **Santo Domingo Church**, which boasts murals and frescoes by local artists. The tribe is most famous for *heishi* (shell bead) jewelry, as well as the huge August 4 **Corn Dances** and a Labor Day weekend **arts & crafts fair** that attracts folks from all over the state.

Pueblo de Cochiti

About 10 miles north of Santo Domingo on NM 22, or 18 miles west of I-25 on NM 16, **Pueblo de Cochiti** (☎ 465-2244; www.pueblo decochiti.org) is known for its arts and crafts, particularly ceremonial bass drums. This is where Helen Cordero came up with those storyteller dolls. These days, ceramicists like Victor Ortiz exhibit ironic modern interpretations of the old arts at Robert Nichols Gallery (p110) in Santa Fe.

Several stands and shops are usually set up around the plaza and 1628 mission, and dances are held on the July 14 **Feast Day of San Buenaventura** and at Christmas. There's no photography allowed here, but snap away at **Pueblo de Cochiti Golf Course** (p86), considered the state's most challenging, or placid **Cochiti Lake** (day use free), favored by boaters, windsurfers and swimmers.

Just a bit past Cochiti Lake, stop at **Dixon Apple Orchards** (Map p191; ☎ 465-2976; 1 La Cañada, Peña Blanca; ☯ 8am-5pm, late Sep-Oct). Come during harvest season, which usually starts in late September, to enjoy an afternoon of apple picking.

Kasha-Katuwe Tent Rocks National Monument

This is a must. Well signed from NM 22 (off I-25 from the Santo Domingo Pueblo) and co-managed by the pueblo and BLM, this bizarre and beautiful geological formation of tent-shaped hoodoos can be explored along **Cave Loop Trail**. But the real treat is **Canyon Trail**, an easy and spectacular 2-mile round-trip, threading a narrow 30ft-tall canyon with walls so close together that you can touch both sides. The steep final leg climbs to a perfect vista overlooking the odd landscape.

ALBUQUERQUE

BALLOON FIESTA: THE EXECUTIVE DIRECTOR'S CUT   Heather Dickson

Back in 1979, a lawyer called Paul Smith bought a balloon ride for a friend. Now, nearly 30 years on, Paul Smith is the executive director of the Albuquerque International Balloon Fiesta – the largest event of its kind in the world – and a passionate balloon pilot.

If you gasp when you see one balloon floating in the sky, imagine what you'll do when you see 700? Since 1972, when just 13 balloons took off, Albuquerque's balloon fiesta has been wowing spectators. No doubt most of them have a pang of envy when the balloons head skywards, but there's something magical about watching a heap of material inflate to become a swaying giant, be it a traditional rainbow-colored one or a comedy cow.

As Paul says, 'it's hard to imagine how incredibly beautiful it can be,' and one of the main attractions is being able to 'wander in and among the balloons.' Ah, just picture it.

One of Paul's favorite fiesta moments occurred on a very calm day, when there was a 'box' (think interesting wind action, where winds blow in different directions at different altitudes) and from the northeast came 'a highway of balloons in the sky' that stretched for a mile and ended down on the fiesta field. Other spectacles to impress the 100,000 spectators include the nightly inflations, which theatrically light the balloons – the burners acting like glowing hearts.

Being a balloon pilot, Paul sometimes gets frustrated being on the ground directing things. However, when he starts thinking 'it would be so much easier to go fly,' he sees 'the kids on the ground with wide eyes, open mouths and big grins,' and says to himself, 'I guess what we do is kinda cool.' Yes, indeed.

For festival details, see p181.

THE TURQUOISE TRAIL

The Turquoise Trail has been a major trade route since at least 2000 BC, when local artisans began trading Cerrillos turquoise with communities in present-day Mexico. Today it's the scenic back road between Albuquerque and Santa Fe, lined with quirky communities and other diversions.

Cedar Crest

Tinkertown Museum (Map p191; ☎ 281-5233; www .tinkertown.com; 121 Sandia Crest Rd; adult/child $3/1; ⏺ 9am-6pm Apr-Nov), just a bit up Sandia Crest Rd (NM 165), is an inspiring assortment of detailed towns, circuses and other scenes that come alive with a quarter. Woodcarver and wisdom collector Ross J Ward built it and surrounded it with antique toys, junque (aka fancy junk) and suggestions that you eat more mangoes naked.

The nearby **Museum of Archaeology** (Map p191; ☎ 281-2005; 22 Calvary Rd, off NM 14; adult/child $3.50/1.50; ⏺ noon-7pm May-Oct) has an 'archaeological site' outdoors (kids dig this) and local Indian artifacts inside. It also runs the adjacent **Turquoise Trail Campground** (tent $13, RV $23, rustic cabins $28-50; Ⓟ), which has hot showers and cool shade. There's national forest access for guests.

Sandia Mountain Hostel (Map p191; ☎ 281-4117; www.sandiamountainhostel.com; 12234 N NM 14; campsite/dm/d $10/14/32; Ⓟ ⊠ ✸), a fine independent hostel, has passive solar-designed common areas, handmade quilts, five friendly donkeys and lots of classic cars (in various states of disrepair) on the woodsy grounds.

Spend the rest of the day exploring Sandia Crest (p182), or continue up the Turquoise Trail, which winds through **Golden**, which has an art gallery, a trading post and lots of gorgeous desert scenery.

Madrid

A bustling company coal-mining town in the 1920s and '30s, Madrid (pronounced *Maa*-drid) was all but abandoned after WWII. In the mid-1970s, the company's heirs sold cheap lots to tie-dyed wanderers who have built a thriving arts community with galleries and wacky shops. It's not nearly as mellow as you'd think, attracting more bikers than New Agers, but that's just part of the appeal.

There are dozens of galleries and shops in this one-horse town, but pay special attention to **Fuse Arts** (☎ 438-4999; 2878 NM 14), with its first-rate abstractions; **Seppanen & Daughters Fine Textiles** (☎ 424-7470; 2879 NM 14), with its tactile and colorful Oaxacan, Navajo and Tibetan rugs; and **Range West** (☎ 474-0925; 2861 NM 14), with its elegant water fountains carved from monolithic granite chunks.

The **Old Coal Mine Museum** (☎ 438-3780; 2814 NM 14; adult/child $4/free; ☻ 10am-5pm, shorter winter hr) preserves plenty of old mining equipment, right where the miners left it. It also hosts the **Madrid Melodrama & Engine House Theatre** (adult/child $10/4; ☻ 3pm Sat & Sun May-Oct), starring a steam locomotive and lots of Wild West desperados, scoundrels and vixens, and stories that leave you feeling good. Admission includes a six-shooter loaded with marshmallows to unload at the villains.

Or chat up modern-day scoundrels and vixens at the 1919 **Mine Shaft Tavern** (☎ 473-0743; 2846 NM 14; dishes $5-11; ☻ noon-midnight). It has live music on weekends and the 'longest stand-up bar in New Mexico.' It was built in 1946 and has been Madrid's favorite attraction ever since.

Mama Lisa's Cafe (☎ 471-5769; NM 14; snacks $6-10; ☻ 11am-4:30pm Fri-Sun) serves good quesadillas and a great red-chile chocolate cake.

Overnight at **Madrid Lodging** (☎ 471-3450; www.madridlodging.com; 14 Opera House Rd; d $110-130; Ⓟ ⓧ ⓧ), which has two two-room suites, an outdoor hot tub and wireless internet.

Cerrillos

A photographer's dream, with unpaved streets threading through an adobe Old West town relatively unchanged since the 1880s, this is the home of the first mine in North America, built to extract turquoise around AD 100.

Cerrillos Turquoise Mining Museum & Petting Zoo (☎ 438-3008; 17 Waldo St; admission $2; ☻ 9am-sunset usually), a top-drawer roadside attraction, packs five rooms with Chinese art, pioneer-era tools, mining equipment dating to 3000 BC, bottles and antiques excavated from an abandoned area hotel, and anything else the owners thought was worth displaying. For $2 more you can feed the goats, llamas and unusual chickens.

Broken Saddle Riding Co (☎ 424-7774; www .brokensaddle.com; off County Rd 57; rides $55-90) offers one- to three-hour horseback rides through juniper-dotted hills and abandoned mines. Along the way, you'll learn about local history and geology; don't forget a camera to capture the spectacular views. Only open by appointment.

Continue north on NM 14 until you hit I-25. From there, it's five minutes north on I-25 heading into Santa Fe.

ALBUQUERQUE

New Mexico Road Trips

We agree that Santa Fe and Taos should probably be the highest priorities on your 'to see and do' list. And maybe you've acquiesced to spending a day or two in Albuquerque to round out your visit. But if you don't veer off that three-destination corridor, you'll be missing some of the finest that New Mexico has to offer: the expansiveness, the quirkiness, the lack of human presence, the sense of timelessness, the diversity of natural experiences.

This chapter covers four circle trips around New Mexico's four quadrants. All routes are best taken in a car and use Albuquerque as a jumping-off and end point; even if you are firmly ensconced in Santa Fe, it will simply mean backtracking for about 60 miles (at worst).

Consider trekking down to Gila National Forest, where you can hike unimpeded and climb into cliff dwellings. Shuttle over to Roswell to check out aliens or to Carlsbad to commune with bats (and stalagmites.) Dip into hot springs in T or C; watch hundreds of thousands of migrating birds at Bosque del Apache; or follow a Route 66 trail of 1950s-era neon. Stand atop a haunting mesa, still home to Acoma Indians, or stand still at Chaco and listen to the winds trying to tell the story of disappearance. Above all, get off the map.

HIGHLIGHTS

- Ride the glorious rail of the **Cumbres & Toltec Scenic Railway** (p221)
- Fang along **Route 66** (p225), where neon and nostalgia reign
- Rub shoulders with stalagmites and bats at **Carlsbad Caverns National Park** (p212)
- Visit **Spencer Theater for the Performing Arts** (p210), where the space is as artful as the performance
- Romp around the dunes at **White Sands National Monument** (p207) at sunrise and sunset
- Follow migrating flocks of birds to **Bosque del Apache National Wildlife Refuge** (p198)
- Indulge yourself at **Sierra Grande Lodge & Spa** (p200)
- Drink in the solitude and scramble around the cliff dwellings at **Gila National Forest** (p202)
- Tour the mesa top and witness the living history at **Acoma Pueblo** (p214)
- Take in the ancient mysteries of **Chaco Culture National Historical Park** (p220)

ROUTE 1: SOUTHWESTERN NM

The Rio Grande Valley runs by the fingerlike Elephant Butte Reservoir to the bubbling hot springs of funky Truth or Consequences and attracts wildlife to Bosque del Apache National Wildlife Refuge. Residents are few and far between and most towns are relatively young, dating to the late 19th century when mining began.

West of I-25, the rugged Gila National Forest is thick with backpacking and fishing adventures. The very wildness of Southwestern New Mexico is perhaps its greatest drawcard, but the breadth of attractions may surprise you. Don't overlook the Gila Cliff Dwellings National Monument, quaint Victorian buildings in Silver City, giant white disks (the VLA) west of Socorro and plenty of ghost towns (and almost-ghost towns) like Chloride and Winston.

SOCORRO & AROUND

☎ 505 / pop 8900 / elev 4585ft

A quiet and amiable layover 75 miles south of Albuquerque via I-25, Socorro boasts a downtown area with a good mix of buildings dating from the 1880s to the late 20th century. Its standout, though, is a 17th-century mission. Still, most visitors are birders drawn to the nearby Bosque del Apache refuge.

SOUTHWESTERN NEW MEXICO

NEW MEXICO ROAD TRIPS

DETOUR: GET THE DISH ON THE VLA TELESCOPE

In some remote regions of New Mexico, TV reception is little more than a starry-eyed fantasy. But about 40 miles west of **Socorro**, 4 miles south of US 60 off NM 52, 27 huge antenna dishes sprout from the high plains like a couch-potato's dream-come-true. Actually, the 240-ton dishes comprise the National Radio Astronomy Observatory's **Very Large Array Radio Telescope** (VLA; www.vla.nrao.edu; admission free; ☺ 8:30am-sunset). Together, they combine to form a very large eyeball peeking into the outer edges of the universe. It would take a 422ft-wide satellite dish to provide the same resolution that this Y-shaped configuration of 82ft-wide antennas offers the observatory.

Sure, the giant 'scope may reveal the relativistic electron movement in the heavens and allow geophysicists to wonder at the wobble of the earth on its axis…But what does it tell the rest of us? Well, without it, Jodi Foster never could have flashed-forward into our future (or was it her past?) in the movie *Contact,* which was filmed here with a little help from Canyon de Chelly. The radio waves collected by these enormous dishes have increased our understanding of the complex phenomena that make up the surface of the sun. They have given us a gander at the internal heating source deep within the interiors of several planets sharing our orbit. They have provided us with just enough information to turn our concepts of time and space inside out as we extrapolate the existence of varieties of matter that, sans satellites, might only exist in our imaginations as we spin through space on the head of this peculiar, little blue-green globe.

Socorro means 'help' in Spanish. The town's name supposedly dates to 1598, when Juan de Oñate's expedition received help from Pilabo Pueblo (now defunct). The Spaniards built a small church nearby, expanding it into the San Miguel Mission in the 1620s. With the introduction of the railroad in 1880 and the discovery of gold and silver, Socorro became a major mining center and New Mexico's biggest town by the late 1880s. The mining boom went bust in 1893. True to its mining roots, New Mexico Institute of Mining & Technology (locally called Tech) offers postgraduate education and advanced research facilities.

The **chamber of commerce** (☎ 835-0424; www .socorro-nm.com; 101 Plaza; ☺ 9am-5pm Mon-Fri, 10am-1pm Sat) is helpful.

Sights

Most of the historic downtown dates to the late 19th century. Pick up the chamber of commerce's walking tour, the highlight of which is the **San Miguel Mission** (☎ 835-1620; 403 El Camino Real), three blocks north of the plaza. Although restored and expanded several times, the mission still retains its colonial feel and parts of the walls date back to the original building.

The funky **Loma Theater** (☎ 835-0965; 107 Manzanares Ave) shows Hollywood movies in a remodeled Victorian store.

Most travelers are naturalists who descend on Socorro because of the **Bosque del Apache National Wildlife Refuge** (entry per car $3; ☺ dawn-dusk). About 8 miles south of town, the refuge protects almost 90 sq miles of fields and marshes, which serve as a major wintering ground for many migratory birds – most notably the very rare and endangered whooping cranes of which about a dozen winter here. Tens of thousands of snow geese, sandhill cranes and various other waterfowl also call this place home, as do bald eagles. The wintering season lasts from late October to early April, but December and January are the peak viewing months and offer the best chance of seeing bald eagles. Upwards of 325 bird species and 135 mammal, reptile and amphibian species have been recorded here.

From the **visitor center** (☎ 835-1828; www .friendsofthebosque.org; ☺ 7:30am-4pm Mon-Fri, 8am-4:30pm Sat & Sun), a 15-mile loop circles the refuge; hiking trails and viewing platforms are easily accessible. To get to the refuge, leave I-25 at San Antonio (10 miles south of Socorro) and drive 8 miles south on NM 1.

Refuge visitors often stop by the **Owl Bar Cafe** (☎ 835-9946; 215 San Antonio; dishes $6-10; ☺ 8am-9pm Mon-Sat; P ♿ V ♨), half a mile east of I-25 near San Antonio, for its green chile cheeseburger. San Antonio, by the way, is the childhood home of hotelier Conrad Hilton.

Sleeping & Eating

Economy Inn (☎ 835-4666; 400 California NE; r $40-44; P X X X) There aren't a lot of options in town. Clean and reasonably well kept, most rooms here have microwaves and small refrigerators.

El Sombrero (☎ 835-3945; 210 Mesquite; dishes $5-11; ☆ 11am-9pm; P X & V ☆) Of Socorro's several very local Mexican restaurants, this cheerful and friendly place is a good bet. Try to get a table in the garden room. Fajitas and enchiladas are quite popular, but mostly it's the sauces (like mole and poblano chile) that cover them. If only they would bottle the stuff.

Socorro Springs Brewing Co (☎ 838-0650; www.socorrosprings.com; 1012 N California St; dishes $6-11; ☆ 6:30am-10pm Mon-Fri, 8am-10pm Sat & Sun; P X & V ☆) In the mood for a relatively sophisticated experience? A breath of fresh, groovy air? Come to this airy, renovated mod place for big calzones, decent pasta dishes, homemade soups and really good pizzas made in a stone oven fired with pecan wood. At times, the selection of brews can be on the minimalist side. Whatever they're serving at the moment, though, is smooth and tasty.

TRUTH OR CONSEQUENCES & AROUND
☎ 505 / pop 7300 / elev 4260ft

Originally called Hot Springs, funky and rustic little T or C (as it's locally known) has more character than most New Mexico towns. Wander around the little hole-in-the-wall cafés downtown, check out the antique, thrift and junk shops, and take a bath, so to speak. Most visitors eventually find time to soak in the hot springs or camp and fish at the three state parks nearby. T or C is 74 miles south of Socorro via I-25.

The **chamber of commerce** (☎ 894-3536; www.truthorconsequencesnm.net; 400 W 4th St; ☆ 10am-5pm Mon-Thu, call first) and **Gila National Forest Ranger Station** (☎ 894-6677; 1804 N Date St; ☆ 8am-4:30pm Mon-Fri) have detailed information.

The 60-sq-mile **Elephant Butte Reservoir** (☎ 744-5421; www.elephantbuttelake.net; per car per day $5, tent sites/hookups $10/14), formed in 1916 by damming the Rio Grande, is the state's largest artificial lake, and is quite popular for fishing, waterskiing and windsurfing. In addition to camping, you can walk a looped 1.5-mile nature trail. The nearby **marina** (☎ 894-2041) rents tackle and boats (as pontoons and for fishing and skiing). Spring and fall are the best seasons for fishing.

Hot Springs

Indians, including Geronimo, have bathed in the area's mineral-laden hot springs for centuries. Long said to boast therapeutic properties, the waters range in temperature from 98°F (37°C) to 115°F (46°C) and have a pH of 7 (neutral). Although the commercial hot baths date from the 1920s and 1930s and look a little worse for wear from the outside, they are acceptably clean inside. Most places charge $5 to $10 per person for a hot bath; private, couple and family tubs are also available. Massages ($50) and other treatments require advance notice.

The swankiest place, by far, is Sierra Grande Lodge & Spa (p200). Other places, though, also offer lodging with their hot springs: **Charles Motel & Bath House** (☎ 894-7154; www.charlesspa.com; 601 Broadway; ☆ 8am-8am) has the hottest water in town and indoor and outdoor tubs, massage, ayurvedic treatments, sauna, reflexology, and holistic healing. Riverbend Hot Springs (p200) has two private outdoor tubs ($15 per

NEW MEXICO ROAD TRIPS

A TOWN BY ANY OTHER NAME

Seems like there's at least one town named Hot Springs in every state of the union – heck, in California alone there are more than 30 of 'em. In 1950, TV game-show host Ralph Edwards wished aloud that a town somewhere in the US liked his show so much that they would name themselves after it. That year, there was one less town named Hot Springs: by a margin of four to one, the 1294 residents of what would become Truth or Consequences voted to change the name. That same year, NBC broadcast the show live for the first time ever from...(where else?) Truth or Consequences to celebrate the town and the popular show's 10th anniversary.

Nowadays, T or C residents live among the sandstone bluffs, basking in the healing springs and the renown of being not only one of the top retirement destinations, but one of the quirkiest-named towns in the country – to heck with the consequences.

person, per hour) by the river (open 8am to 10pm).

Most places in town pump mineral water from wells; a few have natural springs, including **Hay-Yo-Kay Hot Springs** (☎ 894-2228; www.hay -yo-kay.com; 300 Austin St; ☺ 10am-7pm Wed-Fri, noon-7pm Sat & Sun), with five pools and massage.

Winston & Chloride

There's silver in them thar hills. In 1879 Englishman Harry Pye, scrapping together a living as a muleskinner, prospector and freighter for the US army, discovered silver in a canyon between Hillsboro and Camp Ojo Caliente. It took him two years to garner the resources to return and stake a claim. But stake a claim he did, and it set off a silver-mining boom that gave rise to Chloride and Winston, northwest of T or C. Many a town began with a tent like Harry's, pitched beside a mother lode. Few survived as more than rubble and remnants of the rigging erected to extract riches from stone.

Pye didn't live long enough to suffer the consequences of the silver panic of 1893, brought on by the country opting for the gold standard. That plunged the value of silver to about 10% of its prior value and quickly drained the dreams from the boom-towns that had sprung up along the fruitful veins of silver. Pye was killed by a band of Apache Indians in 1881, his death attributed to the fact that his gun jammed.

Chloride is a ghost town these days, while the population of Winston hovers at around 97 souls, down from about 500 in 1886 when Frank H Winston arrived to settle what was then Fairview. He established a store, became a state legislator and a cattleman, and prospected a bit on the side. He also extended generous credit at his store, even when the chances of being repaid were slim. After his death in 1929 the town changed its name to Winston to honor his altruism. To reach the little towns, head west on NM 52 from I-25 just north of T or C.

Sleeping & Eating

Riverbend Hot Springs (☎ 894-6183; www.riverbend hotpsrings.com; 100 Austin St; per person with/without HI/AYH card $18/20, d $39-49, r with kitchenette $69; P ☒ ☒ ☐) Riverside hostel, with friendly hosts, offering dormitory-style accommodations in cabins, trailers and teepees. Private

rooms have kitchenettes and microwaves; several teepees sleep families and small groups. Hot-spring tubs are available morning and evening and are free for guests.

ourpick **Sierra Grande Lodge & Spa** (☎ 894-6976, www.sierragrandelodge.com; 501 McAdoo St; r $105-135; P ☒ ☒ ☐) This is an oasis, not a mirage. It's real and refined and occupies a masterfully renovated 1920s lodge. Guest rooms and suites are luxe, tranquil and furnished with sophisticated touches and attention to detail; mineral-bath privileges are included with the room. Spa treatments (for an additional fee; 5pm to 10pm Wednesday to Sunday) radiate warmth, as does the contemporary kitchen, which prepares light and seasonal spa food (dinner $15 to $25). The wine selection is diverse and reasonably priced.

La Cocina (☎ 894-6499; 1 Lakeway Dr; lunch $6-9, dinner $9-25; ☺ 10:30am-9pm Mon-Thu, 10:30am-10pm Fri-Sun; P ☒ ⊛) For decent Mexican food, fabulous salsa and good steaks, search out the 'Hot Stuff' sign behind the Super 8 motel. Make sure you have time before choosing to sit down; it doesn't have the fastest service in the Southwest.

Los Arcos (☎ 894-6200; 1400 N Date St; dishes $10-23; ☺ 5-9:30pm; P ⊛ Ⓥ ⊛) T or C's most upscale place serves very good steaks, lobsters and locally caught fish dinners. Dine on the pleasant patio or within the hacienda-like interior. There's also a salad bar.

SILVER CITY & AROUND

☎ 505 / Pop 10,500 / Elev 5938ft

The city's name tells the story of a mining town founded in 1870 after the discovery of silver. When that went bust, instead of becoming a ghost town like many others in the area, Silver City tapped its copper reserves. It still mines those reserves today. Is there a name change (à la it's northern neighbor T or C) to Copper City in the works? Nah, locals still sometimes call their town, simply, Silver. Downtown streets are dressed with lovely old brick-and-cast-iron buildings, some Victorian ones, a few adobes and a Wild West air. Silver is also the gateway to outdoor activities in the Gila National Forest. North of Silver City, scenic and mountainous NM 15 heads through Pinos Altos and dead-ends at the Gila Cliff Dwellings National Monument, 42 miles away. Narrow and winding, the road to Gila Cliffs takes almost two hours.

Silver City is 82 miles west of T or C via I-25 and then NM 152 west; most of it is quite scenic. Silver City is about 320 miles from Albuquerque.

Information
Chamber of Commerce (☎ 538-3785, 800-548-9378; www.silvercity.org; 201 N Hudson St; ☯ 9am-5pm Mon-Sat) With so many area artists, the office publishes a map with the city's galleries.

Gila National Forest Ranger Station (☎ 388-8201; www.fs.fed.us/r3/gila; 3005 E Camino De Bosque; ☯ 8am-4:30pm Mon-Fri) Just north of US 180 E at 32nd St.

Library (☎ 538-3672; 515 W College Ave; ☯ 9am-8pm Mon & Thu, 9am-6pm Tue & Wed, 9am-5pm Fri, 9am-1pm Sat) Has free internet access.

Sights & Activities
The heart of this Victorian town is encompassed by Bullard, Texas and Arizona Sts between Broadway and 6th St. The former Main St, one block east of Bullard, washed out during a series of massive floods in 1895. Caused by runoff from logged and overgrazed areas north of town, the floods eventually cut 55ft down below the original height of the street. In a stroke of marketing genius, it's now called **Big Ditch Park**.

The **Silver City Museum** (☎ 538-5921; www.silvercitymuseum.org; 312 W Broadway; suggested donation $3; ☯ 9am-4:30pm Tue-Fri, 10am-4pm Sat & Sun), ensconced in an elegant 1881 Victorian house, displays mining and household artifacts from Silver City's Victorian heyday. It also displays the iconic, highly stylized Mimbres black-on-white pottery. It's usually hemispheric in shape and contains stunning geometric patterns that represent the Mimbres culture (which flourished in this region from about AD 1000 to 1250.) The shop has a good selection of Southwestern books and gifts.

The **Western New Mexico University Museum** (☎ 538-6386; 1000 W College Ave; admission free; ☯ 9am-4:30pm Mon-Fri, 10am-4pm Sat & Sun) boasts the world's largest collection of Mimbres pottery, along with exhibits detailing local history, culture and natural history. The gift shop specializes in Mimbres motifs.

Gila Hike & Bike (☎ 388-3222; 103 E College Ave; ☯ 9am-5pm Mon-Sat,11am-4pm Sun), a friendly and helpful outfitter, rents bicycles, snowshoes and camping equipment for exploring the adjacent National Forest. Ask about a loaner car rack. This rugged country is perfect for backpackers, campers, hunters, anglers, birders, cross-country skiers and other outdoor-sports enthusiasts who are looking for challenging solitude.

Sleeping
Palace Hotel (☎ 388-1811; www.zianet.com/palacehotel; 106 W Broadway; r $44-57, ste $72; P ✗) For a sliver of Silver City's history, this restored 1882 hostelry has 18 rooms that range from small (with a double bed) to two-room suites (with king- or queen-sized beds). Suites are outfitted with modern-day refrigerators and microwaves, but they still have old-fashioned Territorial-style decor. If you want to log on, there's an internet café next door. Rates include breakfast.

Bear Creek Cabins (☎ 388-4501, 888-388-4515; www.bearcreekcabins.com; 88 Main St, Pinos Altos; cabins $119-149; P) These 15 cabins – some with two bedrooms and a kitchenette or balcony – all have fireplaces or wood-burning stoves. Try your luck at gold prospecting; the managers have loaner gold pans for sifting through the silt at nearby Bear Creek.

Bear Mountain Lodge (☎ 538-2538, 877-620-2327; www.bearmountainlodge.com; 2251 Cottage San Rd; r incl breakfast $125-185; P ✗ 🐾 💻) This large ranch house, built in 1928 and set on 160 acres, is operated by the Nature Conservancy. There's plenty of area hiking, and a lodge naturalist can help with suggestions. In addition to 10 rooms and suites, the lodge also rents a guesthouse with a kitchenette. Inquire about other meals that may be arranged.

Eating
Dos Baristas (☎ 388-5952; 112 W Yankie St; dishes under $5; ☯ 7am-5pm Mon-Sat; ✗ 🚼) For easy conversation over a good cuppa gourmet coffee (really good), Dos Baristas has lots of life. It's a sunny, happy place frequented by folks with the same disposition (well, artists and gallery-owners, that is). Hang on the patio in good weather.

Jalisco's Cafe (☎ 388-2060; 100 S Bullard; dishes $6-10; ☯ 11am-8:30pm Mon-Sat; P ✗ 🚼 V 🚼) Family-owned and friendly, this Mexican eatery dishes up large and very good enchiladas and *chile rellenos*. It's a fun, community-oriented, eclectic place in the historic district. Even if you're in the health-conscious camp that thinks fried *sopapillas* are trouble, eat one here.

NEW MEXICO ROAD TRIPS

Vicki's Deli & Eatery (☎ 388-5430; 107 W Yankie St; dishes about $7; ⊗ 11am-3pm Mon-Sat; ⊠ Ⓥ) Fresh feel-good food, simple sandwiches and light meals. Dine outside in good weather.

our pick **Shevek & Mi** (☎ 534-9168; www.gaysilver .org; 602 N Bullard St; lunch $8-12, dinner $10-22, 4- to 9-course dinner prix fixe $28-50; ⊗ 11am-9pm Sun-Tue & Thu, 11am-10pm Fri & Sat; Ⓟ ⊠ ⅋ Ⓥ) Owned by a CIA-trained chef, this delightful eatery is by turns formal, bistro-like and patio-casual. Sunday brunch is decidedly New York, à la Upper West side; dinners range from Moroccan to Spanish to Italian. Enjoy the excellent selection of beer and wine.

Diane's Restaurant & Bakery (☎ 538-8722; 510 N Bullard St; lunch $7-11, dinner $13-26; ⊗ 11am-2pm Tue-Thu, 5:30-9pm Tue-Sat, 9am-2pm Sat & Sun; Ⓟ ⊠ ⅋ Ⓥ) Often referred to as an oasis in the culinary wasteland known as Southwestern New Mexico, Diane's employs elegant touches like white linens to complement her fine eclectic specialties. It's quite popular at lunchtime, but the tempo settles down at dinner, which turns more romantic. Filet mignon ($26) tops out the menu.

Buckhorn Saloon (☎ 538-9911; Main St, Pinos Altos; dishes $15-30; ⊗ bar 3pm, food 4pm, dining room 6pm Mon-Sat; Ⓟ ⊠ ⅋) About 7 miles north of Silver City, this restored adobe eatery offers steaks (a house specialty) and seafood amid 1860s Wild West décor. The big stone fireplaces are warming. Live music (or open mic) livens up the joint on most nights.

Entertainment

Catch a flick at **Real West Cinema II** (☎ 538-5659; 11585 NM 180 E) or belly up to the **Buffalo Bar** (☎ 538-3201; 201 N Bullard St), which hosts occasional dancing in the adjacent nightclub. Without the dancing it's your basic (not particularly salubrious) western bar.

GILA NATIONAL FOREST

If you're looking for isolated, not to mention magnificent, these mountains have it in spades. Northwest of Silver City, NM 180 crosses the Continental Divide and winds through remote and wild country dotted with a few tiny communities. The Gila National Forest and Mogollon Mountains offer some excellent opportunities for backpacking, hiking, camping and fishing. The **ranger station** (☎ 539-2481; www.fs.fed.us/rs/gila/; NM180; ⊗ 8am-4:30pm Mon-Fri, 8am-4:30pm Sat in summer) a half-mile south of Glenwood has details.

From Glenwood head 5 miles east on NM 174 to the **Catwalk** (parking $3), a trail enclosed by a wire walkway hugging the cliff up narrow Whitewater Canyon. It follows water-pipe routes built by miners in 1893. When the pipes needed repair, the miners walked along them (the 'Catwalk'). It's a short but worthwhile hike with some steep spots.

Mogollon, a semi–ghost town, lies 4 miles north of Glenwood and then 9 miles east on steep and narrow NM 159 (mostly accessible during the winter). Once an important mining town, it's now inhabited by only a few people offering 'antiques.' Many buildings lie deserted and empty – it's an interesting but slightly spooky place.

The USFS maintains the **Bighorn** (entry free; ⊗ year-round) campground in Gila National Forest, 0.25 miles north of Glenwood. It has no drinking water.

The area around **Reserve** on US80 is mainly settled by ranchers, cowboys and loggers who particularly loathe federal government interference and environmentalists. It's the kind of place where county officials passed a resolution urging every family to own a gun. This is about as close to the old Wild West as you'll get.

Casitas de Gila Guesthouse (☎ 535-4455, 877-923-4827; www.casitasdegila.com; casitas $120-190; Ⓟ ⊠ 🖳), off US 180, near the town of Gila, is a private and stunningly sited group of five adobe-style casitas that's like a dream come true. If you're stressed out getting here, you won't be within minutes of arriving. Each unit has a fully stocked kitchen, plenty of privacy and one or two bedrooms. Stay a while and use telescopes, an outdoor hot tub and grills. The guesthouse is about two hours from the Cliff Dwellings, but practically right on top of the national forest.

Gila Cliff Dwellings

Mysterious, relatively isolated and accessible, these remarkable cliff dwellings look very much like they would have at the turn of the 1st century. Luckily, the cliffs are not crowded with visitors, so it will be easy for you to step back in time. The influence of the ancestral Puebloans on the Mogollon culture is writ large. Take the 1-mile round-trip self-guided trail that climbs 180ft to the dwellings, overlooking a lovely forested canyon. Parts of the trail are steep and involve ladders. The trail begins at the end of NM 15, 2 miles beyond the **visitors center** (☎ 536-9461; admission $3; ☑ 8am-5pm summer, 8am-4:30pm the rest of the year). Between the visitors center and the trailhead, two small **campgrounds** have drinking water, picnic areas and toilets. They're free on a first-come, first-served basis. A short trail behind the campground leads to other dwellings.

Gila Hot Springs

Used by Indians since ancient times, these springs are 39 miles north of Silver City within the **Gila Hotsprings Vacation Center** (☎ 536-9551; NM 15; www.gilahotspringsranch.com; camping sites without/with hookups $12/17, d $60-75). The center has simple rooms with kitchenettes and an RV park with a spa and showers fed by hot springs. Primitive **camping** (hot pools $3; camping & hot pools $4) is adjacent to the hot pools. You can arrange horseback rides, guided fishing and wilderness pack trips and other outfitting services in advance through the center.

ROUTE 2: SOUTHEASTERN NM

With the exception of the forests surrounding the resort towns of Cloudcroft and Ruidoso, Southeastern New Mexico is marked by seemingly endless horizons and grassy plains. It's also marked by the state's second-largest city (Las Cruces), an awesome expanse of gypsum at White Sands National Monument and a 60-mile cave system at Carlsbad Caverns. Spend dusk at the last two places if you can. Other draws range from thousand-year-old rock etchings at Three Rivers Petroglyph National Recreation Area to ground zero, where the atomic bomb was first detonated. To be sure, Southeastern New Mexico epitomizes quirky and diverse. You'll also encounter alien sightings in Roswell, painter Peter Hurd in Lincoln, and a winery and artists near Alamogordo.

LAS CRUCES & AROUND
☎ 505 / pop 74,000 / elev 3890ft

Nicely sited between the Rio Grande Valley and the fluted Organ Mountains, Las Cruces (Spanish for crosses) acquired its name through death. In 1787 and again in 1830,

Apaches killed bands of travelers camping here, and their graves were marked by a collection of crosses. Settled permanently in 1849, Las Cruces today is New Mexico's second-largest city. Although its next-door neighbor, Mesilla, was more important than Las Cruces in the mid-19th century, it's quieter now than it was then. Poke around Mesilla's shady plaza and surrounding streets; it has lovely 19th-century buildings hung with colorful *ristras*, including a stagecoach stop for the Butterfield Overland Mail Company. Shops on the plaza sell souvenirs ranging from cheap and kitschy to expensive and excellent. New Mexico State University (NMSU) keeps things somewhat lively with about 15,000 students.

Las Cruces is 149 miles south of Albuquerque via I-2 and 69 miles south of Truth or Consequences via I-25.

Information

Chamber of commerce (☎ 524-1968; www.lascruces .org; 760 W Picacho Ave; ☑ 8am-5pm Mon-Fri)
Library (☎ 528-4000; 200 E Picacho Ave; ☑ 8am-9pm Mon-Thu, 8am-6pm Fri, 10am-6pm Sat, closed on Sun in summer) Free internet access.
¡Viva Mesilla! (www.oldmesilla.org) Info on Mesilla.

Sights

For many, a visit to neighboring **Mesilla** is the highlight of their time in Las Cruces. Despite the souvenir shops and tourist-oriented restaurants, the Mesilla Plaza and surrounding blocks are a step back in time. Wander a few blocks beyond the plaza to garner the essence of a mid-19th-century Southwestern town of Hispanic heritage.

The **NMSU Museum** (☎ 646-3739; www.nmsu .edu/~museum; Kent Hall, cnr Solano Dr & University Ave; admission free; ☑ noon-4pm Tue-Fri) is worth a quick look because of changing exhibits focusing on local art, history and archaeology. **NMSU Art Gallery** (☎ 646-2545; www.nmsu .edu/~artgal; Williams Hall; admission free; ☑ 10am-5pm Mon-Sat, 1-5pm in winter, 11am-4pm Tue-Fri, 1-4pm Sat & Sun in summer) has a large permanent collection of contemporary art.

If you're interested in agricultural history, the **Farm & Ranch Heritage Museum** (☎ 522-4100; www.frhm.org; 4100 Dripping Springs Rd; adult/senior/child 6-17 yrs $3/2/1; ☑ 9am-5pm Mon-Sat, noon-5pm Sun) is for you. From prehistoric Indian farming techniques to the life histories of 20th-century ranchers, the exhibits here are well

NEW MEXICO ROAD TRIPS

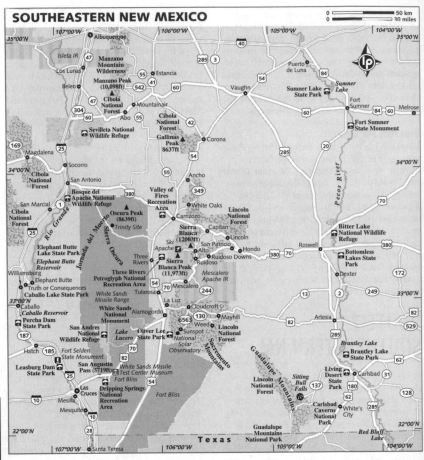

laid out. Children get a kick out of seeing livestock up close and personal. Call ahead about milking and blacksmithing demonstrations. The museum also features a good restaurant.

Dripping Springs National Recreation Area (☎ 522-1219; per car $3; ☉ 8am-5pm), once called the Cox Ranch and now jointly managed by the BLM and the Nature Conservancy, is a great bird-watching and picnicking place about 11 miles from town. Head east on University Ave, which becomes unpaved Dripping Springs Rd.

White Sands Missile Test Center Museum (☎ 678-2250, 678-8824; www.wsmr-history.org; Bldg 200, Headquarters Ave; admission free; ☉ 7:30am-4pm Mon-Fri, 10am-3pm Sat & Sun), about 25 miles east

of Las Cruces along US 70, represents the heart of the White Sands Missile Range. A major military testing site since 1945, it still serves as an alternate landing site for the space shuttle. At the entrance gate, tell the guard you are visiting the museum; you'll need to show your driver's license, proof of car insurance and car registration (or rental papers).

Sleeping

Hilton (☎ 522-4300; 705 S Telshor Blvd, Las Cruces; r $60-109; Ⓟ ⊠ 🐾 🖥 🖃) The town's best and biggest hotel, a seven-story Mexican Colonial structure, has 204 spacious rooms, exercise facilities and good city and mountain views.

Mesón de Mesilla (☎ 525-9212, 800-732-6025; www.mesondemesilla.com; 1803 Av de Mesilla, Mesilla; r incl full breakfast $65-140; P ⊠ ⚡ ☐ 🕭) This stylish and graceful adobe house has 16 guest rooms furnished with antiques, Southwestern furnishings and modern amenities. A short walk from the plaza, the 'boutique-style' house also has a lovely courtyard; attractive gardens surround the house.

Lundeen Inn of the Arts (☎ 526-3326, 888-526-3326; www.innofthearts.com; 618 S Alameda Blvd, Las Cruces; s/d $69/85, ste $95-105, all incl breakfast; P ⊠ ⚡ ☐) This large, turn-of-the-19th-century Mexican Territorial-style inn has 20 guest rooms (all wildly different), an airy living room with soaring ceilings (made of pressed tin) and an art gallery. Some rooms have kitchenettes; some might feature vigas or a kiva fireplace; all have a phone.

Hilltop Hacienda (☎ 382-3556; www.zianet.com /hilltop; 2600 Westmoreland, Las Cruces; r $95-125; P ⊠ ⚡ ☐) Yes, the three antique-filled rooms are comfortable and the B&B offers a common room with VCR and library filled with Southwestern books. But it's the setting, on 18 acres atop a hill with panoramic mountain views, that's the real draw.

Eating

Spirit Winds Coffee Bar (☎ 521-1222; 2260 S Locust, Las Cruces; dishes $3-6; 🕭 7am-7pm Mon-Fri, 7:30am-7pm Sat, 8:30am-7pm Sun; P ⊠ ⚡ V 🕭) Join the university crowd for excellent cappuccino and gourmet tea, as well as good sandwiches, salads, soups and pastries. An eclectic gift and card shop and entertainment on the weekends keeps the students, artsy types and business folks coming back.

Nellie's Cafe (☎ 524-9982; 1226 W Hadley Ave, Las Cruces; dishes $5-8; 🕭 8am-2pm Tue-Sat; P ⊠ ⚡ V 🕭) Without doubt the favored local Mexican restaurant, Nellie's has been around for decades and has a dedicated following. The café's slogan is 'Chile with an Attitude,' and the food is deliciously spicy. It's small and humble in decor, but big in taste.

Chope's Bar & Cafe (☎ 233-3420; NM 28, Mesilla; dishes $5-8; 🕭 11:30am-1:30pm & 5:30-8:30pm Tue-Sat; P ⊠ ⚡ V 🕭) About 15 minutes (or 10 miles) south of Old Mesilla and worth every second of the drive, Chope's isn't anything to look at, but the hot chile will turn you into an addict within minutes. From *chile rellenos* to burritos, you've seen the menu

before; you just haven't had it this good. The adjacent bar is loads of fun.

La Posta (☎ 524-3524; www.laposta-de-mesilla.com; 2410 Calle de San Albino, Mesilla; dishes $8-15; 🕭 11am-9pm; P ⊠ ⚡ V 🕭) The area's most famous Mexican eatery (due to location more than the quality of the food or the table settings) is housed in an early-19th-century adobe house that predates the founding of Mesilla. A Butterfield stagecoach stop in the 1850s, today's restaurant claims to have the largest collection of tequila in the Southwest (with close to 100 varieties). Order enchiladas.

Double Eagle Restaurant (☎ 523-6700; Mesilla Plaza; lunch $9-15, dinner $15-45; 🕭 11am-10pm Mon-Sat; P ⊠ ⚡) A dual-identity eatery offering continental (steaks and seafood) and Southwestern cuisine in an elegant Victorian and Territorial-style setting, Double Eagle doesn't mind if you stroll around to drink in the 19th-century architecture even if you decide not to eat here. It's on the National Register of Historic Places; they don't make 'em like this anymore, with central courtyards, chandeliers and 30ft bars. Lunches revolve around simpler sandwiches, chicken dishes and burgers.

Entertainment

The *Bulletin*, a free weekly published on Thursdays, has up-to-the-minute entertainment information.

Foreign and art films are screened at the **Fountain Theater** (☎ 524-8287; 2469 Calle de Guadalupe; adult/student $6/5). Shoot some pool and down some brews at **Brew Ha Ha** (☎ 647-3348; 2500 Valley Dr; 🕭 3 or 4pm-2am). **Hurricane Alley** (☎ 532-9358; 1490 Missouri Ave) has live rock or DJs and dancing on weekends.

ALAMOGORDO & AROUND

☎ 505 / Pop 35,500 / Elev 4350ft

Despite a dearth of amenities, Alamogordo (Spanish for 'fat cottonwood tree') is the center of one of the most historically important space and atomic research programs in the country. Perhaps more importantly for today's traveler, it's also close to La Luz, a little outpost for artists and craftspeople, and near Tularosa, which has a fine winery.

White Sands Blvd (also called US 54, 70 or 82) is the main drag through town and runs north–south. Addresses on North White Sands Blvd correspond to numbered cross-streets (thus 1310 N WSB is just north

NEW MEXICO ROAD TRIPS

DETOUR: OFF THE BEATEN PATH

The uncrowded **Three Rivers Petroglyph National Recreation Area** (☎ 525-4300; County Rd B30; $2 per car; tent/RV sites $2/10), off US 54, showcases 21,000 petroglyphs inscribed 1000 years ago by the Jornada Mogollon people. The 1-mile hike through mesquite and cacti offers good views of the Sacramento Mountains to the east and White Sands Monument on the horizon. Nearby is a pithouse in a partially excavated village. There are six camping shelters with barbecue grills (free), restrooms, water and two hookups for RVs. The **BLM** (☎ 525-4300) in Las Cruces has details. The site is 27 miles north of Alamogordo on US 54, and then 5 miles east on a signed road.

---

of 13th); addresses on South WSB are one block south of 1st.

To reach Alamogordo from Las Cruces, take US 70/82 east for 62 miles.

Information

Library (☎ 439-4140; 10th St; ☺ 10am-8pm Mon-Thu, 10am-5pm Fri, 11am-5pm Sat, 1-5pm Sun) Free internet access.

Lincoln USFS National Forest Ranger Station (☎ 434-7200; 1101 New York; ☺ 7:30am-4:30pm Mon-Fri)

Visitors center (☎ 437-6120, 800-826-0294; www .alamogordo.com; 1301 N White Sands Blvd; ☺ 8am-5pm Mon-Fri, 9am-5pm Sat & Sun)

Sights

Alamogordo's most important attraction, the four-story **New Mexico Museum of Space History** (☎ 437-2840, 877-333-6589; Hwy 2001; adult/ child 4-12 yrs $3/2.50; ☺ 9am-5pm) is nicknamed 'the golden cube' and looms over the town. It has excellent exhibits on space research and flight. Its **Tombaugh IMAX Theater & Planetarium** (adult $6-8, child $4-8) shows outstanding films about anything from the Grand Canyon to the dark side of the moon.

Established in 1898 as a diversion for railway travelers, the **Alameda Park & Zoo** (☎ 439-4290; 1021 N White Sands Blvd; adult/child 3-11 yrs $2.20/1.10; ☺ 9am-5pm) is the oldest zoo west of the Mississippi. Small but well run, it features exotics from around the world, among them the endangered Mexican gray wolf.

Railroad buffs and kids flock to the **Toy Train Depot** (☎ 437-2855; 1991 N White Sands Blvd; admission $4; ☺ noon-4:30pm Wed-Sun), an 1898 railway depot with five rooms of train memorabilia and toy trains, and a 2.5-mile narrow-gauge train.

Wander around the historical center of town, east of N White Sands Blvd along and just off 10th St. The attractive USFS building at 11th and New York houses Peter Hurd's *Sun and Rain* frescoes, painted in the early 1940s as part of the New Deal's WPA art program.

La Luz, 4 miles north of Alamogordo and worthy of a stroll, remains unspoiled by tourism. Ten miles further north on US 54, the attractive village of **Tularosa** is dominated by the 1869 **St Francis de Paula Church**, built in a simple New Mexican style. **Tularosa Vineyards** (☎ 585-2260; www.tularosavineyards.com; Coyote Canyon Rd; ☺ 9am-5pm Mon-Sat, noon-5pm Sun), a friendly and picturesque winery 2 miles north of Tularosa, off US 54, has afternoon tours and tastings by appointment. **Casa de Suenos** (☎ 585-3494; 35 St Francis Dr; dishes $7-13; ☺ 11am-8pm Mon-Sat, 10:30am-8pm Sun; P X & V ♿), all done up with folk paintings from south of the border, is a festive place with a great outdoor patio. Its New Mexican cuisine is some of the best in the area and the lunchtime buffet is bountiful.

Sleeping & Eating

Satellite Inn (☎ 437-8454, 800-221-7690; www.satel liteinn.com; 2224 N White Sands Blvd; r $40 incl breakfast; P X ✗ 🖥 ⛷) All these simple and clean double rooms have a microwave and refrigerator. It's your typical (albeit above-average) roadside motel.

Compass Rose (☎ 434-9633; 2203 E 1st St; dishes $5-10; ☺ 6:30am-10pm Mon-Thu, 6:30am-11pm Fri, 7am-11pm Sat, 7am-10pm Sun; P X & V ♿) If you're tired of enchiladas and beans, and are overcome by a desire for food with an eclectic American flair, try this healthy and creative place. The family-friendly Compass Rose has a great selection of brews from all around the world, soup and salads. Try the Zinger sandwich with horseradish sour cream, roast beef, green chile, pepperjack and swiss, on a sunflower-seed bread.

Margo's (☎ 434-0689; 504 E 1st St; dishes $5-12; ☺ 10:30am-9pm Mon-Thu, 10:30am-9:30pm Sat, 11am-9pm Sun; P X & V ♿) There's not much to look at inside, but hey, when they offer such good Mexican cuisine at such good prices, who can complain? Family-owned since the late 1970s, Margo's has a robust and tasty combo plate.

Entertainment
Shooters Pizza & Patio Bar (☎ 443-6000; US 70) Shooters has Karaoke Monday through Wednesday; the lineup the rest of the week is hip hop, country or top 40.

WHITE SANDS NATIONAL MONUMENT
These captivating windswept dunes, 5 miles southwest of US 82/70, are a highlight of any trip to New Mexico. Try to time a visit to the oasis-like and ethereal **White Sands** (www.nps .gov/whsa; adult/child 16 yrs & under $3/free) with sunrise or sunset (or both) when it's even more magical than normal. It's here that gypsum, a chalky mineral used in making plaster of paris, covers 275 sq miles. From the **visitor center** (☎ 679-2599; ☿ 8am-7pm Jun-Aug, 8am-5pm Sep-May), drive the 16-mile scenic loop into the heart of the dazzling white sea of sand – get out of the car and climb, romp, slide and roll in the soft dunes. Hike the Alkali Flat, a 4.5-mile (round-trip) backcountry trail through the heart of the dunes, or the simple 1-mile loop nature trail. **Backcountry campsites**, with no water or toilet facilities, are a mile from the scenic drive. Pick up **permits** (adult/child 16 & under $3/1.50) in person at the visitors center one hour before sunset. White Sands is 13 miles southwest of Alamogordo via US 70/82.

CLOUDCROFT & AROUND
☎ 505 / pop 750 / elev 9000ft
Pleasant Cloudcroft, with buildings from the turn of the 19th century, offers lots of outdoor recreation, a good base for exploration and a low-key feel. Situated high in the mountains, it provides welcome relief from the lowlands heat to the east.

Cloudcroft is 25 miles of Alamogordo; take US 54 east to US 82 east. US 82 is the main drag through town; most places are on US 82 or within a few blocks of it. Stop at the **chamber of commerce** (☎ 682-2733; www .cloudcroft.net; ☿ 10am-5pm Mon-Sat).

Sights & Activities
One of the world's largest solar observatories is near Sunspot, 20 miles south of Cloudcroft. Though primarily for scientists, tourists take guided tours (self-guided in the winter) of the **National Solar Observatory** (☎ 434-7000; ☿ visitors center 10am-6pm summer, 10am-4pm winter) on Friday, Saturday and Sunday at 2pm during the summer. The drive to Sunspot, along the **Sunspot Scenic Byway**, is a high and beautiful one, with the mountains to the east and White Sands National Monument to the west. From Cloudcroft, take NM 130 to NM 6563.

Hiking (April to November) is popular in these parts; outings range from short hikes close to town to overnight backpacking trips. Although trails are often fairly flat, the 9000ft elevation can make for some strenuous hiking if you are not acclimatized. The most popular day hike is the 2.6-mile Osha

NEW MEXICO ROAD TRIPS

THE BLAST HEARD 'ROUND THE WORLD
Just two days a year (on the first Saturdays in April and October), the public is permitted to tour the **Trinity Site**, where the first atomic bomb was detonated on July 16, 1945. Thirty five miles west of **Carrizozo**, the eerie tour includes the base camp, the McDonald Ranch house where the plutonium core for the bomb was assembled, and ground zero itself. The test was carried out above ground and resulted in a quarter-mile-wide crater and an 8-mile-high cloud mushrooming above the desert. The radiation level of the site is 'only' 10 times greater than the region's background level; a one-hour visit to ground zero will result in an exposure of one-half to one millorentgen (mrem), two to four times the estimated exposure of a typical adult on an average day in the US. Trinitite, a green, glassy substance resulting from the blast, is still radioactive, still scattered around, and still must not be touched. Resist the urge to add it to your road-trip rock collection. This desolate area is fittingly called **Jornada del Muerto** (Journey of Death) and is overshadowed by 8638ft **Oscura Peak** (Darkness Peak on state maps). Call the **Alamogordo Chamber of Commerce** (☎ 437-6120, 800-826-0294; www.alamogordo.com) for information. Guided trips through the chamber cost $35 to $50 per person (reservations required), but you may also follow the motor coach in and then join a free tour. The entire trip from Alamogordo takes four hours.

Loop Trail, which leaves US 82 from a small parking area 1 mile west of Cloudcroft.

Trails in the Sacramento Mountains offer great mountain biking, and **High Altitude** (☎ 682-1229; www.highaltitude.org; 310 Burro Ave; ☉ 10am-5:30pm) can tell you where to go when they rent you bikes. For horseback riding, contact **Rynyan Ranches** (☎ 687-3136) about 16 miles out of town.

Ski Cloudcroft (☎ 682-2333; www.ski-cloudcroft .com; Hwy 8; lift tickets adult/child under 12 yrs $35/25), about 2 miles east of town, has 24 runs designed mostly for beginning and intermediate skiers. Inner-tubing and snowboarding are also possible.

Sleeping & Eating

Raven Wind (☎ 687-3073; www.ravenwindranch.com; 1234 Hwy 24, Weed; r incl breakfast $85; P ☒) Surrounded by the Lincoln National Forest about 28 miles from Cloudcroft, this ranch-style place offers two basic double rooms (don't expect Southwestern style), comfortable rockers on a huge wraparound porch and a complimentary light lunch. Families can settle into an entire guesthouse. It also offers one week all-inclusive spa vacations that can be booked at www.ravenwind retreat.net.

Lodge Resort & Spa (☎ 682-2566, 800-395-6343; www.thelodgeresort.com; 1 Corona Pl; r $125-175, pavilion r $125-175, ste $250-350; P ☒ ☒ 🖳 🖳) One of the best historic hotels in the Southwest, this grand old lodge was built in 1899 as a vacation getaway for railroad employees. Try to get a room in the main Bavarian-style hotel; these are furnished with period and Victorian pieces. Pavilion rooms are a few blocks away in a separate, less attractive building. The Lodge also rents four more luxurious suites in a mountain home and has a fine restaurant.

Western Bar & Café (☎ 682-2445; Burro Ave; dishes $5-12; ☉ 6am-9pm; P ☒ ☒ 🖳 ☒) This popular place looks like something out of the Wild West.

Rebecca's (☎ 682-3131; 1 Corona Pl; breakfast $6-11, lunch $7-17, dinner $18-34; ☉ 7am-9pm; P ☒ ☒ 🖳 🖳) Within the Lodge Resort, Rebecca's offers by far the best food in town, especially during the Sunday brunch buffet ($17). Kick back on the outside deck that has spectacular views of the mountains and the distant and shimmering White Sands Monument. All in all, it's elegant with good

service and nicely prepared steaks and continental cuisine (and some Mexican dishes of course).

RUIDOSO & AROUND
☎ 505 / pop 8000 / elev 700ft

You want lively in these parts? You want Ruidoso. Downright bustling in the summer and big with bettors at the racetrack, resorty Ruidoso has an utterly pleasant climate thanks to its lofty and forested perch near Sierra Blanca (12,000ft). Neighboring Texans and local New Mexicans escaping the summer heat of Alamogordo (46 miles to the southwest) and Roswell (71 miles to the east) are happy campers here (or more precisely, happy 'cabiners'). The lovely Rio Ruidoso, a small creek with good fishing, runs through town. Summertime hiking and wintertime hiking at Ski Apache keep folks busy, as do a smattering of galleries.

Both the **chamber of commerce** (☎ 257-7395, 800-253-2255; www.ruidosonow.com; 720 Sudderth Dr; ☉ 8:30am-5pm Mon-Thu, 9am-5pm Fri-Sun) and the **Lincoln National Forest Ranger Station** (☎ 257-4095; www.fs.fed.us/r3/lincoln.com; 901 Mechem Dr; ☉ 7:30am-4:30pm Mon-Fri Nov-Apr, Mon-Sat May-Oct) are helpful.

Ruidoso is 85 miles from Cloudcroft through the Apache Reservation via NM 244 to US 70.

Sights & Activities

The fine **Hubbard Museum of the American West** (☎ 378-4142; www.hubbardmuseum.org; 841 US 70 W; admission $6; ☉ 9am-5pm) displays more than 10,000 western-related items including Old West stagecoaches, saddles and American Indian pottery, as well as works by Frederic Remington and Charles M Russell. An impressive collection of horse-related displays, including a collection of saddles and the Racehorse Hall of Fame, lures horse-lovers.

The **Ruidoso Downs Racetrack** (☎ 378-4431; www.ruidosodownsracing.com; US 70; admission free, grandstand 4-seat box $28; ☉ races Thu-Sun late May-early Sep, casino 11am-11pm year-round), one of the major racetracks in the Southwest, hosts the All American Futurity on Labor Day. This is the world's richest quarter-horse race, with a purse of over $2 million.

About 3000 Native Americans live on the 719-sq-mile **Mescalero Apache Indian Reservation**, which lies in attractive country about 17 miles southwest of Ruidoso on US 70. The nomadic Apaches arrived in this area about 800 years ago and soon became enemies to local Pueblo Indians. In the 19th century, under pressure from European settlement and with their mobility greatly increased by the introduction of the horse, the Apaches became some of the most feared raiders of the West. Despite the name of the reservation, the Apaches here are of three tribes: the Mescalero, the Chiricahua and the Lipan.

The **cultural center** (☎ 464-4494; Chiricahua Plaza, Mescalero), off US 70, has a small but interesting exhibit about the Apache peoples and customs. If you're in the area, the annual Apache Maidens' Puberty Ceremony takes place for about five days around July 4. Apart from the sacred rites of the Puberty Ceremony, there is a powwow, rodeo and arts-and-crafts demonstrations. The Inn of the Mountain Gods (see right) is a great place to sleep.

The best ski area south of Albuquerque is **Ski Apache** (☎ 336-4356, snow conditions 257-9001; www.skiapache.com; exit 532, NM 48; all-day passes adult $49-52, child $31-34; �YES 8:45am-9pm), 18 miles northwest of Ruidoso on the slopes of beautiful Sierra Blanca Peak (about 12,000 feet).

Hiking is a popular summertime activity, especially the 4.6-mile day hike from the Ski Apache area to Sierra Blanca Peak, an ascent of 2000ft. Take Trail 15 from the small parking area just before the main lot and follow signs west and south along Trails 25 and 78 to Lookout Mountain (11,580ft). From there an obvious trail continues due south for 1.25 miles to Sierra Blanca Peak. Several other trails leave from the Ski Apache area; the ranger station in Ruidoso has maps and information for more adventurous trips, including the beautiful **Crest Trail**.

Sierra Blanca Peak offers several lookouts with stunning views, especially in the fall – just drive up Ski Area Rd (NM 532) from Alto. Along this road, you'll see signs for the Monjeau Lookout via USFS Rd 117.

Sleeping

There are lots of area cabin rentals, but some of the ones in town are cramped. Most newer, spiffier cabins are located in the Upper Canyon. Generally, cabins have kitchens and grills, and often they have fireplaces and decks. **Central Reservations of Ruidoso** (☎ 257-9171, 888-257-7577; www.4seasonsrealestate.com; 712 Mechem Dr; �YES 8am-6pm; ✕) arranges house, condominium, cabin and lodge rentals. Although Ruidoso hotels are often referred to as 'lodges' or 'inns,' they are basically your standard motel.

Dan Dee Cabins (☎ 257-2165; www.dandeecabins .com; 310 Main Rd; 1-bedroom cabins winter/summer $89/119; P ✕ ▫) One of the friendliest places to stay in New Mexico, these 13 woodsy cabins are spread out over five grassy and forested acres. Constructed at various times beginning in the 1940s, each one is unique, private and comfy.

High Country Lodge (☎ 336-4321, 800-845-7265; www.highcountrylodge.net; 859 NM 48; weekday/weekend r $94/124; P ✕ ▫) Just south of the turnoff to Ski Apache, this older selection of rustic cabins is still among the town's most comfortable. The complex has 32 basic two-bedroom cabins, each with kitchen, fireplace and porch. Other facilities include a sauna, hot tub and tennis courts.

Shadow Mountain Lodge (☎ 257-4886; www .shadowmountainlodge.com; 107 Main Rd; r $109-141; P ✕ ✕ ▫) Geared toward couples, these immaculate rooms feature fireplaces and offer romantic allure. A wooden wraparound balcony overlooks the professionally landscaped grounds; the hot tub is tucked away in a gazebo. Ask about individual cabins.

Inn of the Mountain Gods (☎ 257-5141, 800-545-9011; www.innofthemountaingods.com; 287 Carrizo Canyon Rd; r $159-299; P ✕ ✕ ▫ ▫) This luxury resort hotel on the Mescalero Apache Reservation offers a casino and all kinds of activities including guided fishing, paddleboat rentals and horseback riding. The old Inn of the Mountain Gods was completely leveled in 2003. A new one sprang up in 2004, complete with a fitness room, several restaurants, a nightclub, a sports bar and a championship golf course.

Eating

Hummingbird Tearoom (☎ 257-5100; 2306 Sudderth Dr, Village Plaza; dishes $5-7; �YES 11am-5pm Mon-Sat; P ✕ V ♿) This homey little place specializes in simple soups, salads and lunchtime sandwiches; delectable desserts and rich teas make a lovely afternoon diversion. The owners can be attentive or harried.

Weber's Grill (☎ 257-9559; 441 Mechem Dr; lunch $6-10, dinner $12-24; �YES 11am-9pm Sun-Mon & Wed-Thu, 11am-10pm Fri & Sat; P ♿ V ♿) A kinda

NEW MEXICO ROAD TRIPS

cool and kinda happenin' sort of place that appeals to both families (upstairs) and brew-pub crawlers (downstairs), Weber's is a friendly place to nosh on appetizers and burgers or gravitate toward something more serious like rib-eye steaks. Pizzas and calzones are also popular.

Casa Blanca (☎ 257-2495; 501 Mechem Dr; lunch $6-7, dinner $6-19; ☷ 11am-9pm; Ⓟ ☒ ☒ Ⓥ ☒) Dine on Southwestern cuisine in a renovated Spanish-style house or on the pleasant patio in the summer. The *chile rellenos* are to die for.

Cornerstone Bakery (☎ 257-1842; 359 Sudderth Dr; dishes under $8; ☷ 7am-2pm Mon-Sat, 7:30am-1pm Sun; Ⓟ ☒ ☒ Ⓥ ☒) Stay around long enough and the Cornerstone may become your touchstone. Everything on the menu, from omelets to croissant sandwiches, is worthy.

Café Rio (☎ 257-7746; 2547 Sudderth Dr; pizzas $10-25; ☷ 11:20am-7:50pm; Ⓟ ☒ ☒ Ⓥ ☒) Thick-crust pizza, with your choice of toppings, are wickedly and deservedly popular here, but the stuffed calzones are a good runner-up. Wash it down with the big selection of international and seasonal beer.

Texas Club (☎ 258-3325; 212 Metz Dr; dinner $10-30; ☷ 5-10pm Wed-Sun; Ⓟ ☒ ☒ Ⓥ ☒) One of the busiest and best restaurants in town, decorated with all the bigness you'd expect in a place that takes its name from Texas (think longhorn and cowboy hats). It serves big steaks and has dancing and live entertainment on the weekends. Call for directions since it's a bit hidden and reservations since it's so beloved.

Flying J Ranch (☎ 336-4330; NM 48; adult/child 4-12 yrs $21/12; ☷ from 6pm daily May-Aug, Sat Sep–mid-Oct; Ⓟ ☒ ☒ ☒) If the kids want some entertainment along with their steak, circle the wagons and ride over to Flying J. About 1.5 miles north of Alto, this 'Western village' stages gunfights and offers pony rides with their cowboy-style chuckwagon. Western music tops off the evening.

Entertainment

Spencer Theater for the Performing Arts (☎ 336-4800, 888-818-7872; www.spencertheater.com; Hwy 220, Alto; performances $20-40) Set in a stunning mountain venue, the theater hosts theatrical, musical and dance performances. Rising from its setting to look like equal parts cut diamond, space-ship, pyramid and mountaintop, this Antoine Predock–designed

building is a joy to behold. Performances are elevated simply by their setting.

Farley's Food Fun & Pub (☎ 258-5676; 1200 Mechem Dr; ☷ 11am-10pm Sun-Thu, 11am-11pm Fri & Sat) The most popular hang-out in town; you can enjoy a beer and a game of pool while throwing peanut shells on the floor.

The Texas Club is popular for dancing. **Quarters** (☎ 257-9535; 2535 Sudderth Dr; ☷ 11am-2am Mon-Sat, 11am-midnight Sun) offers DJs and nightly dancing. Hang out at the bar or at comfortable tables. Or hang at its sister establishment across the street, **Win, Place & Show** (☷ 11am-2am Mon-Sat, 11am-midnight Sun), where country-and-western bands play nightly.

LINCOLN
☎ 505 / pop 55 / elev 5700ft

Fans of Western history won't want to miss little Lincoln. Twelve miles east of Capitan along the **Billy the Kid National Scenic Byway** (www.billybyway.com), this is where the gun battle that turned Billy the Kid into a legend took place. Perhaps surprisingly, modern influences, such as souvenir stands, are not allowed in town.

Only about 70 folks still reside in Lincoln, and they're intent on preserving the 1880s buildings; the main street has been designated the **Lincoln State Monument**. You can visit the Tunstall Store (with a remarkable display of late-19th-century merchandise), the courthouse where the Kid escaped imprisonment, and Dr Wood's house, an intact turn-of-the-century doctor's home and office. At the **Anderson Freeman Visitors Center & Museum** (☎ 653-4025; US 380; entry to all 6 houses $5; ☷ 9am-4:30pm) exhibits on the Buffalo soldiers, Apaches and the Lincoln County War explain the town's history. The Tunstall Store and Dr Wood's house are closed from March to November.

Hurd Ranch Guest Homes (☎ 653-4331, 800-658-6912; www.wyethartists.com; 105 La Rinconada Lane, San Patricio; casitas $140-250; Ⓟ ☒ ☒ ☒) This 2500-acre, very rural place in San Patricio, about 14 miles south of Lincoln, rents six lovely casitas by an apple orchard. Furnished with style and grace, and lots of original art, some units sleep up to six people. They are outfitted with modern conveniences.

Owner and artist Michael Hurd runs the **Hurd la Rinconada Gallery** on the premises; he also shows the work of his relatives NC and Andrew Wyeth and Henriette Wyeth.

ROSWELL

☎ 505 / pop 45,000 / elev 3649ft

Conspiracy theorists and *X-Files* fanatics descend from other worlds onto Roswell. Oddly famous as both the country's largest producer of wool and its UFO capital, Roswell has built a tourist industry around the alleged July 1947 UFO crash (p212). The military quickly closed the area and allowed no more information for several decades (although later they claimed it was a balloon). Was it a flying saucer? The local convention and visitors bureau suggests that Roswell's special blend of climate and culture attracted touring space aliens who wanted a closer look! Decide for yourself.

If you're driving east on US 70/380 from the Sacramento Mountains, enjoy the view. Roswell sits on the western edge of the dry plains, and these are the last big mountains you'll see for a while.

The 'Staked Plains' extending east into Texas were once home to millions of buffalo and many nomadic Native American hunters. White settlers and hunters moved in throughout the late 19th century, and killed some 3.5 million buffalo during a two-year period. Within a few years, the region became desolate and empty; only a few groups of Comanche mixed with other tribes roaming the plains, hunting and trying to avoid confinement on reservations. Roswell, founded in 1871, served as a stopping place for cowboys driving cattle.

The main west–east drag through town is 2nd St and the main north–south thoroughfare is Main St; their intersection is the heart of downtown. Roswell is 77 miles east of Ruidoso; take US 70 east.

Information

BLM office (☎ 627-0272; 2909 W 2nd St; ⏰ 7:45am-4:30pm Mon-Fri)

Library (☎ 622-7101; 301 N Pennsylvania Ave; ⏰ 9am-9pm Mon-Tue, 9am-6pm Wed-Sat, 2-6pm Sun) Free internet access.

Roswell Visitor Center (☎ 624-0889, 888-767-9355; www.roswell-usa.com; 426 N Main St; ⏰ 8:30am-5:30pm Mon-Fri)

Sights & Activities

The excellent **Roswell Museum & Art Center & Goddard Planetarium** (☎ 624-6744; www.roswellmuseum .org; 100 W 11th St; admission free; ⏰ 9am-5pm Mon-Sat, 1-5pm Sun) deserves a visit. Seventeen galleries showcase Southwestern artists including Georgia O'Keeffe, Peter Hurd and Henriette Wyeth. An eclectic mix of Native American, Hispanic and Anglo artifacts means there's something for everyone. As you might imagine, a major focus is space research. Robert H Goddard, who launched the world's first successful liquid fuel rocket in 1926, spent more than a decade carrying out rocket research in Roswell. His laboratory has been reconstructed at the museum, and a variety of early rocketry paraphernalia is on display.

Serious followers of UFO phenomena (not to mention skeptics or the merely curious) will want to check out the **International UFO Museum & Research Center** (☎ 625-9495; www .iufomrc.org; 114 N Main St; adult/child $2/1; ⏰ 9am-5pm). Original photographs and witness statements form the 1947 Roswell Incident Timeline explain the great cover-up. The library claims to have the most comprehensive UFO-related materials in the world. And we have no reason to be skeptical.

Housed in the 1910 mansion of local rancher James Phelp White, the **Historical Center for Southeast New Mexico** (☎ 622-8333; 200 N Lea St; donation; ⏰ 1am-4pm) is well worth seeing. It's on the National Register of Historic Places, and the interior has been carefully restored to its original early-20th century decor with period furnishings, photographs and art.

Water birds gather at the 38-sq-mile **Ritter Lake National Wildlife Refuge** (☎ 622-6755; www.fws .gov/southwest; Pine Lodge Rd; admission free; ⏰ sunrise-sunset); many remain to nest in the summer, but the fall and winter are definitely the most active times to see them. A 7-mile self-guided auto-route makes viewing a snap. To reach the refuge, about 15 miles northeast of Roswell, follow the signed roads from either US 380 or US 285/70.

Festivals & Events

Roswell has a couple quirky festivals.

New Mexico Dairy Day Features the Great Milk Carton Boat Race on Lake Van, 20 miles south of Roswell, as well as cheese-sculpting contests, 36ft-long ice-cream sundaes, games and sporting events. Held early June.

UFO Encounter Centers on alien-costume competitions and lectures about UFOs. Held around July 4.

Eastern New Mexico State Fair (☎ 623-9411) The main annual event is this early October fair, with rodeo, livestock and agricultural competitions and chile-eating contests.

NEW MEXICO ROAD TRIPS

IDENTIFY THIS!

It was a heady time, the summer of 1947. Several UFOs were sighted around the country, but none like the one that fell into the desert near Roswell sometime during the first week of July. In a press release, the government identified the object as a crashed disk. A day later it claimed the disk was really just a weather balloon, confiscated all the previous press releases, cordoned off the area as all the debris was collected, and posted armed guards to escort curious locals from the site of the 'weather-balloon' crash. A local mortician fielded calls from the mortuary office at the government airfield inquiring after small, hermetically sealed coffins for preventing tissue contamination and degeneration after several days of exposure to the elements. To this day, eyewitness accounts, rumor and misinformation continue to swirl, fueling all manner of speculation over what really happened in the desert that day.

Sleeping & Eating

Heritage Inn (☎ 748-2552; www.artesiaheritageinn .com; 209 W Main St, Artesia; r $80; P ⊠ ✂ ▣) The nicest area place to stay is actually not in Roswell. If you're traveling between Roswell and Carlsbad and in the mood for slightly upscale digs (this is Southeastern New Mexico, don't forget), this c 1900, in-town establishment offers 11 Old West–style rooms about 36 miles south of Roswell.

Sally Port Inn (☎ 622-6430, 800-528-1234; 2000 N Main St; r $85-95; P ⊠ ✂ ▣ ▣) As good as it gets in Roswell, this Best Western has limited spa facilities and 124 standard-issue rooms (some with refrigerators and microwaves.)

Wellhead (☎ 746-0640; 332 W Main St, Artesia; dishes $6-23; ✆ 11am-9pm Mon-Sat; P ⊠ ✂ ✂) If you're traveling between Roswell and Carlsbad, you'll find the region's best food and drink at this modern brewpub restaurant and bar. Housed in a 1905 building and reflecting the town's origins, it's decorated with an oil-drilling theme and serves burgers ($8) and tenderloins ($23). Artesia is about 36 miles south of Roswell.

Peppers Bar & Grill (☎ 623-1700; 500 N Main St; lunch $5-7, dinner $7-15; ✆ 11am-10pm Mon-Sat; P ⊠ ✂ ✂) Part bar, brewpub and restaurant, Peppers has good old-fashioned American dishes (and requisite Mexican ones). Try the steak au poive ($15) or catfish ($10). But the real draw just might be the live music and dancing on weekends. The patio is nice in summer.

Farley's (☎ 627-1100; 1315 N Main St; dishes $7-12; ✆ 11am-midnight, until 2am Fri & Sat; P ⊠ ✂ ✂) A boisterous barnlike place, Farley's has something for everyone: burgers, pizza, chicken and ribs. It's family friendly except on Friday and Saturday nights, when kids might grow impatient at the wait.

Cattle Baron (☎ 622-2465; 1113 N Main St; dishes $7-15 ✆ 11am-9:30pm Mon-Thu, 11am-10pm Fri & Sat, 11am-9pm Sun; P ⊠ ✂ Ⓥ ✂) This efficient and friendly place specializes in consistently good and reasonably priced beef. With a name like that, whaddaya expect? And yet the salad bar would give any vegetarian a run for their money. Hang your spurs at the full bar before or after dinner.

CARLSBAD CAVERNS NATIONAL PARK

Drive for hours across the desert just to see a cave? But it's not just any cave; it's a truly astonishing and immense system of caves, one of the world's greatest. Once visitors get a glimpse, even the most skeptical are impressed. A visit is, without a doubt, a highlight of any Southwestern journey. But wait, there's more. The cave's other claim to fame is the 250,000-plus Mexican free-tail bat colony that roost here from April to October. Visitors flock here at sunset to watch them fly out to feast on a smorgasbord of bugs.

The park covers 73 sq miles and includes almost 100 caves. Visitors can take a 2-mile subterranean walk from the cave mouth to an underground chamber 1800ft long, 255ft high and over 800ft below the surface. Exploration for experienced spelunkers only continues at the awe-inspiring **Lechugilla Cave**. With a depth of 1567ft and a length of about 60 miles, it's the deepest and third longest limestone cave in North America.

The park entrance is 23 miles southwest of Carlsbad. A three-day pass for self-guided tours to the natural entrance and the Big Room (send a postcard from the lunchroom, 829ft below the surface!) costs $6 for adults and $3 for children, and passes are honored. The **park** (☎ 785-2232, 800-967-2283; www.nps.gov/cave; 3225 National Parks Hwy; 🕙 8am-5pm, until 7pm late May–mid-Aug) also has a variety of ranger-led tours ($7 to $8 for scenic tours that depart four times daily, $20 for technical caving tours that are booked two months in advance); call for advance reservations. If you want to scramble to lesser-known areas, ask about Wild Cave tours. The last tickets are sold two to 3½ hours before the visitors center closes. Wilderness backpacking trips into the desert are allowed by permit (free); the visitors center sells topographical maps of the 50-plus miles of hiking trails.

There are no accommodations within the park, but the comfortable, small and resort-like **Best Western Cavern Inn** (☎ 785-2291, 800-228-3767; www.bestwestern.com; 6 Carlsbad Hwy, White's City; r $100; P X X X R) is the most decent place to stay near the park; it's a quarter-mile from the entrance and offers free wireless internet in its 63 good-sized guest rooms. Ask for a room in the Guadalupe building.

It's 74 miles from Roswell to Carlsbad via US 285 south and then another 16 miles west to White's City and the park entrance via US 62/180.

CARLSBAD
☎ 505 / pop 25,600 / elev 3120ft
When Carlsbad Caverns was declared a national monument in 1923, a trickle of tourists turned into a veritable flash flood. Today, hundreds of thousands of visitors come through annually. Situated on the Pecos River about 30 miles north of the Texas state line, Carlsbad's main thoroughfare is US 285, which becomes Canal St, then S Canal (south of Mermod St) and then National Parks Hwy at the southern end of town.

Information
Chamber of commerce (☎ 887-6516, 800-221-1224; www.carlsbadchamber.com; 302 S Canal St; 🕙 9am-5pm Mon, 8am-5pm Tue-Fri, 9am-3pm Sat late May-early Sep)
Library (☎ 885-6776; 101 S Halagueno St; 🕙 10am-8pm Mon-Thu, 10am-6pm Fri & Sat, 2-6pm Sun) Free internet access, but computers are turned off 30 minutes prior to closing.
National Parks Information Center (☎ 885-8884; 3225 National Parks Hwy; 🕙 8am-4:30pm Mon-Fri) Information on both Carlsbad Caverns National Park and Guadalupe Mountains National Park.

Sights & Activities
On the northwestern outskirts of town, off US 285, **Living Desert State Park** (☎ 887-5516; www.friendsofthelivingdesert.org; 1504 Miehls Dr; adult/child 7-12 yrs $5/3; 🕙 8am-8pm May-Aug, 9am-5pm Sep-Apr, last entrance to park at 6:30pm) is a great place to see and learn about cacti, coyotes and wildlife with evocative Southwestern names such as agave, javelina, ocotillo and yucca. The park has a good 1.3-mile trail that showcases different habitats of the Chihuahuan Desert.

North of Bataan Bridge, a system of dams and spillways on the Pecos River creates the two-mile **Lake Carlsbad**, which has a pleasant 4.5-mile trail along its banks. At the north end of Park Dr, **Carlsbad Riverfront Park** has a beach and swimming area. At nearby **Port Jefferson** (☎ 887-8343; 🕙 10am-dark Sat & Sun, noon-dark Mon-Fri late May-early Sep) you can rent a paddle-wheel boat or kayak ($10 per hour) to tool around the river.

Sleeping & Eating
The nearby national park and mild winters make this a year-round destination; always ask for the best rates. Sorry, folks, but it's mostly chain motels in Carlsbad.
Executive Suites & Hotel (☎ 885-8500; 601 S Canal St; r incl full breakfast $70-105; P X X R R) This two-story place is the only full-service hotel downtown; the 150 rooms are spacious and have a faux Southwestern feel.
Best Western Stevens Inn (☎ 887-2851, 800-730-2851; 1829 S Canal St, r $79-99; P X X R R) Carlsbad's largest hotel has more than 200 rooms, some with kitchenettes or microwave/refrigerator combos.
Casa Milagro (☎ 887-2188, 866-332-0743; www.casa-milagro-nm.com; 1612 N Guadalupe St; r $95; P X X R) On the edge of town, this comfortable old homestead from the turn of the 20th century rents five pleasant rooms that are the pride of the owner. Plan your day on the porch or stay a while and read.
Lucy's (☎ 887-7714; 701 S Canal St; dishes $5-12; 🕙 11am-9pm Mon-Sat; P X & V 🕙) The most popular place in Carlsbad, Lucy's is usually packed with devoted locals *and* visitors. Apart from a great Mexican menu, it serves up tasty margaritas and a good selection of microbrews. (Admittedly that may be one reason the place is jumpin'.)
Blue House Bakery & Cafe (☎ 628-0555; 609 N Canyon Rd; dishes under $8; 🕙 6am-3pm Mon-Sat; P X & V 🕙) This sweet Queen Anne

NEW MEXICO ROAD TRIPS

house perks the best coffee and espresso in this quadrant of New Mexico. The baked goods are pretty darn good too. At lunchtime, this cheery place has good sandwiches made with fresh breads.

Red Chimney Barbeque (☎ 885-8744; 817 N Canal St; dishes $9-11; ☺ 4:30-8:30pm Mon-Fri; P ⊠ ⚒ ⚐) Barbecue aficionados will agree: Red Chimney has one of the most unusual sauces you'll ever encounter. It just may have you dreaming about secret ingredients.

Entertainment

Fiesta Drive-In Theater (☎ 885-4126; www.fiesta drivein.com; 401 W Fiesta; per person $4 or per carload $10; ☺ shows at 8:30pm Fri-Mon, 11pm Sat & Sun) Head here to soak up some nighttime desert air and experience a form of American entertainment that has almost disappeared.

ROUTE 3: NORTHWESTERN NM

Dubbed 'Indian Country' for good reason – huge swaths of land fall under the aegis of the Navajos, Pueblo, Zuni, Apache and Laguna tribes – this quadrant showcases remarkable ancient Indian sites alongside modern Native American settlements. Since about 1075, the mesa-top Acoma Pueblo has commanded a simply spectacular site; since about the mid-16th century, the Zunis have carved out homes around their pueblo. From excavated dwellings at Chaco Culture National Park to unexcavated ones at Aztec Ruins National Monument, the mysteries of the land are carried on the wind. While Farmington may serve as the regional business hub, Gallup reigns as its heart, a crossroads trading center for tribes and tourists.

It's not all Native Americans all the time, though. In Chama, it's all aboard. The Cumbres & Toltec Scenic Railroad transports travelers into the mid-19th century on a classic locomotive train trip through the mountains. And for driving fans, US 64 east to Tres Piedras is hard to beat.

ACOMA PUEBLO

Journeying to the top of 'Sky City' is journeying into another world. There are few more dramatic mesa-top locations; the village sits 7000ft above sea level and 367ft above the surrounding plateau. One of the oldest continuously inhabited settlements in North America, people have lived here since the later part of the 11th century. In addition to a singular history and a dramatic location, it's also famous for pottery, which is sold by individual artists on the mesa. There is a distinction between 'traditional' pottery (made with clay dug on the reservation) and 'ceramic' pottery (made elsewhere with inferior clay and simply painted by the artist), so ask the vendor.

The stunning 40,000-sq-ft **Sky City Cultural Center, Haak'u Museum** and **Yaak'a Café**, which opened in June 2006 at the bottom of the mesa, are the starting point for **guided tours** (☎ 800-747-0181; tours adult/child 6-17 yrs $10/7, cultural center & museum $4; ☺ 8am-6:30pm, last tour at 4:30pm Apr-Oct, 8am-5pm, last tour at 3pm Nov-Mar). Tours are offered daily about every 45 minutes, except for July 10–13, occasional other days, and either the first or second weekend in October, when the pueblo is closed to visitors. Though you must ride the shuttle to the top of the mesa, you can walk down the rock path back to the visitors center on your own. Definitely do this.

Festivals and events include a Governor's Feast (February), a Harvest Dance on San Esteban Day (September 2) and festivities at the San Esteban Mission (December 25–28). Photography permits cost $10; no videos are permitted.

The visitor center is 13 miles south of I-40 exit 96 (15 miles east of Grants) or I-40 exit 108 (50 miles west of Albuquerque).

Sky City Casino Hotel (☎ 552-6123, 877-552-6123; www.skycityhotel.com; exit 102, I-40; r/ste $89/120; P ⊠ ⚒ ⚐), the pueblo's modern casino, has 132 motel-style rooms and suites dressed up in Southwestern decor. Amenities include live entertainment, dining, room service and a pool.

Acoma is 75 miles west of Albuquerque; take I-40 to NM 23.

EL MALPAIS NATIONAL MONUMENT

Volcanic badlands in New Mexico? El Malpais (pronounced el mahl-pie-ees, meaning 'bad land' in Spanish) consists of almost 200 sq miles of lava flows abutting adjacent sandstone. All told, five major flows have been identified; the most recent one is pegged at 2000 to 3000 years old. Prehistoric Native Americans may have witnessed

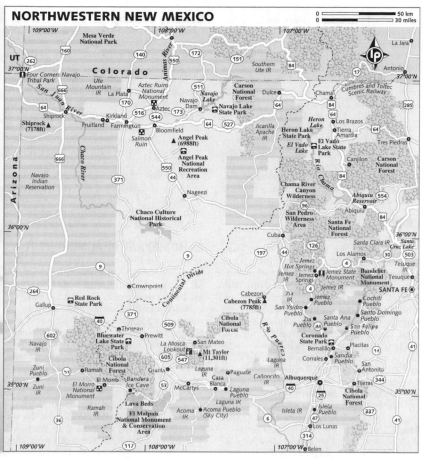

NORTHWESTERN NEW MEXICO

the final eruptions since local Indian legends refer to 'rivers of fire.' Scenic NM 117 leads modern-day explorers past cinder cones and spatter cones, smooth *pahoehoe* lava and jagged *aa* lava, ice caves and a 17-mile lava tube system.

El Malpais is a hodgepodge of National Park Service (NPS) land, private land, conservation areas and wilderness areas administered by the BLM. Each area has different rules and regulations which change from year to year. The **BLM** (☎ 287-7911) in Grants and the **BLM Ranger Station** (☎ 528-2918; NM 117; ⏲ 8:30am-4:30pm), 9 miles south of I-40, have permits and information for the Cibola National Forest. The **El Malpais Information Center** (☎ 783-4774; NM 53;

www.nps.gov/elma; ⏲ 8:30am-4:30pm), 22 miles southwest of Grants, is easiest to reach by phone. Staff can assist you when the BLM Ranger Station can't be reached. **El Malpais National Monument** (☎ 285-4641; www.nps.gov /elma; 123 E Roosevelt Ave, Grants; ⏲ 8am-4:30pm Mon-Fri) has permits and information for the lava flows and NPS land. Backcountry camping is allowed, but a free permit is required.

Sights & Activities

Though the terrain can be difficult, there are several opportunities for **hiking** through the monument. An interesting but rough hike (wear heavy shoes or boots) is the 7.5-mile (one way) **Zuni-Acoma Trail**, which leaves from NM 117 about 4 miles south of the ranger station. The trail crosses several lava flows and ends at NM 53 on the west side of the monument. Just beyond **La Ventana Natural Arch**, visible from NM 117, 17 miles south of I-40, is the Narrows Trail, about 4 miles (one way). Thirty miles south of I-40 is Lava Falls, a 1-mile loop.

County Rd 42 leaves NM 117 about 34 miles south of I-40 and meanders for 40 miles through the BLM country on the west side of El Malpais. It passes several craters, caves and lava tubes (reached by signed trails) and emerges at NM 53 near Bandera Crater. Since the road is unpaved, it's best to have a high-clearance 4WD.

GRANTS
☎ 505 / pop 8800 / elev 6400ft

You can hear the sounds – boom, bust, bust, boom – if you listen carefully. They are the sounds of Grants' up-and-down history. These days it's simply a strip, with several motels that make it a convenient, albeit uninteresting, base from which to explore the region. Originally an agricultural center and railway stop founded in the 1880s, Grants experienced a major mining boom when uranium was discovered in 1950. The town is 75 miles due west of Albuquerque via I-40.

The **chamber of commerce** (☎ 287-4802, 800-748-2142; www.grants.org; 100 N Iron Ave; ☾ 9am-4pm Mon-Sat) and **Cibola National Forest Mount Taylor Ranger Station** (☎ 287-8833; 1800 Lobo Canyon Rd; ☾ 8am-noon & 1-5pm Mon-Fri) provide more detailed information if you need it.

In the same building, the **New Mexico Mining Museum** (☎ 287-4802; adult/child 7-18 yrs $3/2; ☾ 9am-4pm Mon-Sat) bills itself as the only uranium-mining museum in the world. Although the mine no longer operates because of decreased demand, it remains America's largest uranium reserve. You can go underground on a self-guided tour by elevator in a miner's cage.

The 11,301ft peak of **Mt Taylor** is the highest in the area, and the mountain offers great views and hiking. Head northeast on Lobo Canyon Rd (NM 547) for about 13 miles to where it changes into gravel USFS Rd 239. For a great view follow 239 and then USFS Rd 453 for another 3.3 miles to 11,000ft **La Mosca Lookout**, about a mile northwest of Mt Taylor's summit.

Sleeping & Eating
Cimarron Rose (☎ 783-4770, 800-856-5776; www.cimarronrose.com; 689 Oso Ridge Rd; ste $110-130; P ☒ ☒) Although it's 30 miles southwest of Grants, this B&B is conveniently located on NM 53 between El Malpais and El Morro in the Zuni Mountains. With hiking in the Cibola National Forest just off the 20-acre property, it's a peaceful and pleasant rural alternative to the chain hotels in Grants or Gallup. Cimarron Rose offers two Southwestern-style suites, with tiles, pine walls and hardwood floors (one has a kitchen).

El Cafecito (☎ 285-6229; 820 E Santa Fe Ave; breakfast $3-5, lunch & dinner $5-8; ☾ 7am-8:30pm Mon-Sat; P ☒ ☒ V ☒) Great local hang-out lively with families chowing down on enchiladas and burgers in a comfortable setting.

EL MORRO NATIONAL MONUMENT
Throughout history travelers have liked to leave their mark, as in 'Catherine was here.' El Morro is proof positive of that. Also known as 'Inscription Rock,' it's been a travelers' oasis for a few millennia. Well worth a stop, this 200ft sandstone outcrop is covered with thousands of carvings, from pueblo petroglyphs at the top (c 1250) to inscriptions by Spaniard conquistadors and Anglo pioneers.

To reach **El Morro** (☎ 783-4226; www.nps.gov/elmo; adult/child $3/free; ☾ 9am-5pm visitors center & bookstore, trail closes 4pm winter & 6:45pm summer), head 43 miles southwest of Grants or 52 miles southeast of Gallup on NM 53. Of the two trails that leave the visitors center, the paved, half-mile loop to **Inscription Rock** is wheelchair accessible. The unpaved 2-mile **Mesa Top loop trail** requires a steep climb to the pueblos. Trail access stops one hour before closing.

The only real area dining option is **Ancient Way Café** (☎ 783-4612; 4018 NM 53; dishes $6-10; ☾ 10am-6pm Mon-Sat, 10am-4pm Sun) in pleasant little Ramah, a few miles west of El Morro. It's a no-frills place, a place to sustain your metabolism rather than fill your soul. Think along the lines of hash browns, fry bread, pork chops and chicken strips.

GALLUP
☎ 505 / pop 20,200 / elev 6515ft

This crossroads feels like a real town; walk the downtown area – it's suffused with a Native American and wildish West feel. Gallup serves as the Navajo and Zuni peoples' major trading center. Because of that, you'll

NEW MEXICO ROAD TRIPS

find many trading posts, pawnshops, jewelry shops and arts-and-crafts galleries in the historic district. It's arguably the best place in New Mexico for top-quality goods at fair prices. Although Gallup's economy relies on trade and tourism, it's pretty darn quiet (especially in the winter). Gallup grew up in 1881 when the railroad arrived, and when coal was discovered soon thereafter, it remained an important mining town until the mid-20th century.

Developed in 1926, the famous Route 66 proudly struts its stuff here, serving as the main drag and running parallel to and south of I-40, the Rio Puerco and the railway line. Gallup is 68 miles due northwest of Grants via I-40.

Information

Library (☎ 863-1291; 115 W Hill Ave; ☺ 9am-8pm Mon-Fri, 9am-6pm Sat) Offers free internet access.
Chamber of Commerce (☎ 722-2228; 103 W Route 66; ☺ 8am-5pm Mon-Fri) Next to the Gallup Cultural Center; has a great permanent exhibit on the Navajo code talkers of WWII.

Sights

Gallup is lined with about 20 downtown structures of historic and architectural interest, all built between 1895 and 1938. Most are along 1st, 2nd and 3rd Sts between Route 66 and Hill Ave, and detailed in a brochure found at the visitor center. Among these is the small **Gallup Historical Museum** (☎ 863-1363; 300 W Route 66; admission by donation; ☺ 8:30am-3:30pm Mon-Fri), which occupies the renovated, turn-of-the-19th-century Rex Hotel.

The **Gallup Cultural Center** (☎ 863-4131, 722-3730; www.southwestindian.com; 201 E Route 66; ☺ 8:30am-4:30pm Mon-Fri) houses a small but well-done museum with Indian art, including excellent collections of both contemporary and old kachina dolls, pottery, sand painting and weaving. A 10ft-tall bronze sculpture of a Navajo code-talker honors the sacrifices made by many men of the

---

KICKIN' IT DOWN ROUTE 66 WEST OF ABQ

Never has a highway been so symbolic as **Route 66**. Snaking across the belly of America, this fragile ribbon of concrete pavement first connected the prairie capital of Chicago with the California dreamin' of Los Angeles in 1926. Along the way, lightning-bug towns sprouted up with neon signposts, motor courts and drive-ins, all providing the simple camaraderie of the road.

Called the 'Mother Road' in John Steinbeck's novel Grapes of Wrath, Route 66 came into its own during the Depression years, when hundreds of thousands of migrants escaping the Dust Bowl slogged westward in beat-up old jalopies painted with 'California or Bust' signs. Meanwhile unemployed young men were hired to pave the final stretches of muddy road. They completed the job, as it turns out, just in time for WWII.

Hitchhiking soldiers and factory workers traveled the route next. Then amid the jubilant post-war boom, Americans took their newfound optimism and wealth on the road, essentially inventing the modern driving vacation. And so the era of 'getting your kicks on Route 66' was born.

But just as the Mother Road hit her stride, President Dwight Eisenhower, a US army general who had been inspired by Germany's autobahn, proposed a new interstate system for the US. Slowly but surely, each of Route 66's 2200-plus miles was bypassed. Towns became ghosts and traffic ground nearly to a halt. The highway was officially decommissioned in 1984.

A movement for preservation of the Mother Road resulted in the **National Historic Route 66 Association** (www.national66.com). Every year another landmark goes up for sale, but more are rescued from ruin.

Today this phoenix-like highway relies on travelers daring enough to leave the interstate behind for a combination of blue-line highways and gravel frontage roads. You can still spy relics of the original road, stay in a jewel of a 1930s motor court, revel in sunsets over the Painted Desert or splash in the Pacific Ocean. This is not just your mother's Mother Road. It's yours.

New Mexico revels in all 475 miles of its Route 66 legacy. From quirky **Albuquerque** head west to **Grants** and hard-edged **Gallup**, the unofficial capital of Indian country. In addition to publishing a quarterly magazine, the active **New Mexico Route 66 Association** (☺ 224-2802; www .rt66nm.org; 1415 Central Ave NE, Albuquerque) has archives, news and event calendars on its website.

Navajo Nation in WWII. A tiny theatre screens films about Chaco Canyon and the Four Corners region.

Six miles east of town, beautiful **Red Rock State Park** (☎ 722-3839; 8:30am-4:30pm Mon-Fri) has a little museum with modern and traditional Indian crafts, hiking, a campground and a **trading post** (☎ 863-9330; 7am-6pm). Call the trading post to make camping reservations.

Festivals & Events

Thousands of Native Americans and tourists throng the streets of Gallup and the huge amphitheater at Red Rock State Park for **Inter-Tribal Indian Ceremonial Gallup** (first week of August). It includes a professional all-Indian rodeo, beautifully bedecked ceremonial dancers from many tribes and a powwow with competitive dancing. Book accommodations as far ahead as possible for this and several other annual events that fill hotel rooms quickly.

Sleeping & Eating

It's a seller's market during ceremonial week and other big events, when hotel and motel prices can double.

El Rancho (☎ 863-9311, 800-543-6351; www.elranchohotel.com; 1000 E Route 66; $69-86; P X R) Gallup's most historic hotel opened in 1937 and quickly became known as the 'home of the movie stars.' Many of the great actors of the '40s and '50s stayed here including Humphrey Bogart, Katharine Hepburn and John Wayne. El Rancho features a superb Southwestern lobby, a restaurant, a bar and an eclectic selection of 76 simple rooms, including suites that sleep up to six. Next door, a modern 23-room motel is under the same ownership and has cheaper, though less-interesting, rooms.

Earl's Restaurant (☎ 863-4201; 1400 E Route 66; dishes $6-15; 6am-9pm Mon-Fri, 7am-9pm Sat; P X V) Earl's has been serving great green chile and fried chicken (but no alcohol) since the late 1940s. And the locals know it, as this fast-food, dinerlike place is packed on weekends. Perhaps you'll even get some shopping done here; Navajos sell goods at the eatery to tourists passing through.

Coffee House (☎ 726-0291; 203 W Coal Ave; dishes under $10; 7am-10pm Mon-Thu, until 11pm Fri & Sat; P X V) With local art on the walls, overstuffed couches and newspapers, this place has the feel of a small college-town hang-out. But there's no mistaking its Southwestern roots – a pressed-tin ceiling and a historic building speak to that. As you might imagine, it serves strong espresso, soups, chicken salads, turkey sandwiches and homemade desserts.

El Rancho Restaurant (☎ 863-9311; 1000 E Route 66; breakfast & lunch $6-12, dinner $6-24; 6:30am-10pm; P X V) For real old-world Western atmosphere, this hotel eatery rules. Photos of old-time movie stars plaster the walls; heavy furniture dots the landscape. It's straight out of a movie set. As for the food, it tends towards upscale diner grub like pancakes, burgers and steaks.

ZUNI PUEBLO

This pueblo, 35 miles due south of Gallup via NM 602, is well known for its jewelry. You can buy beautiful pieces at little shops throughout the town along NM 53. Other than that, there's not much going on, which is precisely why you might want to spend a little time driving around its housing developments. It'll give you a bare bones hint of modern reservation life, albeit from the outside looking in.

Information is available from the extremely helpful **Zuni Tourism Program Office** (☎ 782-7238; 8:30am-5:30pm Mon-Fri, 10am-4pm Sat & Sun), which dispenses photography permits. The office also offers daily tours ($10 to $200, depending on the tour and the number of people), walking past stone houses and beehive-shaped mud ovens to the massive **Our Lady of Guadalupe Mission**, featuring impressive locally painted murals of about 30 life-sized kachinas. The church dates from 1629, although it has been rebuilt twice since then. The program office can also arrange for a traditional meal to be cooked for groups of 10 or more ($10 per person) with advance reservations.

The **Ashiwi Awan Museum & Heritage Center** (☎ 782-4403; Ojo Caliente Rd; donation; 9am-5pm Mon-Fri) displays early photos and other tribal artifacts. Next door, **Pueblo of Zuni Arts & Crafts** (☎ 782-5531; 9am-6pm Mon-Fri, 9am-5pm Sat) sells locally made jewelry, baskets and other crafts.

The friendly **Inn at Halona** (☎ 782-4547, 800-752-3278; www.halona.com; 1 Shalako Dr; r $85; P X X) , decorated with local Zuni arts and crafts, is the only place to stay on the pueblo. Since each of the eight pleasant rooms is very different, try to check out as many as you can to see which fits your fancy. Full breakfasts are served in the common dining room or in the flagstone courtyard, weather permitting; room service is provided by the adjoining grocery store (where you check in).The inn is located behind Halona Plaza, south from NM 53 at the only four-way intersection in town.

FARMINGTON & AROUND

☎ 505 / pop 38,000 / elev 5400ft

Well sited for an overnight, Farmington is 123 miles north of Gallup. Farmington, the region's largest town, serves as a pleasant base for excursions to nearby sites. Farmington itself has nice parkland on the San Juan River, a quaint downtown and some good trading posts, but most visitors hang around because they're visiting Shiprock, Salmon Ruin and Aztec Ruins (p220) just a few miles from Farmington. It's also the best place to stay when visiting the remote and desolate Chaco Culture National Historical Park (p220), located about two hours' drive south of Farmington.

Information

Farmington Museum (☎ 599-1174; ⏲ 8am-5pm Mon-Sat) At the visitors bureau.

Library (☎ 599-1270; 2101 Farmington Ave; ⏲ 9am-7pm Mon-Thu, 9am-5pm Fri-Sat, 1-5pm Sun) Free internet access.

Visitors Bureau (☎ 326-7602, 800-448-1240; www .farmingtonnm.org; 3041 E Main; ⏲ 8am-5pm Mon-Fri)

Sights & Activities

Shiprock, a 1700ft-high volcanic plug and a lofty landmark for Anglo pioneers, is also a sacred site to the Navajo. It rises eerily over the landscape west of Farmington. It's certainly visible from US 64, but there are better views from US 666 and Indian Hwy 13, which almost skirts its base.

An ancient pueblo similar to the Aztec Ruins, **Salmon Ruin & Heritage Park** (☎ 632-2013; adult/child 6-16 yrs $3/1; ⏲ 8am-5pm Mon-Fri, 9am-5pm Sat & Sun) features a large village built by the Chaco people in the early 1100s. Abandoned, resettled by people from Mesa Verde and again abandoned before 1300, the site is named after George Salmon, an early settler who protected the area. Check out the adjoining park, which has remains

of the Salmon homestead, petroglyphs, a Navajo hogan, an early Puebloan pithouse, a teepee and a *wickiup* (a rough brushwood shelter). To reach it, take US 64 east toward Bloomfield.

Several trading posts offer high-quality Indian crafts, including Navajo rugs. **Fifth Generation Trading Company** (☎ 326-3211; 232 W Broadway; ⏲ 9am-5:30pm Mon-Sat), founded in 1875, displays a big selection.

E3 Children's Museum (☎ 599-1425; 302 N Orchard St; ⏲ noon-5pm Tue-Sat) features a play room for kids under six and science exhibits on topics like dinosaurs, magnetism and light designed for kids under 12.

Riverside Nature Center (☎ 599-1422; Animas Park; ⏲ 1-6pm Tue-Sat, 1-5pm Sun; admission free, fees for some special programs), a constructed wetland off Browning Pkwy, is home to more than 100 species of birds and other wildlife. Daytime and evening programs include guided nature walks, birding tours and hands-on workshops.

Sleeping & Eating

Knights Inn (☎ 325-5061; 701 Airport Dr; r $45; P ⊠ ⊠) This place, with 21 large rooms and weekly rates, has the cheapest, simplest and cleanest rooms in town. It fits the bill, nothing more, nothing less.

Silver River Spa Retreat & Adobe B&B (☎ 325-8219, 800-382-9251; www.silveradobe.com; 3151 W Main St; r $115-175; P ⊠ ⊠) Three miles from downtown, this lovely two-room cottage offers a peaceful respite among the trees on the San Juan River. Fall asleep to the sound of the river, wake to organic blueberry juice and enjoy a morning walk to the prairie dog village. The additional guesthouse is attractively rustic, made of adobe and timbers.

Kokopelli's Cave (☎ 325-7855; www.bbonline.com /nm/kokopelli; r $220-260; P ⊠) For something truly unique, this incredible 1650-sq-ft cave is carved 70ft below the surface into the sandstone above La Plata River. Equipped with a kitchen stocked for breakfast and lunch, a VCR with videos and a hot tub, this spacious cave dwelling offers magnificent views over the desert and river. The isolation is magnificent. It requires a 1.5-mile drive on dirt roads and a short hike to reach it.

Main Street Bistro (☎ 334-0109; 122 N Main St; dishes under $10; ⏲ 7am-4pm Mon-Fri, 7am-noon Sat; P ⊠ ⅍ V ⅍) Yes! It seems like such a simple request: great coffee and a muffin to match. But it's all too rare outside Santa Fe, Taos and Albuquerque. This wonderful place has vegetarian sandwiches, good quiches and creative soups. You might just want to move in.

Three Rivers Eatery & Brewhouse (☎ 324-2187; 101 E Main St; dishes $7-26; ☺ 11am-10pm Mon-Sat, noon-9pm Sun; P ⊠ ⚅ V ♿) Managing to be both trendy *and* kid-friendly, this hippish place has good food and its own microbrews. If you're really hungry, try the tantalizing full rack of hickory-smoked ribs ($26). More moderate appetites will be sated with any of the spiffy sandwiches and soups.

Clancy's Pub (☎ 325-8176; 2703 E 20th St; dishes $8-16; ☺ 11am-10pm; P ⊠ ⚅ V ♿) Popular with 20- and 30-somethings, Clancy's offers a fine selection of imported beers to wash down hefty hamburgers, Mexican food and other pub grub. Or get more exotic at the dinnertime sushi bar. Dine inside, where the rock music is loud, or on the patio (overlooking, unfortunately, a strip).

AZTEC
☎ 505 / pop 6400 / elev 5600ft

Although Aztec is primarily on the traveler's map because of the reconstructed Great Kiva at Aztec Ruins, the old downtown of Aztec still has several interesting buildings from the turn of the 19th century, many on the National Register of Historic Places. Cruise the pleasant tree-lined residential district too.

NM 516 from Farmington (14 miles northeast) becomes Aztec Blvd through town and continues as NM 173 toward Navajo Lake State Park. For more details, the **visitors center** (☎ 334-9551, 888-838-9551; www.aztecnm.com; 110 N Ash; ☺ 8am-5pm Mon-Fri) is helpful.

An alternative to the bigger and more visited sites like Chaco (below) and Mesa Verde, the 27-acre **Aztec Ruins National Monument** (☎ 334-6174; www.nps.gov/azru; adult/child 15 & under $5/free; ☺ 8am-5pm, until 6pm Jun-Aug, closed Thanksgiving, Dec 25, Jan 1) features the largest reconstructed kiva in the country, with an internal diameter of almost 50ft. Let your imagination

---

DETOUR: CHACO CULTURE NATIONAL HISTORICAL PARK

Chaco, the center of a culture that extended far beyond the immediate area, was connected to Aztec (above) and Salmon Ruins (p219) by carefully engineered 30ft-wide roads. Very little of the road system is easily seen today, but about 450 miles have been identified from aerial photos and ground surveys. Clearly, this was a highly organized and integrated culture.

The **park** (www.nps.gov/chcu; per vehicle/bike $8/4; ☺ sunrise-sunset) contains massive and spectacular Puebloan buildings, evidence of 5000 years of human occupation, set in a remote high-desert environment. The largest building, Pueblo Bonito, towers four stories tall and may have had 600 to 800 rooms and kivas. None of Chaco's sites have been reconstructed or restored. If you like isolation and using your imagination, few places compare. If you've visited Mesa Verde in Colorado, you may be disappointed here, especially considering how long it takes to reach the site. You'll need a whole day for a trip here.

Be sure to check the website in advance for any road closures. All park routes involve rough and unpaved dirt roads, which can become impassable after heavy rains or snow. Park rangers prefer that visitors enter via NM 44/US 550 on the north side. About three miles south of the Nageezi Trading Post on NM 44/US 550 and about 50 miles west of Cuba, turn south at mile marker 112.5 on CR 7900, which is paved for 5 miles. Continue on the marked unpaved county road for 16 miles to the park entrance. Because this route includes 20 miles of rough dirt roads, it is not recommended for RVs, and can be very difficult and slippery for any vehicle during rains.

Park facilities are minimal – no food, gas, auto repair or supplies. The nearest provisions are along NM 44, 21 miles from the **visitors center** (☎ 786-7014; www.nps.gov/chcu; ☺ 8am-5pm), where free backcountry hiking permits (no camping) are available. Inquire here about night sky programs (April to October).

The 49-site **Gallo Campground** ($10), 1 mile east of the visitor center, operates on a first-come, first-served basis and is often full by 3pm April to October. There are no hookups and no showers, but toilets, grills and picnic tables are available. Bring your own wood or charcoal. Water is available at the visitors-center parking lot only.

wander as you sit inside the Great Kiva. Rangers give early afternoon talks at the c AD 1100 site about ancient architecture, trade routes and astronomy during the summer months. They're very informative.

The small but excellent **Aztec Museum & Pioneer Village** (☎ 334-9829; 125 N Main Ave; donations requested; ☺ 9am-5pm Mon-Sat, 10am-4pm winter) features an eclectic collection of historical objects, including telephones, barbershop chairs and a great display of late-19th-century regional photographs. Outside, a small 'pioneer village' shows off original or replica early buildings, such as a church, jail and bank.

Built in 1907 as the American Hotel, **Miss Gail's Inn** (☎ 334-3452, 888-534-3452; www.cpt net.com/~missgail; 300 S Main St; r $58-88 incl breakfast; ⓟ ✗) is a historic and ramshackle two-story brick structure decorated with early photographs and period pieces. Rooms may be too frilly and Victorian for some folks; others may think them charming and sweet.

Stop by for big portions of reasonably priced Mexican and American fare at the **Aztec Restaurant** (☎ 334 9586; 107 E Aztec Blvd; lunch $3-7, dinner $7-11; ☺ 6am-9pm; ⓟ ✗ ⓖ Ⓥ ⓖ), including a decent T-bone steak ($11).

CHAMA
☎ 505 / pop 1200 / elev 7880ft

Only recently has the small mountain community of Chama been ever so slightly rediscovered. Even with first-ever sidewalks, it still feels like an outpost. Sure, Indians lived and hunted here for centuries, and Spanish farmers settled the Chama River Valley in the mid-1700s, but it was the arrival of the Denver & Rio Grande Railroad in 1880 that really put Chama on the map. Although the railroad closed, the prettiest part later reopened as one of the most scenic train trips in the Southwest.

East of the Jicarilla Reservation, US 64 joins US 84, crosses over the Continental Divide and drops into Chama. Downtown is 1.5 miles north of the so-called Y junction of US 84/64 with NM 17. The main street is variously called Main, Terrace Ave or Hwy 17; the intersection, known as the Y, is the main reference point in town. A handy **information center** (☎ 756-2235; www .chamavalley.com; 2375 NM 17; ☺ 8am-6pm) is located at the Y.

Chama is 102 miles east of Farmington via US 64. It's another 89 beautiful miles east to Taos from Chama.

Sights & Activities
The **Cumbres & Toltec Scenic Railway** (☎ 756-2151, 888-286-2737; www.cumbresandtoltec.com) is the longest (64 miles) and highest (over the 10,015ft Cumbres Pass) authentic narrow-gauge steam railroad in the US. It's a beautiful trip through mountains, canyons and high desert, especially in September and October during fall foliage. Some carriages are fully enclosed; none are heated. Dress warmly.

The train runs between Chama and Antonito, Colorado, every morning from late May to mid-October. Several options for riding the train are offered. You can take a van to Antonito (a 1½-hour drive) and then take the six-hour train ride back to Chama (adult $59 to $72, child aged 2 to 11 $30 to $36, parlor car per person $15). Alternatively, go to the midpoint of Osier, Colorado, then return to your starting point (same fares, six hours). In July and August, on Thursdays only, the Cinder Express offers shorter rides (adult/child with box lunch $44/22). Whatever you do, make reservations two weeks in advance. A snack bar and rest room are available on board, and the train makes a lunch stop in Osier.

Several outfitters specialize in winter activities, including **Chama Ski Service** (☎ 756-2492; 1551 Alamo Rd); it can outfit you with skis and provide information on ski touring. You can park along the local highway, ski into pristine national-forest lands at a number of entry points, and often not cross paths with another person all day, but you need to know the best spots. It also provides backcountry touring equipment including snowshoe ($10 per day) and ski ($12 per day) rentals, and a nearby **rental cabin** (Porter's Guest House; www.mdvrentals.com; $130-160). **Cumbres Nordic Adventures** (☎ 888-660-9878; www.yurtsogood.com) offers backcountry ski tours in the snowy San Juan Mountains and deluxe backcountry yurt rentals for $100 to $115 per night.

Sleeping & Eating
Foster Hotel (☎ 756-2296; 393 S Terrace Ave; r $53; ⓟ ✗ ✗ ▢ ▣) If you're looking for local culture, look no further. Built in 1881 as a bordello, this hotel is the only building in Chama that wasn't wiped out by a massive

NEW MEXICO ROAD TRIPS

fire in the 1920s. A few of the rooms are said to be so haunted that the management doesn't rent them.

Elkhorn Lodge & Café (☎ 756-2105, 800-532-8874; www.elkhornlodge.net; NM 84; r low season/high $45/85, cabins low season/high $69/135; P ⊠ ⌂) Choose one of 22 simple but spacious motel rooms in the main log cabin or one of the 11 free-standing cabins with a kitchenette (great for families), then join other guests and the folks who run the lodge for a riverside chuck-wagon barbecue dinner on Saturday nights in summer (adult/child $18/9), when the evening includes old-time cowboy music.

Chama Trails Inn (☎ 756-2156, 800-289-1421; www.chamatrailsinn.com; 2362 NM 17; r $65-75; P ⊠) More than a roadside motel with wireless internet; has 16 rooms with character – thanks to an abundance of handmade Southwestern furniture, local artwork and hand-painted tiles. A few rooms are further warmed with a gas fireplace. A communal hot tub and sauna come in handy after hiking.

Gandy Dancer B&B (☎ 756-2191, 800-424-6702; www.gandydancerbb.com; 299 Maple Ave; r $119-149; P ⊠) Ensconced in an early 1900s house, this ultra-tasteful bird-watcher's haven offers seven pristine and stylish rooms, an outdoor hot tub and views. The helpful hosts provide information, wireless internet, breakfast, reservations and dinners (November to March) or box lunches on request.

High Country Restaurant & Saloon (☎ 756-2384; 2289 S NM 17; Sun breakfast buffet $9, lunch $6-11, dinner $8-24; ⊙ 11am-10pm Mon-Sat, 8am-10pm Sun; P ⊠ ⅋ Ⓥ ⅋) Wild West saloon serving burgers, Mexican food, steak and seafood.

CUBA
☎ 505 / pop 600 / elev 6950ft

Mountainous Cuba is a convenient stop on the way to or from Chaco Culture National Historical Park, since accommodations closer to Chaco are limited. Cuba is still about 50 miles from the turnoff to Chaco. Look for the **ranger station** (☎ 289-3265; ⊙ 7am-4:30pm Mon-Sat) and **visitors center** (☎ 289-3808; ⊙ 9am-1pm & 2-4pm Mon-Fri), both on NM 44.

Set in 360 beautiful acres in the Nacimiento Mountains 5 miles north of Cuba, just off US 550, friendly and recommended **Circle A Ranch** (☎ 289-3350; www.circlearanch.info; dm $25, s $35-55, d $50-70; ⊙ May–mid-Oct; P ⊠ ⌂) is a gem. The lovely old adobe lodge, with exposed beams, grassy grounds, lots of hiking trails and a

kitchen for guests, is peaceful and relaxing. Choose between private bedrooms (some with quilts and iron bedsteads), shared bunkrooms, or the apartment with living room, kitchen and space for four ($150).

Cuba is 102 miles south of Chama via US 84 east to NM 96 west. It's another 80 miles to Albuquerque from Cuba via US 550 east to I-25 south.

ROUTE 4: NORTHEASTERN NM

The Santa Fe Trail, along which pioneer settlers rolled in wagon trains, ran from New Mexico to Missouri. And you can still see the wagon ruts in some places off I-25 between Santa Fe and Raton. Because of this trade route, Las Vegas and Raton became important centers in the late 1800s, and both towns retain the flavor of that era in their many well-preserved buildings. If you're looking for a bit of the Old West without a patina of consumer hype, this is the place. Another scenic byway, Route 66 (p225), more or less parallels I-40 east; it's a nice stretch from Santa Rosa to Tucumcari. As if that weren't enough, the region is also dotted with small lakes and beautiful canyons. East of Santa Fe, the lush Sangre de Cristo Mountains give way to high and vast rolling plains.

LAS VEGAS & AROUND
☎ 505 / pop 14,656 / elev 6470ft

Not to be confused with its wild-n-crazy namesake in Nevada, Las Vegas is one of the loveliest towns in New Mexico. It has a strollable downtown, shady plaza and some 900 gorgeous buildings – most of them not adobe – listed in the National Register of Historic Places. The classic Western backdrop is the perfect spot for a high-noon shootout, an ambiance exploited in cowboy flicks like *Wyatt Earp* and *The Ballad of Gregorio Cortez*.

Home to the Comanche people for some 10,000 years, Las Vegas was founded by Mexico in 1835 as a stop along the Santa Fe Trail and later the Santa Fe Railroad. It quickly grew into one of the biggest, baddest boomtowns in the West.

Today Las Vegas retains a sienna-tinted elegance and social whirl, thanks in part to

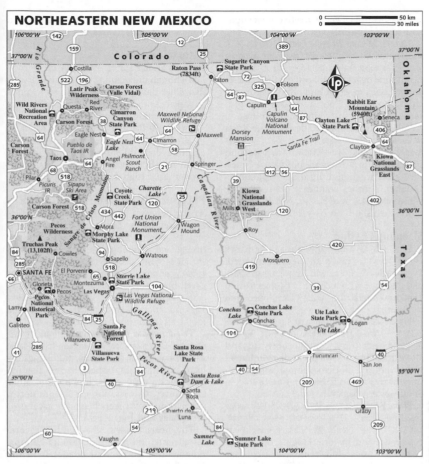

NORTHEASTERN NEW MEXICO

the city's two universities. It's the gateway to two wilderness areas: Pecos Wilderness and Las Vegas National Wildlife Refuge.

Las Vegas is about an hour east of Santa Fe on I-25 and three hours (90 miles) south of Angel Fire and the Enchanted Circle on NM 518, which makes for a great trip through backcountry New Mexico.

Information

Carnegie Public Library (☎ 454-1401; 500 National St; 8am-5pm Mon-Fri, 8am-noon Sat) Historic library with free internet access.

Chamber of commerce (☎ 425-8631, 800-832-5947; www.lasvegasnm.org; 701 Grand Ave; 9am-5pm Mon-Fri) Free maps, suggested walking tours and a wall of flyers.

Sights & Activities

Las Vegas' main in-town attraction is strolling the beautiful neighborhoods surrounding the plaza and Bridge St.

Rough Riders Memorial Collection (☎ 454-1401; 727 Grand Ave; donations appreciated; 9am-4pm Mon-Fri, plus 10am-3pm Sat & noon-4pm Sun summer) is a small, informative museum chronicling the fabled cavalry unit led by future US President Theodore Roosevelt in the 1898 fight for Cuba. More than one-third of the volunteer force came from New Mexico, and here you'll see their furniture, clothes and military regalia.

Santa Fe Trail Interpretive Center & Museum (☎ 425-8803; 125 Bridge St; admission free; 10am-3pm Mon-Sat) features vintage photos and unique artifacts from Las Vegas' heyday as a rough-and-tumble trading post.

Tapetes de Lana Weaving Center (☎ 426-8638; www.tapetesdelana.com; 1814 Old Town Plaza; admission free; 🕙 8am-5pm Mon-Fri, 10am-5pm Sat) is a non-profit rural development project that teaches area villagers to weave and offers visitors the chance to watch. Your purchases help preserve small, self-sustaining communities.

Take a break from the desert in **Las Vegas National Wildlife Refuge** (☎ 425-3581; 🕙 refuge dawn-dusk daily, office 8am-4:30pm Mon-Fri), a wetland preserve with a driving loop, nature hikes, rare waterfowl and hunting September-October, 6 miles southeast of town: take I-25 to exit 345, head east on NM 104 for 1.5 miles, then south on Hwy 281 for 4 miles.

Sleeping & Eating

El Fidel (☎ 425-6761; 500 Douglas St; r/ste $62/84; P X X 🖳) This is an elegant, if faded, 1920s belle of a hotel, with character to spare and a lounge with a coffee bar (open 8am to 7pm) and a pub, the Wolff's Den (open 6pm to 11pm).

Inn on the Santa Fe Trail (☎ 425-6791, 888-448-8438; 1133 N Grand Ave; r $80-105; P X X 🖳 🖳) A good restaurant, central courtyard and shaded grounds anchor this well-maintained place with 30 modern rooms (some with microwaves and refrigerators) decorated in Southwestern hacienda-style.

Plaza Hotel (☎ 425-3591, 800-328-1882; www .plazahotel-nm.com; 230 Old Town Plaza; d & ste incl break-fast $129-179; P X X 🖳) Las Vegas' most celebrated and historic lodging opened in 1882 and was carefully remodeled a century later. The elegant brick building now offers 36 comfortable accommodations in antique-filled rooms with wireless internet.

Cheap eats are along Mills Ave, but look downtown to find local favorites, most concentrated around the plaza and Bridge St.

Semilla Natural Foods (☎ 425-8139; 510 University Ave; 🕙 10am-6pm Mon-Fri, 10am-5pm Sat; & V 🛦) This natural grocery outpost has organic treats galore.

Estella's Café (☎ 454-0048; 148 Bridge St; dishes $4-8; 🕙 11am-3pm Mon-Wed, 11am-8pm Thu & Fri, 11am-7pm Sat; P X & V 🛦) Estella's devoted patrons treasure the homemade New Mexican fare offered by the Gonzalez family since 1950 in this crowded gem.

Charlie's Bakery & Cafe (☎ 426-1921; 715 Douglas St; dishes $5-12; 🕙 6:30am-5:30pm Mon-Sat, 7am-3pm

Sun; P X & V 🛦) Cheerful, casual and usually crowded, thanks to a great bakery.

Entertainment

Byron T's Saloon (☎ 425-3591; 230 Plaza; 🕙 noon-2am) Though the nightlife can't compare with that *other* Las Vegas, mosey on over to this cozy place with live music Thursday through Sunday evening at the Plaza Hotel.

Fort Union Drive-In (☎ 425-9934; 3300 7th St; 🕙 May-Sep) One of New Mexico's few remaining drive-in movie theatres lies just north of town and has great views of the surrounding high desert.

PECOS NATIONAL HISTORICAL PARK

At the gateway to the **Pecos Wilderness**, administered by the Las Vegas Ranger Station and with almost unlimited opportunities for hiking and camping, is this historical **park** (☎ 737-6414; www.nps.gov/peco; per person $3; 🕙 9am-4:30pm), centered on the windswept remains of a well-preserved 700-room pueblo, including a rebuilt kiva and spectacularly dilapidated 1717 mission. All are reached along a 1-mile loop trail from the visitors center.

The **Pecos-Las Vegas Ranger Station** (☎ 757-6121; NM 63; 🕙 8am-5pm Mon-Fri, 8am-4:30pm Sat in summer) has flyers, free maps and listings for local outfitters that specialize in fishing, horseback riding, rock climbing and other adventures. Cowles, about 18 miles north, is where serious hikers begin the ascents of **Pecos Baldy** and **Truchas Peak**.

The nearby town of Pecos has several restaurants and accommodations options, ranging from a handful of motels to the **Pecos Benedictine Monastery** (☎ 757-6415; www .pecosmonastery.org; NM 63; s $65-75 donation), which has small hermitage rooms perfect for the aspiring ascetic looking for a retreat.

CIMARRON

☎ 505 / pop 900 / elev 6430ft

Cimarron has a wild past. Once a stop on the Santa Fe Trail, it attracted gunslingers, train robbers, desperados, lawmen and other Wild West figures like Kit Carson, Buffalo Bill Cody, Annie Oakley, Wyatt Earp, Jesse James and Doc Holliday. The old St James Hotel alone saw the deaths of 26 men within its walls. Today, Cimarron is a peaceful and serene village with few street signs. Poke around to find what you need, or ask the friendly locals. The **chamber of**

KICKIN' IT DOWN ROUTE 66 EAST OF ABQ

Due east of Albuquerque, Santa Rosa and Tucumcari were once key stops along old Route 66. Today, freeways mean most travelers don't travel Route 66, but since most hotels and restaurants still lie along the old Route 66, you'll be traveling the mother road for services. Still, there's not much going on here, these days, though.

Santa Rosa

The **Santa Rosa Chamber of Commerce** (☎ 472-3763, www.santarosanm.org; 486 Route 66; 🕑 8am-5pm Mon-Fri) has more information than you'll ever need.

Santa Rosa's modern claim to fame is, oddly enough, as the scuba-diving capital of the Southwest. One of the 10 best spots to dive in the country is the bell-shaped, 81ft-deep **Blue Hole**. Get permits from the **dive shop** (☎ 472-3370; 🕑 8am-5pm Sat & Sun), located right at the hole.

The **Route 66 Auto Museum** (☎ 472-1966; 2766 Old Route 66; adult/child under 10 $5/free; 🕑 7:30am-6pm May-Aug) pays homage to the mother of all roads. It boasts upwards of 35 cars from the 1920s through the 1960s, all in beautiful condition, and lots of 1950s memorabilia. It's a fun place; enjoy a milkshake at the '50s-style snack shack.

Route 66 nostalgia lines the walls of popular **Joseph's Bar & Grill** (☎ 472-3361; 865 Route 66; dishes $6-12; 🕑 7am-10pm; P ✕ ⚫ V), family owned since its inception in 1956. Many of the bountiful Mexican and American recipes (like country fried steak; $9) have been handed down through the generations. Burgers and steaks are as popular as anything smothered in green chile. Joseph's also mixes the best margaritas on Route 66.

Tucumcari

The biggest town on I-40 between Albuquerque (173 miles west) and Amarillo (114 miles east), Tucumcari boasts one of the best-preserved sections of the myth-laden road. Not surprisingly, it still caters to travelers with inexpensive motels, several classic Route 66 buildings and souvenir shops like the Tee Pee Curios. A **chamber of commerce** (☎ 461-1694; www.tucumcarinm.com; 404 W Tucumcari Blvd) keeps sporadic hours.

Several rooms of the **Tucumcari Historical Museum** (☎ 461-4201; 416 S Adams St; adult/child $2.50/0.75; 🕑 8am-5pm Mon-Sat) consist of reconstructions of early Western interiors, such as a sheriff's office, a classroom and a hospital room. It's an eclectic collection, to say the least, displaying a barbed-wire collection alongside Indian artifacts.

Well worth a visit is the **Mesalands Dinosaur Museum** (☎ 461-3466; 222 E Laughlin St; adult/child $5.50/3; 🕑 10am-6pm Tue-Sat), which showcases real dinosaur bones and has hands-on exhibits. Casts of dinosaur bones are done in bronze (rather than the usual plaster of paris), which not only shows fine detail, but also makes them works of art.

Listed on the State and National Registers of Historic Places the beautifully restored Route 66 **Blue Swallow Motel** (☎ 461-9849; www.blueswallowmotel.com; 815 Route 66 Blvd; s $38-41, d $43-71; P ✕ ⚫ 🖳) has a great lobby and a neon sign that's been featured in many articles about Route 66.

If your arteries can take the hardening, chicarones (fried pork skins) are a **Rubees** (☎ 461-1463; 605 W Tucumcari Blvd; dishes $4-8; 🕑 7am-7pm Mon-Fri, 7am-4pm Sat & Sun; P ✕ ⚫ V 🍴) New Mexican specialty.

Del's Restaurant (☎ 461-1740; 1202 Route 66 Blvd; dishes $5-15; 🕑 7am-9pm Mon-Sat; P ⚫ V 🍴) is popular in these here parts for its hearty salad bar.

Odeon Theater (☎ 461-0100; 123 S 2nd St; adult/child $5/4) is a renovated, cool old place screening movies.

For weekend drinks and dancing, **Lizard Lounge** (☎ 461-0500; Best Western Pow Wow Inn, 801 W Tumcumcari Blvd) has two-steppin' to live country and western.

NEW MEXICO ROAD TRIPS

DETOUR: ONWARD TOWARD TRES PIEDRAS

From Chama take US 84/64 11 miles south to see the spectacular cliffs in scenic **Brazos Canyon**. Stay a while in extreme privacy. Set on 400 acres heading into the canyon, the handsome **Timbers at Chama** (☎ 588-7950; www.thetimbersatchama.com; NM 512; r $200, guesthouse with kitchen $225; ☒) has an authentic mountain lodge aesthetic, five double rooms and a private cabin; rates include a hearty breakfast.

Just south of Los Brazos in Los Ojos, visit **Tierra Wools** (☎ 588-7231 888-709-0979; www.handweavers .com; 91 Main St; r $65-85), a 100-year-old weaving cooperative in a rustic, century-old building. On weekends, village artisans carry on the Hispanic weaving tradition, hand spinning, dying and weaving. In addition to a two-suite guesthouse, Tierra Wools also offers weaving classes (March to October).

From tiny TA (as Tierra Amarilla is locally known), head east on scenic US 64 over a 10,000ft pass in the Tusas Mountains to Taos, 80 miles away. This road is closed in winter.

---

commerce (☎ 376-2417; www.cimarronnm.com; NM 64; ♥ 9am-5pm Mon-Fri) has a bit of information (phone before visiting).

Most historic buildings lie south of the Cimarron River on NM 21. Find the historic **St James Hotel** and you'll find the old town plaza, Dold Trading Post, the Santa Fe Trail Inn (which dates to 1854), Schwenk's Gambling Hall, a Wells Fargo Station, the old jail (1872) and the **Old Mill Museum** (Aztec Mill; admission $2; ♥ Jun-Aug), built in 1864 as a flour mill. Today it houses historical photographs and local memorabilia.

The town is located on US 64, 54 winding miles east of Taos and 94 (mostly speedy) miles north of Las Vegas.

Sleeping & Eating

Casa del Gavilan (☎ 376-2246, 800-428-4526; www .casadelgavilan.com; NM 21; r incl hot breakfast $80-110, guesthouse $140; ℗ ☒) This magnificent Pueblo Revival–style house, built in 1908 and set on 225 acres, offers four double rooms decorated with Southwestern antiques and art. Complete with high ceilings, vigas and thick adobe walls, the house is a treat. A two-room guesthouse sleeps up to four people.

St James Hotel (☎ 376-2664, 866-472-5019; www .stjamescimarron.com; NM 21; historic rooms $95-130, modern rooms $70-150; ℗ ☒ ☒) A saloon in 1873, this well-known place was converted into a hotel in 1880 and then renovated 100 years later. It's a toss up between the 13 simple historical rooms or the modern annex, which has 10 rooms equipped with TVs and phones. Within the hotel, you'll find a decent midrange restaurant and a cozy bar with a pool table. Just for fun, count the bullet holes in the period pressed-tin ceiling. Dorothy, you're not in Kansas anymore.

Directory

CONTENTS

ACCOMMODATIONS

Accommodations range from the disturbingly downscale to the obscenely luxurious, running $450 or more a night for every possible amenity. Don't discount B&Bs, practically an art form in prime destinations, where there are good midrange deals as well as luxury properties. There are also plenty of wackier options, like earthships and old communes, and a decent network of hostels. RV parks and campsites are plentiful, but keep in mind that nights are cold from October through May.

Lodging isn't cheap, and this book defines budget rooms as under $100 per night; midrange $100 to $175; and top-end $175 and over. Don't be afraid to bargain. If your road karma is good (tipping hotel staff helps), you may be able to talk proprietors down on weekdays and in off-season, particularly at luxury properties. Too shy? When you're quoted a rate, simply ask, 'Do you have

anything cheaper?' AARP, AAA and other discounts are also common, so ask. You can also ask for discounts on multinight stays. One caveat: late summer and the Christmas holidays are high season. Make reservations as far in advance as possible.

B&Bs

B&Bs run the gamut from glorified hotels ($100) to absolutely stunning antique-filled properties ($150 and up), complete with full hot breakfasts, fabulous amenities and evening refreshments. The **New Mexico Bed & Breakfast Association** (☎ 800-661-6649; www.nmbba.org) has listings and links for statewide B&Bs.

Campsites & RV Parks

RV parks, most of which allow tent camping, are plentiful and usually located on the outskirts of town. Campgrounds on public lands generally run $10 per night for tent sites and $17 to $20 with hookups. Not all public campgrounds have running water. Backcountry camping is free. The ranger stations administrating each region are noted throughout the text. Check for fire restrictions before you camp. Most Santa Fe National Forest sites do not allow charcoal or wood fires during the season. The Public Lands Information website publishes a daily 'Know Before You Go' newsletter that includes all restrictions and has maps and guides for hiking trails.

The **Public Lands Information Center** (Map p62; ☎ 505-438-7542, 877-276-9404; www.publiclands .org; 1474 Rodeo Rd, Santa Fe; ☼ 8:30am-4:30pm Mon-Fri) has information on all outdoor recreation including camping, biking, hiking, caving and fishing. You can't reserve campsites on federal land, but **New Mexico State Parks** (Map pp64-5; ☎ 505-476-3355, 888-667-2757, reservations 877-664-7787; www.nmparks.com; 141 E DeVargas St, Santa Fe; campsite/RV $10/14; ☼ 8am-5pm Mon-Fri) takes reservations for the 29 state parks that allow camping.

If you're on a budget and looking for free accommodations, there's the **CouchSurfing Project** (http://couchsurfing.com), where you can find a couch to crash on worldwide. The 'project' touts 86,000 members from 205 countries. It's a relaxed way to learn about the local culture and exchange resources.

For information on renting an RV, see p242.

Hostels

Hostels are few and far between, but all are festive and fairly well kept, with bunks running about $15 to $25 per night, private rooms about $25 to $35 a night. None have lockout and all offer full use of kitchen facilities. Those covered in this book:

Abominable Snowmansion (p157) In Arroyo Seco, north of Taos.

Circle A Ranch/Hostel (p222) In Cuba, near Bandelier National Monument.

River Bend Hot Springs (p199) In Truth or Consequences, south of Albuquerque.

Route 66 Hostel (p181) In Albuquerque.

Sandia Mountain Hostel (p182) In Sandia Crest, north of Albuquerque.

Santa Fe International Hostel (p95) In Santa Fe.

Hotels & Resorts

Hotels on the commercial strip, further from downtown, usually run $80 to $150 a night, but those within walking distance of the plaza are much pricier, with basic rooms starting at $150 a night and reaching up into the stratosphere.

Invariably decorated in the Southwestern style, they often have pools, on-site restaurant-bars, in-room coffeemakers and a continental breakfast. Kitchenettes and fireplaces are often available for around $20 more, while basic suites run $40 to $50 extra.

For resort-style accommodations with Pueblo Revival architecture, spas, concierges, fireplaces and generally better locations, expect to tack on an extra $75 – at least. True resorts (those out in the country) can include everything from horseback riding and childcare to natural hot springs. Prices vary widely.

Motels

Motels tend to be well kept and basic, and in ski areas they often have rooms sleeping six, a great deal for a group or family.

Motels are generally less expensive the further you are from downtown, and often offer a continental breakfast, replete with plastic-wrapped pastries. The cheapest motels, including many on Central Ave in Albuquerque and in central Española, may also serve as flophouses for down-on-their-luck locals. Seasoned budget travelers who don't mind those conditions can get rooms for under $40. Most entries listed in this book hover around $75, with prices skyrocketing in high season.

Rental Properties

Many people maintain vacation homes near Taos and Santa Fe, which they rent out through various agencies. Rentals range from tiny adobe casitas to huge ranch-style homes, and you'll get better deals by staying a week or more. Some agencies:

Kokopelli Property Management (☎ 505-988-7244, 888-988-7244; www.kokoproperty.com)

Management Group (☎ 505-982-2823, 866-982-2823; www.santaferentals.com)

Santa Fe Stay (☎ 505-820-2468, 800-995-2272; www.santafestay.com)

BUSINESS HOURS

Many businesses close entirely on Sunday or, at the very least, keep shorter hours. Small businesses may also close for lunch. Particularly in rural areas, but even in Santa Fe, businesses may close for a day or week unannounced – hey, everyone needs a vacation. Businesses geared to tourism and museums (particularly in Taos) may also keep shorter hours in winter and other off-season periods.

Shops and galleries are generally open 9am to 5pm Monday through Saturday and noon to 5pm on Sunday, but sometimes they take off Sunday or Monday completely; some galleries keep longer hours Friday evening for art openings. Bars are usually open from 11am until 2am Monday through Saturday, closing at midnight Sunday by law.

Restaurant hours vary widely, and many close from 2pm to 5pm – ah, siesta culture. Most restaurants close early, around 9pm or 9:30pm; even bars close their kitchens at that time.

Indian pueblos may close to visitors with just a few hours' notice for religious purposes. Casinos are open 8am to 4am Sunday through Thursday, and remain open round the clock from Thursday morning until Sunday night. On feast days, almost all businesses at that particular pueblo are closed.

CHILDREN

New Mexico is an extremely kid-friendly destination. Between the strong Catholic and hippie traditions, most folks are comfortable with rambunctious children just about anywhere. Local parents are quick to recommend sights, activities and restaurants to visitors, so don't be shy. Lonely Planet's *Travel with Children* has lots of tips and advice for keeping kids happy and healthy on the road.

Practicalities

Museums and other attractions generally offer discounts for children (the age varies widely, however) as well as a range of children's activities. Only the most exclusive restaurants will turn up their noses at kids, and a high proportion have children's menus.

Some B&Bs do not accept children, but this is more the exception than the rule. Call ahead. Many other lodging options have large family rooms and casitas with kitchenettes, hide-a-beds and even playgrounds outside. In larger cities, services will send sitters to your hotel room; check the yellow pages.

New Mexico Kids Childcare Resource & Referral (☎ 505-277-7900, 800-691-9067; www.newmexicokids .org) helps parents find childcare in New Mexico and has a comprehensive list of licensed providers. Breastfeeding is legal and, in general, acceptable throughout New Mexico.

Keep in mind that children are more sensitive to sunburn, dehydration and altitude sickness than adults: slather them with sunscreen and make sure they wear hats and are getting enough liquids. Allow them to acclimate for a few days before taking on any serious activities.

Ensure that they stay well away from sick or dying animals, particularly groundhogs and other rodents, many of which carry diseases.

Most car-rental companies (p240) lease child-safety seats, but they don't always have them on hand; reserve in advance if you can.

Sights & Activities

Every newspaper and free weekly includes listings for children's events and activities. Pick up the free bi-monthly **New Mexico Kids!**

(www.newmexico-kids.com), which has information on kids' stuff in Albuquerque and throughout the state, and the quarterly *Tumbleweeds,* covering Santa Fe and the surrounding area.

Brief rundowns of attractions geared toward kids are included in the Santa Fe (p89), Taos (p146) and Albuquerque (p179) chapters.

New Mexicans take pride in their tricultural community, and showcase Native American culture, Hispanic history and Anglo arts with a focus on inclusiveness and understanding, making it a great place to inoculate your children against smallmindedness while they're still young.

Outdoor activities are another highlight: between oddball opportunities like llama excursions and hot-air balloon rides, and short hiking trails that feature not only wildlife but also petroglyphs and caves, your child will remember this vacation for a long time.

CLIMATE CHARTS

Don't like New Mexico weather? Just wait a minute. This is a land of extremes, and in fall or spring you may have snow on the ground in the morning and T-shirt weather by afternoon. Even summer visitors should bring jackets. For more information, check out p12.

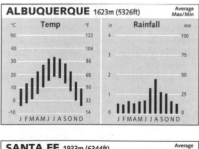

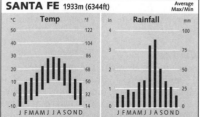

DANGERS & ANNOYANCES
Crime
New Mexico ranks near the bottom of US states in personal income, yet it attracts wealthy tourists who often flash their cash around. You do the math.

Yep, New Mexico ranked (in 2000) as the third worst state in the USA for overall crime, second for burglary, fifth for murder. Sure, you'll be helping support the local economy if you park your gear-packed car in an isolated spot (this most definitely includes trailheads) or carry all your cash in a cute handbag, but why not buy more art instead? Keep the car clean, and stash emergency money and credit card contact information somewhere other than your wallet – perhaps in your luggage or under the seat of your car.

Rio Arriba County, just north of Santa Fe, has the highest rate of heroin overdose in the country (in 2004 anyway). While the situation is improving, don't count on criminals to be predictable, just desperate. And though Chimayó and Española get most of the press, drug addiction and the attendant criminal activity is a statewide problem. Stay alert.

Weather
Desert temperatures are extremely variable, easily varying by 50°F (28°C) between day and night. Carry an extra layer when hiking, even in summer. Don't underestimate the effects of dehydration: you may not realize how much you're sweating (it evaporates quickly) and become disoriented. Folks have died getting lost on a day hike. No kidding. Bring and drink a gallon of water per person, per day.

Thunderstorms roll in regularly, but not exclusively, on summer afternoons, when you should try to be below the tree line at higher elevations. And even if you haven't had a drop of rain, a wall of water can come barreling down a dusty arroyo with little or no warning. Never camp in anything resembling a waterway, no matter what the forecast.

Wildfires
Between the drought, the piñon bark beetle and long-term fire suppression, New Mexico is currently undergoing a massive ecosystems overhaul, courtesy of Mother Nature and morons who flick cigarettes out of cars. Wildfires over the past few years have been devastating.

The **National Interagency Fire Center** (www .nifc.gov) has up-to-date information on wildfires and regions affected. And for heaven's sake, make sure your campfire is absolutely, 100% completely out.

Wildlife
Scorpions and tarantulas in this region are not deadly, though they do leave nasty welts. More worrisome are potentially deadly (particularly for kids) black widow and brown recluse spiders, both of which enjoy outhouses and other shady spots. If bitten, get to a doctor.

Rattlesnakes, with diamond-shaped markings, easily have enough venom to kill. They enjoy sunbathing on rocks and roads on chilly mornings, when you're most likely to surprise them. Generally they strike only when threatened, so just give them their space. If bitten, refer to the Health chapter for first-aid instructions, and get to a hospital as quickly as possible.

Black bears can be pesky but are smart enough not to bother you. If you see one up close, back away slowly, speaking softly, to let them know you mean no harm. Pack up all foodstuffs when you leave a campsite, and don't leave any food, toothpaste or other tasty-smelling treats in the tent.

DISABLED TRAVELERS
Although laws requiring all businesses to be wheelchair-accessible are in place, centuries-old areas like downtown Santa Fe and Taos still have some prohibitively narrow sidewalks and doorways. Steps are being taken, if slowly, to live up to regulations.

Public parking is free for anyone with a disabled placard. Most better hotels maintain at least one wheelchair-accessible room, and guide dogs are welcome at all businesses. Some B&Bs keep pets and livestock, and while legally bound to accept your well-behaved pooch, owners may be uncomfortable with how their own animals will act. Call first.

The **Governor's Commission on Disability** (☎ 505-827-6465, 877-696-1470, TTD 505-883-0381; www.gcd.state.nm.us; 491 Old Santa Fe Trail) lists accessibility resources on their website. The New Mexico State Parks TTD is ☎ 800-659-1779 or 800-659-8331.

New Mexico's **Adaptive Ski Program** (☎ 505-995-9858; www.adaptiveski.org), at Santa Fe Ski Basin and Sandia Ski Park, offers lessons including special equipment, if required, for folks with a wide range of disabilities. Make reservations two weeks in advance for lessons ($50 to $65).

Wheelchair Getaways (☎ 505-247-2626, 800-408-2626; www.wheelchairgetaways.com), in Albuquerque, rents wheelchair-accessible vans.

DISCOUNT CARDS

Many motels and hotels offer discounts to holders of **AAA** (☎ 800-874-7532; www.aaa.com) and **AARP** (☎ 800-424-3410; www.aarp.org) cards, while student IDs can often score you savings at attractions.

The **Traveler Discount Guide** (☎ 800-222-3948; www.roomsaver.com) is available at any visitors center or by internet, and contains coupons (many downloadable) offering substantial savings on chain hotels.

The **New Mexico Department of Tourism** (www.newmexico.org) has a free visitors' guide and the New Mexico Discount Card, which has deals on more than 400 businesses.

FESTIVALS & EVENTS

New Mexico loves a good party, and special events involving everything from upscale wine tastings and studio tours to motorcycle rallies and exploding 50ft-tall puppets are just part of the fun. For more information, see Santa Fe (p91), Taos (p146) and Albuquerque (p180). Newspapers, visitors' guides and free weeklies provide much more comprehensive listings.

FOOD

New Mexican cuisine is a highlight of any visit. The Food & Drink chapter (p53) has a rundown on all the delicious dishes waiting in store. You can fill up at budget spots for under $10, while midrange restaurants serve quality cuisine in the $10 to $20 range. Top-end spots start at $20 for dinner, but often serve the same fine food far more cheaply at lunch.

GAY & LESBIAN TRAVELERS

Gays and lesbians can travel more openly in northern New Mexico than almost anywhere else in the country, though sadly hate crimes are not unknown. Unless it will compromise your integrity, consider refraining from public displays of affection in quiet neighborhoods after dark, particularly in rural areas. Neither Taos nor Santa Fe (p107) has a real 'gay scene,' but Albuquerque (p186) has a few gay and lesbian bars, and the Nob Hill area has a cluster of gay-friendly businesses. But the region is so integrated that establishing gay neighborhoods has never really been necessary.

Good national guidebooks include *Damron Women's Traveller*, providing listings for lesbians; *Damron Men's Travel Guide*, for men; and *Damron Accommodations*, with listings of gay-owned or gay-friendly accommodations nationwide. All three are published by the **Damron Company** (☎ 415-255-0404, 800-462-6654; www.damron.com).

National resources include **National AIDS/HIV Hotline** (☎ 800-232-4636; www.ashastd.org), **National Gay/Lesbian Task Force** (☎ 202-393-5177; www.thetaskforce.org) in Washington, DC, and **Lambda Legal Defense Fund** (☎ NYC office 212-809-8585, LA office 213-382-7600; www.lambdalegal.org).

With the exception of Massachusetts (which recognizes gay marriage), New Mexico boasts the most comprehensive legal protection in the country for gays and lesbians, going so far as to guarantee equal treatment not only for sexual orientation but also sexual identity. Several organizations have more information:

Albuquerque Pride (☎ 505-873-8084; www.abqpride.com) Links to New Mexico resources.

Coalition for Gay & Lesbian Rights in New Mexico (www.qrd.org/qrd/www/usa/nm/coalition)

Parents, Families & Friends of Lesbians & Gays (☎ 505-424-8951; www.pflag.org)

HOLIDAYS

On some religious holidays, like Christmas and Easter, some businesses close for a week, about how long it takes to walk to Chimayó.

New Year's Day January 1
Martin Luther King Jr Day Third Monday in January
Presidents' Day Third Monday in February
Easter A Sunday in March or April
Memorial Day Last Monday in May
Independence Day July 4
Labor Day First Monday in September
Columbus Day/Dia de la Raza Second Monday in October
Veterans Day November 11
Thanksgiving Fourth Thursday in November
Christmas December 25

DIRECTORY

INTERNATIONAL VISITORS
ENTERING THE COUNTRY
Welcome to Fortress USA: security protocols at all points of entry into the country are tightening, with new procedures being added almost monthly. These range from increasingly invasive baggage checks and searches to stricter visa requirements. Contact your US embassy or log on to the US Department of Homeland Security's website for **Customs & Border Protection** (www.customs .ustreas.gov) for the latest safety and security measures, and expect long waits at the airport.

Passports
At press time, seven nations were identified by the US government as state sponsors of terrorism: North Korea, Cuba, Syria, Sudan, Iran, Iraq and Libya. Visitors from these countries must fill out giant stacks of paperwork and arrange an interview with a US consulate. If you have passport stamps from these countries, you will not be automatically denied entry into the USA, but it will probably be noted.

New Mexico has three border crossings with Mexico, but the most convenient is at El Paso, Texas, and Ciudad Juarez, Chihuahua. Mexican nationals and travelers from other countries must have a passport (and nonimmigrant visa) to cross into the USA. Because of the Terrorism Prevention Act of 2004, Canadians and US citizens must now have a valid passport to enter/re-enter the United States by air or sea.

Visas
Visitors from all countries must have a valid passport to enter the United States and many visitors also must have a US visa.

Citizens of these 27 countries can participate in the Visa Waiver Program, which allows visitors with round-trip, nonrefundable tickets to visit for 90 days without a visa: Andorra, Australia, Austria, Belgium, Brunei, Denmark, Finland, France, Germany, Iceland, Ireland, Italy, Japan, Liechtenstein, Luxembourg, Monaco, the Netherlands, New Zealand, Norway, Portugal, San Marino, Singapore, Slovenia, Spain, Sweden, Switzerland and the UK.

As of October 2004 all visitors on this program must have a Machine Readable Passport (MRP) to participate, which includes your biographical information digitally encoded into the passport. Otherwise you will need a nonimmigrant visa. Check with the State Department Visa Services (http://travel.state.gov) for the latest information.

If you need a visa, begin the procedure as early as possible. Many foreign nationals who could previously obtain visas by mail are now required to report to a US embassy for a personal interview, which may need to be scheduled weeks in advance. Reports of regular visitors to the USA being suddenly denied visas have become ridiculously common. Plan ahead.

International Driver's License
An International Driving Permit is a useful accessory for foreign visitors in the USA. Local police are more likely to accept it as valid identification than an unfamiliar document from another country. Your national automobile association can provide one for a nominal fee. They're usually valid for one year.

Customs
US Customs allows each person over the age of 21 to bring 1L of liquor and 200 cigarettes duty-free into the USA, and non-US citizens can bring in $100 in gifts and US$10,000 in cash, traveler's checks and money orders; you must declare excess amounts. Visitors must also declare all purchases and gifts received while in the USA when leaving the country; bring your receipts. Each person is allowed to transport $800 worth of goods duty-free. For more information, contact the **US Custom Service Albuquerque Field Office** (☎ 505-346-6425).

EMBASSIES & CONSULATES
USA Embassies & Consulates
Some US diplomatic offices abroad:
Australia Canberra (☎ 02-6214-5600, 21 Moonah Pl, Yarralumla ACT 2600); Sydney (☎ 02-9373-9200, MLC Centre, Level 10, 19-29 Martin Pl, Sydney NSW 2000); Melbourne (☎ 03-9526-5900, 553 St Kilda Rd, Melbourne, Victoria)

Canada Ottawa (☎ 613-238-5335, 490 Sussex Dr, Ottawa, Ontario K1N 1G8); Vancouver (☎ 604-685-4311, 1095 W Pender St, Vancouver, BC V6E 2M6); Montréal (☎ 514-398-9695, 1155 Rue St-Alexandre, Montréal, Québec H3B 3Z1)
France (☎ 01 43 12 22 22, 2 Ave Gabriel, 7582 Paris Cedex 08)
Germany (☎ 30-8305-0, Neustädtische Kirchstrasse 4-5, 100117 Berlin)
Ireland (☎ 1-668-8777, 42 Elgin Rd, Ballsbridge, Dublin 4)
Israel (☎ 3-5197575, 71 Hayarkon St, Tel Aviv 63903)
Japan (☎ 3-3224-5000, 1-10-5 Akasaka, Minato-ku, Tokyo 107-8420)
Mexico (☎ 5-080-2000, Paseo de la Reforma 305, Colonia Cuauhtémoc, 06500 Mexico City)
New Zealand (☎ 64 4 462 6000, 29 Fitzherbert Tce, Thorndon, Wellington)
Spain Madrid (☎ 91587- 2200, Serrano 75, 28006 Madrid); Barcelona (☎ 93 280 22 27, Paseo Reina Elisenda de Montcada 23, 08034 Barcelona)
UK London (☎ 020-7499-2000, 24 Grosvenor Sq, London W1A 1AE); Edinburgh (☎ 031-556-8315, 3 Regent Tce, Edinburgh EH7 5BW); Belfast (☎ 28-9038-6100, Danesfort House, 223 Stranmillis Rd, Belfast BT9 5GR)

Other US embassies and consulates can be found on the government's website at http://us embassy.state.gov.

Embassies & Consulates in New Mexico
Most countries maintain embassies in Washington, DC. The closest consulates for the UK, Canada, France, Italy and Australia are in Los Angeles or Houston (and the addresses and contact information always seem to change). The **New Mexico Council on International Relations** (☎ 505-982-4931; www.santafecouncil.org; 227 E Palace Avenue, Suite D) in Santa Fe provides welcoming services.
German Consulate (☎ 505-796-9600; mesersmith@aol.com; 4801 Lang Ave NE, Ste 110, Albuquerque 87109)
Japanese Consulate (☎ 505-293-2322; ikukosnm@aol.com; Albuquerque 87123)
Mexican Consulate (☎ 505-247-2147; 1610 4th St NW, Albuquerque 87102)

MONEY
US currency is based on the dollar. Bills come in denominations of $1, $5, $10, $20, $50 and $100. The dollar is divided into 100 cents. Coins are the penny or cent (1 cent), nickel (5 cents), dime (10 cents), quarter (25 cents) and half-dollar (50 cents). Dollar coins and two-dollar bills are rarely used.

Traveler's checks can be changed at any bank, and most banks in Santa Fe, Taos and Albuquerque will exchange foreign currency. ATMs are common, and you can use debit cards at most businesses, including restaurants.

PRACTICALITIES
- The USA uses the National TV System Committee (NTSC) color TV standard, which is incompatible with other standards (PAL or SECAM) used in Africa, Europe, Asia and Australasia.

- The USA uses 110V and 60 cycles, and the plugs have two (flat) or three (two flat, one round) pins. Most European appliances will require voltage converters and plug adapters.

- Distances are in feet (ft), yards (yds) and miles (m or mi). Three feet equal 1 yard; 1760 yards or 5280 feet equal 1 mile (1.61 kilometers).

- Dry weights are in ounces (oz), pounds (lb) and tons (16 ounces are 1 pound; 2000 pounds are 1 ton), but liquid measures differ from dry measures. One pint equals 16 fluid ounces; 2 pints equal 1 quart, a common measure for liquids like milk, which is also sold in gallons (4 quarts).

- Gasoline is dispensed in US gallons, about 20% smaller than imperial gallons. Pints and quarts are also 20% smaller than imperial ones. There is a conversion chart on the inside front cover of this book.

DIRECTORY

INSURANCE

Medical care in the United States is prohibitively expensive, and while New Mexico has clinics and programs for uninsured people, you'll be taking a serious risk with both your health and pocketbook if you go without travel insurance. Health insurance, discussed further on p243, is imperative.

Travel insurance should cover you for medical expenses, emergency care and evacuations, luggage theft or loss, cancellations or delays in your travel arrangements, and everyone should be covered for the worst possible case, such as an accident requiring hospital treatment and a flight home. Buy insurance as early as possible, and take a copy of your policy, in case the original is lost.

INTERNET ACCESS

Almost every New Mexico library offers internet access for free or a nominal charge. Youth hostels, visitors centers and senior centers also often offer internet access. Most New Mexico branches of Kinko's/FedEx offer 24-hour internet access ($12 per hour). Internet cafés, which charge similar prices, are a growing business, but are hard to find outside Santa Fe, Taos and Albuquerque.

LEGAL MATTERS

If you are stopped by the police for any reason, remember that there is no system of paying fines on the spot, and offering to do so constitutes bribery. Smile, be friendly and cooperate, and provide photo identification when asked. If you are arrested, you have the right to remain silent until speaking to an attorney, and are presumed innocent until proven guilty. Note that all pueblos and Indian reservations are basically sovereign nations, with their own police and laws.

You must be 16 years old to drive, 21 years old to drink alcohol, and are considered a drunk driver at 0.08% blood alcohol content – roughly two alcoholic drinks. Ask the bartender to call you a cab.

Marriage licenses are easier to get in New Mexico than a taxi: the bride and groom must each appear in person and present a driver's license, passport or birth certificate, plus $25 in cash, to the **Santa Fe County Clerk's Office** (☎ 505-986-6280; 102 Grant Ave; ☾ 8am-5pm Mon-Fri). That's it – no blood test, and no need for residency – the clerk's office will even help find a judge.

MAPS

The maps provided in this book are fine for paths more traveled, and all visitors centers stock free maps of varying (usually subpar) quality. Folding street maps, usually $4 at any gas station, are a good investment. *The Horton Family Map,* a locally produced atlas of street maps covering Santa Fe and the surrounding communities, is worthwhile if you'll be in the area for a while.

If you plan to get out into the wilderness, the *New Mexico Road & Recreation Atlas* is indispensable. The **Delorme Mapping Company** (☎ 207-846-7100; www.delorme.com) publishes great atlas-style state maps for about $20 – nothing compares for delving into backcountry roads. Serious hikers should get regional USGS topos; these are available at ranger stations and map stores, or for free online through **LANL** (http://sar.lanl .gov/maps_by_name.html).

Travel Bug (Map pp64-5; ☎ 505-992-0418; www .mapsofnewmexico.com; 328 S Guadalupe St), in Santa Fe, and **Holman's** (Map pp170-1; ☎ 505-449-3810; 6201 Jefferson St NE), in Albuquerque, have the best selections of maps in the state.

POST

Postage rates increase every few years, and at press time it cost 39¢ for letters and 24¢ for postcards. International rates were 84/75¢ for letters/postcards, slightly less to Canada and Mexico. For rates and zip-code information, contact the **United States Postal Service** (☎ 800-275-8777; www.usps.gov).

Mail (poste restante) can be sent general delivery to any post office that has its own five-digit zip code. Mail is usually held for 10 days before it's returned to sender; request that your correspondents write 'hold for arrival' on their letters. Mail should be addressed like this:

Name
c/o General Delivery
Albuquerque, NM 87106.

SENIOR TRAVELERS

Travelers aged 50 years and older can expect to receive cut rates and benefits. Be sure to inquire about such rates at hotels, museums and restaurants. The National Park Service issues Golden Age Passports that cut costs greatly for seniors. Other organizations worth looking into include the following:

American Association of Retired Persons (AARP; ☎ 888-687-2277; www.aarp.org) This advocacy group for Americans 50 years and older is a good resource for travel bargains.

Elderhostel (☎ 800-454-5768; www.elderhostel.org) This nonprofit organization offers folks 55 years and older one- to three-week tours throughout the USA and Canada, including meals and accommodations.

Grand Circle Travel (☎ 617-350-7500, 800-959-0405; www.gct.com) This group offers escorted tours and travel information, mainly for mature travelers.

SOLO TRAVELERS

Travel, including solo travel, is generally safe and easy. In general, women need to exercise more vigilance in large cities than in rural areas. Everyone, though, should avoid hiking, cycling long distances or camping alone, especially in unfamiliar places. For more safety advice, see Women Travelers (p236) and Dangers & Annoyances (p230).

TELEPHONE

Currently New Mexico uses only the 505 area code but may introduce the 575 area code for areas outside Albuquerque and Santa Fe before this book is updated. If so, a recorded message will tell you how to re-direct your call.

All phone numbers within the USA consist of a three-digit area code followed by a seven-digit local number. If you are calling locally, just dial the seven digit number. If you are calling long distance, dial 1 + the three-digit area code + the seven-digit number. If you're calling from abroad, the international country code for the USA is ☎ 1.

For nationwide directory assistance, dial ☎ 411.

The 800, 888 or 877 area codes are for toll-free numbers within the USA; some work from Canada. Call ☎ 800-555-1212 to request a company's toll-free number. The 900 area code is for numbers for which the caller pays a premium rate.

Local calls usually cost 50¢ at pay phones, and hotels often add a hefty surcharge for local calls made from their rooms. The best plan is to invest in a phone card, which allows purchasers to pay $5, $10, $20 or $50 in advance, with access through an 800 number. Rates vary widely, so be sure to ask.

To make an international call direct, dial ☎ 011 + the country code + the area code + the phone number.

TIME

The Southwest is on Mountain Time, which is seven hours behind Greenwich Mean Time. When it's noon in Santa Fe, it's 11am in Los Angeles, 2pm in New York City, 7pm in London and 4am in Sydney. Daylight saving time begins on the first Sunday in April, when clocks are put forward one hour, and ends on the last Sunday in October, when the clocks are turned back one hour.

TOILETS

Relatively speaking, it's not hard to go in New Mexico – as long as you don't mind wandering freely into a hotel or resort and availing yourself of the facilities (generally without fear of being stopped.) As a general rule, gas stations and convenience stores are your best bet, though. Public toilets are few and far between, and even when you do eventually find them, you will find you probably don't really want to use one.

TOURIST INFORMATION

State and regional tourist offices include the following:

Indian Pueblo Cultural Center (www.indianpueblo .org) Schedules of events and dances, plus cultural information, for all 19 Indian pueblos.

New Mexico Department of Tourism (www.new mexico.org) Information and links to accommodations, attractions and other great websites.

New Mexico's Cultural Treasures (www.nmculture .org) A fabulous searchable and comprehensive listing of every last museum and cultural attraction.

North-Central New Mexico Guide (www.new mexiconorth.com) Museums, missions, landmarks and pueblos, plus links and recommended driving tours in the Santa Fe–Taos region.

TOURS

Several tour operators provide a range of guided tours catering for both groups and individuals; most tours cost less if you share accommodations.

Known World (☎ 800-983-7756; www.knownworld guides.com) Enjoy outdoor adventures – including bike treks, fly-fishing, rafting and kayaking – with vegetarian meals.

Open Roads, Open Minds (☎ 530-345-7825; www
.openroadsopenminds.com) Tour Anasazi ruins and
modern Native communities via steam train, raft and
muleback.

Rojo Tours & Services (☎ 505-474-8333; www.rojo
tours.com) Arranges corporate, group and custom trips to
Native American sites, artist studios, outdoor attractions
and more.

Royal Road Tours (☎ 505-982-4512; www.royal
roadtours.com; 826 Camino del Monte Rey, Ste A-3, Santa
Fe) A nonprofit agency with customized group tours empha-
sizing art, architecture and historical sites.

Santa Fe Destinations (☎ 505-995-4525; www.santa
fedestinations.com; 309 W San Francisco St, Santa Fe)
Specializes in providing groups of 10 to 1200 with upscale
packages.

World Outdoors (☎ 303-413-0938, 800-488-8483;
www.theworldoutdoors.com) Raft the Taos Box, bike the
Enchanted Circle and hike, too.

WOMEN TRAVELERS

The first thing female visitors younger
than, say, 70, will notice upon visiting New
Mexico are the wide variety of catcalls from
passing cars. Generally, this is not meant to
be threatening; in fact, loosely translated it
means, 'Golly, you're attractive.'

There are three ways to deal with it: smile
(may invite further interaction), become
frustrated and indignant (may cause high
blood pressure) or ignore it (recommended).
Or you could stay in your hotel room.

Women should note that New Mexico
ranks third in the country for reported
rapes, so take all the precautions you would
in a major city downtown, no matter how
quaint-seeming the village: park in well-
lit areas, stick to populated neighborhoods
after dark and trust your gut at the bar.

Transportation

CONTENTS

GETTING THERE & AWAY

The region covered by this book has been isolated by geography, which is why it's such a fascinating, relatively untouched place. To reach these settlements along the Rio Grande – basically a long, slender oasis through an otherwise sparsely populated desert – you're either going to spend several hours on the road or rails from other US population centers, traversing some fairly boring stretches of scrub, or take a plane.

AIR

Unless you live in or near the Southwest, flying to the region and renting a car is the most time-efficient option.

Airports & Airlines

The main hub for all air travel in New Mexico is the low-key Albuquerque International Sunport.

ALBUQUERQUE INTERNATIONAL SUNPORT

The attractive Pueblo Revival–style **Albuquerque International Sunport** (ABQ; ☎ 505-244-7700; www.cabq.gov/airport; 2200 Sunport Blvd) is easy to navigate, with two small terminals, lots of art and a visitors center on the 2nd floor. Though the Sunport doesn't offer connecting flights to Santa Fe or Taos, bus shuttles make the run to both cities several times daily.

Eight major carriers and two regional airlines serve the Sunport. More than half of all flights are operated by **Southwest Airlines** (☎ English 800-435-9792, Spanish 800-826-6667; www.southwest.com), which serves most of the country from here. The following are others serving Albuquerque, along with their most popular direct flights:

American (☎ 800-433-7300; www.aa.com) Chicago and Dallas–Fort Worth.

Continental (☎ 800-525-0280; www.continental.com) Newark and Houston, connecting to international flights.

Delta (☎ 800-221-1212; www.delta.com) Salt Lake City, Cincinnati and Atlanta, connecting to international flights.

Frontier (☎ 800-432-1359; www.flyfrontier.com) Denver.

Great Lakes (☎ 800-554-5111; www.flygreatlakes .com) Silver City and Clovis.

Mesa Air (☎ 800-637-2247; www.mesa-air.com) Colorado Springs and several New Mexico cities including Roswell, Carlsbad and Farmington.

Northwest (☎ 800 225 2525; www.nwa.com) Minneapolis-St Paul, connecting to international flights.

United (☎ 800-241-6522; www.united.com) Denver, Los Angeles, San Francisco and San Antonio, connecting to international flights.

US Airways (☎ 800-235-9292; www.usairways.com) Phoenix and Las Vegas, Nevada.

There are eight rental-car agencies at the Sunport. Note that you'll pay an extra 10% concession fee for the privilege of renting

---

THINGS CHANGE

The information in this chapter is particularly vulnerable to change – prices, routes and schedules change, special deals come and go, and rules and visa requirements are amended. Check directly with the airline or travel agency to make sure you understand how a fare (or a ticket you may buy) works. Get opinions, quotes and advice from as many airlines and travel agencies as possible before you part with your hard-earned cash. The details given in this chapter should be regarded as pointers: they are not a substitute for careful, up-to-date research.

CLIMATE CHANGE & TRAVEL

Climate change is a serious threat to the ecosystems that humans rely upon, and air travel is the fastest-growing contributor to the problem. Lonely Planet regards travel, overall, as a global benefit, but believes we all have a responsibility to limit our personal impact on global warming.

Flying & Climate Change

Pretty much every form of motorized travel generates CO_2 (the main cause of human-induced climate change), but planes are far and away the worst offenders, not just because of the sheer distances they allow us to travel, but because they release greenhouse gases high into the atmosphere. The statistics are frightening: two people taking a return flight between Europe and the US will contribute as much to climate change as an average household's gas and electricity consumption over a whole year.

Carbon Offset Schemes

Climatecare.org and other websites use 'carbon calculators' that allow travelers to offset the level of greenhouse gases they are responsible for with financial contributions to sustainable travel schemes that reduce global warming – including projects in India, Honduras, Kazakhstan and Uganda.

Lonely Planet, together with Rough Guides and other concerned partners in the travel industry, support the carbon offset scheme run by climatecare.org. Lonely Planet offsets all of its staff and author travel. For more information check out our website: www.lonelyplanet.com.

---

directly from the airport. Consider renting from these agencies' city locations, many of which will drop off the car to any Albuquerque address. For more off-site choices, see p240.

Advantage (☎ 505-247-1066; www.arac.com) With an additional location near UNM.

Alamo (☎ 800-327-9633; www.alamo.com)

Avis (☎ English 800-331-1212, Spanish 800-874-3556; www.avis.com) With an additional location near UNM.

Budget (☎ 800-527-0700; www.budget.com) With several other Albuquerque locations.

Dollar (☎ 800-800-4000; www.dollar.com)

Enterprise (☎ 800-736-8222; www.enterprise.com) With several other Albuquerque locations.

Hertz (☎ 800-654-3131; www.hertz.com)

National (☎ 800-227-7368; www.national.com)

Thrifty (☎ 800-847-4389; www.thrifty.com) With another office right down the street from the airport.

Albuquerque's public bus system, SunTran, serves the airport, while **Airport Shuttle** (☎ 505-765-1234) and **Sunport Shuttle** (☎ 505-883-4966, 866-505-4966) both run between the Sunport and Albuquerque addresses from 4am to 11pm.

Several shuttles make the run from the Sunport to Santa Fe:

Faust Transportation (the airport ☎ 505-758-3410, 888-830-3410; www.newmexiconet.com/trans/faust/faust.html; ticket $25; ☉ 7am-7pm) Also connects to Taos ($50).

Sandia Shuttle Express (☎ 888-775-5696; www.sandiashuttle.com; ticket $25; ☉ 7am-6pm)

Santa Fe Shuttle (☎ 888-833-2300; www.shuttlesantafe.com; ticket $23; ☉ 8am-8pm)

Twin Hearts Shuttle (☎ 800-654-9456; ticket $20; ☉ 7am-9pm) Also to downtown Albuquerque and to Taos ($45). Call for reservations at least 24 hours in advance.

SANTA FE MUNICIPAL AIRPORT

This slightly larger **airport** (SAF; ☎ 505-955-2908; 2511 Camino Entrada) is served only by **Great Lakes Air** (☎ 505-473-4118, 800-554-5111; www.greatlakesav.com), a United Airlines partner, with two to three flights a day to Denver International Airport for $250 to $350 round-trip.

Two car-rental agencies are located at this airport: **Avis** (☎ 505-471-5892, 800-331-1212; www.avis.com; Airport Rd) and **Hertz** (☎ 505-244-7211, 800-654-3131; www.hertz.com; Aviation Dr). **Roadrunner Shuttle** (☎ 505-424-3367; one way/round-trip $15/26) meets all incoming planes and provides service to any Santa Fe address.

LAND
Bus

Greyhound (☎ 800-231-2222; www.greyhound.com), the USA's major bus service, operates throughout New Mexico in conjunction with **Texas New Mexico & Oklahoma** (TNM&O; ☎ 806-763-5389; www.tnmo.com), a regional carrier that has expanded to cover parts of

Colorado, Kansas and Wyoming. Buses connect many larger cities and will drop you off in smaller towns along the way.

Meal stops, usually in inexpensive and unexciting cafés, are made on long trips; you pay for your own food. Buses have on-board toilets, and seats recline for sleeping. Smoking is not permitted. Long-distance bus trips are often available at bargain prices if you purchase or reserve tickets in advance.

Tickets can be bought over the phone or online with a credit card and mailed to you if purchased 10 days in advance. They can also be picked up at the terminal with proper identification. Greyhound terminals also accept traveler's checks and cash. Reservations are made with ticket purchases only.

Fares vary tremendously. Sometimes you can get discount tickets if you buy them three, seven or 21 days in advance. At press time, tickets ran between $10 and $35 for travel within New Mexico, $60 for any journey under 1000 miles and $129 to $199 for any journey of 1000 to 3000 miles, if purchased two weeks in advance. Generally, bus terminals are served by local public buses, but take a cab to your hotel if you arrive after dark.

GREYHOUND DISCOVERY PASSES

These passes offer unlimited travel on Greyhound buses and other regional carriers. US citizens pay between $250 for seven days and $700 for 60 days, with discounts for students and seniors.

Foreign tourists can buy International Discovery Passes, which are about 20% cheaper, usually online or through a travel agency. A variety of passes covering different regions of the USA and Canada are accepted by many regional carriers. TNM&O honors AmeriPass (covering the USA) and CanAmPass (which includes Canada).

Car

Two major interstates cross in Albuquerque. I-25 (north–south) roughly traces the old Camino Real, connecting Taos with Mexico City. From Albuquerque, I-25 South runs 270 miles (four hours), officially ending at the USA–Mexico border crossing at El Paso, Texas, and Ciudad Juárez, Chihuahua. The road continues to Ciudad Chihuahua and points south as M-45D.

From Santa Fe, I-25 North actually dips southeast for a 65-mile (one-hour) drive to Las Vegas, New Mexico, then turns north for a 300-mile (five-hour) stretch to Denver, Colorado, and points north.

Interstate 40 (east–west) runs basically from sea to shining sea, connecting Albuquerque to Los Angeles, California, via an 800-mile, 12-hour slog passing Flagstaff, Arizona, and the Grand Canyon (330 miles, 5½ hours). Heading east, I-40 runs 1800 miles to Durham, North Carolina, just a few hours from the Atlantic Ocean.

Train

Amtrak (☎ 800-872-7245; www.amtrak.com) runs its *Southwest Chief* between Chicago and Los Angeles daily, with stops in **Las Vegas** (☎ 800-872-7245); **Lamy** (☎ 505-466-4511), 18 miles south of Santa Fe; and **Albuquerque** (☎ 505-842-9650; 214 1st St SW). Travel within the state runs from $20 to $30 one way.

Tickets should be booked in advance. Only the Albuquerque station has regular facilities, and trains stop in Lamy and Las Vegas, New Mexico, only if you have purchased a ticket in advance. You can arrange a shuttle in advance between Lamy and Santa Fe.

For non US citizens, Amtrak offers various USA Rail Passes that must be purchased outside the USA (check with a travel agent).

GETTING AROUND

New Mexico has a fairly well-developed bus system, augmented by private shuttles that can get you around the corridor between Albuquerque, Santa Fe and Taos, including the (pricey) option of arranging transport into the immediate wilderness areas. At press time, plans were afoot to operate a train between Albuquerque and Santa Fe. That said, renting a car is by far the quickest and easiest way to see the state, and the only way you'll be able to see many smaller towns and pueblos.

AIR

The Albuquerque International Sunport (p237) is the major air hub for New Mexico and offers connecting flights to cities throughout the region. **Mesa Air** (☎ 800-637-2247; www.mesa-air.com) serves several New

Mexico cities including Roswell, Carlsbad and Farmington.

You can catch shuttles to Santa Fe from the Sunport, but to fly into Santa Fe Municipal Airport (p238) you'll have to make the connection in Denver.

BICYCLE

Bicycle activism is huge in New Mexico, where you'll spot stickers reading 'Bikes not Bombs' and 'One Less Car' plastered all over cycles competing with cars for the roadways. Urban areas, in particular Albuquerque, have developed elaborate bike paths and multiuse trails, and most public buses have front-loading bicycle racks.

Scenic highways, including the Enchanted Circle and the Turquoise Trail, are popular among road bikers, and some locals traverse the entire state without internal combustion year-round.

The state boasts some of the finest mountain biking anywhere, including summertime downhill runs in ski areas, which keep their lifts open for the occasion. Several outfitters offer guided bicycle trips.

A couple of caveats to this two-wheeled wonderland: aridity, altitude and heat conspire to fell newbies. Allow yourself time to acclimate before taking on any serious rides, and drink more water than you ordinarily would. Also keep in mind that New Mexico ranks near the top of traffic deaths – be careful out there!

Bicycle rentals are available in most urban areas and are noted within the text. Some hostels and B&Bs also rent bikes. Cyclists must follow the same traffic laws as auto drivers, and technically you are required to have a bicycle license and bell, plus a light for night rides.

For more information, contact the **Traffic Safety Department** (☎ 505-827-3349; 1120 Cerrillos Rd, Santa Fe), which issues bicycle licenses, good for one year, or the **Bike Coalition of New Mexico** (www.bikenm.org).

BUS

It's possible, though somewhat inconvenient, for travelers with time on their hands to tour most of New Mexico's major population centers by bus. Greyhound and TNM&O buses (p238) connect many city centers (like Santa Fe, Taos, Albuquerque, Española and Las Vegas) with the rest of

the country. Many stops have convenient connections with public bus systems.

CAR

The very best way to explore New Mexico is by car. Many smaller towns and pueblos, as well as the vast wilderness areas that deserve your full attention, are unreachable by public transportation, and arranging a private shuttle or guided tour can be inconvenient and expensive. Note that New Mexico ranks near the top of traffic deaths, drunk-driving arrests and overall accidents. Drive carefully!

Whether you rent a vehicle or bring your own, begin your trip by stocking up with at least a gallon of water per person, a blanket or jacket, extra medication and any other provisions you might need if stranded for a day or two. Always carry a spare tire, and know how to put it on. And note that cell phones don't always work in the hinterlands.

The **American Automobile Association** (AAA; ☎ 800-222-4357, in Santa Fe 505-471-6620; www.aaa .com), for $26 to $51 annually, provides free maps, roadside assistance, towing and low-cost insurance. It can book car rentals, air tickets and hotel rooms at discount prices.

The **State Highway & Transportation Department** (☎ 800-432-4269) has a toll-free line with information about weather, state travel laws and road advisory updates.

Rental

Shop around, and make reservations at least two weeks in advance. Many chains also offer far better deals on weekly rentals rather than on two- or three-day rentals. You can find good deals on **Orbitz** (www.orbitz.com), **Expedia** (www.expedia.com) and **Travelocity** (www .travelocity.com).

Don't limit yourself to the convenient locations at the Albuquerque Sunport, either. You'll often get better rates elsewhere, and most companies can arrange to drop off the car at your hotel. (Yes, you'll have to take a taxi to your hotel first, though.)

Rental rates skyrocket from late July through early September, as well as during the Albuquerque Balloon Fiestas and the Christmas holidays. Make reservations at least a month in advance, if possible.

In general, you'll need to be 25 years old and have a US driver's license or international driver's permit, as well as a major credit card (or ability to make a large cash deposit), to rent a car. Smaller, independent companies are more likely to make exceptions, however.

Rates usually include unlimited mileage, but make sure they do. If there is a mileage charge, your costs can go up disconcertingly quickly. You are expected to return the car to the same place where you picked it up; you can sometimes arrange to drop the car off elsewhere, but there is often a large surcharge. Be aware that the person who rents the car is the only legal driver, and in the event of an accident only the legal driver is covered by insurance. However, when you rent the car additional drivers may be signed on as legal drivers for a fee, usually $5 per day per person.

You will be offered a variety of insurance options, most of which insured US drivers don't need. Review your own policies before committing to collision insurance (CWD). If you don't have uninsured driver's insurance, however, go ahead and invest – one-fifth of New Mexicans drive uninsured. Basic liability insurance, which will cover damage you may cause to another vehicle, is required by law and comes with the price of renting.

Many credit cards will cover collision insurance if you rent for 15 days or fewer and charge the full cost of rental to your card. If you have collision insurance on your personal car insurance policy, this will often cover rented vehicles. The credit card will cover the large deductible. Call and make sure.

Note that many rental agencies stipulate that damage a car suffers while being driven on unpaved roads is not covered by the insurance they offer. Check with the agent when you make your reservation.

In addition to the nationally known agencies, try these smaller chains and independent rental companies (all but one of which is in Albuquerque), which usually offer better rates, more flexibility for younger drivers and, best of all, no 10% airport concession tax:

ABC Car Rental (Map p176; ☎ 505-256-1169; 2501 Lead Ave SE, Albuquerque) Rents to under 21-year-olds and folks without credit cards.

Beaver Toyota-Scion (Map p62; ☎ 505-982-1901; www.beavertoyota.com; 1500 St Michaels Dr, Santa Fe)

Capps Van & Car Rental (☎ 505-848-8267; www.cappsvanrental.com; 2200 Renard Pl SE, Albuquerque) Rents huge vans.

Rent-A-Wreck (Map pp170-1; ☎ 505-232-7552; 2001 Ridge Crest SE, Albuquerque) Despite the name, the cars are nice.

Thunderbird Harley-Davidson/Buell (Map p191; ☎ 505-856-1600; www.thunderbirdhd.com; 5000 Alameda Blvd NE, Albuquerque) Rents touring models.

Road Rules

Foreign motorists and motorcyclists (traveling with their own foreign vehicles) will need the vehicle's registration papers, liability insurance and an international driver's permit in addition to their domestic license. Canadian and Mexican driver's licenses are accepted.

The speed limit on New Mexico highways tops out at 75 miles per hour. You are expected to yield to pedestrians and cyclists in cities and towns, and all accidents resulting in damages more than $500 must be reported.

Road Conditions

Also known as the 'Orange Barrel State,' New Mexico generally performs road construction and maintenance in the spring and fall, though summer months see their share of bypasses and impasses.

Generally, road conditions in urban centers and along major arteries are excellent, but stray much off the beaten path and many roads remain unpaved. Most of these roads are dirt, not gravel, and after rain may become temporarily impassable to folks without 4WD. Such roads on public land may be heavily rutted throughout the year, which can be hard on a car.

HITCHHIKING

Hitching is never entirely safe in any country in the world, and we don't recommend it. Travelers who decide to hitch should understand that they are taking a small but serious risk. You may not be able to identify the local rapist/murderer before you get into the vehicle. People who do choose to hitch will be safer if they travel in pairs and let someone know where they are planning to go. Ask the driver where he or she is going rather than telling the person where you want to go.

LOCAL TRANSPORT

Several cities offer public buses, most of which run from around 7am to 7pm daily, with limited service on Sunday. They charge a nominal fee for one-way rides, and offer

TRANSPORTATION

day and week passes. All have convenient connections to Greyhound except for the Los Alamos entry, which connects with Española Transit.

Albuquerque Ride (p190) Daily service to most tourist areas, plus trolleys.

Española Transit (p122) Also serves San Juan and Santa Clara Pueblos, plus connections with Los Alamos Public Transit.

Los Alamos Bus System (p133)

Santa Fe Trails (p113) On-demand transit for folks with ADA-certified disabilities and anyone older than 60.

Taos Chile Line (p155) Serves the Ski Valley and Arroyo Seco in winter only.

Taxis serve Santa Fe, Taos, Las Vegas and Albuquerque. Generally, they don't cruise the streets, so you'll have to call for pickup.

MOTOR HOME (RV)

Touring by recreational vehicle can be as low-key or as over-the-top as you are. Rentals range from ultra-efficient VW campers to plush land yachts that resemble suites at the Bellagio in Las Vegas. Whatever mode you choose, what you've bought is freedom (except when you venture into big cities, when freedom's just another word for a parking nightmare).

After the size of the vehicle, consider the impact of gas prices, gas mileage, additional mileage costs, insurance and refundable deposits; these can add up quickly. It pays to shop around and read the fine print. Given the myriad permutations in rental choices, it's incredibly hard to generalize, but to get you started, you might expect a four-person vehicle with 1000 'free' miles to run $1100 to $1400 weekly in the summer, plus 32¢ each addition mile. Get out a good map and a calculator to determine if that's too steep a price for freedom. Perhaps tent camping in a rental car doesn't sound so bad after all?

Before heading out, consult www.rvtravel .com for tips galore, including wi-fi locations on the road. Then purchase a campground guide from **Woodall's** (www.woodalls.com), which also has a great all-round website, or **KOA** (☎ 406-248-7444; www.koa.com), and hit the road.

For RV rentals contact the following:

Adventure Touring Rentals (☎ 866-814-0253; www.usarvrentals.com)

Cruise America (☎ 800-327-7799; www.cruiseamerica .com)

TOURS

For when you just don't feel like organizing everything yourself, you have options:

Enchanted Lands Luxury Bicycle Vacations (☎ 505-661-8687; www.enchantedlands.com) Customized bicycle tours through canyons and mesa landscapes.

Native Sons Adventures (☎ 800-753-7559; www .nativesonsadventures.com) Guided rafting, biking, hiking, ATV and snowmobile tours in northern New Mexico.

Santa Fe Detours (☎ 800-338-6877; www.sfdetours .com) Walking and hiking tours of Bandelier National Monument, Santa Fe and Taos.

Health David Goldberg MD

CONTENTS

New Mexico encompasses a wide range of climates and temperatures, from the blistering heat of the desert summer to several 12,000ft-plus peaks where snow lingers almost year-round. Because of the high level of hygiene here, as in the rest of the USA, infectious diseases are rarely a significant concern for most travelers.

BEFORE YOU GO

INSURANCE

The United States offers possibly the finest health care in the world. The problem is, it can be prohibitively expensive. If you're coming from abroad, buy supplemental travel health insurance if your regular policy doesn't cover you for overseas trips. If you are covered, find out in advance if your insurance plan will make payments directly to providers or reimburse you later.

Domestic travelers who have insurance coverage should check with their insurance company for affiliated hospitals and doctors. US citizens who don't have regular health coverage can purchase domestic travel insurance.

Bring any medications you may need in original containers, clearly labeled. A signed, dated letter from your physician describing all medical conditions and medications, including generic names, is a good idea.

INTERNET RESOURCES

The World Health Organization publishes a superb book called *International Travel and Health,* which is available online at no cost at www.who.int/ith. Another website worth visiting is **MD Travel Health** (www.mdtravelhealth.com), which provides (free) health recommendations for travel in every country.

Also consult your government's travel health website before departure, if one is available:

Australia (www.smartraveller.gov.au)
Canada (www.hc-sc.gc.ca)
UK (www.doh.gov.uk)
United States (www.cdc.gov/travel)

IN NEW MEXICO

AVAILABILITY & COST OF HEALTH CARE

In general, if you have a medical emergency, find the nearest public hospital emergency room. If the problem isn't urgent, call a nearby hospital and ask for a referral to a local physician, which is usually cheaper than a trip to the emergency room if you have insurance. Avoid stand-alone, for-profit urgent-care centers, which tend to perform large numbers of expensive tests.

Pharmacies are abundantly supplied, but international travelers may find that some medications that are available over-the-counter at home require a prescription in the US, and as always, if you don't have insurance to cover the cost of prescriptions, they can be shockingly expensive.

INFECTIOUS DISEASES

In addition to more common ailments, several infectious diseases are unknown or uncommon outside North America. Most are acquired by mosquito or tick bites.

West Nile Virus

These infections were unknown in the US until a few years ago, but have now been reported in almost all 50 states. The virus is transmitted by Culex mosquitoes, active in late summer and early fall and which generally bite after dusk. Most infections are mild or asymptomatic, but the virus may infect the central nervous system, leading to fever, headache, confusion, lethargy, coma and sometimes death. There is no treatment.

HEALTH

Rabies

Rabies is a viral infection of the brain and spinal cord that is almost always fatal. The rabies virus is carried in the saliva of infected animals and is typically transmitted through an animal bite, though contamination of any break in the skin with infected saliva may result in rabies. In the US, most cases of human rabies are related to exposure to bats. Rabies may also be contracted from raccoons, skunks, foxes and unvaccinated cats and dogs.

If there is any possibility that you have been exposed to rabies, you should seek preventative treatment, which consists of rabies immune globulin and rabies vaccine and is quite safe. If you wake up to find a bat in your room, or discover a bat in a room with small children, precautionary treatment may be necessary.

Giardiasis

This parasitic infection of the small intestine occurs throughout North America and the world. Symptoms may include nausea, bloating, cramps and diarrhea and may last for weeks. To protect yourself from giardiasis, you should avoid drinking directly from lakes, ponds, streams and rivers, which may be contaminated by animal or human feces. Giardiasis is easily diagnosed by a stool test and readily treated with antibiotics.

HIV/AIDS

As with most parts of the world, HIV infection occurs throughout New Mexico. You should never assume, on the basis of someone's background or appearance, that they're free of this or any other sexually transmitted disease. Be sure to use a condom.

Plague

While rare, plague (aka the Black Death, the little flea-borne bacterium that killed some 25 million Europeans in the 1350s) still infects about a dozen people in New Mexico each year, usually between April and November.

Plague has an incubation period of two to seven days and rather nonspecific symptoms: headache, chills, high fever and painful, swollen lymph nodes in the groin, armpit and/or neck. If you display these symptoms shortly after your vacation, tell your doctor that you've been in a plague area and ask them to test for the disease.

Plague is usually contracted by hikers and campers bitten by fleas shared with infected rodents and small animals, in particular rock squirrels and gophers. Stay on trails, avoid stirring up the undergrowth in piñon forests, and give wide berth to sick, slow-moving or disoriented animals.

ENVIRONMENTAL HAZARDS
Altitude Sickness

Visitors from lower elevations undergo rather dramatic physiological changes as they adapt to New Mexico's high altitude, and while the side effects are usually mild, they can be dangerous if ignored. Some people – age and fitness level are not predictors of who these will be – will feel the effects strongly, others won't even notice.

Symptoms, which tend to manifest after four days and continue for about two weeks, may include headache, fatigue, loss of appetite and/or nausea, sleeplessness, increased urination and sometimes hyperventilation due to overexertion. More severe cases, which usually affects those who hiking at over 10,000ft and didn't take time to acclimate, display extreme disorientation, breathing problems and vomiting. These folks should descend immediately and get to a hospital.

Drink plenty of water (dehydration exacerbates the symptoms) and take it easy – at 7000ft, a pleasant walk around Santa Fe can wear you out faster than a steep hike at sea level. Put off serious hiking and biking for a few days, if possible.

Dehydration

Visitors to the desert may not realize how much water they're losing, as sweat evaporates quickly and increased urination (to help the blood process oxygen more efficiently) can go unnoticed. The prudent tourist will make sure to drink more water than usual – think a gallon a day if you're active. Parents can carry fruits and fruit juices to help keep kids hydrated.

Severe dehydration can easily cause disorientation and confusion, and even day hikers have gotten lost and died because they ignored their thirst. So bring plenty of water even on short hikes, and drink it!

Bites & Stings

Commonsense approaches to these concerns are the most effective: wear boots when hiking to protect from snakes, wear long sleeves and pants to protect from ticks and mosquitoes. If you're bitten, don't overreact. Stay calm and follow the recommended treatment.

MOSQUITO BITES

Keep yourself covered (wear long sleeves, long pants, hats, and shoes rather than sandals) and apply a good insect repellent, preferably one containing DEET, to exposed skin and clothing. Don't overuse the stuff, though, because neurologic toxicity – though uncommon – has been reported from DEET, especially in children. DEET-containing compounds should not be used at all on kids under age two.

Insect repellents containing certain botanical products, including oil of eucalyptus and soybean oil, are effective but last only 1½ to two hours. Products based on citronella are not effective.

TICK BITES

Ticks are parasitic arachnids that may be present in brush, forest and grasslands, where hikers often get them on their legs or in their boots. Adult ticks suck blood from hosts by burrowing into the skin and can carry infections such as Lyme disease (uncommon in New Mexico).

Always check your body for ticks after walking through high grass or thickly forested area. If ticks are found unattached, they can be brushed off. If a tick is found attached, press down around the tick's head with tweezers, grab the head and gently pull upwards – do not twist it. (If no tweezers are available, use your fingers, but protect them from contamination with a piece of tissue or paper.) Do not rub oil, alcohol or petroleum jelly on it. If you get sick in the next couple of weeks, consult a doctor.

ANIMAL BITES

Do not attempt to pet, handle or feed any wild animal, no matter how cuddly looking; most injuries from animals are directly related to people trying to do just that.

Any bite or scratch by a mammal should be promptly and thoroughly cleansed with large amounts of soap and water, followed by application of an antiseptic such as iodine or alcohol, and possibly an antibiotic. The local health authorities should be contacted immediately for possible post-exposure rabies treatment, whether or not you've been immunized against rabies.

SNAKE BITES

There are several varieties of venomous snakes in the USA, but unlike those in other countries they do not cause instantaneous death, and antivenins are available. First aid is to place a light constricting bandage over the bite, keep the wounded part below the level of the heart and move it as little as possible. Stay calm and get to a medical facility as soon as possible. Bring the dead snake for identification if you can, but don't risk being bitten again.

SPIDER & SCORPION BITES

Although there are many species of spiders in New Mexico, the main two that cause significant human illness are the black widow and brown recluse. The black widow is black or brown in color, measuring about 15mm in body length, with a shiny top, fat body and a distinctive red or orange hourglass figure on its underside. It's usually found in barns, woodpiles, sheds, harvested crops and bowls of outdoor toilets. The brown recluse spider is brown, usually 10mm in body length, with a dark violin-shaped mark on the top of the upper section of the body. It's active mostly at night and lives in dark sheltered areas such as under porches and in woodpiles, and typically bites when trapped.

If bitten by a black widow, you should apply ice or cold packs and go immediately to the nearest emergency room. Complications of a black widow bite may include muscle spasms, breathing difficulties and high blood pressure. The bite of a brown recluse typically causes a large, inflamed wound, sometimes associated with fever and chills. If bitten, apply ice and see a physician.

If stung by a scorpion, you should immediately apply ice or a cold pack, immobilize the affected body part, and go to the nearest emergency room. To prevent scorpion stings, be sure to inspect and shake out clothing, shoes and sleeping bags before use, and wear gloves and protective clothing when working around piles of wood or leaves.

HEALTH

Glossary

Although American English is most widely spoken, the state's constitution designates New Mexico as officially bilingual, and about 30% of New Mexicans speak Spanish at home. Visitors are likely to hear 'Spanglish,' in which speakers switch smoothly between Spanish and English, even within the same sentence. You'll also see Spanish and Native American terms on menus, in galleries and at historical sights. The following list should help you translate, as well as make sense of some of the government acronyms and New Age terminology you'll hear in these parts.

abierto – Spanish for 'open.' So come on in.

acequia – ancient irrigation ditches. Still used in Santa Fe and throughout the Rio Grande Valley, these were communally owned and maintained by local landowners for centuries before plumbing was introduced. Today they are maintained by associations that operate in much the same fashion.

adobe – a building material originally made with bricks cut directly from root-filled sod by Pueblo Indians, and later improved by mixing straw and mud by the Spanish. Today it refers to almost any building material designed to resemble adobe.

AIPC – All Indian Pueblo Council. This is an intertribal governmental organization comprising the 19 New Mexico pueblos: Acoma, Cochiti, Isleta, Jemez, Laguna, Nambé, Ohkay Owingeh (formerly San Juan), Picuris, Pojoaque, Sandia, San Felipe, San Ildefonso, Santa Ana, Santa Clara, Santo Domingo, Taos, Tesuque, Zia and Zuni.

arroyo – a usually dry ditch or waterway, which can fill quickly and violently even if there's no rain in your area. As schoolteachers say, 'Ditches are deadly, stay away.'

Avanyu – the water serpent motif popular on pueblo pottery. It symbolizes the prayer for rain and flowing water.

ayurveda – an Indian (as in India) holistic healing philosophy based on balancing three body types, or *doshas*. This can be accomplished in a variety of ways at spas, restaurants and holistic healing centers throughout the state.

Aztlán – Nahuatl for 'Place of the Blue Herons,' and ancestral home of the Aztec peoples, probably Northern New Mexico. It also refers to those parts of the American Southwest annexed during the Mexican-American war, including New Mexico, Arizona, Texas, California and parts of Wyoming and Colorado.

barrio – Spanish for 'neighborhood.' It is used to describe primarily Hispanic parts of town.

bienvenidos – Spanish for 'welcome.'

biscochito – the New Mexico state cookie! It is simple and sweet with a hint of anise, traditionally made around Christmas.

bolo – a replacement for a man's tie (often worn by women) that cinches a thick cord with a silver disc or semiprecious stone. Around here, it counts as formal wear.

bosque – Spanish for 'forest.' It refers to the wooded area along rivers that flow year-round.

breakfast burrito – a burrito usually filled with scrambled eggs, sausage or bacon, cheese and chile.

bultos – carved Catholic saints. These are often roughly hewn from wood.

burnish – the Native method of bringing unglazed pottery to a high sheen, using special smoothed rock tools often handed down for generations.

Camino Real – Spanish for the 'Royal Highway.' Here it refers to the old route that has connected Santa Fe and Mexico City since before the time of the Aztec empire, and which has since been used by Indians, Spanish and NAFTA truck drivers for trade.

carne adovada – pork cooked until it's so tender you barely have to chew it. It's then marinated and baked in a rich mixture of red chile and spices.

casita – Spanish for 'little house.' B&Bs and hotels use it to designate small, usually freestanding accommodations, often suite-style with a full kitchen.

cerrado – Spanish for 'closed.' Sorry, folks.

ceviche – sort of Mexican sushi. It's fish that's not cooked per se, but soaked in citrus juices and other ingredients that catalyze a similar chemical reaction.

chakra – seven power points in the human body that often need to be re-aligned by experienced metaphysicians.

Chicano – sometimes traced to a Spanish corruption of the Nahuatl word for 'poorest of the poor.' This was almost a racial slur for Hispanic Americans until adopted in the late 1950s by young Latinos as a badge of pride, and later popularized by the Chicano Civil Rights Movement of the 1960s.

chicharones – Spanish for 'pork rinds.'

chile – the correct spelling for the fruit of the chile plant, despite what editors elsewhere in the USA would have you think.

chile relleno – poblano or green chiles stuffed with cheese and sometimes meat or other fillings, then breaded and deep fried.

chili – a meat and bean stew eaten primarily in Texas, or the incorrect spelling of the word 'chile' (see above).

chorizo – spicy Mexican sausage often served at breakfast.

churro sheep – the sheep originally brought here by Spanish settlers and used for wool, milk and, in times of desperation, meat. They were almost entirely replaced by generic meat sheep in the last century, until the recent weaving renaissance inspired more interest in preserving this unique and historic breed.

concha – Spanish for 'shell.' Generally refers to the thin silver discs, usually with scalloped edges and decoratively engraved, used to make those Navajo-style belts and hat bands you see everywhere.

descansos – small shrines, usually by the side of the road, marking where travelers have died; drive extra carefully when you see one.

Diné – the more proper name for the Indian tribe more often referred to as Navajo, or the language thereof.

DOE – the Department of Energy. This administrates LANL (Los Alamos National Laboratory) and was headed by Governor Bill Richardson during the Clinton administration.

enchiladas – corn tortillas either rolled (Mexican style) or stacked (New Mexican style) with cheese, chile sauce and often meat.

ENIPC – Eight Northern Indian Pueblos Council. An organizing body for the pueblos of Nambé, Ohkay Owingeh (formerly San Juan), Picuris, Pojoaque, San Ildefonso, Santa Clara, Taos and Tesuque.

farolito – paper bags weighted with sand and illuminated with candles, usually around Christmastime. They're also often referred to as luminarias.

fetish no, not that, silly. These are the carved stone animals that some Zuni Indians believe impart their carrier with the traits of the critter portrayed: a bear for strength, frog for fertility etc. Different rituals may be required to activate their powers, usually described in the brochures provided by the shops and galleries that sell them.

fiesta – Spanish for 'celebration.' This usually refers to weeklong parties throughout New Mexico that nominally honor Catholic saints.

fonda – Spanish for inn. 'La Fonda' is often the oldest hotel in town.

gray water – recycled water from sinks and showers that's been purified by natural and/or artificial means. This is typically used to water lawns and gardens.

green chile stew – the barometer of competitive home cooks. This is stew made of green chile and usually ground beef, potatoes and other vegetables.

hacienda – Spanish-style house built around a courtyard. This refers to anything adobe of mansion-sized proportions.

horno – a beehive-shaped outdoor adobe oven, originally used by Spanish settlers and still popular among many Pueblo Indians. It also refers to the chewy bread baked after heating the oven with coals, then removing them.

huevos rancheros – eggs cooked to order atop lightly fried corn tortillas and swimming in chile, served with beans and potatoes.

Indian taco – also 'Navajo taco.' It consists of soft fry bread often topped with beans, meat, cheese, lettuce, tomato and chile.

jerga – a type of weaving popular among Spanish colonists and usually used as a wall hanging, characterized by streaks of colorful yarn without the geometric patterns favored by Native weavers.

kachina (or katsina) – religious dolls carved primarily by the Hopi from the root of a cottonwood tree, representing the spirits and spirit dancers sacred to the tribe. Cheap knockoffs abound but are still pretty neat.

Kokopelli – the flute-playing rain deity you'll see on advertisements, corporate logos and sometimes Native crafts.

kiva – a circular, partially underground Native American house of worship, or a bulbous fireplace built into a corner and boasted about by B&Bs.

LANL Los Alamos National Laboratory, the USA's top weapons lab.

lowrider – a car with lowered suspension, clean paint, nice rims and often a plush interior and hydraulics that lift the car up and down. This also refers to the driver thereof, as well as the art, fashion and style associated with folks who build such fine cars.

mañana – not just Spanish for 'tomorrow.' It's the word that sums up the New Mexico lifestyle.

Manhattan Project – the top-secret WWII project that built the first atomic bomb.

menudo – a spicy tomato-based breakfast stew of tripe (yes, animal intestines, and if that grosses you out, consider what sausage casings are made with) and other ingredients, long venerated as a hangover cure.

micaceous clay – clay flecked with sparkling mica and made into cooking vessels by potters at Picuris, Taos and other pueblos. Many New Mexicans consider micaceous kitchenware to be the ultimate pots in which to cook beans.

milagrosa – a small tin charm usually representing a body part you hope to heal.

morada – a chapel or meeting place for *penitentes* (see below).

ojo – literally, Spanish for 'eye.' In New Mexico it usually refers to an artesian spring. An *ojo caliente* is a hot spring, while an *ojo sarco* is a clear spring.

paraje – Spanish for 'campground' or stopping place.

passive solar energy – a term coined in New Mexico that refers to architectural elements that maximize use of the sun for heating, cooling and other purposes.

pawn – items traded for cash on a short-term loan that couldn't be paid back. Also used to refer to Native American jewelry traded as such.

penitentes – a secretive Catholic sect that became popular in Northern New Mexico after the Franciscans more or less closed up shop. Though known for self-flagellation, the actual rituals involved are not advertised to the general public (thus most of what you hear is probably not true).

petroglyph – line drawings etched into rock. Usually this refers to those that are centuries old.

photovoltaic cells – plates of silicon alloy specially treated to absorb sunlight and then allow free electrons to migrate to the surface, creating a negative charge on top while leaving behind a positive charge on the bottom. The resulting imbalance creates a voltage potential that can be used to generate solar electricity.

piñon – a high-desert tree indigenous to Northern New Mexican deserts, or its rich nut.

piñon bark beetle – *Ips pini*, the rice-grain-sized beetle currently devouring piñon trees throughout the Southwest.

placita – Spanish for 'small square.' These are plazas usually fortified by being entirely surrounded with strong adobe structures to protect them from attack. The plaza in Chimayó is a good original example.

posole – a usually tomato-based stew made from hominy (corn soaked in lye until it gets puffy) and other ingredients.

pueblo – literally, Spanish for 'people' or 'town.' This is used to designate the villages or reservations of the 19 tribes along the Rio Grande, or the multistoried adobe buildings built by these tribes.

Pueblo Revival – modern architecture based on the look of pueblo buildings.

rajas – the rough cedar sticks closely packed at 45-degree angles to vigas, making a popular ceiling for Pueblo Revival (see above), or actual pueblo, interiors.

raza – Spanish for 'race' and used to describe the Spanish-speaking peoples of the Americas. It is a reference to José Vasconcelos' essay *La Raza Cósmica*.

recuerdo – a memory or souvenir.

reredo – a series of religious paintings, as on an altar.

retablo – a religious painting, usually of a saint or the Virgin Mary. These are done in Spanish colonial style.

ristra – a string of vegetables, usually red chiles, designed for drying. These are both decorative and delicious.

santero/a – a person who makes reredos, retablos or bultos (see above).

sopapilla – flaky pillows of delicately puffed fried dough, perfect with honey.

squashblossom necklace – the heavy silver necklaces, once considered an integral part of Santa Fe style, with several flower-shaped beads and a central crescent-shaped pendant, called a *naja*, which represents both the moon and female spirit.

storyteller doll – a popular style of ceramic figure depicting an adult swarming with small children. These dolls were originally created by Cochiti artist Helen Cordero.

tilde – the accent above the 'n' in Española. The letter 'ñ' is called an eñe.

viga – a substantial roof beam used in Spanish adobe architecture, often carved into decorative patterns.

virga – rain, visible to the naked eye, that evaporates before it hits the ground.

WPA – Works Progress Administration. Created in 1935 as part of President Franklin D Roosevelt's 'New Deal' to lift the country out of the Great Depression, the WPA provided public funds for a variety of projects and professions nationwide, playing patron to some 5000 artists who produced more than 200,000 works of art, including many of the Taos Society of Artists, Patrociño Barela and many other New Mexico masters.

xeriscaping – landscaping using only drought-resistant plants, and usually lots of rocks (which are very drought-resistant).

zia – New Mexico's state symbol for now (see p83). The sun sign that's all over everything.

Behind the Scenes

THIS BOOK

This 2nd edition of *Santa Fe, Taos & Albuquerque* was researched and written by Kim Grant. Paul Smith, Director of the Albuquerque International Balloon Fiesta, was interviewed by Heather Dickson for the boxed text entitled 'Balloon Fiesta: The Executive Director's Cut.' The Health chapter was adapted from text by Dr David Goldberg. The 1st edition of the book, entitled *Santa Fe & Taos*, was researched and written by Paige Penland. Thanks also to boxed-text writers Beth Penland, Annette Rodriguez and Bridgette Wagner. This guidebook was commissioned in Lonely Planet's Oakland office, and produced by the following:

Commissioning Editors Heather Dickson & Suki Gear
Coordinating Editors Simon Williamson & Kyla Gillzan
Coordinating Cartographers Ross Butler & Emma McNicol
Coordinating Layout Designer Pablo Gastar
Assisting Editor Janet Austin
Managing Cartographer Alison Lyall
Cover Designer Rebecca Dandens
Project Manager Nancy Ianni

Thanks to Greg Benchwick, Sally Darmody, Jennye Garibaldi, Mark Germanchis, Kathie Leyendecker, Katie Lynch, Kate McDonald, Raphael Richards, Paul Smith & Celia Wood

THANKS FROM THE AUTHOR
KIM GRANT

With each passing edition, it takes a bigger and bigger pueblo to pull together a Lonely Planet guidebook. I'm grateful beyond compare for the assistance and support of so many. First among them is Catherine Direen, who unearthed essential shards of information and wrangled many an unruly steer. Thanks for the cappu-frosties and lemon-lime drinks. May your day job – strategic planning and communications – push the landlocked boundaries of New Mexico toward regular visits to the Atlantic and Pacific. Thanks to Clare Innes and Colby Cedar Smith, who came through once again. To Tess Houle and all my Albuquerque friends. To Paige Penland, who wrote a witty and insightful first edition. And to Commissioning Editor Heather Dickson, who got the ball rolling for Suki Gear, who came in for the late-inning stretch. They both make LP a better place to work.

OUR READERS

Many thanks to the travelers who used the last edition and wrote to us with helpful hints, useful advice and interesting anecdotes:

Naomi Brennan, Roger R Conant, Caryn Davidson, Lillian Hall, Shirley Isgar, Laura Koller, Ann Lippmann, Iain McCormick, Whitney Owens, Barrie Robbins, Chaim Schlezinger, Lynette Stewart, David Wedlan

THE LONELY PLANET STORY

The story begins with a classic travel adventure: Tony and Maureen Wheeler's 1972 journey across Europe and Asia to Australia. There was no useful information about the overland trail then, so Tony and Maureen published the first Lonely Planet guidebook to meet a growing need.

From a kitchen table, Lonely Planet has grown to become the largest independent travel publisher in the world, with offices in Melbourne (Australia), Oakland (USA) and London (UK). Today Lonely Planet guidebooks cover the globe. There is an ever-growing list of books and information in a variety of media. Some things haven't changed. The main aim is still to make it possible for adventurous travellers to get out there – to explore and better understand the world.

At Lonely Planet we believe travellers can make a positive contribution to the countries they visit – if they respect their host communities and spend their money wisely. Every year 5% of company profit is donated to charities around the world.

SEND US YOUR FEEDBACK

We love to hear from travellers – your comments keep us on our toes and help make our books better. Our well-travelled team reads every word on what you loved or loathed about this book. Although we cannot reply individually to postal submissions, we always guarantee that your feedback goes straight to the appropriate authors, in time for the next edition. Each person who sends us information is thanked in the next edition – and the most useful submissions are rewarded with a free book.

To send us your updates – and find out about Lonely Planet events, newsletters and travel news – visit our award-winning website: **www.lonelyplanet.com/contact**.

Note: We may edit, reproduce and incorporate your comments in Lonely Planet products such as guidebooks, websites and digital products, so let us know if you don't want your comments reproduced or your name acknowledged. For a copy of our privacy policy visit www.lonelyplanet.com/privacy.

Index

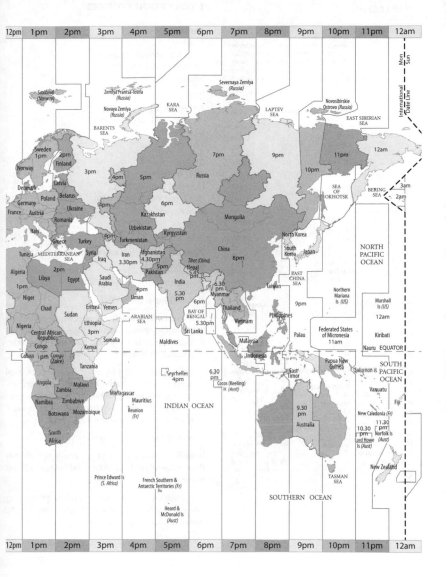

MAP LEGEND

ROUTES

Tollway	One-Way Street
Freeway	Mall/Steps
Primary	Pedestrian Overpass
Secondary	Walking Tour
Tertiary	Walking Tour Detour
Lane	Walking Trail
Under Construction	Walking Path
Unsealed Road	Track

TRANSPORT

Bus Route	Tram
Rail	

HYDROGRAPHY

River, Creek	Water
Intermittent River	Lake (Dry)
Canal	Lake (Salt)

BOUNDARIES

International	Regional, Suburb
State, Provincial	Cliff

AREA FEATURES

Airport	Land
Area of Interest	Mall
Beach, Desert	Market
Building	Park
Campus	Reservation
Cemetery, Christian	Rocks
Cemetery, Other	Sports
Forest	Urban

POPULATION

◉ CAPITAL (STATE)	○ **Large City**
● Medium City	○ Small City
○ Town, Village	

SYMBOLS

Sights/Activities
- Beach
- Christian
- Islamic
- Monument
- Museum, Gallery
- Point of Interest
- Pool
- Pub/Bar
- Ruin
- Skiing
- Winery, Vineyard
- Zoo, Bird Sanctuary

Eating
- Eating

Drinking
- Drinking
- Café

Entertainment
- Entertainment

Shopping
- Shopping

Sleeping
- Sleeping
- Camping

Transport
- Airport, Airfield
- Bus Station

Information
- S Bank, ATM
- Hospital, Medical
- Information
- @ Internet Facilities
- Police Station
- Post Office, GPO
- Toilets

Geographic
- Lookout
- ▲ Mountain, Volcano
- National Park
-) (Pass, Canyon
- Waterfall

LONELY PLANET OFFICES

Australia
Head Office
Locked Bag 1, Footscray, Victoria 3011
☎ 03 8379 8000, fax 03 8379 8111
talk2us@lonelyplanet.com.au

USA
150 Linden St, Oakland, CA 94607
☎ 510 893 8555, toll free 800 275 8555
fax 510 893 8572
info@lonelyplanet.com

UK
72–82 Rosebery Ave,
Clerkenwell, London EC1R 4RW
☎ 020 7841 9000, fax 020 7841 9001
go@lonelyplanet.co.uk

Published by Lonely Planet Publications Pty Ltd
ABN 36 005 607 983

© Lonely Planet Publications Pty Ltd 2007

© photographers as indicated 2007

Cover photograph by Lonely Planet Images: Mass ascension at the International Balloon Fiesta, Adina Tovy Amsel. Many of the images in this guide are available for licensing from Lonely Planet Images: www.lonelyplanetimages.com.